Matrix of Mystery

MATRIX OF MYSTERY

*Scientific and Humanistic Aspects
of rDzogs-chen Thought*

Herbert V. Guenther

SHAMBHALA
Boulder & London
1984

SHAMBHALA PUBLICATIONS, INC.
Boulder CO 80306

ISBN: 1-57062-649-9

Library of Congress Cataloging in Publication Data
Guenther, Herbert V.
  Matrix of Mystery.
  Bibliography: p.
  Includes index.
  1. Rdzogs-chen (Rñiṅ-ma-pa) 2. Rñiṅ-ma-pa (Sect)—
Doctrines. I. Title.
BQ7662.4.G83 1983   294.3'923   83-2306

Leslie and Toyo Kawamura

friends of many years

Preface

This book constitutes a phenomenological approach to the problem of man and human creativity in terms of the self-organization of living systems. It also attempts to bridge the gap and to overcome the mutual antagonism between scientific and humanistic probings. Both are necessary and should be mutually inclusive for gaining deeper insight into our origins and our place in an evolving universe. Science makes it possible for us to know, but with an ever increasing store of knowledge comes an ever growing sense of awe and mystery, although, of course, awe and mystery are not scientific terms. Though phenomenological in character the presentation does not subscribe to the growing dogmatism of the discipline called "phenomenology"; and though it bases itself on original source material it eschews any philological reductionism, which itself is based on the narrow and often erroneous interpretation of basic operational norms which, in turn, had their philosophical justification embedded in nineteenth century conceptions of the nature of linguistics. Lastly, since the texts utilized were written in Tibetan by Tibetans who interpreted the terms they used according to how they applied them in their language, reference to non-Tibetan language(s) has been minimal and restricted to those instances where the Tibetan authors referred to a non-Tibetan (Sanskrit) word. (Any other such references do not help understanding what the Tibetans wanted to convey, but merely restate, in a ponderous manner, what everybody knows: that different languages have different vocabularies.)

It is obvious that the author of a book like this, even if it ventures into as yet unchartered and unexplored territory, owes much to others, either through their writings or through conversations with them. In particular I wish to express my gratitude to the late Erich Jantsch who carefully read the whole manuscript and was always helpful in the formulation and clarification of crucial problems. Similarly I am deeply indebted to Steven D. Goodman for the many valuable suggestions as to the presentation of the vast material covered in this book and for the meticulous drawing of all diagrams.

Special thanks go to Sylvia Hellman and her staff, without whose unfailing support and genuine interest publication would not have been possible.

I am grateful to Rick Cowburn for his continual help in compiling and arranging the bibliographies. Most of all, I acknowledge a great debt to my wife Ilse who, since the inception of this project, has been the unseen sustaining force.

Herbert Guenther

Saskatoon, Saskatchewan
1983

Contents

1. Introduction to the Scope of Being

[1]

Simply put, this book probes the following: how is it that man is both the encodement (as preserver) and the encoder (as transmitter) of essential insights into the structure of Reality? Stating it in another way, how are we to understand that fantastically improbable complexity termed "man" so that that equally complex notion of "tradition"—as that which preserves and transmits essential insights—is itself comprehensible?

Here, "essential" is to be understood as that which is relevant to the actuality of man's existential predicament. As such it has nothing to do with cultural artifacts, museum pieces, and other playthings of those in the humanities who have failed to distinguish between that which can still make a claim on contemporary man in all his situational complexities and those fossilized cultural patterns which survive merely by virtue of gathering dust. It is this failure that accounts, to a very large part, for the growing suspicion and hence fear—completely justified—that the humanities are in fact no longer relevant.

Whether or not the so-called "insights" of any tradition are essential, will be determined by the extent to which they are, firstly, *comprehensible* to whomsoever chances to focus on them and, *implementable,* that is experientially accessible, so that they may become relevant to one's own life by allowing for the means by which those who seek a more satisfactory, and less fragmented mode of being, can open up their limited and limiting perspectives regarding what is, in fact, experientially possible. With respect to comprehensibility this means that the language used to explicate such putatively essential insights must be culturally consonant with both the cognitive and aesthetic complexities of the person trying to probe these insights. In addition, the process of making comprehensible such insights necessarily entails a concerted confrontation with the pregiven prejudices that have sedimented—and continue sedimenting—into and as one's "natural attitude" toward both what "we" are and what the "world" is supposed to be.

One cannot implement or experientially access that which one does not understand (is not made comprehensible). Although implementation necessarily lies outside the scope of this book, the fact that comprehensibility is so closely intertwined with implementation, makes reference to the latter unavoidable. Here, however, only a few general remarks need to be made. It is a mistake to assume that accessing in the light of a new perspective can occur in isolation, for man by his very nature is always situated with-others and hence "experiences" (even himself) in the midst of and in relation to others. Any attempt to artificially fabricate a lifestyle that would cut one off from social situatedness is based on a lack of comprehension of what the tradition under consideration regards as valuable and healthy. This does not mean, however, that one will have to continue being enmeshed in a social situatedness with one's natural attitudes intact. Indeed, it cannot be emphasized enough, that to comprehend essential insights means, at the very least, to be forever severed from one's former (natural) attitude. It is equally, and perhaps even more damagingly, a mistake to assume that accessing the essential insights of a tradition means fixating one's activities on another person judged (more properly speaking, prejudged) to be the locus within which such insights inhere, and that accessing these insights will occur merely by being in the presence of such a "special" locus. These two mistaken approaches to the problem of "how to" access the value and meaning of a tradition are, in fact, avoided only to the extent that one has honestly and carefully acknowledged what is and what is not comprehensible in the light of one's own experience, for it is only in the light of such sincere acknowledgment of one's own engagement with the task of opening up that one becomes sensitive to, and can thereby accurately identify, those growth-enhancing patterns which are reinforced by other like-minded individuals. It is only when such sensitivity begins to stir that one finds the "seemingly" inner dimension of spiritual growth "outwardly" mirrored in others and recognizes this mirroring as an incentive to further accessing. Indeed, it is the community of such individuals, sensitively attuned to the essential insights of a tradition, who sustain, by having become the existential embodiment of that tradition, that ongoing process which, like a beacon light, guides man in his attempt to open up to the full measure and value of being human.

Having made these above remarks, by way of a general orientation, we may now proceed to a discussion of the specific task before us in this book, namely, to make comprehensible those "insights" preserved and sustained by that tradition called rDzogs-chen,[1] which have been regarded as essential by the most creative geniuses within this tradition.

Tradition, as understood by Buddhist thinkers, always involves two complementary aspects—authoritative texts *(lung)* and the understanding *(rtogs)* which results from accessing the meaningfulness of what these texts have to say.[2] Authoritative texts are usually taken to mean those literary works that constitute the corpus of the Buddhist teaching.[3] Yet there is a more thoughtful interpretation in which such texts are understood to be the embodiment of that "fundamental concern" *(don-nyid)* which took shape in and as the manifold literary expressions of these texts. This fundamental concern is the ever active energizing matrix *(snying-po)* which operates throughout the whole of Reality so as to refine *(byang)* and optimize *(chub)* the functional intelligence which inheres, however dimly, in each and every sentient being.[4]

With respect to understanding, as the experiential accessing of that which the authoritative texts merely encode, there are two modes. These two "reality modes" are: (1) a conventional mode of accessing, based on objectifying, representational thinking, and (2) an ultimate mode of accessing, which is nonegological and beyond the confines of the psycholinguistically bound operations of the intellect.[5] These two modes, however, are neither mutually exclusive—like the "two horns on the head of an ox"[6]—nor contradictory. Indeed, their inseparability, in the sense of an inextricably relational functioning, is itself due to the self-structuring process of Reality-as-such,[7] whose expressive immediacy is that fundamental concern that comes to the fore as encounters with the inexhaustible source of possibilities of meaning, thereby prompting and engendering interpretive responses.

That such experiential accessing and interpretive response can take place at all is an undeniable and irreducible mystery.

Once one begins to probe the essential insights of this fundamental mystery—as understood by the rDzogs-chen tradition—one is immediately faced with a seemingly insurmountable obstacle to comprehensibility. We refer to a subtle, pervasive simultaneity of complexity, interconnectedness, and dynamic high-energy processes, which is so alien to any "natural attitudes" that one might well be tempted to give up in despair. Nevertheless we shall attempt to make as comprehensible as possible, in the chapters that follow, a number of the most essential insights into this matrix of mystery. Thus, we shall deal with such features as the configurational complexity *(dkyil-'khor)* of this mystery; its patterning as formal gestalt *(sku)*; its communicative structuring as authentic utterance *(gsung)*; its cognitively sensitive thrust as vibrant spirituality *(thugs)*; its resource dynamics as creative potential *(yon-tan)*; its intrinsic ability to initiate optimally executed modes of activity *(phrin-las)*; and its auto-presencing *(snang-ba)* by virtue of its inherent modalities and their images *(lha)*.

Although more exhaustively explicated in Chapter Two, in the remainder of this chapter, however, we shall have to present the reader with an overall perspective of how this mystery itself is understood to constitute that fundamental pervasive, unified, holistical process whose highly energized dynamics set up the variety of subprocesses and their associated structures which are so feebly indicated by the term "Reality." In doing so it will be necessary to introduce a number of totally unfamiliar terms, for these terms name unfamiliar perspectives and insights. Although difficult at first, because the nature of that which we are probing is most difficult for thought, it is hoped that mentally moving into this admittedly foreign terrain will become easier as the implications and interconnections of these new perspectives are drawn out. To aid in this task we will frequently resort to analogies with phenomena and patterns of thought already explored, and hence available, within the Western intellectual traditions of science and philosophy. These analogies are meant to stimulate comprehensibility, yet given the "arcane" nature of the most fundamental aspects of the mystery, one must preserve the essential insight which these aspects reveal in a manner that will show the subtlety and complexity of their "message." One cannot expect to find here, therefore, either a simplistic or "for the beginners" approach. Instead, being faithful to the fundamental concern that is preserved in authoritative texts, one will find in these explications that follow only that complexity and subtlety which was intended by the rDzogs-chen tradition itself. Given the fact, however, that this tradition has to-date been virtually unknown outside of a small group of highly specialized and trained individuals, the explications that follow necessarily represent "first attempts." Whether or not there follow further attempts, of course, will depend entirely on the extent to which the message and insights embodied in this tradition can be made compellingly comprehensible to that growing world community of cognitively sensitive individuals. It is to them and their future, as well as to the rDzogs-chen thinkers of the past, that this present book is dedicated.

[2]

The problematic nature of what we have termed mystery *(gsang-ba)*— Reality as a dynamic holistic process—has been of central interest to the rDzogs-chen tradition. Indeed, extensive explications regarding the matrix of this mystery *(gsang-ba'i snying-po)* are to be found in that commentarial tradition which takes as its most authoritative text a work which itself is entitled *The Matrix of Mystery*.[8] The name given to this mystery in its foundational and dynamically pervasive modalities is the Ground *(gzhi)*, whose nature will be discussed in detail in the following chapter. Here we shall only indicate a few crucial points with respect to how one is to understand what is meant by this term. Insofar as it is the ground and reason for everything, always retaining its thoroughly dynamic character, it is as a unified holistic process "responsible" for the variety of structures, things, and experiences that are said to make up Reality, yet it must never be confused nor identified with the variegated nature of that which comes into presence. We will "translate" this most elusive and important term *(gzhi)* as Being, thereby indicating the similarity in philosophical understanding between the rDzogs-chen view of Reality's dynamic holistic *ground* and that of Martin Heidegger's view of Reality's nonreductive, essentially open character termed "das Sein." It is crucial to avoid associating the term Being as we shall use it throughout, with any determinate, isolatable, static essence or thing; indeed, Heidegger named all such associations "ontic" and constantly cautioned against reducing the fundamental dynamics of Being to the ontic.[9] How it is that Being lends itself, as it were, to such a reduction, and what the experiential implications of this is, will be addressed in the chapters that follow.

By its very nature Being, in its totality, tends to structure itself in and as the unifying continuity which most decisively determines the uniquely experiential character of being human. This unifying continuity which determines experience as such, we shall name Existenz. To indicate that this continuity is always suffused, as it were, by the highly energized processes of Being, we shall use the term Being-*qua*-Existenz.

A fundamental property of Being's mystery is what is termed its communicative thrust *(sngags)*.[10] This is itself a process in which there is an inextricable relational functioning of two modes. The one termed the operational mode *(thabs)* names the auto-regulative nature of Being's communicative thrust, thereby indicating that this thrust is entirely due to Being's intrinsic dynamics. The other mode, termed appreciative discrimination *(shes-rab)*, names the cognitively and aesthetically accessible nature of Being's thrust. Although analytically separable into two modes, functionally these modes operate as a coherent, unified process. Moreover, this process simultaneously presents three interrelated facets termed communicative thrust-*qua*-mystery *(gsang-sngags)*, communicative thrust-*qua*-comprehensibility *(rig-sngags)*, and communicative thrust-*qua*-signal maintenance *(gzungs-sngags)*. All of them operate so as to ensure optimization of Being's communicative thrust. Thus, the communicative thrust-*qua*-mystery is that facet which protects the inherent cognitive capacity of an individual to access Being's mystery by eliminating tendencies toward errant mental functioning; the communicative thrust-*qua*-comprehensi-bility is that facet which ensures the awareness (and hence comprehensibility) of the fundamental value of Being's mystery by eliminating misunderstanding about it; and the communicative thrust-*qua*-signal maintenance is that facet which assures the continued monitoring of the full richness of the apprehended "signal" in such a manner that it may be received just as it was transmitted by those in the tradition who have faithfully implemented, by existentially embodying, the import of Being's mystery. Such signal maintenance occurs through the elimination of weaknesses in signal reception. Hence, the operation of each facet exhibits a dual function of lessening and eliminating negative forces and enhancing and sustaining positive forces. [11]

Most importantly, these facets of Being's communicative thrust also account for the possibility of experientially accessing Being's mystery. Such accessing, however, is not to be likened to the flipping of a switch so that when the switch is in the on-position the message of Being's mystery is completely accessed and when in the off-position nothing of Being's mystery comes through. There is no off-position for, by virtue of simply being alive, one is always (at least minimally) accessing Being's mystery. Hence there are always but degrees of accessing. Indeed, one may speak of a relatively optimized experiential accessing, but this is never to be understood as indicating a maximum level—for part of Being's mystery is that there is no upper limit to accessing. If there were a limit it would be something localized or localizable and this is precisely not the case because of Being's utter openness.

Although the communicative thrust of Being's mystery is primarily related to and representative of Being's authentic utterance, it encompasses much more than this because of the holistic character of the process. The thrust itself presences in symbols which are sensory-specific and whose presence is felt as having a masculine and/or feminine quality, which is imaged anthropomorphically. Thus Being's operational mode in its communicative thrust expresses itself through and as the shape, color, and posturing of those compelling forces, which are termed gods *(lha)*; whereas the appreciative and sustaining modes of this thrust express themselves through and as the shape, color, and posturing of those coherence-ensuring forces which are referred to as goddesses *(lha-mo)*. [12]

It is these formulated energies as gods and goddesses—as much imaged feelings as felt images—that initiate aesthetic creation and enjoyment and constitute an essential aspect of human life. As formulated energies these gods and goddesses are neither representations of some abstract idea, located in some metaphysical realm, nor replicas of the commonplace. In the process of taking shape these energies merely stand out in relief, as it were, never losing their connectedness with the whole and always continuing as a source of infinite possibility in sensuous disclosure. And it is these same formulated energies that urge man to look and listen, to imagine and restructure, to access and relive the creative process which is Being's mystery. This accessing may occur through that first utterance which, with reference to Being's "speaking," we shall call gnosemic language.[13] Although it asserts nothing, it opens up the configurational complexity *(dkyil-'khor)* of man's existential situatedness, prior to his reduction into a subject-*thing* amongst a welter of object-*things*. Accessing also may occur through that first utterance which, with reference to Being's sensuous auto-presencing, is the first act of form-giving—the form being a possibility actualized within such media as stone, metal, and paint on canvas. Indeed, it is worth noting that that spiritual movement known by the Sanskrit name Guhyamantrayāna, which evolved in the wake of this communicative thrust of Being's mystery by eliciting man's responsive attunement to it, has been of greatest significance in the development of Buddhist art.

[3]

So far we have just given the barest indications of the dynamic processes constituting Being's mystery. Two important facts regarding the processes must now be addressed: (1) they exhibit a functional complementarity *(dbyer-med)*, which makes futile any attempt to demarcate a separable functioning of cause and effect components and a separable functioning of an ultimately valid and a conventionally valid reality mode; and (2) they are intrinsic to (not derivative from) Being's mystery. It is admittedly difficult to express these facts accurately without being able to resort to the use of a complex symbolism for process-thinking such as developed by mathematicians, for our everyday language is so geared to mechanistic thinking. Not having access to such symbolism those in the rDzogs-chen tradition who themselves were deeply concerned with the communicative thrust of Being's mystery (Guhyamantrayāna), addressed the fact of Being's complementarity in highly concise and cryptic language. Rong-zom-pa Chos-kyi bzang-po discusses this complementarity as follows:[14]

> [The Guhyamantrayāna] (1) views the ultimately valid as "cause" and the conventionally valid as "effect"; (2) it views the "cause" as (the individual's present) status and the "effect" as a configuration of regents;[15] (3) it views (one's) actions and comportment as (evidence of Being's) resources;[16] and (4)

it views, by virtue of the existential value (of Being's mystery) even in the domain of the conventionally valid, "cause" and "effect" as (indivisibly) complementary.

One should carefully note that in Buddhist thought what is here rendered as cause *(rgyu)* refers to what is, more properly speaking, the momentum of a process and as such indicates both momentum thrust and momentum conservation. Similarly, what has been rendered effect *('bras-bu)* is to be understood as a nonfinal climaxing. Using the analogy of a wave, this climaxing can occur as either upward-directed (the crest) or downward-directed (the trough). As indicated in the above quotation, the "trough" is what is termed the conventionally valid, a cover-term for the whole of what is processed by egocentered dichotomizing mentation, which is felt to be unsatisfactory because of its self-limiting effect. It is precisely this unsatisfactoriness (as effect) which, as cause, triggers an optimizing movement leading to that nonfinal climaxing termed "configuration of regents." It is within the very dynamics of optimization that one's actions and comportment—experienced as "doing something about" unsatisfactoriness—bear evidence of Being's rich resources. For what is termed Being's resources *(tshogs)* is that which makes *possible* such experiences as "doing something about one's situation," the possibility being provided by the atemporally abiding fact of Being's auto-presencing in utter openness as its pure potential. Finally, the above passage makes the important observation that, even conventionally speaking, what from one perspective may be judged to be cause, can from another perspective be regarded as effect—both terms referring to complementary experiential phases embedded in the self-regulating dynamics of Being itself.

Being's mystery is not only characterizable as an indivisible complementarity of modes or processes. The processes themselves are intrinsic to (not derivative from) Being's mystery and as such cannot even be said to take place in time. As processes of Being's very mystery they have, in a sense, always been taking place—yet they are not to be thought of as eternally operating.[17] To indicate this special sense of always taking place without having had a temporal onset with the latter's rather automatic association of temporal sequence, we shall use the phrase atemporally abiding. To summarize, indivisible complementarity and atemporal abiding are ways of pointing to, not explaining, Being's mystery and in this sense only may be regarded as pervasive features.

Furthermore, Being's dynamic character simultaneously exhibits three atemporally abiding aspects: (1) Being's essentially open (that is, nonreductive) character, termed utter openness *(stong-pa)*; (2) what may be conceived of as Being's high-energy radiating, termed sheer lucency *(gsal-ba)*; and (3) the intrinsic intelligence of Being as a whole whose excitatory nature gives it a highly active disposition which cognitively "shapes," as it were, the unbroken continuity of that which makes experience possible. This is termed Being's excitatory intelligence *(rig-pa)*, an active intelligence which is present at every phase of Being's auto-unfoldment into and as the variety of structures which are collectively termed the universe and its inhabitants. The creative dynamics of this excitatory intelligence operates as a pristine—in the sense of an atemporally abiding and hence ever fresh—cognitiveness. It is this pristine cognitiveness *(ye-shes)* which, in a sense, accounts for the possibility of any and all cognitive acts. As such it may be regarded as the cognitively dynamic facet of Being-*qua*-Existenz. Insofar as it functions as the ground and reason for all possible experiences, it is Experience-as-such *(sems-nyid)*. The essentially nonreductive character of Experience-as-such, itself a reflection of Being's mystery, is expressed by Klong-chen rab-'byams-pa as follows:[18]

> Experience-as-such as an atemporally abiding sheer lucency, dissipatively expands *(sangs-rgyas-pa)*[19] into a triad of configurations,[20] in no way amenable to being established as a substance or quality.

This terse statement expresses an essential insight into the nature of Experience-as-such. As being the ground of all possible experience, one might reasonably be tempted to think of it as simply an essential possibility or as a rather metaphysical hypostatization. Yet as should be clear from the quoted passage, Experience-as-such is quite the contrary; it is an active unfolding into configurational complexities which preserve and transmit Being's mystery by having all tendencies toward reductive and restrictive structuring dissipate.

The abstract diction of the above quotation is, then, illustrated by simile, essence, and indication; Experience-as-such is likened to the cloudless autumn sky, a vast expanse of blue which draws us further and further into infinite realms; its "essence" is self-existent pristine cognitiveness; and its "indication" is the lucidity present in the variety of cognitive processes.

Thus, although we have seen that probing Being's mystery entails moving into rather "alien" terrain, paradoxically this very mystery is always "available" to us, operating in the all too familiar forms of our cognitive processes. In fact, our cognitive processes are relatively low-level instantiations of Being's pristine cognitiveness. Yet even such low levels are not present as some finitely fixed amount of pristine cognitiveness. Indeed, as beings endowed with a cognitive capacity, we constitute a special, locally bound nexus, a nodal point on the surface of Being itself, through which the full energy of pristine cognitiveness tends toward optimization. This optimizing thrust of pristine cognitiveness, however, is often felt—from the vantage point of the nexus itself (the individual experiencer)—as the strain of conflicting thoughts, feelings, and projects. This felt tension of being human, however, is itself due to modulations in the dynamic unfolding of Being's mystery. Simply by virtue of *being* a human being, then, one is caught in a complete, yet special, presentation of Being's mystery. Experientially accessing this fact and all its attendant implications is precisely what is meant by Being's thrust toward optimization. The thrust itself operates so as to dissipate *both* locally generated entropy, experienced as the welter of affective disturbances, collectively termed Saṃsāra, *and* locally bounded negentropy, experienced as the variety of hypostatized states of bliss and happiness, collectively termed Nirvāṇa. In effect, then, Being's optimization is an ever active, renormalizing movement in which nonoptimal perturbations are dampened.

[4]

Being's optimizing movement sets up the necessary condition for what might be termed its auto-elucidation whereby its essentially open and thoroughly dynamic character automatically unfolds as a coherent structuring, which precisely because of its coherence and lucidity is amenable to experiential accessing. The accessing is itself but Being's resonating concern *(thugs-rje)*, impellingly moving toward optimization in its operation within the limited horizon of an individual. From the perspective of an individual, coming to an understanding of Being's mystery is synonymous with experiential accessing and involves probing what is technically termed Being's essentially diaphanous *(dag-pa)* and self-same and identical *(mnyam-pa)* character. In the diction of the *gSang-snying* such coming to an understanding is expressed as follows:[21]

> By understanding the physical world, the structured organisms and the
> (cognitive patterning by) Existenz as diaphanously pure,
> Through two ordinary identities and two extraordinary identities (Being's
> configurational character is experienced as) Kun-tu bzang-po field.

This terse statement indicates that Being's essentially diaphanous character is to be understood with respect to three themes—the physical world, the organism (sentient beings) living in this world, and Existenz itself.

Regarding the first two themes, however, an adjustment in one's natural attitude toward the relationship between inanimate environment and animate organisms within that environment is necessary. For here what one calls the inanimate and the animate both derive from the same elemental (organizing) forces *('byung-ba)*; and their difference merely lies in the mode of operation. The inanimate is that mode in which the radiating energy of Being progressively congeals, "turning into" matter. The animate, by contrast, is that mode in which Being's radiating energy is still vibrant.[21a] Bearing in mind the basically relational character of the inanimate and animate, we can now proceed to discuss what diaphanous purity with respect to these themes indicates.

The physical world, constituted by the elemental forces, is, in its diaphanous purity, a process which one comes to understand properly, in profoundly human terms, as the feminine; and the organisms structured out of these forces into what is termed the psychosomatic constituents, one comes to understand as the masculine.[22] As directed processes, the masculine may be said to aim at solidity of structure, whereas the feminine keeps the processes of change (and evolution) going on. In short, one comes to experience, through refined discernment, Being's mysterious complementarity operating throughout the whole of Reality as the sensitive interaction of masculine and feminine forces, which one feels pervading one's own being.

The diaphanously pure nature of the physical world may also be experienced as a wondrous and dazzling palace, while the diaphanous purity of the inhabitants of this world is, correspondingly, experienced as palace residents—stunning gods and goddesses.[23]

Whether one focuses on what is taken to be the physical world as a relatively stable environment, or on those relatively dynamic structures which as sentient beings inhabit the world, all such experiences are due to that continuity of Being's mystery that operates as one's Existenz. Although one's Existenz is usually experienced as simply being an ensemble of cognitive and affective processes, one may deepen this experience by coming to understand oneself, that is, one's Existenz, as the diaphanous purity of Being's pristine cognitiveness which operates as a configurational complexity of five pristine cognitions. This complexity itself is, in its diaphanous purity, an atemporally abiding dissipative structure wherein all that which works against optimization continuously dissipates and all that which ensures the fullness of Being continuously expands.

Having briefly indicated those special understandings associated with three diaphanous purities—the environmental world, the sentient beings therein, and one's Existenz (as that which makes possible embodied

consciousness and its being-in-a-world)—we must now address the meaning of the two ordinary and two extraordinary identities. The two ordinary
identities refer to those special understandings that relate to the two reality
modes. All that can be said to exist—subsumed under the terms Saṃsāra
and Nirvāṇa (as interpretations of what is but a sheer coming-into-
presence)—is identical from the viewpoint of the ultimate reality mode,
insofar as it is identically Being itself that has no specifiable on-set. From
the viewpoint of the conventional reality mode, all that can be said to exist,
is identical insofar as it is Being's apparition-like auto-presencing. In other
words, these two ordinary identities illustrate the fact that Being "just is"
("having no specifiable on-set"), and that it yet dynamically presences as
the paradox of a something-yet-nothing ("apparition-like").[24]

The two extraordinary identities are so named because they relate to that
extraordinary phenomenon of man himself as the continuity of lived
experience (Existenz).[25] This continuity as the organized pattern of psychophysical constituents is itself understood to be identical to Being's auto-
presencing through formal gestalt images termed Tathāgatas.[26] From
among the psychophysical constituents the ensemble of cognitive and
affective processes termed perceptive functioning (rnam-par shes-pa) is of
primary importance, for it reflects and in this reflecting makes accessible
Being's inherent intelligence. This ensemble, therefore, is understood as
identical with Being's pristine cognitiveness.

Because of the importance of these four identities and the subtleties
involved in correctly understanding them, we shall discuss them from a
slightly different perspective.[27] One may come to see and actually experience that everything that may be said to exist is, in fact, identical insofar
as it is impossible to establish any ontic principle that would ensure its
status as real and hence as different from everything else. Stated differently,
everything said to exist is, in fact, identical insofar as it presents Being's
ceaseless auto-presencing. Furthermore, inasmuch as everything that may
be said to exist is, as Being's auto-presencing, only a coming-into-presence
in what is the excitatoriness of Being's intelligence, it is identical in being
able to initiate contextually regulated sequences; and in view of the fact
that all such coming-into-presence is due to a concatenation of determining
circumstances, there is identity in just such presencing. Thus, although one
may speak of four identities, one must understand them as but aspects of
that ultimate identity (mnyam-pa chen-po) which is Being's unitary nature
operating in and as the complementarity of Being as such and everything
that is. Indeed, it is the manifold of that which is, which serves as evidence
of Being's abiding mystery.

Being's mystery is also evidenced through a fourfold deeply probing understanding *(rtogs),* which makes this mystery amenable to experiential accessing. These four in-depth probings are summed up in *gSang-snying* as follows:[28]

> Through a fourfold deeply probing understanding (of Being's mystery)—
> As being a holistic process; as presencing in gnosemic nuclei;
> As pervaded by a sustaining and stabilizing force; as constituting an unmediated meaning-value—
> All and everything (is realized to be) the monarch (presenting Being's) complete evidence.

It bears emphasizing that the symbol of a monarch for the intrinsic value and evidence of Being's mystery intimates that man's fundamental nature is one of dignity and integrity. It is this—man's fundamental nature—that is brought to light by a fourfold deeply probing understanding.

The in-depth probe termed holistic process *(rgyu-gcig-pa)* deals with the difficulty of gaining that privileged experiential accessing that will bring to light, in all its holistic complexity, the unitary nature of Being's mystery as the complementarity of conventional and ultimate reality modes. In the words of the eighth-century rDzogs-chen master Padmasambhava:[29]

> Everything that is, in an ultimate sense, has no on-set *(ma-skyes-pa)* and (hence) is not discretely specifiable; and in a conventional sense, it exhibits an apparitional character and (hence) is not discretely specifiable either. The very fact of having no (specifiable) on-set, yet presencing as variegated apparitions—such as the reflection of the moon in water—is (what makes possible) the initiating of contextually regulated sequences; and this very fact (of being present as variegated) apparitions does not entail its having an ontic status, and since there is no specifiable on-set (in either aspect) there is the indivisible complementarity (of Reality as) conventional and ultimate reality modes. And this is what is meant by understanding Reality as a holistic process.

The in-depth probe termed gnosemic nuclei *(yig-'bru)* deals with the difficulty of gaining that privileged mode of accessing in and through which we, as concretely embodied individuals, bear evidence of Being's mystery as operating through the preprograms for optimum attainment standards, termed authentic utterance *(gsung),* formal gestalt *(sku),* and vibrant spirituality *(thugs).* As Padmasambhava states:[30]

> The fact that everything that is has no specifiable on-set is symbolized by the (gnosemic nucleus graphically represented as) ཨ (pronounced *A*)—the (preprogram of) authentic utterance.
> The very fact that all that is has no specifiable on-set, yet presences as

(variegated) apparitions initiating contextually regulated sequences, is symbolized by (the gnosemic nucleus graphically represented as) ཨ (pronounced *O*)—the (preprogram of) formal gestalt.

That intelligence which understands (Reality) in this manner, being that apparition-like cognitiveness, which has neither periphery nor center, is symbolized by (the gnosemic nucleus graphically represented as) ཨཾ (pronounced *OM*)—the (preprogram of) vibrant spirituality.

While the first two in-depth probings deal with the ever present mystery of Being as the source of all that is, and the manner in which all that is is given intelligible form through gnosemic language, the third in-depth probing termed sustaining-stabilizing force *(byin-gyis brlabs)* is concerned with Being's mystery felt and experienced as the individual's progressive attunement to his truly holistic nature. Padmasambhava states:[31]

> Just as the power to transform a white cloth into a red one and then to maintain it in this state inheres in the dye, so also the power to transform all that is into a dissipative structure and to maintain it as such is understood to be the capacity inherent in the holistic process itself and the gnosemic nuclei.

This sustaining-stabilizing force is an auto-stabilization which climaxes in and as the fourth in-depth probing termed unmediated meaning-value *(mngon-sum)*. This probing and understanding does not proceed via such mediated modes as hearsay, belief, or axiomatic predications, but occurs as the unmediated apodictic presentation of Being's mystery, which as such is never reducible to the three traps of metaphysical expression, causally sequential explication, and inference schemata. As Padmasambhava says:[32]

> The fact that all that is atemporally abides as a dissipative structure neither contradicts authentic texts and oral instructions nor is dependent on mere texts and words, for it is a fact assuredly based in the depths of (one's) mind through the intelligence of Being itself. And this is what is meant by the unmediated meaning-value understanding.

Taken together these four in-depth probings constitute a single process that reflects man's drive toward comprehension of the irreducible mystery of his own existence. Such a drive defines man's spiritual character as a meaning-seeking creature. The unavoidably problematic nature of contingent situatedness, which such meaning-seeking entails, is the subject matter of the next chapter.

II. The Problem Situation

[1]

There are many kinds of problems which confront man in his meaning-seeking activities, but the major and disquieting one is that he himself is intrinsically problematic, not only for others, but above all for himself. This disturbing fact, more often than not, causes man to evade facing up to his problematic nature by seeking refuge in a variety of easy "solutions," which, of course, solve nothing, because the basic questions concerning man's problematic nature have not been squarely addressed.

It seems, however, that there have always been special situations in which people wondered why they exist at all, and more specifically, exist as they do. It is not necessary to assume, as has been done by some Western existentialist thinkers, that questions concerning man's existence are raised most authentically at moments of despair, when everything seems to have become meaningless and frightening.[1] Quite the contrary, the mood of despair prevents rather than stimulates any balanced questioning, for such moods not only foster misunderstanding the very source of that which prompts the questioning, but also obscure and undermine the urge to know. Consequently, the actual source of the questioning is clouded over even before it has been authentically experienced. The result is then a merely "subjective mood," which usurps the genuine impulse to know. The question of existence is thereby reduced to and channelled through a subjective feeling of emptiness and vacuity and a sense of futility and hollowness with its attendant denigration of all that is. Certainly, to exist so as to view life from an unlimited perspective, whereby meaning is given to all actions and experience, is neither the same as, nor something reducible to, the distorted and clouded glimpses from limited (subjective) viewpoints.

It is therefore more likely that such questions as "Why is man a problem?" and "What does it mean to be?" are most authentically raised during or after feelings of exaltation, when man has been "most himself," has experienced himself as perfect, whole, and complete, and has been able to perceive perfection, wholeness, and completeness both in others and in the world around him so that he feels *impelled* to recover, that is, more appropriately speaking, to re*dis*cover that experientially all-pervading wholeness. Although we may speak of man as having been "most himself" in such moments, we must be cautious not to confuse this experience with a mood of hysterical elation, for this is the other extreme to the anxiety and death preoccupations of the earlier existentialist thinkers, and is in no way less radically subjective and egocentric.

Probing the question "What does it mean to be?" necessarily involves experiential understanding which, apart from being thoroughly qualitative, goes beyond any conceptual framework. Furthermore, the questions "Why is man where he is?" and "What does it mean to exist?" are not restricted to any single questioning person within a specific cultural milieu. These are questions that involve humanity as a whole. As such, they are attuned to the ever present dynamics of Being, of which each individual is a concretely active presentation.

As already discussed in Chapter I it is necessary to distinguish Being and Existenz.[2] The former names what may be called the enduring reality in the latter. Existenz, by contrast, is a pulsation, fluctuation, and "projection" of Being, in the sense that each and every pulsation reveals a different possibility of Being's infinite openness *(stong-pa)*, a program, as it were, of its own readout through what functions as deep-structure program selectors operating as our "individual" sensory and mental processors. Being-as-such, an enduring reality in Existenz, is not only open and radiating *(gsal-ba)*, it is also intelligent *(rig-pa)*. It is so in the sense that it presents a pervasive excitatory-responsive mode that generates the structures or standing-wave patterns of both knowledge and opinion—the former aids one's creative unfoldment by disposing one to meaningfulness, whereas the latter merely perpetuates one's biases. Both, however, are alike in being available modes that ultimately derive from a "critical state," an "interference pattern" of the spontaneous being there *(lhun-grub)* and resonating concern *(thugs-rje).*[3]

It is primarily the radiating aspect of Being *(gsal-ba)* which, in presenting challenges and eliciting responses, constitutes Existenz. As such, this aspect serves as the ground and creative source of those interpretive notions with which we organize our experience. One such notion is "subjectivity," which, far from being primary, merely mimics Existenz. Subjectivity tends to connote an entity (the subject) existing alongside other entities (understood as those objects with which the subject variously interacts). Existenz, however, is neither thing nor essence; it is no more concretizable than Being itself. As an operational mode *(thabs)*, Existenz brings into prominence man's abiding concern for creative unfoldment, which constitutes the value and reality of one's being *(don)*, and initiates this concern by making it articulate.[4] Whether we see Existenz as man's abiding value or as a mode of operation, such "seeing" presupposes the working of intelligence as a charge or excitation that is pervasively present. This intelligence *(rig-pa)* marks out horizons of possible lifeforms, both determining their functional scope and radiating into each and every aspect of these forms. It is present throughout all such horizons while yet always remaining utterly open.

The triadic dynamics of Being—openness opening-up *(stong-pa)*, lucency radiating *(gsal-ba)*, and excitatory intelligence *(rig-pa)*—actively structure Existenz *(rang-bzhin)* specifically through the excitation that goes with lucency,[5] thereby constituting Existenz in the specific sense of being the matrix of an individual's unfolding experiences. This process may also be spoken of in terms of interactional features called a ground, a path, and a goal,[6] which derive their significance from Being, manifesting itself in and through that dynamic invariant which accommodates specific elucidations. In the words of Klong-chen rab-'byams-pa:[7]

> Existenz *(rang-bzhin-gyi rgyud)* means (the triad of) ground, path and goal;
> as has been stated in the *Mu-tig phreng-ba*:[8]
>
>> "Since it is necessarily to be apprehended in (its phases of) ground, path
>> and goal,
>> It is Existenz."

Here, its facticity is the dynamic invariant's openness, lucency, and excitatory intelligence, subsumed under the (triad of) ground, path, and goal; its definition is that it is all-encompassing and that it is precisely that which ensures the realization of Buddhahood; and its division is into ground, energy bursts, and (spiritual) concentrate.

As ground *(gzhi)*, Existenz is the excitatory intelligence of (and as) that which has, since its beginning (which is no beginning in the ordinary sense), been utterly pure *(ka-dag)* in (and as the) triad of facticity, actuality, and resonating concern. Moreover since facticity has remained utterly pure from the very beginning, the designation stepped-down excitatory intelligence *(ma-rig-pa)*[9] does not apply, nor has it been experienced as (something) existent which could be labelled as going astray. Since actuality is (Being's) spontaneous presence, excitatory intelligence radiates in (specific) light values (throughout).

Since resonating concern is all-encompassing it does not cease in its activity of providing for the possible emergence (of world perspectives) from which either Saṃsāra or Nirvāṇa originates.

As energy bursts *(snying-po)*, Existenz means that the triadic (hierarchical) organization of pristine cognitiveness[10] has become the (vitalizing) energy (residing) in the heart (of each living being). It is the dynamics of Existenz (in its aspect as) ground, which as Being's coming-into-presence shines forth from (a person's) eyes (in the formulated energy of) four lamps.[11] It is, therefore, the path as the direct vision of four light-intensities[12] making themselves felt in their coming-into-presence.

As spiritual concentrate *(bcud)*, Existenz means maturation (which is) the goal (or climax) of experiencing the (intensity of) excitatory intelligence as it comes-into-presence. Moreover, since its facticity is open, it does not involve a belief in an eternal (something) and has nothing to do with a materially particular existent. Since this fact of being open has been there in such a manner as to make its presence felt all by itself, it is not an absolute nothing. Rather, since the very indivisibility of this being open and being lucent is the quintessence of excitatory intelligence, it is in view of having matured into its optimal value, that one speaks of Existenz having become distilled into a spiritual concentrate.

Apart from indicating the undividedness and indivisibility of the ground (Being and Existenz), this passage talks about holistic processes, which have only recently become a major field of research in the physical and biological sciences. First of all, the "ground" (Being), discussed in the above passage is nonlocalizable (nowhere and everywhere); it is like a quantum field always active, coming-into-presence, that is, auto-presencing by radiating in all directions. Secondly, in this process of auto-presencing, the ground becomes "distilled" into a spiritual concentrate, constituting what may be likened to the quantum mechanical notion of a particle, which as an excitation of the field, is never independent of but always in constant interaction with it. And just as there are no actual fundamental particles as such—the very notion of particle being a carryover from classical physics—but only interactional field effects, so also that which is termed excitatory intelligence operates in terms of man's experience as the field effect of resonating concern and not as an allegedly fundamental or "higher" self. Therefore intelligence is never independent of the field *(dbyings)* of which it is its fluctuation.[13] This interdependence is technically termed *dbyings-rig*. Here *dbyings* indicates a vibrant continuum "feeding" as it were, what becomes the multidimensional texture of Experience-as-such. It has also been likened to a field in which, like plants in the soil, insight can germinate and grow.[14] And it has also been described as "a lambency expanding and developing into five hues such as brilliant azure."[15] In this context *rig-pa* is the excitation or, in terms of experience, the cognitiveness of and in this field such that "although essentially an interiority previously described it is this lambency in its outward-directed brilliance, a coming-into-presence as a continuum welling-up."[16] Furthermore, the field and its excitation operate in such a manner that "neither can be joined to nor separated from the other, (being similar to) the sun and its rays."[17] In its dynamics, this complex whole is a process that makes itself felt in its variegated intensities and intentionalities.

[2]

The dynamic character of Existenz with its interactional and interpenetrating features of being open *(stong-pa)* and lucent *(gsal-ba)* is quite similar to the modern ideas of a vacuum field and of electromagnetic-gravitational fields as fluctuations of the vacuum, respectively. In addition, however, there is the always operative excitatory field *(rig-pa)*, which allows for Existenz to be processed as that holistic configuration which we commonly associate with what we term experience.[18] Insofar as the dynamic processes of Existenz are comparable to a vacuum field and its fluctuation, one might introduce a distinction (though not an actual separation) between Existenz and experience so as to conceive of the former as a coding agency and of the latter as a decoding procedure. This allows for, on the one hand, the acceptance of the familiar distinction between the inanimate and the animate, while, on the other hand, accounting for the possibility of these processes becoming holistically self-organizing or, more precisely, reorganizing.

Once one has accepted and understood the distinction between Existenz and experience, what may now be appropriately termed a "problem situation" tends to emerge. Its configurational character involves both structure and process; and while the latter may be understood to be evolutionary (in the sense that it organizes itself in the direction of higher regimes), the former may be viewed as both a horizontally expanding network and a vertically stacked hierarchy. The horizontally expanding network is a result of the dynamics of a fivefold display process *(phun-sum-tshogs)* which, however, also participates in the vertically stacked hierarchy of pristine cognitions *(ye-shes sum-brtsegs)*.

The horizontal network (constituting Existenz) provides the information input for what specifically becomes the human problem situation—as a readout of the input—through experience (trial runs). In either case the network consists of five vectorial connections, which are termed the place, teacher, audience, teaching, and time. The fact that such a network is understood to belong both to Existenz and experience implies two things: first, the existence of a pattern that dynamically informs every part of itself and, second, the omnipresence of this pattern throughout its individualized manifestations.[19] Hence it is said:[20]

Wherever there occurs Existenz (its) teacher is certain to voice (his teaching) to his audience; and on this occasion there certainly is a place (where this happens), and where all this concurs time is implicitly operating.

Specifically, in the case of an individual, as the experiential embodiment of Existenz, it is stated:[21]

When the material and mental are in intimate union, (the person's) body is the site and therefore considered as the "place." Within this field of perceptible qualities consciousness (perception) is the "teacher" around whom ideas gather as the "audience." Feeling is the "content" (of the teaching) and motivation is the "time" (of this live situation).

As is evident from these two passages—the first referring to a phase of and in experience, which is as yet undisturbed by explicit thematization, and the second referring to thematically explicit determinations—the five vectorial bonds that make up the problem situation all work simultaneously.

Additionally, each of these bonds also interfaces with a hierarchically stratified order reflecting the dynamics of Being. Three passages may serve to clarify this point. The first states:[22]

Since (Being's) facticity is open it is not given as either substance or quality; since (its) actuality is lucent it does not shed its character of auto-presencing as an atemporal outward directed glow; and since (its) resonating concern is excitatory-intelligent, it is unceasingly there as the reason (ground) for the emergence of its sensitivity expanding into pristine cognitions.

The second passage highlights the indivisibility of Being's structural features:[23]

Facticity is the indivisibility of being open and lucent; actuality is the indivisibility of being lucent and open; and resonating concern is the indivisibility of being excitatory-intelligent and open.

The third passage sums up the inseparability of these structural features with respect to the manner in which they are experienced:[24]

Although facticity, actuality, and resonating concern are discussed as being distinct, they do not involve separability. As is stated in the *Thal-'gyur:*[25]

"Pristine cognitions in this (hierarchical) order are triple but inseparable."

Hence, from the viewpoint of the nonthematic, one speaks of facticity, and this is open and thematically inaccessible; from the viewpoint of the thematic, one speaks of actuality, and this is a coming-into-presence as yet not amenable to concretization; and from the viewpoint of the unity (of the nonthematic and the thematic) one speaks of resonating concern, and this is (the indivisibility of) being excitatory-intelligent and being open, and it defies any congealing into (something) eternally existing or (something) eternally nonexisting.

[3]

Because excitatory intelligence is a pervasive feature of Existenz (as the coming-into-presence of Being), and is capable of assuming specific aspects according to its contextual operation within the hierarchical order of each of its levels, the figure of a teacher, as one of the vectorial bonds in any problem situation, gains prominence. It is "he" who initiates the information input and, as it were, determines the character of the situation as a whole. It is therefore permissible to speak of an overall plan as it already exists on the level of Being's facticity being activated in specific situations by the contextually determined teacher. However, inasmuch as facticity is an utter openness—seething with activity and tending to become actuality—any situation together with the vectorial bonds holding it can only be a complex of virtual processes from among which the one figuratively spoken of as teacher assumes a gestalt or virtual existence *(chos-sku)*, in a virtual field *(chos-dbyings)*, and communicates an overall plan virtually (nonverbally) to a virtual audience constituted by the directionality of the intentional (cognitive) operation at a virtual moment. What happens may be conceived of as a first stirring within Being, which then tends to arrange itself in a vertically structured hierarchy.[26]

These virtual processes, however, are inseparable from the actual or, more exactly, self-actualizing processes through which Being radiates in and as Existenz. This radiant and lucent actuality is the spiritual sphere in the sense of an appreciated or felt reality, a presentational immediacy that is yet neither a here nor a now. It is a realm in which the teacher is a gestalt still participating in the virtual while mediating between a downward acting movement of the virtual existence and an upward acting movement that operates from Being's level of resonating concern, where the teacher is both the ideal toward which man strives and the initiator of this urge to find this ideal, which is active on social and cultural planes. These three levels—virtual, mediating, and social-cultural—imaged to be stacked one on top of the other, yield the notion of a vertical hierarchical order. In a person's life these levels are lived simultaneously.

It is the dynamics of Being that makes Being transform itself into a gestalt becoming progressively modified. Its appreciation is already a kind of interpretation which is due to Being's character of concern, responding to and resonating, as it were, with its own actuality so that this gestalt, inseparable from its awareness, is an eminently creative movement. Nevertheless, this very responsiveness and resonance, dealing creatively with the auto-presencing actuality of Being, is a critical moment—creative cognition, an exciting and excited awareness, can take the lead, or the excitement can be lost, in which case cognition becomes ever more dull in the stifling maze of its own constructs, figuratively expressed by saying that the light goes out.

It seems that at the one extreme of the experiential spectrum there is a high-energy optimal awareness *(rig-pa)* operating in and as a pristine cognition *(ye-shes)* coincident with a formal gestalt as the external expression of an inner meaning *(sku)*, carrying with it the feeling of certainty and undivided wholeness. At the other extreme there is a stepped-down awareness *(ma-rig-pa)*, which manifests as the thingness of thought and its reductionist programs through which the world is seen as but a collocation of separable entities, with the attendant sense of uncertainty and unsatisfactoriness. The former is associated, in the Buddhist tradition, with an experiential interpretation termed Nirvāṇa,the latter is associated with an experiential interpretation termed Saṃsāra.It would be hard to overestimate the significance of this extraordinary state of affairs. The inevitable consequence is that Saṃsāra and Nirvāṇa are expectation values, rather than quantitatively determined end states. This suggests that all human uncertainty with its attendant anxiety is due to the unrestricted and unrestrictable freedom of Being constituted in and as Existenz.[27]

[4]

The immense complexity of the self-structuring process discussed above manifests itself as configurational fields within a hierarchy as it specifically relates to man's physical existence which, in the light of the dynamics of Being-*qua*-Existenz, necessitates a reinterpretation of what is commonly termed the body *(lus)*. Most often, we use the term body to refer to a physical object in space and time, and consider it as an aggregate of the disparate elements into which it can be analyzed. By contrast, when we speak of the body as experienced, we do not think of it as being simply the physical object amenable to analytical investigation by the various branches of science. Rather, we experience it actively and imaginatively in many ways, and we do so because the body is itself an active embodying process. As such it acts as an orientational point in terms of which and around which the surrounding world in all its richness and variety is structured and organized. Furthermore, the existence and cognizance of such an orientational point implies that there also is operative a spatio-temporal singling-out process. This process of singling out points to an intelligent agency of which the body *(lus)* as observed and felt is a concrete actualization of a formal gestalt *(sku)*. In this process, which is likened to water turning into ice, the intelligence loses much, though not all, of its excitatory character.

This active character of the body along with its ability to constitute a sequence of "new" (singled-out) transmutations, is clearly brought out in the following quotation:[28]

> Body is so called because there is a running around in circles, an adaptive arrangement, a leaving behind, a not remaining the same. Body is so called because there is a going onward after having left the present (body) behind, in view of the fact that, with any body, after having left behind the previous body constituted by the four elemental forces and their atoms, one recognizes the present body as not being the previous one and that even hereafter, in not recognizing this state of affairs, one will take up (a new body) which is not this present body.

The manner in which intelligence is pervasively present in the body, whereby it acquires the particular global meaning for this intelligence of which it is its embodiment, may be illustrated by a reference to perception in art. Just as aesthetic meaning is experienced as pervading and belonging to the whole texture and pattern of a work of art (be this a poem, a painting, a sonata, or a ballet), so also the existential meaning of the body is inseparable (aesthetically indistinguishable) from the body itself. In perception mediated by concepts and categories, we perceive the body as a collocation of many different units, but in immediate and existentially significant perception we perceive the body as a gestalt of meaningful evidence and the awareness *of* this meaningfulness is pervasively *in* the gestalt. It is this difference of mediated empirico-analytical perception versus immediate existentially significant perception, which is hinted at in the statement in the *sGron-ma snang-byed*:[29]

> The foundation and site of excitation *(rig-pa)* is the body;
> If there is no body, there is no (excitation).

If there is, there is certainly pristine cognition *(ye-shes)*.
If one were to search for it in the body
From head to toe
With the various methods of investigation
Using concepts by postulation
One would not find it.
Neither would one find it by looking for it
By means of various prognostications.
Does this then mean that it does not exist at all?
It does not mean that it does not exist at all
But that it is clearly present when bodily and verbal preoccupations have
    ceased.[30]
Just as blood pervades the body:
If a stupid person were
To search.the (surface of the) body for blood
He would not find it anywhere.
Does this then mean that there is no blood in the body?
It does not mean that there is no blood in the body
(Which) depends on the blood pervading it all.
But if a skillful person
Were to let blood from a vein, blood would come out.
It is the same with the pristine cognition residing in the body.

The key-term in this passage is "pristine cognition" *(ye-shes)*, which is
more of a prethematic possibility rather than a content-terminated cognition.[31] What this term refers to derives directly from the self-excitatoriness
(rang-rig) of the field as the universe of and for experience, and as such
denotes a sensitivity and alertness that makes cognition possible as such on
every level of the biosphere.[32] This pristine cognition has a self-referential
intentionality of atemporal primordiality *(ye)*, which is indicated in the
statement:[33]

(Its) actuality has been spontaneously there atemporally *(ye)*;
From this, then, understanding comes to the fore.
This is the definition of pristine cognitiveness *(ye-shes)*.

In particular, primordiality is the value and, by implication, the meaning[34]
that goes with existence, as is stated in the following quotation:[35]

The definition: (we speak of) pristine cognition *(ye-shes)* because
The value (of existence) that has been there atemporally *(ye)* is known
    (shes) as such.

The excitatory character of pristine cognition pervades the whole organism. Consequently, an organism cannot but express this excitation which, in turn, indicates the system's ability to grow and to achieve optimization of its potential. This is illustrated in the statement:[36]

> Pristine cognitiveness (deriving from the) self-excitatoriness (of the system) is present in the body[37]
> Like oil in sesame seeds;
> The body's healthy complexion and glowing appearance
> Is constituted by the moisture of pristine cognitiveness.

From the perspective of experience, therefore, our body embodies many meanings. Only when the experience of this process of embodiment is channelled into representational thinking by becoming filtered through a system of concepts, categories, and constructs which, in turn, are sustained by the wayward character of affective processes, usually termed emotions, do we fail to attend to these meanings, being content with the notions we have about the body as an object. This tendency to reduce a vivid and expressive experience to an impassive system of concepts, and to dissect and fragmentize its presentational immediacy, prevents us from perceiving and appreciating the full meaning and value of the body. It very often leads to denial of the body and to a treatment of it as something from which one must dissociate oneself. Concepts imply selection; that is, some aspects of what we perceive are contrasted with others, some are even suppressed, and the emotions assist in further distorting that which is perceived, because they, too, are denied their scope.[38] In the context of our body this state of affairs is termed the body of sedimented drives and tendencies (initiated by and filtered through) a system of concepts and discursive ventures *(rnam-rtog bag-chags-kyi lus).*[39]

While perception geared to such a system tends to distract from what is immediately present and to become increasingly lost in the maze of its projective ventures, which are amenable to quantification, measurement and control, intrinsic perception and nonrepresentational thinking not only free feeling and imagination from the narrowness of representational and conceptual confines, but also give perception a wider scope and depth. In such perception, which is as much cognition as it is feeling retaining throughout its operation a freshness and originality not found anywhere else, the body is not perceived as an opaque object for discursiveness. Rather, it is known and felt as if it were there for the first time—transparent and iridescent as an apparition or a phantom, fascinating, charming, enchanting, and supremely beautiful. Its perception is a "letting things be" with no attempt to control entering into the situation. This state of affairs is termed the body in its magic of being there phantom-like in and for a pristine cognition *(ye-shes sgyu-ma'i lus)*.[40]

But this phantom-like, dream-like body seems to point to a still deeper layer or source from which it has emerged gradually taking on form and shape. This source is felt to be a preciousness that cannot be likened to anything precious we ordinarily know. It is also felt to be a mystery, though not in the sense that something remains hidden, but in a more fundamental sense. What is mysterious *(gsang-ba)* is the inexplicable yet undeniable and problematic thrust of a deep-structured dynamic into the limited domain of one's individual existence in such a manner that the boundary of this personal existence is broken from within, thereby resulting in a surpassed yet integrated organization of a more complex array of interactional forces. This preciousness and mystery is certainly not some transcendental "thing" located in an unattainable realm; it is the preciousness of what has been termed Existenz, the manner in which the mystery that is Being makes its presence felt. This level of embodiment is termed the mystery body of and as pure preciousness *(rin-po-che gsang-ba'i lus)*.[41] This level abides as a first stirring, which eventually and almost inevitably leads to the origination of two universes—a qualitative (experiential) and a quantitative (thematically discursive)—which yet continue to interact. It is as yet an inner light which, although absorbed and withdrawn into itself, is not at all faint or dim. It tends to radiate into an as yet nonexistent outside and therefore is not simply an interiority. Although it has not yet moved away from its interiority, yet tends to do so, it is also as yet not an exteriority.[42] It is the realm where dreams are born—nothing as yet and yet all that is to evolve.

The above three embodying levels, as distinct experiences, display a marked gradation in what may be called insubstantiality (the qualitative) on the one hand, and massiveness (the quantitative), on the other, depending on the direction into which one inquires.[43] This gradation in itself points to the existence of a hierarchical order within the ongoing process of experience. However, these body experiences are also part of a topological process inasmuch as each is a readout or translation (into biophysical processes) of its underlying invariant which, in contrast with the embodying level *(lus)*, is technically termed a formal gestalt *(sku)*.[44] Topology, as a branch of modern mathematics, deals with the relations between points and those fundamental properties of a figure that remain invariant when the figure is twisted out of shape. In the context under discussion here, there is bending and twisting, technically termed a going astray *('khrul-pa)* or stepped-down excitation *(ma-rig-pa)*, which does not, however, compromise the dynamic invariance of the formal gestalt. In particular, there is a twisting or going astray of the gestalt into the shape of a body[45] such that a vast expanse is crumpled into a tight sheath and a transparent and open presence is mistaken (misread) as some thing which, as an isolated or more exactly a self-isolating system, now begins to exert its gravitational pull.[46]

These topological processes start with Existenz, which presents the three structural features of Being—facticity *(ngo-bo)*, actuality *(rang-bzhin)*, and resonating concern *(thugs-rje)*—to its own intelligence for a readout as gestalt possibilities. This phase is marked by uncertainty. The intelligence can either recognize these gestalt possibilities or invariants for what they are and embark on a process in which these invariants are preserved, or it can fail to do so and engage in topological transformation and transmutation. Existenz is thus truly creative in making use of these transformations and their invariants, which are mutually related processes taking place simultaneously in all the different structural sublevels of an integral system such as a living individual. Inasmuch as invariance (the qualitative as formal gestalt) is not amenable to measurement or quantification, we may speak of it as being virtual. Yet this virtual energy is quite "real" insofar as it can profoundly affect the body (as that which is tangibly amenable to quantitative and quantifiable analysis). The virtual is thus the inexhaustible "treasure chest" that makes life worth living.[47]

This inexhaustible energy is the very mystery of man's existence. It reaches into each of us through Existenz, which comes as a disclosure of Being. It comes and is there as an open pure possibility, eliciting a response precisely by its being there. The response, proceeding from the spirituality and intelligence inherent in Existenz, and sharing in and pervading all of its openness and lucency, is an indeterminacy and ambiguity. It can be revealing, creating a world that is felt to be meaningful and sensuously delightful, and which in this imaging activity is also felt to be thoroughly liberating. But it also can be concealing and restrictive. In a response that is revealing, mystery is allowed to unfold and is transfigured by understanding; whereas in a response that allows itself to slip into determinateness, mystery is lost, and with its loss man's life congeals into a frozen pattern of dismal impoverishment. Even so, the mystery remains:[48]

> Just as under the floor in the house of a pauper
> There lies an inexhaustible treasure;
> Yet the man does not know it and the treasure also
> Does not tell him "Here I am."
> So it is with the priceless treasure (life's mystery) embedded in one's mind:

It is flawless, nothing need be added nor removed from it.
Since this man does not understand, he will only
Feel the multitudinous hardships of poverty.

[5]

In speaking of Being's inexhaustible energy as a mystery, an element of wonder is introduced, which itself is not separable from the dynamic character of experience. This mystery also carries with it a sense of reverence and tenderness, which one feels called upon to protect against profanation.[49]

Wonder is made up of two features which, though analytically distinguishable, require each other's presence in the intentional structure of lived experience. The one refers to whatever excites astonishment or amazement, be it by its beauty, greatness, or inexplicableness (the object phase of the intentional structure). The other denotes the amazement and wonderment (the act phase) that intends this wonder.[50] Yet because neither phase can claim priority over the other, wonder is ineluctably intentional in structure. There can be no wonder (the intentional object) without the act of wondering that specifically intends wonder, just as there can be no intentional act of wondering without the intended wonder. As an intentional act, wondering directs itself onto an object which presents itself as sheer possibility. This does not mean that the intentional structure of wonder cannot be indicated with some degree of descriptive precision. Whatever is intended by and presents itself to the act of wondering is considered in its possibility for its own sake, and not for the sake of something extrinsic, such as its (possible) concretization into the fully determinate and thematic structure which constitutes empirical reality. As a matter of fact, in wonder, the possible (providing extra freedom of action and appreciation) ranges so widely that any form of determinateness is experienced as a constraint, a fetter, and an impoverishment. Therefore, the intentional structure of wonder (through which mystery manifests itself) carries with it an auto-solicitation that triggers the release of the mind from the confines of self-imposed determinateness. It also triggers the opening up of experience to realms of the possible—such realms being amenable to destruction if taken as objects. Wonder is a bliss-filled presence, which is neither the result of a formally valid inference nor the product of a judgment about some quality controlled by empirical reality—wonder is an exclamatory exuberance:[51]

E-ma-ho:
    This marvelous and wondrous fact
    Is the mystery of all perfect Buddhas:
    From that which has no origin, everything (that is) has taken its origin;
    Yet in so having taken its origin, it remains that which has no origin.

E-ma-ho:
    This marvelous and wondrous fact
    Is the mystery of all perfect Buddhas:
    From that which never ceases all that ceases (seems to come);
    Yet in ceasing it remains that which never ceases.

E-ma-ho:
    This marvelous and wondrous fact
    Is the mystery of all perfect Buddhas:
    From that which has no locus all that is located comes;
    Yet in being so located it remains that which has no locus.

E-ma-ho:
    This marvelous and wondrous fact
    Is the mystery of all perfect Buddhas:
    From that which is unobjectifiable all that is objectifiable comes;
    Yet in being so objectifiable it remains that which is unobjectifiable.

E-ma-ho:
    This marvelous and wondrous fact
    Is the mystery of all perfect Buddhas:
    From that which neither comes nor goes all that comes and goes
        proceeds;
    Yet in so coming and going it remains that which neither comes nor
        goes.

Of the five above mentioned examples illustrating the "mystery of all perfect Buddhas," the first modality of mystery is intended to point out that what we would refer to as the "universe" is not something that happens against a background other than itself, nor is it dependent on a principle outside itself. The second modality suggests that the kaleidoscopic array of empirical reality is the realization of a formal structure, the transmutation and transformation of gestalt invariants. The third modality specifies the indivisibility of the openness of Being and its ceaseless presencing in all its manifestations. The fourth modality intimates the working of energy unfolding, an overall evolutionary principle, a creativity which is

Experience-as-such *(sems-nyid)* as the builder of universes, in which the individual self-centered world is but a tiny ripple, a drop believing itself to be the ocean. The fifth modality is to be understood as wonder's holistic nature.

These five examples, moreover, illustrate particular possibilities which, each in its own way, are intentional correlates to an intending act, previously termed pristine cognition *(ye-shes)*. In itself it involves two operations: a pristine cognitiveness as an overall sensitivity, and pristine cognitions as sensitivities to particular forms.[52]

The exclamatory exuberance, which expresses and is also the expression of the mystery of Being through its dynamics of Existenz, sets in motion a series of related processes that are aimed at unravelling the exigency inherent in the human condition. There is the feeling of distress at not understanding this mystery which is yet so vital for a full life. This distress, too, prompts an exclamation, at once enigmatic and emblematic, thereby immediately pinpointing the modalities in which mystery is elusively operative:[53]

> E-ma-ho:
>> A mystery from the very beginning;
>> A palpable mystery in what presents itself in various shapes;
>> A fundamental and hence deep mystery;
>> A mystery so profound that nowhere is anything more profound.

It is this feeling of distress that initiates an awareness of the basis of failure to understand the mystery and, as a consequence, to be caught in a network of restrictive forces. This growing awareness is pervaded by tenderness, a capacity for expressing such gently responsive emotions as love and compassion with a delicacy and gentleness, which are especially thrilling to those concerned. And so it is love that exclaims:[54]

> E-ma-ho:
>> It is from the thrust toward Being[55]
>> That (beings) drift away by their own notions as driving force.
>> As to their various embodiments and sensory enjoyments and
>> Their stations in life as well as their experiences of (happiness and)
>>> sorrow:
>> They entertain the separating notions of I and mine.

Thematization, as is apparent from this quotation, introduces a division into the primordial unity of experience, and is seen to develop into the customary subject-object dichotomy. This development takes place in such a manner that the distinct separation of the interiority of a constituted subject and the exteriority of a constituted object is a later phase. Even in this separation, however, subject and object are held together by an intentional act in which a subject grasps, appropriates and holds on to its object, which is placed into the reach of the subject as something to be grasped, appropriated and held on to. In this context the intentional act acquires the character of what Heidegger so appropriately has called *Jemeinigkeit* (in each and every instant mine). The dynamic character of this intentional act precludes the possibility of falsely hypostatizing entities. As is stated in the *gSang-ba snying-po*:[56]

> Nobody has ever fettered (anyone);
> Neither is there anything (that could be called) a fetter;
> Nor is there (anyone) to be fettered!
> (Fettering) is done by the divisive notion which holds to a self
> Tying and untying knots in (an imaginary rope in) the open sky.

Such a process is also able to disconnect itself from the concrete concerns and particular projects of life-world activities, which all suffer, through their ego-centeredness, from errors of overestimation, misapplication, and mislocation. In effecting this disconnection, which goes beyond the predications of bondage and freedom, compassion—not as a mere sentimentality, but as the enactment of a resonating concern which is Being manifesting itself through Existenz—comes into full play:[57]

> In order to disclose Buddhahood
> Which has been there from all beginning in utter perfection,
> Having nothing to do with fettering and freeing,
> (Being's resonating concern) arranges various displays.

These displays are both incentives to find oneself and one's endeavors to understand what man has been and most authentically is. These endeavors have found their expression in the various spiritual pursuits, not as ends in themselves but as beacons.

III. The Recognition of the Problem Situation as the Evolutionary Zero Point

[1]

The preceding chapter has dealt with the problem situation as the starting point of man's endeavors to secure a meaningful life. Its analysis showed that the problem situation is already a manifestation of Being's projectivity as Existenz and as such is pervaded by inherent intelligence which, as resonating concern, gives each situation a distinct flavor. Even so, any such situation remains a dynamical whole and can never become a static end-state. Moreover, the vectorial tendencies within this whole are not externally related units out of which the situation is additively built up; nor is the individuality of these vector forces absorbed or dissolved in an undifferentiated unity of the situational whole. This is admittedly difficult to grasp because of our ingrained habit of thematizing thinking—made explicit by the discrete signifiers of our language, whose fixity masks and obscures the dynamic undercurrent of meanings—in which the differentiations so established are taken to be actually separate and hence separable things. It must be emphasized, therefore, that there is no functional distinction between Being and Existenz. To understand this, dichotomizing mental habits must be given up and replaced by a dynamic notion of experience, whose intentional structure reveals an open-ended process constituting both the source and continuity of being human. We can guard ourselves against tendencies toward dichotomizing by recognizing that analytic differentiations merely refer to the vectorial tendencies within the source and continuity of experience itself. It is because of this, the experiential character of Being and Existenz, that it is permissible to speak of Existenz (continuity) as the projectivity of Being (source), which is felt as an immediate presence, an ever-present challenge that can never be reified. In this challenging situation the felt awareness is pervasively present. With this precaution not to solidify what is translucently present in and as experience, the import of the following quotation should become readily apparent:[1]

The concrete presence (of experience) is Existenz as ground, in the sense that both the state of being a Buddha and that of being a sentient being are born from it. Therefore it is justifiable to speak of Existenz as ancestress or as ground. It is through understanding that one hastens to Existenz (as the experiential continuity termed) the state of being a Buddha, and through nonunderstanding to Existenz (as the experiential continuity termed) the state of being a sentient being. Therefore it is also justifiable to speak of Existenz as ground because of having made Existenz itself the ground.

Understanding is here seen as *residing* in Being-*qua*-Existenz as the vividness of experiential continuity; it is not brought from somewhere else. In a certain sense, understanding is an evaluative term. We value only that which we can understand and which, therefore, has meaning. By contrast, what we do not understand can have no meaning and, by implication, also no value (unless ignorance). Meaning and value, therefore, turn out to be experientially synonymous and, because of their dynamic character, fluctional. Whether there is understanding or nonunderstanding, each in its own way colors the nature of experience. Wherever and whenever understanding is involved, whether we speak of value or of meaning, the fact remains that neither can be reduced to something else, which then elicits its own response. In other words, intelligence (revealing itself in understanding and concealing itself in nonunderstanding) is inherent in the process of Being's auto-projective coming-into-presence as its own actuality. Intelligence, as here understood, is never an afterthought nor a by-product of random motions of matter.

In the human context, intelligence *reaches* into man's life as his spirituality, constituting itself as human subjectivity *(yid)*.[2] The latter, therefore, is not immutable essence, rather it is a product of an overall evolutionary force moving in an optimizing direction, thereby enabling the subject to transcend itself by overcoming its limited domains. This force is felt as giving meaning to man's life and is experienced as having existential significance. It is of primary importance to recognize this *presence* as a *process,* which is both thematic and nonthematic in inseparable fusion. Regarding the indivisibility of the thematic and nonthematic aspects of reality, Klong-chen rab-'byams-pa says:[3]

> Here,[4] first of all, it is important to know how (Being) is abidingly there (as a presence).
> Although it displays many facets according to the (spiritual) pursuits (of it),
> Its unequivocal dynamics, the indivisibility of (the two) reality modes,
> Is the mysterious treasure-house of the Buddhas.

Its actuality is a pristine cognitiveness in sheer lucency;
Since time without beginning it has been of a deeply tranquil nature, not
  marred by verbal-mental proliferations,
A spontaneous presence, uncontrived, like the sun in the sky.[5]
Since this actuality has been there atemporally *(ye-nas)* in utter purity,
There is no divisibility in its presencing and openness; it can neither be
  affirmed nor denied; it neither comes nor goes.

This indivisibility of reality is not such that it can be affirmed or denied;
  rather,
Since it is beyond the differentiations pertaining to the qualifications of
  the conventional and therefore
Beyond the two realities postulated (by the philosophical systems), all
  thematizations have come to rest.
Since in the continuum (of sheer lucency), presencing and openness are
  not (there as) two (entities),
This reality is correctly said to be the indivisibility of reality.

If a division into two reality modes is made, as is done in common
  parlance,
All the mistaken identities subsumed under (the term) Saṃsāra,
Constitute what is conventionally held to be real, despite the fact that it is
  (actually) unreal and deceptive.
Whereas all that is profound, serene, and a sheer lucency, subsumed
  under (the term) Nirvāṇa,
Is claimed to be an unchanging actuality and real in the ultimate sense.

All that presents itself in such variety and is held conventionally to be real
Is like a magic show, the moon's reflection in water, a phantom, a fictive
  image.
If one thoroughly analyzes that which is a presence without actually being
  anything,
(One will find it) to be open like the sky and having no denotation at all.[6]
But if one does not analyze (this), one experiences various delights which,
  like a magic show,
Have their origin in the combined operations of deceptive tendencies—
They are like the hallucinations experienced when a person has eaten
  Dātura.

Because all this, open in its actuality and without any ontic character,
Is the manner in which the ultimate abides,
It is said to be the ultimately real, while its presencing is the convention-
  ally real.
Since from the time it presences onward it has nothing about it which

could be asserted to have come into existence and so on,
Its actuality, being this, is the indivisibility of reality.

Since actuality, pure from the very beginning, and
Sheer lucency, the ultimately real, are such as not to be divisible into two
   (separable) entities,
Saṃsāra and Nirvāṇa are indivisible, and not two separate realities.

Despite the fact that there is a presence, it has nothing about it to make it
   an (ontic) actuality, because Saṃsāra is not found as such,
And since this cannot be divided and separated into something distinct
   from the ultimacy of Being,
Saṃsāra and Nirvāṇa are indivisible and shown to be alike (in their
   identity with Being).

To conceive of (reality) in any other way (indicates) a warped mind
Which is completely muddled about what is meant by Being abiding.

(However) as long as there is a presencing from the perspective of mistaken identities, cause and effect are (operationally valid notions),
And therefore it is important to know what is good and bad, what to
   accept and reject.

That which remains unchanging, ultimately real,
Is a sheer lucency, a spontaneously present pervasive thrust towards bliss
   supreme.[7]
The very indivisibility of openness, lucency, and excitation.

This, (Being's) spontaneously present actuality is a configuration—
Atemporally it has been spontaneous and complete, possessed of the
   energy (coming from and leading to) limpid clearness and consummate perspicacity,
Diaphanously pure, defying all thematization, free from any partiality,
Profound and calm, the inseparableness of formal gestalt and pristine
   cognitiveness.

The analogies for its existence in all living beings
Are known by the wise as
A treasure under the earth, a flame within a jar, and the unfolding display
   of a lotus flower.

Just as a pauper remains destitute by not knowing
That a precious treasure lies beneath the floor of his house,
So we remain continually destitute due to the evils of the world

Because the ever-present Buddhahood within ourselves
Is obscured by the overlay of an eightfold cognitive ensemble[8] (functioning as one's) body, speech, and mind.

Just as magnificent wealth would be available for us and others
If we were to unearth it when a person with divine eyes,
Having seen this treasure would show us the means to dig it out,
So also Buddhahood would be realized by ourselves if and when we
    implemented this experience of Being as
Taught by competent persons,
And its most excellent value, as it exists for ouselves as well as for others,
    would then turn into the Wish-Fulfilling Gem.

Just as a light within a jar, however bright it may be,
Is rendered invisible by the jar and does not shine outward,
So also the meaningfulness of our existence, pervading every one of our
    pores, though residing within us
Is rendered invisible by the jar of our (intellectual and affective) veils and
    does not shine outward,
But just as the light would shine brightly if the jar were broken,
So also, when we have become free from the obscurations that mar the
    (various) spiritual stages,
We shall make the lamp shine everywhere throughout the world.

Just as in a lotus flower Buddha-nature
Does not shine outward, since it is shut in by the petals,
So also the capacity for Buddhahood, shining in its own light, cannot be
    seen
Since it is concealed by the thousand petals of subject-object constructs.
But just as the flower is there in its brightness once the petals open,
So also when we are free from the foliage of mistaken identifications that
    come due to the subject-object division,
The triple structure of our existentiality in limpid clearness and consum-
    mate perspicacity shines by itself.[9]

Therefore be sensitive to the presence in yourself
Of the continuum that is the internal logic of Being, the ultimately real, a
    sheer lucency.

There are many names for it:
It is termed a (continual) source because Saṃsāra and Nirvāṇa spring
    from it;
It is named a spontaneously present actuality because it has existed
    atemporally,

It is acclaimed, by sages who have eyes to see,
As intrinsic (potential) energy,[10] because its (radiation) is rendered
  invisible by impurity;
As ultimate reality because it is Being's presence;
As a flawless sheer lucency because it has been pure since its very
  beginning;
As the very still-point because (the localized presence) of the two extremes
  have been eliminated;
As the transcending function of appreciative discrimination because it
  passes beyond thematic confines;
As the indivisibility of the two reality modes, which are the purity of
  openness and lucency;
As the internal logic of Being, suchness, because it neither moves away
  from nor changes into something other (than itself).

Although those who do not know how all this works and cling to utter
  emptiness
Make big noises about it as being dissociated from the limiting (notions)
  of existence and nonexistence;
Not knowing the reason (ground) for dissociation (from these notions),
  and holding views which seem lofty (but still are worldly),
They stand outside this teaching here,
And well deserve to smear their empty-mindedness with ashes.

What here the Teacher has said to be the treasure of life's meaning,
Is the omnipresent vitalizing sheer lucency, the path supreme,
The (way) in which Being as the ground (of our existence) spontaneously
  abides.

He who knows this ultimate, (seen) through a vision more profound than
  profound,
Is freed from pitfalls and obscurations, and unaffected by (the two
  extremes of) eternalism and nihilism,
His realization will be meaningful, quickly he will spiritually grow.
He will possess the eye that sees the (real) meaning of all Sūtras and
  Tantras.
Therefore, grow sensitive to (this) sheer lucency, the manner in which
  Being abides.

[2]

In the above lengthy quotation, which epitomizes the multifaceted
nature of experience, two themes stand out. One is that of indivisibility

(dbyer-med), the other that of configuration *(dkyil-'khor)*. Both, however, are intimately related.

As we have seen in a previous chapter, indivisibility, also referred to as nonduality, names the functional operation of complementarity. It does not indicate the obliteration of differentiations, nor does it imply a fusion of disparate entities. Rather it emphasizes the presence of a continuum from which, speaking negatively, dichotomies such as exterior and interior, subject and object are suspended.[11] More positively stated, these dichotomies are seen and felt to interpenetrate "like the reflection of the moon in water."

The indivisibility of Being and Existenz can be illustrated by analogies taken from the realm of science, which speaks of the indivisibility of energy and its radiation and of the vacuum and its fluctuations. But in rDzogs-chen thought there is the additional factor of intelligence which inheres in the very dynamics of the unfolding universe itself, and which makes primordiality of experience of paramount importance.[12] The atemporal onset of this unfoldment occasions the emergence of various intentional structures, thereby allowing felt meanings to occur. Since this onset is structurally prior to any functional splitting, one speaks of the indivisibility of openness and its presencing, which involves the gauging of what will become the "world" (as the specific horizon-form of lived-through experience):[13]

> From out of the reach and range of the initially pure *(ka-dag)*, which is open, lucent, uncompounded, and like the clear blue sky, there comes the presenc-ing of a spontaneously available *(lhun-grub)* lucency which is there as a quincunx of light-values of pristine cognitions, an internal glowing, like the sun, moon, and the stars, never ceasing (to shine in the sky), and (it is there) as resonating concern possessed of the energy of excitation.

Resonating concern *(thugs-rje)*—the excitatoriness and resonance of the field which is Being-*qua*-Existenz, marking and sustaining pristine cogni-tions in all their primordiality—determines whether the world is to be experienced within and as an authentic or inauthentic horizon-form. In so experiencing a world we find ourselves within, never outside, a presence which, regardless of whether we experience it authentically or not, already belongs to the conventionally accepted *(kun-rdzob)*, and not to the ulti-mately valid *(don-dam)* domain of reality. Strictly speaking, the latter domain is no localizable domain at all, it is Being itself, which we cannot authentically describe without falsification. However, insofar as the ulti-mately valid, Being as an utter openness, is nowhere else than in its lucency, or Existenz, the unifying still-point for the horizon-forms of the authentic and inauthentic, which both constitute the domain of our conventionally accepted reality, it exhibits both the ultimately valid and the conventionally accepted reality modes in an indivisible manner.

Being's lucency, which is the ceaseless auto-presencing of that which in a certain sense is the "real" (that with which we can and do deal), initiates an "auto-investigation" sparked by the pervasiveness of intelligence. Consequently, this very auto-presencing of lucency in the ceaseless manifold of presence-*cum*-interpretation[14] supplies, as it were, the formative (back) ground against and within which the question, "What does it mean to be?" is automatically (and repeatedly) formulated. Lucency, therefore, can be understood as the process character of conventionally accepted reality, which, figuratively speaking, comes before any ontic specifications. This lucency elicits responsive perturbations from within the auto-presencing, thereby giving rise to the distinction between what is authentic conventional reality *(yang-dag kun-rdzob)* and what is inauthentic conventional reality *(log-pa'i kun-rdzob)*. Both these reality modes primarily involve distinctions of direction and deployment of organizational tendencies. Authentic conventional reality is a mode in which the discriminating, disruptive, and disconcerting determinations set up by representational thought and its rigid subject-object structuring have been suspended. Its operation is undisturbed, that is, unimpeded in utter purity, by such rigidity so that "the whole of reality comes into presence as the merriment of configuration patterning":[15]

> Pristine cognitions make merry in pristine cognitiveness,
> This very merrymaking by pristine cognitions is an open-textured
> plenum.[16]

By contrast, inauthentic conventional reality is a mode that has gone wrong in that it operates (perceptually and experientially) in terms of bogus dichotomies, thereby converting the open texture of reality into an assortment of insular entities.

Lucency never loses its process character, yet the possibility of making operational distinctions between different conventional reality modes allows each such mode to take on a certain ontic quality. The process character of lucency is paradoxical, for it carries with it a sense of magic which, on the one hand, is kept alive by the freshness of pristine cognition preserving existential evidence values, while, on the other hand, the freshness of the magic is dissipated in ever more rigid self-propagating absurdities *(log-rtog)*. It is not as though the freshness of pristine cognition provided the raw material for what is then organized into accumulations of discretely sensed input. Rather, both movements within lucency have their "own" organizational features, and both have their own indivisibility in the sense that the movement of each, in its presencing and openness, is like the indivisibility encountered in the reflection of the moon in water. The fact that each movement has its own direction[17] does not contradict the fact that each is an embedded tendency within experience abiding in the lucency of Being, and that each reality mode, be it the authentic or the inauthentic conventional, surges as an ongoing process, effectively blocking any attempt at reducing the open-texture nature of Experience-as-such into discrete isolatable data. Although in its openness, each movement "shares" in the ultimately valid reality mode *(don-dam)*, in its presencing as the conventional reality mode two directions open and may be freely followed:[18]

> All the mistaken notions that make up what is called the world [as the impure presencing of the without and within, the environment and the beings, are like dream images, as well as that] stepped-down intelligence [which does not recognize Being's presence as an atemporally operative dissipative structure], hold man in deep sleep.
> Due to the bifurcating notions of the apprehendable and apprehending [as determinants there comes-into-presence the infinite variety of]
> External [objects] and internal [subjects so that sentient beings] move about in a nexus [of the without and within, which is the result of mistaken presencing due to the momentum in the process, and which may be likened to a wheel's rotation].
> The incongruity [of the dynamics of presencing and the reification into objects] is felt as happiness and suffering [respectively so that there appears the movement from one bounded state to another so characteristic of Saṃsāra].
>
> [Nevertheless, Being's] actuality [in its coming-into-presence as Saṃsāra] has not slipped from [what is the] internal logic [of Being, an atemporal freedom that remains self-same and whole, because Being's actuality is Being's very openness].
> [Despite the fact that there is such a coming-into-presence as Saṃsāra without this presencing being something as such] it is the authenticity [of Being-*qua*-Existenz] that [in its conventional setting] is there in two magic-like modes; [for]
> There is nothing else [that could be said to be] a subject and a subject's [interpretation of its experience, just as the dream and the dreamer's mind are not two different entities; it is Experience-as-such that presences itself as dream and dreamer].

[Hence what is the temporal coming-into-presence as Saṃsāra is some-
thing] aspectwise pure and of the same [atemporal] nature as [the
internal logic of] Being [which in its auto-presencing remains pure as
Being's continuum. This means that Being's intentionality (expressing
itself in) the spontaneity and completeness of its meaning-saturated
gestalt, is the overarching reality that atemporally encompasses each
and everything referred to as Saṃsāra and Nirvāṇa].

All [differentiations introducing] otherness [between] a subject and a
subject's [interpretation of its experience]
Are but absurd constructions [and nothing else].
[If one investigates these absurd constructions one finds that] they have
no subtle status of their own nor is there anything profound about
them [as something existing apart from them, because these constructs
are (the logic of) Being].
While it is the absurd construct [of a subject] that is busily engaged with
the absurd construct [of an object—this subject-object dichotomy
constituting Saṃsāra and proceeding dream-like]
There has [in this process] been no moving away [from Experience-as-
such, the as-is, Being's presential mode, just as the transformations
and transmutations of the four elemental forces do not move away
from "space" (which holds them together), and just as the mental
operations of affirmation and negation do not move away from the
"mind" (whose manifestations they are)].

The import of this quotation is that, whether we find ourselves experiencing what we may assess as the magic of higher and purer realms, or
what we decry as the magic of dismal and impure worlds of ordinary life,
each experience is inseparable from the process that constitutes it and that,
ultimately, is the indivisibility and dynamics of Being-*qua*-Existenz. The
recognition of indivisibility counters the naive belief in abstractable attributes and localizable features and refers back, instead, to Experience-as-
such, which (structurally speaking) antedates every speculation about
specific entities and their supposed nature.

As already hinted at by speaking of a deployment of the organizational
tendencies, operative within experience, the magic of higher and "purer,"
that is, more authentically lived realms (such as the Buddha-realms and
even Nirvāṇa) does not derive from the magic of dismal and impure
(absurdly fragmented) worlds (commonly referred to as Saṃsāra). The
former is already copresent with the latter as a possibility that may be
activated and which, by this activation, facilitates an attunement to the
energizing force as the whole. This activation occurs through understanding

which, though subject to the danger of being misunderstood as something concrete, has the character of a visionary ensemble of forces auto-presencing in wondrous images of configurational interactions which exert a strong pull.

[3]

While indivisibility carries with it a certain sense of abstractness, configuration is imbued with a more vividly descriptive character. The technical term for configuration is *dkyil-'khor*. This is the Tibetan rendering of the more familiar, (but in no way more clearly defined or more easily understandable) Indian term *maṇḍala*.

The manner in which this term was hermeneutically understood within the Tibetan tradition, has been outlined by Rong-zom-pa Chos-kyi bzang-po:[19]

> Maṇḍala means a concentration of energy or a circle; *la* means to take up and to hold. This is its meaning as ground (Being). Therefore, since energy is the foundation for setting up a reign of meaningfulness, it is by taking up this energy that one speaks of *dkyil-'khor*. If rendered literally, this term has the meaning of completely globular and wholly encircled. In this sense one uses the term *dkyil-'khor* as referring to where a center (or principal figure) is surrounded by a circle of attendants. Further, *ma* means beautiful, and *la* beautified . Thus, the Exalted One[20] is enhanced in beauty by his residence, attendants, and so on. Further, *ma-da* means to overwhelm or to be resplendent, and *la* means to provide a foundation. By this meaning the place of residence is termed *dkyil-'khor*.

Rong-zom-pa's account, however, merely summarizes a long history of hermeneutical interpretation in which experience, which itself was seen to be a configurative presence, played the dominant role. Thus, the *sNang-srid kha-sbyor bdud-rtsi bcud-thigs 'khor-ba thog-mtha' gcod-pa'i rgyud* has this to say:[21]

> Center *(dkyil)* is a meaning-saturated gestalt *(chos-sku)*, an invariant,
> The creativity of excitatory intelligence, a ceaseless (operation) is the periphery *('khor)*;
> Therefore configuration *(dkyil-'khor)* is completeness in (and as) experience.[22]

> Nonmistakenness is the center, nonartificiality is the periphery;
> This configuration of nonmistakenness and nonartificiality
> Is complete in (and as Being's) internal logic *(chos-nyid)*, as the impulse

(toward) limpid clearness and consummate perspicacity.

Energy is the center, the coming-into-presence is the periphery;
Energy and coming-into-presence is complete in (and as) experience.

Invariance is the center, nonartificiality is the periphery;
Invariance and nonartificiality are complete in (and as) experience.

Unorigination is the center, noncessation is the periphery;
The nonduality of unorigination and noncessation is configuration.

Indivisibility is the center, presence-*cum*-interpretation is the periphery;
Indivisibility and manifoldness is configuration.

Nonduality is the center, nonpremeditation *(rtsis-med)* is the periphery;
Nonpremeditation and nonduality is configuration.

In this dynamic unity presented as configurations, the center may also be conceived of as a point that has no extension; it may be qualified as a point of origin or departure in relation to both the manifestation itself and to the ensuing circle, the attendant audience becoming aware of this unitary emergence. In this manifestation of the point, a departure from its source is indicated, and this departure expresses itself in the experienced (relished) relationship of the central ("original") point and the peripheral ("moving") point becoming an arc which, as it closes on itself, becomes the circle of ("encircling") attendants. Thus, it appears as an enlivening geometrical configuration imbued with the experience of beauty. This is the idea expressed in the *Rin-po-che 'phags-lam bkod-pa'i rgyud:*[23]

> Since the auto-excitatory intelligence has neither a periphery nor a center,
>   it is a point *(dkyil)*;
> Since it is this that is experienced, it is the attendant circle *('khor)*.
> Since the auto-excitatory intelligence beautifies itself, it is a *dkyil-'khor*
>   (configuration),
> (Its beauty) does not depend on configurations prepared by colored
>   stone-dust.

From among these many and varied interpretations Klong-chen rab-'byams-pa has favored the one that sees the *dkyil-'khor* as a center or point having a circumference whereby it is enhanced in beauty.[24]

This idea of the enlivening beautiful configuration as a circle (in 2-space) or a sphere (in 3-space) implies a radial organization in which there is activity directed both away from, and also toward, a center as dominant focus. The circle or sphere, therefore, is a radically symmetrical organization of forces and not a static array. Although imaged as a circle or sphere, since this configuration is characterized as having "neither (peripheral) limit nor center" *(mtha' dang dbus med-pa)*, it more correctly corresponds to a pseudosphere which, by definition, has an infinite surface (negative curvature) with no privileged position that could be considered its center.

The fundamental inherent dynamics of such a configuration is self-existent pristine cognitiveness *(rang-byung-gi ye-shes)*—it is cognitive operation that does not happen but simply is, and its operation is a configuration-making process:[25]

> There is in all sentient beings self-existent pristine cognitiveness; this is there as the three configurations[26] of (Being's) sheer lucency.

The three configurations mentioned in this passage without being specified as to their distinct character, each in its own manner, present a phase of and in a process which, in moving toward more complex articulation, yet retains its wholeness in each of its articulated phases. Of primary importance in this context, however, is the configuration that serves as the starting point of its own movement—the spontaneous presence of Being in the sheer lucency of Existenz. Its special holistic character presences as the preprogram of three optimum attainment standards as a gestalt triad *(sku gsum)* in the light of which the system, the human individual, organizes itself. In terms of experience this basic configuration has to do with existential evidence values,[27] which cannot but be imaged in terms of a formal gestalt *(sku)* and which, in a bootstrap-like manner, contribute to the emergence of forcefields operating between themselves in such a manner that the whole process leads to bound systems as the encodement of these very values.

There is, first of all, a meaning-saturated gestalt *(chos-sku)*, which as the external expression of an inner meaning is Being itself in its very meaningfulness. It is irreducible to anything and is utterly open *(stong-pa)*. It cannot be limited and is hence devoid of any unvarying and exhaustively specifiable mode of some kind of being. This gestalt character of Being, indeed, is expressive of Being's undivided wholeness in which, in terms of experience, the experiencer is not separable from the experienced. This is to say that gestalt is both the organizing principle of and the so organized universe of meaning. It is important to note and to remember that whenever the texts speak of a gestalt this both-and is always implied. The consequence is that, in concrete terms, the experiencer is an active participant in Being's unfoldment, never a detached observer. This participatory character, which surreptitiously introduces the notions of space and time, expresses itself more noticeably in and as the sheer lucency *(gsal-ba)* in which Being radiates and manifests as Existenz, thereby projecting out of itself, as it were, a realm which serves as the potential for a lived through experience with others as focal points. It is this complexity, being both a realm (space) and a process (time) that constitutes (and is experienced as) Being's scenario gestalt *(longs-sku)*. Out of this truly existential patterning, as yet virtual and prethematic, the universality of psychic life tends to manifest itself in the multiplicity of ideas and ideals ceaselessly *('gag-pa med-pa)* stimulating and assisting mankind in its evolutionary course. Such guiding principles, deeply rooted in (Being's) resonating concern, are collectively termed Being's cultural norms display gestalt *(sprul-sku)*, which releases in the persons experientially engaging this gestalt, the richness of their own diverse responses that relate back to Being's scenario gestalt through which meaning "reaches into" man's world. From such a process-oriented perspective, meaning is purpose stimulating a living system's self-realization in conformity with its optimum attainment standards, which act as a program of controls. The whole process is induced by and guided from what seems to be a higher (more dynamically complex) level, which is figuratively spoken of as a "vassal king" or "regent" *(rgyal-ba)*. This higher level itself is configurational:[28]

> This configuration *(dkyil-'khor)* which just is,
> Is the intentionality of a regent (imaged as) a gestalt triad:
> Excitatory intelligence as the center *(dkyil)* and pristine cognitions as the periphery *('khor)*
> Indicate (what is meant by) the facticity and definition of Being's meaning-saturated gestalt *(chos-sku)*.
> A principle figure as the center, and spiritual forces (figured in images of a) male-female polarity as the periphery,
> Indicate (what is meant by) the facticity and definition of Being's scenario gestalt *(longs-sku)*,
> The globally pervasive substratum *(kun-gzhi)* as the center, and the eightfold cognitive ensemble as the periphery,
> Indicate (what is meant by) the facticity and definition of Being's display gestalt *(sprul-sku)* as cultural norms.

[4]

Having briefly dealt with the meaning of configurations, we must now turn to the explication of the term self-existent pristine cognitiveness. It denotes the actional character inherent in Being-*qua*-Existenz, which initiates a plurality of programs due to its excitation. It is said to be self-existent *(rang-byung)* [29] because it is present even before it crystallizes into the organizing and interpretive notions that constitute what we ordinarily understand by consciousness. And since it operates within the ubiquitous field character of Being-*qua*-Existenz, self-existent pristine cognitiveness is discussed in precisely the same terms that are applied to Being-*qua*-Existenz. Several passages may serve to illustrate this point:[30]

> This self-existent pristine cognitiveness, dissociated from the restrictive (labels thematized as eternally existent or nonexistent) functions such that it cannot be localized as any thing since its facticity is openness; it never ceases coming-into-presence because its actuality is lucency; and it provides the ground (and reason) for the emergence of any and all (thematic) features because as resonating concern *(thugs-rje)* it never ceases providing for (ever-new) possibilities, and is therefore the ever-present existential reality.

Another passage states:[31]

> Self-existent pristine cognitiveness is that which—as (Being's) excitatory intelligence, open, lucent, dissociated from mental-verbal proliferations, and like a transparent crystal—has come into existence as pure fact not allowing itself to be discursively constituted as an object. Although (this cognitiveness) is there in its aspect of providing the ground (reason) for the emergence (of thematization), in itself it is nothing that could be characterized as some thing that has or has not arisen; it shimmers in its own lucency, vibrates in its openness, and dissolves in the diaphanously pure ultimate. That aspect (of this cognitiveness), which arises as a manifold out of its (own) reach and range, constitutes the structured horizon of subject-object dichotomizing. Since what underlies this arising in its nakedness and this dissolution (in the diaphanously pure ultimate)—the excitatory aspect (of cognitiveness)—is there as pristine cognitiveness, one speaks of self-existent pristine cognitiveness precisely because it is not amenable to objectification.

And, finally, another passage states:[32]

> In all living beings this self-existent pristine cognitiveness resides without ever increasing or decreasing.

This pristine cognitiveness itself derives from the excitatory intelligence of the field as the effect of this very excitation, yet it does so merely as an effect without prior cause, since there is no preexisting "space," "time," "matter," or even "mind" to contain this cause. It is a special and unique feature operating at a point of high intensity termed a virtual singularity *(nyag-gcig)*. This special highly energized singularity, exhibited through the self-existent character of pristine cognitiveness, has been explicated as follows:[33]

> Self-existent *(rang-byung)* is (what is meant by) excitatory intelligence, it is free from causes and conditions, open, lucent, and spontaneously there; pristine cognitiveness *(ye-shes)* is the former's ceaseless lucency. Singularity *(nyag-gcig)* means that although there is lucency this is not something in itself, for what is meant is the indivisibility (of the three facets: facticity, actuality, and spirituality).

This central notion of a virtual singularity is laconically indicated in the following passage:[34]

> That which is open, lucent, invariant, a point-instant, virtual, singular,
> Is the root of everything (subsumed by the terms) Saṃsāra and Nirvāṇa.
> If the (real) meaningfulness of self-existent pristine cognitiveness is understood,
> One becomes knowledgeable regarding the entirety (of reality) through comprehending (the import) of this singularity.

Only when read in conjunction with its commentary, however, does this last statement reveal its significance:[35]

> The nature of auto-excitatoriness is the facticity of Being, an utter openness; the outward-directed glow of this openness is lucent in ceaseless radiation, yet in whichever manner it radiates it is not found as a duality (of something open and something lucent). This fact is the point-instant virtual singularity *(thig-le nyag-gcig)* and (this term is so coined because) as a point-(instant) *(thig, ti)* it is the unchanging (invariant) ground (Being-as-such) and, since it remains unbroken and cannot be sectioned, it is termed a (point)-instant *(le, la)*.[36] Since it is not something as such, in view of its subtleness it is termed virtual *(nyag)*, and since there exists nothing that does not gather in it, it is termed singular *(gcig)*. It is like the root or the seed from which all (that which is encompassed by the terms) Saṃsāra and Nirvāṇa sprouts.

After having explicated the meaning of the term self-existent pristine cognitiveness the text further elaborates the meaning of virtual singularity:[37]

> So also it is stated in the *Klong-gsal*:
>
> > The virtual singularity is the foundation of all (encompassed by the terms) Saṃsāra and Nirvāṇa;
> > The self-existent pristine cognitiveness (always) has been self-operating;

Comprehending this is said to be this very pristine cognitiveness.

"If the (real) meaningfulness is understood," means that by envisioning the meaningfulness of this pristine cognitiveness, the belief in an ego having neither foundation nor root dissolves by itself. It is when the internal logic of Being, in which no mistaken identifications have ever been experienced, is understood that the statement "one becomes knowledgeable regarding the entirety (of reality) through comprehending (the import of this) singularity" holds true. This means that when one understands and knows that the basis of all that exists is this (very) self-existent pristine cognitiveness—an invariance, a point-instant, and a virtual singularity—(then) one becomes knowledgeable regarding all that exists. Why? Because all that exists has sprung from the creativity of excitatory intelligence.

Inasmuch as the singularity is a highly charged point within the field of Being-*qua*-Existenz, which itself is open, it is possible to conceive of a veritable multitude of intense activity centers, which are virtual, yet also there (as point-instants) before there is space and time (as formalizable properties of the empirical world). However, it should be borne in mind that such terms as there and before are ineluctably tied to notions of space and time which, at the singularity, cease to have any significance. Hence, we have to be cautious not to give too much credence to what are merely linguistic expressions of natural language, for they may become handicaps for deeper probing. This virtual singularity, therefore, marks the beginning and origin of the universe as it exists for us as alive participants. It is this participation, rooted in and deriving from excitatory intelligence, that gradually splits up the evolving universe into a material-physical realm and a mental-spiritual one, each one then believed to have relatively autonomous existence.

The creativity of the singularity lies in its lucency or radiating character that pervades and is inseparable from its field or continuum *(dbyings)*. The field character of the creativity of thof the virtual singularity possesses both homogeneity, the property of being independent of position and open *(stong-pa)* throughout, and isotropy, the property of being totally independent of direction and lucent *(gsal-ba)* with equal intensity in all directions. This lucency or isotropic radiation *(mdangs)* [38] is excitatory intelligence *(rig-pa)*, which is inseparable from the field and all-encompassing *(kun-khyab)*.

It may be helpful to diagram the process so far described:

FIGURE 8

Omnidirectional isotropic radiation oscillating
outward from the singularity
(as represented in 2-space)

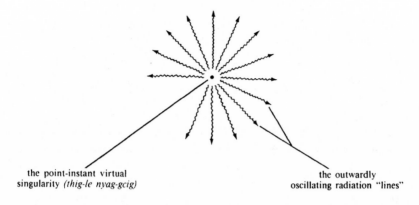

the point-instant virtual
singularity *(thig-le nyag-gcig)*

the outwardly
oscillating radiation "lines"

FIGURE 9

Close-up view of one oscillation "line" showing the complexity
of the interactive processes

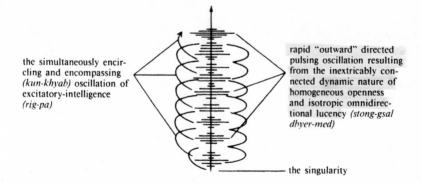

the simultaneously encir-
cling and encompassing
(kun-khyab) oscillation of
excitatory-intelligence
(rig-pa)

rapid "outward" directed
pulsing oscillation resulting
from the inextricably connected dynamic nature of
homogeneous openness
and isotropic omnidirec-
tional lucency *(stong-gsal
dbyer-med)*

the singularity

FIGURE 10

Side-view of oscillating isotropic radiation

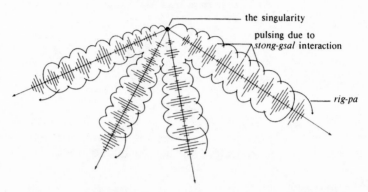

FIGURE 11
The envelope-like meaning-saturated field of pristine cognitiveness
ranging over two outward-pulsing radiating field lines *(gdangs)*

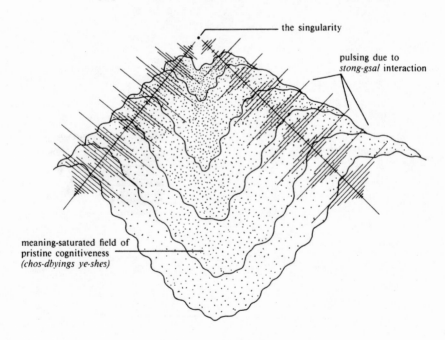

FIGURE 12

View showing rippling of meaning-saturated field of pristine
cognitiveness [dotted area]

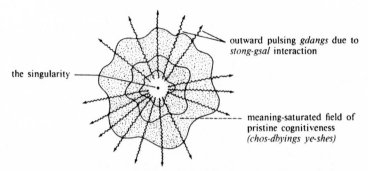

the singularity

outward pulsing *gdangs* due to
stong-gsal interaction

meaning-saturated field of
pristine cognitiveness
(chos-dbyings ye-shes)

It is excitatory intelligence that provides the necessary programming
information for initiating a dramatic unfolding process (the "big bang")
tending towards ever greater degrees of complexity (the evolving universe)
while simultaneously, throughout all of its phases, retaining the intelligence that initiated the process. When this big bang occurs, the surging
(rtsal) of intelligence-*qua*-isotropic radiation *(mdangs)* develops a special
envelope-like[39] structuring of radiation field *(gdangs)*[40] such that there is
simultaneously constituted both a unitary (unbroken) process and a
branching of four additional modes. Both are termed pristine cognitions
(ye-shes).

The unitary process as an envelope-like structure which results from this
surging of intelligence is termed the meaning-saturated field as pristine
cognitiveness *(chos-kyi dbyings-kyi ye-shes)*. This field envelope exhibits
an intentional structure, constituted both as an intending act phase and an
intended object phase (as content *qua* any and all presencing or a coming-
into-presence). Additionally, there occurs a branching phenomenon in
which four other pristine cognition fields are also simultaneously operative, each such field having special features. These branches are (1) the
quasi-mirroring pristine cognitiveness *(me-long lta-bu'i ye-shes)* as that
pristine cognition field which, through its operation, accounts for the
possibility of Being-*qua*-Existenz to effect an auto-encountering that is
prismatic;[41] (2) the specificity-initiating selective mapping pristine cognitiveness *(so-sor rtog-pa'i ye-shes)* as that pristine cognition field which,
through its operation, accounts for the possibility of pinpointing local
regions for discursive elaborations; (3) the auto-reflexive identity pristine

cognitiveness *(mnyam-nyid-kyi ye-shes)* which, through its operation, yields reflexively identical results; and (4) the precisely actualizing pristine cognitiveness *(bya-ba nan-tan-gyi ye-shes/bya-ba grub-pa'i ye-shes)* which, through its operation, effectuates contextually determined, necessary, and appropriate performances. The operation of this unitary yet branching pristine cognitiveness is cryptically indicated in the following quotation:[42]

> A virtual singularity, a lucent (isotropic) radiation, five pristine cognitions.

The commentary to this statement unpacks the complex meanings embedded therein as follows:[43]

> The root (of our material-mental universe) is this self-existent pristine cognitiveness, a point-instant virtual singularity; since (its) facticity is open-dimensioned and not discernible as any (concrete) thing, it is a meaning-saturated field as pristine cognitiveness *(chos-kyi dbyings-kyi ye-shes)*. The radiation field of this open dimension is the intrinsic photic character of pristine cognitiveness. Since this is there in its own lucency (with its prismatic character) as yet undiffracted into color values, it is the quasi-mirroring pristine cognitiveness *(me-long lta-bu'i ye-shes)*. Since these (modes of) pristine cognitiveness have one and the same (operational) source, differing only in name, (this facet is termed) the selective mapping pristine cognitiveness *(so-sor rtog-pa'i ye-shes)*. Since these (modes of) pristine cognitiveness are self-existent, identical with respect to their lucency and indivisible, (this facet is termed) the auto-reflexive identity pristine cognitiveness *(mnyam-nyid-kyi ye-shes)*.[44] Since by understanding correctly the meaning-value of this (cognitive character of Being) all intentional ideation is actualized spontaneously and (this facet is termed) the precisely actualizing pristine cognitiveness *(bya-ba nan-tan-gyi ye-shes)*. It is from this pentad of pristine cognitions as the (operational) source (of the intelligible universe) that the eighty-(four) thousand portals (to life's) meaning open up.

The commentary next links up its discussion of pristine cognitiveness with the three following lines in the basic text:[45]

> All the differences with (each of) the (spiritual) levels, paths and pursuits,
> The eighty-four thousand portals (to life's) meaning and so on,
> Expand from the (operational) source, the point-instant singularity

and explicates these lines as follows:[46]

> At this virtual singularity, self-existent pristine cognitiveness as the (operational) source (of the intelligible universe), the isotropic radiation of excitatory

intelligence expands into four (modes of) pristine cognitiveness as its dynamic facets. From each of these four facets, twenty-one thousand portals open up so that there is a total of eighty-four thousand. The inconceivable variety of spiritual levels, paths, and pursuits have all sprung from the (operational) source, the thrust toward limpid clearness and consummate perspicacity, a sole point-instant virtual singularity. So also in the *Klong-gsal* it is stated:

> All that exists, without exception, each and every thing, the whole (of reality)
> Has sprung from the one point-instant that is the (operational) source.

The passages so far discussed have spoken of the point-instant virtual singularity *(thig-le nyag-gcig)* as the operational source *(rtsa-ba)* for the dynamic pulsing of pristine cognition fields *(ye-shes)*[47] and the emphasis has been on Being's singular and unique character as excitatory intelligence *(rig-pa)* whose high energy is termed sheer lucency *('od-gsal)*.[48] The operational unit within the dynamics of sheer lucency is the discrete photon-like radiating packet *('od)*, which occurs as an outward-directed glow of excitatory intelligence *(rig-pa'i gdangs)*; as a peak value it is said to be the determinant *(rkyen)* for the process termed "becoming enlightened" *(sangs-rgya-ba)*.[49] Furthermore, this lucency has a field character *(dbyings)* that is termed center *(dkyil)* when the field is conceived of as having centripetal movement, and it is termed a turbulent vortex *(klong)* when it has centrifugal movement. Furthermore, this field exhibits several operational modalities, from among which the deep-structured one is said to be a function of both the photon-like radiating packet *('od)* and *thig-le* which, in this context, can best be understood as system-dynamics.[50] The system here is the whole of Being-*qua*-Existenz, with respect to which *thig-le* is said to be both invariant *(mi-'gyur)* and to range over its entirety *(kun-khyab)*. The emphasis on the invariant and holistic (all-encompassing) nature of the system-dynamics is borne out by the following quotations:[51]

> *thig* is invariant, *le* is all-encompassing,

and[52]

> *thig* is sheer invariance,
> Atemporally it has been dissociated from any artificiality;
> *le* is the ultimate overarching,
> In it whatever will come-into-presence is perfectly complete.

and[53]

> *thig* is such that there is no change (variation) involved.
> *le* is the all-encompassing, (allowing) the coming-into-presence of thematized domains.

and[54]

> Its facticity is such that, since it cannot be differentiated and abides all-alone, it is without a rival. Its definition is: *thig* is invariant and *le* is all-encompassing due to its overarching (character).

The invariant and holistic nature of this system-dynamics indicates the impossibility of actually separating the system Being-*qua*-Existenz into discrete isolatable entities. The unbroken wholeness of this system has an absolute value that is its actional character, termed *ye-shes*. In this context the term *ye* emphasizes the fact that this action is constant throughout the entire system, and the term *shes* indicates that the action has a "cognitive torquing" as a quantum of action. This torquing is a function of a certain momentum coupled with its distance (radius) from a point around which it spins. In the terminology of the Tibetan texts, this torquing occurs as the circling *('khor)* around a center *(dkyil)*, the whole constituting a configuration *(dkyil-'khor)*.

We have already seen (figures 1-5) how *stong-gsal* interaction pulses as wave-like oscillations outwardly directed as a radiating field *(gdangs)*. Yet this same *stong-gsal* interaction also exhibits discrete photon-like radiating packets *('od)* which, by encircling *('khor)* a point *(dkyil)* on an orienting axis around which they spin, constitute those special configurations *(dkyil-'khor)* previously mentioned. Moreover, in addition to being affected by photon-like radiating packets, these special configurations are also effected by the torquing of excitatory intelligence *(rig-pa)* in its field pulsing *(rtsal)* of pristine cognitiveness *(ye-shes)*. This torquing of pristine cognitiveness is a function of the magnitude of the quanta of action *(thig-le)*, and these quanta, in turn, affect the structure of the various configurations *(dkyil-'khor)*. The notion of quanta of action adds a special feature to the deep-structured dynamics of that system Being-*qua*-Existenz which, in addition to being constituted in special configurational wholes, may now also be seen to operate in quantum jumps. These complex processes may be diagrammed as follows:

FIGURE 13

Relation between magnitudes of quanta of action *(thig-le)* and
the orientation of dynamically constituted special
configurations *(dkyil-'khor)*

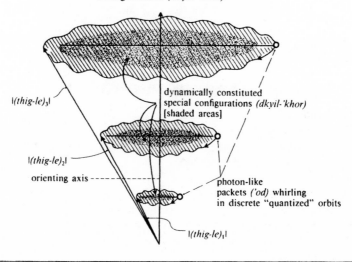

|(thig-le)₃|

dynamically constituted
special configurations *(dkyil-'khor)*
[shaded areas]

|(thig-le)₂|

orienting axis

photon-like
packets *('od)* whirling
in discrete "quantized" orbits

|(thig-le)₁|

|(thig-le)$_n$| length of arrows represent the magnitudes of the quanta of action *(thig-le)*, which itself
is a measure of the "torquing" of pristine cognitiveness

The jumping of these quanta of action *(thig-le)* occurs in four discrete
modes, which have been discussed with respect to their facticity *(ngo-bo)*,
an illustrative analogy *(dpe)*, an unambiguous definition *(gtan-tshig nges-
pa)*, and their targets *('gro-sa)*.[55]
    The first quantum jump relates to the level of thematic reflection:

    (Its) facticity: the eightfold cognitive ensemble;[56]
    (Its) analogy: a blind man and a turquoise.
    The unambiguous definition:
        thig is the eightfold cognitive ensemble as the unit of consciousness;
        le encompasses the three levels of thematic experiencing.[57]
    (Its) target: the limit of the thematically comprehensible universe.[58]

The second quantum jump relates to the interplay of thematic reflection
and nonthematic modalities in experience. It differs from the first quantum
jump in that its scope is wider insofar as it accesses the fundamental source
of the eightfold cognitive ensemble:

(Its) facticity: the fundamental source as a basis of consciousness;
(Its) analogy: a mixture of earth and water.
The unambiguous definition:
    thig is the fundamental source as the basis of consciousness;
    le encompasses the six possible life forms.
(Its) target: the state of having passed and not having passed beyond.[59]

The third quantum jump involves an indeterminacy which characterizes the paradox of there being nothing, yet also a presencing:

(Its) facticity: the fundamental indeterminate source;
(Its) analogy: curds and milk.
The unambiguous definition:
    thig is the fundamental source, nothing;
    le is the presencing in consciousness of all and everything.
(Its) target: no target certainty.

The fourth quantum jump is the most energized, for it involves the operational source of pristine cognitiveness, termed point-instant virtual singularity, discussed previously. The targeted region for this quantum jump is completely nonlocalizable. It is the optimization of the entire system Being-*qua*-Existenz:

(Its) facticity: the point-instant virtual singularity;
(Its) analogy: the sun's energy.
The unambiguous definition:
    thig is dissociation from defects, which are the sedimentations (of experience);
    le is the purity of the affective processes (restored to pristine cognitiveness).
(Its) target: the whole itself.[60]

[5]

We have seen how the mysterious structure of the system termed Being-*qua*-Existenz has been traditionally explicated with reference to such technical concepts as virtual singularity, pristine cognitiveness, quanta of action, and configuration. It should be stressed here that these concepts and their complex interaction were primarily intended as heuristic aids meant for helping one in the adventuresome exploration of the mystery of Being. As the exploration of the mystery proceeds, ever new levels dynamically emerge, each new level retaining its open, lucent, and excitatory intelligence character. What is termed an individual (the prober) is never separated from the multileveled facets of the mystery (the probed). Moreover, this exploratory probing, as a growth *(lam)*, reveals the operation of various configurations or dynamic regimes, which together constitute the complexity of a living individual and function as a preprogrammed ensemble. This preprogram has been described as follows:[61]

A basic ultimate configuration
Is present in the center of the *tsitta*[62] of each and every individual.
Furthermore, configuration means the following:
Self-existent excitatory intelligence is the center;
The coming-into-presence of a quincunx of luminous intensities is construed as the circumference.
This is the basic ultimate configuration number one.

In the white *dung-khang*[63] of each and every individual
A point-instant singularity, pure with respect to discernible facets, is the center;
Flaring point-instant particles are construed as the circumference.
This is the basic ultimate configuration number two.

In the still-point of Being's turbulent vortex, the open dimension of the internal logic of Being, pure with respect to discernible facets,
A continuous welling-up[64] is the center;
The field incandescence[65] is construed as the circumference.
This is the basic ultimate configuration number three.

There are other configurations as well:
The configuration (unfolding as) a formal gestalt *(sku)* is the unchanging (still-point) in Being's turbulent vortex;
The configuration (unfolding as) authentic utterance *(gsung)* is ceaseless expansivity;
The configuration (unfolding as) vibrant spirituality *(thugs)* is a (limitless) range in which there is no (limiting) conceptualization.

These (three) configurations (unfolding as) formal gestalt, authentic utterance and vibrant spirituality
Each have a center and a circumference.
Neither going toward nor coming from, nor changing (in any way),
They just abide in and as the field which is each and every person's *tsitta*.

Thus, the program (set up by) these ultimate configurations
Is complete, (in-built) within the living body of each and every person.

Several important points must be made regarding this somewhat lengthy and highly technical passage. First, the system referred to as the preprogrammed ensemble exhibits what may be called a modular hierarchy in which each module, termed a configuration, is both a functional whole (indicated by the phrase "each configuration has a center and a circumference") and also a contingent structural facet within the indivisible, interconnected ensemble of Being-*qua*-Existenz.

Secondly, two incandescent emitting regions, termed lamps *(sgron-ma)*, are said to be operative with respect to the so-called configuration number three. The first such lamp, termed field incandescence *(dbyings-kyi sgron-ma)*, is intimately related to the welling-up of excitatory intelligence, a phenomenon that engenders the operation of a quantum of action within a field thereby rendered incandescent. This incandescent field becomes polarized into an outward continuum *(phyi'i dbyings)*, likened to the expanse of a cloudless sky, and into an inward continuum *(nang dbyings)*, likened to a lamp spreading its light simultaneously in both directions.[66] From an experiential viewpoint, the interrelated polarization into an outward and inward continuum indicates that there is an interconnected contexture of possible ways of acting in and with the lived world. These possible ways of acting already constitute, as the inner continuum of the field, the prestructured horizon of this lived world. When these possible ways of acting are acted out, behavioral patterns are established through such action, and the pattern as the outer continuum of the field, constitutes the actively structured feature of the lived world.

A second lamp is involved as a consequence of the quantum of action and the vacuum field *(thig-le stong-pa'i sgron-ma)*.[67] The reference to two lamps as localized emitting regions of incandescence, may be likened to a certain effect of electromagnetic radiation. Such radiation has its source in the acceleration or deceleration of charged particles, consisting mostly of electrons that are capable of emitting and absorbing photons of energy ΔE over the time Δt such that the product $\Delta E \Delta t = h$ (where h is Planck's constant). This activity is termed a virtual process and the photons, having such an evanescent existence, are termed virtual photons. Furthermore, these virtual photons can, in turn, engender virtual processes by momentarily decaying into virtual electron-positron pairs, the life of such pairs being 10^{-21} seconds. Thus an electron moves about in a center of a cloud of photons and electron-positron pairs. While the electron is electrostatically repelled by its parent electron, the positron is attracted, the consequence being that the electron electrically polarizes the vacuum (of the field).[68]

This special effect of electromagnetic radiation may now be analogously applied to this situation in which two lamps are said to operate. The polarization of the vacuum is to be seen as similar to the polarization of the incandescent field into an outward and inward continuum. And the presence of the localized emitting regions of incandescence, the lamps, is similar to the existence of electron-positron pairs. This paired relationship between these two lamps is figuratively referred to as a brother and sister[69] who are sent forth by their parents, yet rather than being annihilated (as are the electron-positron pairs), they are welcomed back after their mission is completed.

In a less technical register, the ceaseless activity of the vacuum field with the two lamps is beautifully illustrated by analogies with our natural environment:[70]

> In the vastness of space, so pure (in being) pristine cognitiveness,
> There lies embedded excitatory intelligence, without dichotomizing concepts, lucent,
> Just as in the center of the open sky
> The sun's orb lies embedded.
> In (this) space, pure and open,
> Two lamps lie embedded, shining ceaselessly.
> Just as in the great ocean
> All the rivers flow together,
> So in the center of (this) excitatory intelligence, unborn,
> All that is external, internal, and mysterious gathers.
> Just as in a mirror:
> Whatever is held up before it seems to come there,
> So in (this) excitatory intelligence (vast as) space (which is) the openness
> (of Being),
> The light of the lamps, never ceasing,
> Is present in lambency and lucency.

Such ceaseless activity, analogous to the dynamic processes in the vacuum of the electromagnetic field, is prerequisite for the operation of what was termed above "basic configuration number one" and "basic configuration number two." With the emergence of these configurations, an element of localizability is introduced. Localizability is indicated by the terms *tsitta* and *dung-khang*, which are associated with the heart and head, respectively; *tsitta* and the heart region are associated with processes described as quiet, tranquil, calm, and calming *(zhi-ba)*, whereas *dung-khang* and the head region, more specifically the brain, are associated with processes that are agitated and fierce *(khro-bo)*. This localizability, however, is primarily of a self-referential nature in the sense that excitatory intelligence experiences itself as being a central orientational point within a horizon. The interaction between the center and environing horizon holistically structures a world experienceable and experienced in a multiplicity of versions. These versions are, at first, luminous intensities which may be seen and felt as either a calm glow or as angry flashing.

This new context, in which an element of localizability operates, still retains the character of the whole system termed a preprogrammed ensemble. In such a context the coming-into-presence of varied luminous intensities assumes the character of distinct color values. This process is experienced as presenting a formal gestalt which, as the existential center of the world, is neither independent of nor isolated from those vectorial radiations spreading outward from it. Furthermore, there seems to exist an intimate relationship between chromatic and sonic intensities such that what on one level is experienced as color is, on another level, experienced as sound.[71] Thus, analogously put, insofar as color presents an existential evidence value as a formal gestalt *(sku)*, sound presents an existential communication value *(gsung)* so that the formal gestalt is a vibration made chromatically distinct—nothing in itself and yet a lucency—and sound is this same vibration sonically processed as the melodic and musical features of speech, through which a gestalt announces and communicates its presence. Thus the *Rang-shar* declares:[72]

> Residing in light *('od)* as (my) formal gestalt *(sku)*, I frolic in its rays *(zer)* as "my" authentic utterance *(gsung)*.
> Therefore one speaks of "light-rays" *('od-zer)*.

Here one should note that both formal gestalt and authentic utterance are manifestations (not derivatives) of a projective intentionality termed vibrant spirituality *(thugs)*.[73] The interconnectedness of these three unfolding regimes is itself a configuration:[74]

> My ultimate configuration is there as:
> Light is (my) formal gestalt, (its) rays are (my) authentic utterance, and
> Projective intentionality is (my) vibrant spirituality.

How should one understand the repeated reference to a triadic ensemble of configurations, each of which may be dealt with separately? It would seem suggestive of the mathematical notion of a *set* as a collection of discrete elements, which in this case consists of three configurations. Yet there is also operative an intrinsic affinity among these elements termed configurations, each of which partakes of the whole set. This fact may be likened to the notion that sets also contain an element called the identity *(I)*, such that for any element a, b, c of the set the following is true: $Ia = aI = a$, $Ib = bI = b$, and $Ic = cI = c$. One additional notion found in set theory will be helpful for illumining the operation of the three unfolding regimes of formal gestalt, authentic utterance, and vibrant spirituality. For every element a of the set there is an element a^{-1} (called the inverse of a) such that $a^{-1} = a^{-1}a = I$. And this holds for every element of the set. For the context under discussion, let a be formal gestalt *(sku)* and a^{-1} be concrete corporeal appearance *(lus)*; let b be authentic utterance *(gsung)* and b^{-1} be talk *(ngag)*; and let c be vibrant spirituality *(thugs)* and c^{-1} be mind *(yid)*. The following passage should make evident the implication of the expression $aa^{-1} = a^{-1}a = I$:[75]

> Hi! The teacher of teachers, the king (who is) the creator of universes
> Has patterned the energy (that is his) as a gestalt *(sku)* configuration so
>   that
> The whole of reality as it is present in discrete visible units
> Stays patterned as the dynamic reach and range of (Being's) meaning-
>   saturated field which has nothing to do with coming-into-existence.
>
> He has patterned the energy (that is his) as a speech *(gsung)* configuration
>   so that
> The whole of reality as it is present in discrete audible sounds
> Stays patterned (in such a manner that) in this field which has no origin,
>   talk remains (authentic).
>
> He has patterned the energy (that is his) as an excitatory intelligence
>   *(rig-pa)*[76] configuration so that
> All the notions, each and every one, of the cognitive process
> Remain the excitatory intelligence of this creator of universes who has not
>   come into existence (as a hypostatized agent) in this operation.

This passage indicates that what we term body, speech,[77] and mind are the inverse of formal gestalt, authentic utterance, and excitatory intelligence (the source of vibrant spirituality). Furthermore, what is termed a sentient being may be conceived of as an abstract group S consisting of the triadic ensemble of body, speech, and mind *(lus, ngag, yid)*, and what is termed a Buddha may be conceived of as an abstract group B consisting of the triadic ensemble of formal gestalt, authentic utterance, vibrant spirituality *(sku, gsung, thugs)*.

One should emphasize the fact, however, that each configuration has its basis in what we have called Being-*qua*-Existenz. It operates in configurational modes that are felt to proceed in blissful ease:[78]

> Hi! Center *(dkyil)* is the energy of a reality-value (imaged as the creator of universes), which does not make any mistakes.
> Circumference *('khor)* is bliss supreme in utter perfection (before it lapses into either) Saṃsāra or Nirvāṇa.[79]
> This (bliss) is the root of all and everything, configuration, energy, for Here all configurations are understood to come together.

In an ultimate sense, Being-*qua*-Existenz is itself a configuration process that permits itself to be interpreted in terms of Saṃsāra and Nirvāṇa, without being reducible to either:[80]

> Hi! Center *(dkyil)* is the energy of the reality-value, which does not make any mistakes.
> Circumference *('khor)* is all-pervasive dominance over Saṃsāra and Nirvāṇa.

To summarize, the above analysis of Reality's many facets indicates that complex processes are involved, for which the technical term configuration *(dkyil-'khor)* is but a convenient symbol.

One further feature of such configurations may be explicated. It involves what are technically termed symmetry transformations of the system Being-*qua*-Existenz, meaning that the formal properties of the system remain invariant throughout its transformations.[81] An initial state A, described as open *(stong-pa)* undergoes a symmetry transformation into state B, described as lucent *(gsal-ba)*, which state yet remains indistinguishable from state A. Furthermore, it is possible for state B to undergo a symmetry transformation into state C, described as excitatory intelligence *(rig-pa)*, and this state C is indistinguishable both from state B and state A. The whole process, as a combined transformation, is a symmetry and identity transformation.

In a philosophical and experiential idiom these transformations involve movements from configuration A, B, and C, where

> A is the ontological configuration as the first stirring of resonating concern *(thugs-rje)* inherent and pervasive of Being;
> B is the existential configuration as program dynamics or Existenz; and
> C is the experiential configuration of ground-path-goal dynamics through which the program is worked out individually.

Schematically this may be represented as follows:

FIGURE 14

Transformations of the system
Being-*qua*-Existenz

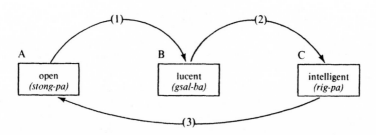

Here (1) is the first symmetry transformation, (2) is the second symmetry transformation, and (3) is the combined transformation as a symmetry-*cum*-identity transformation.

Because of the principle of indeterminacy that pertains to excitatory intelligence in the system and pervades it as a whole, the process of working out the program can follow one of the two courses: either (1) the course of an identity transformation meaning that the result of the operation is indistinguishable from the initial state or phase; or (2) the course glides off into a more radical transformation in which everything seems drastically altered and is felt as a going astray.[82]

However, precisely because of the indeterminacy pertaining to the excitatoriness of intelligence—indeterminacy meaning essentially irreducible to something definitive and static—what from one perspective may be seen as a symmetry transformation, may from another perspective be seen as what Ilya Prigogine has termed a symmetry-breaking dissipative structure.[83] It is not without interest that three aspects are always linked in dissipative structures: the function, referred to in this context as the dynamics of Being (Being-*qua*-Existenz); the structure, referred to as the space-time scenario of Being; and the fluctuations, referred to as the cultural norms (rooted in intelligence) which trigger the instabilities in which Being manifests. Thus, if being-a-sentient-being or being-a-Buddha evolves like a dissipative structure, Being itself is then comparable to a giant dissipative structure. Symmetry transformations and symmetry breaks are not contradictory, but complementary to each other.

It is through these symmetry and symmetry-breaking transformations that Being "speaks," as will be explicated in the following chapter.

IV. Interlude

[1]

Once the existence of a problem has been pointed out, an attempt can be made to deal with it; in concrete terms, an individual can then "address" himself to the task before him. He can do so firstly, because he has been "spoken to" and "called upon," although this "speaking" and "calling" has occurred in an inaudible manner; and, secondly, he can do so because he has been listening, attuned to the sounds and voices of this silent speaking beyond the cacophony of routinized mentation. Within this process constituted by such a speaking and listening, the active structuring of that communicative medium termed "language" is of paramount significance. Within such a rich medium the "sounds" that we hear are not merely phonemic clusters, they are commanding utterances whose phonemic "shapes" delineate existentially relevant messages. Further, within such a medium the words we speak are not mere segmented morphemes, they are the bearers of meaning having become embodied, embedded in the form of words. Within such a medium, therefore, speaking and listening are understood to be meaning-acts that emerge from the intelligence of Being-*qua*-Existenz. Such a speaking and listening, moreover, concretely occurs as a thinking *in* (specific) languages *of* and *about* that which presents itself as worthy of attention; in this presencing it "speaks" to man only to the extent that man "listens." In short, speaking and listening, as formulated processes of understanding, have great existential significance.

The active structuring of the communicative medium here termed language occurs both as highly energized meaning-bearers or "gnosemes" *(yi-ge)*[1] and as formulated encodements of such meaning-bearers taking on specific forms as morphemes and sememes *(ming, tshig)*. The former aspect is suffused by excitatory intelligence *(rig-pa)* and may be described as wordless speaking whose voices are pregnant with significance. The latter aspect includes voiceless (written) words, which relate back to and presuppose the former aspect. It is the gnosemic language medium that provides the context out of which the manifold and pervasive intentionalities of experience come to expression, for it is a modality of Being-*qua*-Existenz itself, and its range of variability is as wide as the polyphony of experience. The gnosemic language medium, however, is not restricted to any single dimension of experience. For example, it may range over the domain of formal gestalt *(sku)* where it becomes embodied, gestural language.[2] In the fullness and contextural nature of experience, various domains and dimensions overlap. For example, the experience termed tonality has both a phonic (aural) and prismatic (visual) aspect:[3]

> The (phoneme) *A* is like a lion's yawn, the (phoneme) *KA* is like pleated silken banner strips.

In a sense, the gnosemic language medium is already a tending-toward the disclosure of Being-*qua*-Existenz into distinct voices so that the ensuing disclosure provides an operational basis for participating in areas of concern by mediating between the "infinity of the unsaid"[4] and what is said in and as the disclosure of this infinity. Just as Being is nowhere else than in and as Existenz, so also the gnosemic language medium operates nowhere else than in and through the intelligence of Existenz, which, because of its highly energized indeterminate nature, is free either (1) to deal with this disclosure meaningfully, or (2) to transform it into progressively less meaningful constructs. Hence this intelligence is nowhere else than in those very interpretive endeavors appearing, magic-like, as perturbations and fluctuations of a localized determinate nature, yet always operating within the global indeterminate field. Furthermore, just as radiation vibrates, with ever varying frequencies, within the region of the visible spectrum into variegated chromatic intensities, so also the gnosemic language medium voices itself (operates), in modulated tones, over the whole region of its voiced (interpreted) disclosure. This voiced disclosure is heard (apprehended and experienced) as a sentient being *(sems-can)* or a Buddha *(sangs-rgyas)*.[5] About the nature of the gnosemic language medium Klong-chen rab-'byams-pa says:[6]

> Experience-as-such *(sems-nyid)*,[7] a primordial transparency, discloses itself as gnosemic language *(yi-ge)* and this serves as the basis (for interpreting experience) as a richly ornamented system (whose components of) formal gestalt, authentic utterance, and vibrant spirituality are inexhaustible. (This gnosemic language medium)—operationally dependent on the information input *(thig-le)* moving in the interior of the structuring channels *(rtsa)* within the four processing centers *('khor-lo)*[8]—is differentially present in what is said to be a Buddha or a sentient being. Moreover, when the chromatic and

qualitatively active aspects are bright, the individual's perceptive capacity is clear, his senses are keen, and great success will come to him. But when the modulation of the gnosemic language medium *(yi-ge'i gzugs)* is blurred, there is dull-wittedness and failure. Through having cultivated (this gnosemic language) within the heart and the other processing centers, its colors and qualities are enhanced; and so it provides the momentum for spiritual realizations.

Elsewhere, Klong-chen rab-'byams-pa has discussed the intimate relationship between Experience-as-such and the gnosemic language medium as a process that defines itself through its creativity on various operational levels. Of primary import is the existential or ontological phase, experience as a dynamic field or source, felt and seen as a value. Here, as is the case with all process thinking, two seemingly contradictory experiences are fused: the lucency of experience bright as the sky, and the cloudy mist that spreads over the sky. This mist is lucency's speaking. Thus Klong-chen rab-'byams-pa says:[9]

Experience-as-such, in itself a sheer lucency and self-existent pristine cognitiveness—in its pure facticity beyond (such predications as) eternally existent *(rtag)*, eternally nonexistent *(chad)*, receding *('gro)*, or approaching *('ong)*—is called the gnosemic language medium which is (and conveys) the internal logic of Being, the ultimate (meaning) continuum. As is stated in the *sGyu-'phrul gsang-snying:*[10]

Experience as such is gnosemic language;
Gnosemic language is the Wish-Fulfilling Gem Cloud.

To understand the import of the rich imagery in this passage one should remember that excitatory intelligence *(rig-pa)* pervasively inheres in Being-*qua*-Existenz and auto-presences as sheer lucency becoming diffracted through the dynamics of its coming-into-presence. It is through the interaction of what is heuristically described as being just (spontaneously) there *(lhun-grub)* and resonating concern *(thugs-rje)* with respect to this spontaneous presence, that the ensuing cognition acquires its specific photic (color) and phonic (resonance) character. Both photic and phonic aspects are meaningfully valuable—because of the pervasive inherence of excitatory intelligence—and are part of that movement that gives hue and shape to the invisible, and timbre and pitch to the inaudible. This photic-*cum*-phonic movement shapes itself as the coming-into-presence of specific experiences for us which, however, are already prefigured in the ground and field out of which such movement surges.

In particular, the shape and shaping of sound is intimately connected with the configurative development of man as the experiencer who is housed in his body, engulfed in his speech (voicing and articulating the manner in which he is in his life-world), and occupied in the midst of his thoughts. In addition, such mental occupation is interlaced with both speech (articulating the intentionality of thought) and embodiment (as lived in bodily deportment and gesture). This triadic intertwined development and ensemble of embodiment, speaking, and mentation derives from the dynamics of sheer lucency, which is both photic and phonic. Furthermore, this triadic ensemble is itself the result of a kind of gravitational collapse. Figuratively speaking, what we term embodiment, speaking, and mentation are collapsed congealments. Thus, the vividness of a formal gestalt *(sku)* is collapsed and warped into the solidity of embodiment *(lus)* as a localized aggregate; authentic utterance *(gsung)* with its repertoire which it sings in melodic cadenzas, vibrant with life, is collapsed and warped into the dissonance and mundane cacophony of everyday chatter *(ngag)*; and the openness of vibrant spirituality *(thugs)* is collapsed and warped into the narrow region of divisive, affectively toned, ego-centered mentation *(yid)*.

Despite such collapse, the living individual is still understood to be a complex, vibrating ensemble, which in its dynamic operation establishes and exhibits symmetry programs—axial *(kun-'dar-ma)*, bilateral *(ro-ma* and *rkyang-ma)*, and rotational *('khor-lo)*—for which there are photic and phonic "readouts." Thus:[11]

> In the center of the four control centers *('khor-lo)* there are three conductors *(rtsa)*: the *ro-ma, rkyang-ma* and *kun-'dar-ma* constituting the body structure by functioning as pillars (that is, the structural support system). Inside them there are the three self-existent gnosemes (phonically operative as) *OM, ĀH, HŪM*, and (photically operative as) white, red, blue, respectively. They provide the operational basis for what is, externally, the triadic ensemble of embodiment, speaking, and mentation; internally, the triple poison of affective forces; and arcanely, the triadic ensemble of formal gestalt, authentic utterance, and spirituality.

Since the experience of being human is primarily conditioned and "controlled" by the processes of embodiment, speaking, and mentation, three so-called control centers are of major importance. They are associated with the head, throat, and heart regions, which are not primarily anatomically localizable networks of nerves—they are properly understood to be "areas" constituted by a self-structuring process involving transformations and presentations which, sonorously, maintain the living individual and resound in gnosemic language. Thus:[12]

In the head, throat, and heart regions there is the triad of *OM, ĀḤ, HŪM,* respectively, in the heart the forty-two peaceful (deities) "speak," and in the head the fifty-eight blood-drinking (deities) "speak." Together with the three levels of gnosemic language (pertaining to) formal gestalt, authentic utterance, and vibrant spirituality there are one hundred and three gnosemes.

What is here termed the heart and the head is elsewhere, in a more technical language, referred to as *tsitta* palace and *dung-khang* palace, respectively. The use of this latter terminology eliminates the confusion of virtual (not concretely localizable) places being concrete localizations suggested by such terms as heart and head. That these regions are to be understood figuratively, is evident from the context under consideration. When it is further stated that the heart *(snying-ga)* is the seat of the peaceful deities, while the head *(spyi-bo),* sometimes even specified as the brain *(klad-pa),* is that of the fierce deities, one may be tempted to interpret this division as a figurative statement indicating the polarity between feeling (peaceful, heartfelt) and thinking (aggressive, headstrong). Indeed, most would agree that love, kindness, joy, happiness, serenity, and bliss are feelings associated with and hence "belonging" to the heart. When one looks at Buddhist sculptures and paintings of calm and peaceful figures, a serene smile playing around their lips, eyes filled with tender love in a gentle face, one can understand and appreciate the gentle power of such images to touch the heart of the beholder. And once the heart is open to such images it resonates with feelings of love and kindness, happiness and bliss, revealing and sharing such experiences with anyone coming into this peaceful heartfelt aura, beckoning and "speaking" to those who are sensitively attuned. Such peaceful heartfelt language is a radiating presence, which in its glow conveys and sustains an abiding steadiness: radiance without glare, a softness which, photically, imparts mellowness of hue and, phonically, imparts mellowness of timbre. In addition, this photic-*cum*-phonic glow in its outwardly directed radiation may also flare, photically experienced as blazing flashes and phonically experienced as a deafening rumble and roar, as an intense activation associated with fierceness and fury. This flaring distinguishes the fierce deities in the head (or brain) from the calm deities in the heart. Yet one should remember that both are the image and the voice of pristine cognitiveness, the dynamics of Being-*qua*-Existenz. It is only one's dichotomic fixation that causes one to think that a quiet heart and a noisy head are necessarily antagonistic or unrelated experiential modes. Thus it is said:[13]

It is the outward glow of the five affinities with Being, (imaged as) the calm deities in the heart which shine forth in and as the (same) five affinities (imaged as) the fierce deities in the head.

We may illustrate this intimate relationship between the tranquil (nearly stationary) glow, which yet extends outward in all directions, and the angry (fiercely flaring) energy bursts by an analogy with solar phenomena. It is well established that the center of the sun's disc is noticeably brighter than its edges, a phenomenon termed limb-darkening. An interesting parallel to this phenomenon is that the calm and tranquil deities in the heart, as the center of man's lived existence, comparable to the quiet center of the sun's disc, exhibit a bright and steady glow; whereas the angry and agitated deities in the head or brain, comparable to the edge or limb of the sun's disc, flare as darkening blazes. Just as the solar phenomena of surface granulation, chromosphere, corona, and solar wind, are all highly energized occurrences tending to concentrate in active regions, the edges of the sun's disc, so also the fierce deities as agitated cognitions occur in the active region, the brain or the *dung-khang* palace, the site of activity bursts many times stronger than the steady glow of the quiet region, the heart or the *tsitta* palace.

[2]

Being-*qua*-Existenz, as a self-structuring process, assumes the form of a network of conductors *(rtsa)* and may be likened to the morphogenetic unfolding of a territory termed the lived body, within which those formulated energies termed deities, occupy certain command posts. These command posts, in turn, are subordinate to a "central intelligence" which, for human beings, is termed the Buddhahood of mankind. This central authority speaks to man, forcing him (by the exigency and prestige of its tone, figuratively termed the "lion's roar") to experience himself as an open-ended project, a localized nexus of forces requiring responsive elucidation and exploration, rather than as some already determined and unalterably programmed automaton. The language of such a process speaks and works in miraculous ways; through it the wonder that is Being expresses itself. Such expression both sets the tone (gnosemic voicing) as well as documents (gnosemic writing) its own play. This play, moreover, is acted out in the interplay of what we as embodied beings image as the masculine *(yab)* and the feminine *(yum)*. In the domain of language, the gnosemic voicing of *A* is the openness of Being (imaged as being of a feminine quality, Kun-tu bzang-mo) intoned together with *KṢA*, the pristine cognitiveness inherent in Being's openness (imaged as being of a masculine quality, Kun-tu bzang-po).[14] Thus, in gnosemic voicing, the carrier-wave resonating as *A* (the openness of Being) conveys the message *KṢA* (the content of Being's cognitiveness). In other words, gnosemic voicing expresses, on the level of authentic utterance, Being's paradoxical character of being both something and nothing. The something is attested to by the fact that there is a presencing; the nothing by the fact that this is not of some thing or other. Gnosemic voicing is meaning-engendering activity. As is stated:[15]

> While *A* is neither vacuous nor nonvacuous
> Nor even objectifiable as a middle (position between these extremes),
> All (things and notions "exist") merely as labels (due to signifying activity) and [this fact is the intentionality of] the whole of Buddhahood
> Abiding in [the very dynamics of] the garland of gnosemes.

This transformative process is furthermore to be understood as the meaning-saturated gestalt *(chos-sku)* in which the internal logic of Being's spontaneity auto-presences.[16] As a dynamic matrix, however, this process involves a consecutive self-transformation, which is indicated as follows:[17]

> This very *A* auto-presences in various transformations
> Encompassing (and pervading) all linguistic features [consisting of vowels and consonants]:
> *KA* and the rest, totalling forty-two
> Definitively [constituting the operational domain of] *A* the king [Buddhahood] making his presence totally felt.

This gnosemic transformation is known as Being's scenario gestalt *(longs-sku)* through which Being is accepted and in this acceptance, which implies an engagement and involvement, is also thoroughly enjoyed.[18] This active participatory mode is associated with the masculine aspect in the tension field that is Being *becoming* Existenz.

This joyous engagement, which is primarily virtual, initiates a further transformation that involves the articulation of what is experienced ("enjoyed") in concretely lived situations which are emblem-engendering. As a complex process it tends toward ever more concrete forms all of which carry with them a specific kind of wonderment. Two major transformations are discussed. In the first, the magic of Being's transformational character holds within itself both the elements of natural language (nouns, adjectives, and verbs) and the capacity to arrange such elements in well-formed strings (sentences). Thus it is said:[19]

(Its) great magic is: the wonder *(e-ma-ho)* that the pure fact of Being is
   there as the experienceable and experienced meaning-saturated
   gestalt; the miracle *(ngo-mtshar)* that Being's actuality auto-presences
   as its scenario gestalt through which Being can be "enjoyed"; and the
   marvel *(ya-mtshan)* that Being's concern makes itself felt in and as a
   cultural norms display gestalt which presents mankind's aspiration
And it abides as possessing, without exception, the words and phrases
   (which have) forty-five (constitutive elements)[20]
Through which the great import of the various (spiritual pursuits) is
   voiced and exhibited.

The second major transformation allows for the whole life of mankind to
unfold in wondrous richness. Thus:[21]

Experience naturally operating as gnosemic language, which is not a
   discrete thing
And is not objectifiable, having no ontic status and being free from
   limitations [set by the linguistic horizon], yet
Through the grouping of words into shapes and colors
Conjures up and exhibits a show suited to the capacity of the experiencing
   beholder.

Thus, the transformation of Being *becoming* Existenz, through the
magic of gnosemic language initiates specific experiences of wonderment
similar to what Martin Heidegger has characterized as the meaningful act
in which "language speaks."[22] Our innermost nature "goes out" to com-
municate something of great significance. Yet, in this going out, the very
source (as a point of departure) intrinsically abides as pristine cognitiveness, ranging over the whole of Being-*qua*-Existenz, and is configuration-
ally active so that each configuration forms a "whole within a whole," each
being complete with its "own" gnosemic language. Thus it is said:[23]

Forty-five configurations[24] (constituting a grand ensemble consisting of
   triple ensembles of)
Formal gestalt, authentic utterance, and vibrant spirituality [each of
   which is itself an ensemble of five (vectorial tendencies)] of pristine
   cognitiveness as the dominant (factor in intelligent life),[25]
Ranging over the ten spatial directions and the quaternary of temporality,
Are complete with respect to the (set of) gnosemes [beginning with] *A* and
   [ending in] *KṢA*.

Gnosemic language issues forth from the realm of the "unspoken," yet this realm is not to be construed as the cause; for gnosemic language is an auto-presencing, and all experiencing is contained within this act of issuing forth. Thus:[26]

> The dynamics of experience as such is gnosemic language;
> Gnosemic language is not a discrete thing.

Precisely because it is neither a discrete thing nor a "no-thing," gnosemic language is infinitely variable and never loses its diaphanous character of sheer lucency and intelligence.
As is said:[27]

> This very fact that it is not objectifiable allows for its variations
> (Which are) the glorious gyrations of formal gestalt, authentic utterance,
>   and vibrant spirituality.
> Formal gestalt, authentic utterance, and vibrant spirituality are conjured
>   up in the great miracle of
> (Being's) wondrous [presence] and marvelous [intentionality].

In this coming-into-presence the gnosemic language medium constitutes a contextuality which ultimately stems from (and remains) related to the domain of the internal logic of Being, which now exhibits an experientially tangible range. This process occurs in the gnosemic language medium as an auto-documentation, gnosemic language writing (about) itself. Such documentation requires a capability to do so, and this capability is the intelligence in Being-*qua*-Existenz, operative as pristine cognitiveness. Thus, ultimately speaking, Being writes its own libretto, and in this act of writing, gnosemic language manifests as its (own) written text. Thus:[28]

> Being is written by Being;
> Therefore one speaks of (gnosemically lucent) graphemes.

With this statement we are brought into the center of a special representational activity, which attempts to make articulated sound carry the messages of expressed thought. This activity does not necessarily involve objectifying mentation that delimits and labels reified domains of experience. Rather, such activity makes one attuned to one's existentiality, alerting one to the possibility of self-understanding. This activity, as a gnosemic performance, embodies both a cognition (whose message is encoded within gnosemically lucent graphemes) and an aid (to proper cognition). This is the true import of the term *sngags* (Sanskrit *mantra*) which Rong-zom-pa Chos-kyi bzang-po explicates as follows:[29]

> The term *sngags* is used with reference to that which has both cognitive (quality) and aiding (capacity). Thus, in the word *mantra*, the *man(a)* means *avabodhana*,which means impressing upon oneself through deep understanding; and *tra* means to protect. Since it involves protection and aiding, most texts speak of it as the unified domain of appropriate action and discriminative appreciation, or as that which has a result.

Gnosemic language, even if it inevitably writes its own libretto, thereby transforming itself into grapho-phonemic levels (written and spoken words), never takes a position or maintains a viewpoint—it asserts nothing and demonstrates nothing, yet nevertheless initiates every meaningful expression. Through the gnosemic language medium Being-*qua*- Existenz announces itself and, in this act, gnosemic performance constitutes itself as a polarized field in which there occurs a special interaction between a subject and an object in such a way that the subject becomes the object (of its own concern), this object itself being the subject, auto-presencing and auto-announcing.

In this peculiar interaction intelligence (the vibrant spirituality of Being-*qua*-Existenz) achieves an actualized self-presence by addressing itself to its copresent partner with whom it can (and does) achieve cognitive appreciative union. In this gnosemic performance the magical act of uttering the world is staged as a phantasmic show *(sgyu-'phrul)*, held together in a web *(dra-ba)*[30] of appreciation. Only in the later scenes does this play lose its coherence, becoming thematically fragmentized. The intentional structure of this magical act involves a conversion of the utterly open field of Being-*qua*-Existenz into the radiance of a polarized field. This radiant polarized field is described as the interaction between virtual charged pairs, themselves surrounded by additional charged pairs. Iconically envisioned, these charged pairs are masculine and feminine in resonantly interactive embrace *(yab-yum)*. Although these pairs have opposite charges (masculine-feminine), they are identical in their properties of being open *(stong-pa)* and coming-into-presence *(snang-ba)*. Because of the highly charged polarity of the field, there are erotically resonating interactions that are due to the inherent spirituality of Being-*qua*-Existenz, active as resonating concern *(thugs-rje)*. In the actual human individual this concern speaks the existential language of compassion *(snying-rje)*.

V. In-Depth Appraisals and Configurational Processes

[1]

We have seen how the virtual, yet thoroughly actional, triadic modality of formal gestalt *(sku)*, authentic utterance *(gsung)*, and vibrant spirituality *(thugs)* fluctuationally collapses into man's concretely lived situation of the triadic ensemble of embodiment *(lus)*, speaking *(ngag)*, and mentation *(yid)*. All these modalities are inextricably related to the evocative and expressive play performed by gnosemic language *(yi-ge)* in the sense that, even in their virtual state, these existential modalities are already gnosemic modulations. As such they exhibit the double character of being both the expression and (re-)discovery of Experience-as-such.

Discovery always occurs in a world into which it brings a new tremor—a note is struck which, expressing the discovery, reverberates into the world and its inhabitants, who are thus given the power to recognize and assimilate that which has been discovered, because they are already attuned to it. Discovery, however, does not merely occur in an already constituted world; it involves the return to a source which, though lying forgotten and untapped, in its hiddenness calls for its discovery. This source is Experience-as-such; in ontological terms, it is Being-*qua*-Existenz which, as ground, is itself neither grounded in or on something, nor localizable as a region among other regions. The persistent presence of Experience-as-such is the very ground which makes possible the search for and rediscovery of itself. The rediscovery process is the ground's dynamic upsurge, the announcement of itself by itself through gnosemic language, assuming and conveying ever fresh meanings. These meanings, which are thus conveyed in the act of discovery and expression, are interpretive, because they involve world-comprehension and world-interpretation. The "worlds," which thus become disclosed in their being rediscovered, are interpreted as Saṃsāra and Nirvāṇa, each presenting a pervasive possible mode of existing, of being installed in *a* world. Here, such interpretation implies two things: (1) that there is a coming-into-presence (as that which will be interpreted) and (2) that there is a response to this presence (the interpretive act itself). Both facets constitute the dynamic character of experience which may then specifically be accessed in an in-depth appraisal *(ting-nge-'dzin).*[1] Such an appraisal is itself an interpretive grasping of lived experience in which understanding takes precedence over thematization. The possibility for such remarkable activity carries with it a sense of felt wonder, which itself indicates the active participation in the dynamics of Experience-as-such by the experiencing individual. As embodied beings we tend to image the qualitative character of this accessing in concretely personal terms through which we sense these forces that shape us. These forces "speak" in us and to us. We, in turn, can learn to get on "speaking terms" with them—a process that carries with it a sense of wonder. Such wonder has a double nature: it is, in a sense, our outgoing nature—the virtual creativity that permeates man and his cosmos—and, in another sense, the accessing process of our inquiry into this nature, which reveals ever greater wonders. The mystery of Being coming into presence in and for us as Existenz admits of contrasting interpretations. As a feeling of expansion, this wonder has been expressed as follows:[2]

A-ho!
   The gyration of gnosemes signifies that the cloud mass of resonating concern through which (Being as) teacher delights in (being active for the) welfare of living beings by its (his) pristine cognitiveness that is out of the ordinary, as it evolves out of the dynamic reach and range, which is appropriate action as self-existent concern and appreciative discrimination as having passed beyond the limiting notions (of something eternally existent or eternally nonexistent), is the momentum in the ensemble[3] (of aspects of the) intent on limpid clearness and consummate perspicacity. (This momentum) as an inexhaustible ornamented gyration matures into the grand configuration of forty-two royal personages (which) is the atemporally existent climax (of the process). It is out of this (auto-)presencing process that the forty-two gnosemic codes, such as *KA* and the rest, come into presence as the momentum through which the welfare of sentient beings is spontaneously effected by the issuing forth of display gestalts (acting as cultural norms). This (auto-)presencing is not something that has been made up as something new (and hitherto unknown) by (ad hoc postulated) causes and conditions, (rather) it is the facticity of Being; (but) since (Being's) self-existent concern for the welfare of sentient beings comes into presence out of the dynamics that have been (Being's) atemporal spontaneity, the gyration that takes place seems to be something that has been made up. (Actually) it is an indestructibility that is

nothing less than the facticity (of Being), which does not admit of displacement and transformation. Since this indestructibility (of the spontaneous presence of Being's facticity) cannot but bring forth the fifty-five odd configurations (referred to by such terms as) formal gestalt, authentic utterance, vibrant spirituality, creative potential, and optimally executed activity, (its integrity being such as) never to shirk its great responsibility to produce and to display configurations, is like the (nature of the) sun, which does not fail to emit rays. This coming-into-presence of configurations occurs automatically just as the reflection of a face (is automatically present) when a mirror is held to it. So also, when in the wake of the gyrating gnosemes the self-existent pristine cognitiveness has been roused, each and every projectivity such as the configuration of (Being's) auto-presencing and the configuration of living beings being educated (thereby), ranging over the ten regions (of the universe), occurs automatically. Since this coming-into-presence has occurred through the enormous power (which lies in the combination) of momentum, the cloud of gnosemes, and the determinants, the presencing of both pristine cognitiveness and those who are to be educated, it constitutes a miracle that prompts the exclamation *(A-)ho.*

Moreover, this wonder can be experientially released within ourselves. This is due to the fact that we are programmed[4] for the possibility of such releasement and, for this reason, bring to life felt images as tuning-in processes that are appropriately termed in-depth appraisals. There are three major in-depth appraisals that operate throughout the self-organizing, autopoietic system Being-*qua*-Existenz[5] they are termed As-is In-depth Appraisal *(de-bzhin-nyid-kyi ting-nge-'dzin),* World-spanning Presence In-depth Appraisal *(kun-tu snang-ba'i ting-nge-'dzin),* and Gnosemic Language Momentum In-depth Appraisal *(yi-ge rgyu'i ting-nge-'dzin),*[6] and constitute symmetry transformations of the state → image kind, the image (the in-depth appraisal) of the state being just that state itself (Being-*qua*-Existenz). Not only has the system Being-*qua*-Existenz the highest degree of symmetry, it also remains identical with itself throughout any and all transformations (appraisals).

However, the pervasive presence of intelligence in the "state" Being-*qua*-Existenz—we are using here "state" interchangeably with "system"—introduces a feature which effects seeming symmetry breaks by calling attention to and interpreting the "image" (in-depth appraisal) as constituting a new order. The experience of such a symmetry break describes an intuited and felt deviation from the identity of the total system as it unfolds, whereby a certain directedness becomes apparent. The imperturbable calm and wondrous serenity of the as-is, in its being appraised as calm and serene, is made to shine forth. And this shining forth, when so appraised, indicates that a symmetry break has occurred. As a world-spanning presence, which now fills the universe of experience, this lighting-up prompts a further appraisal, which expresses itself in that first utterance within which the total momentum of gnosemic language is gathered. As this appraisal becomes expressed in being uttered, another symmetry break has occurred. Seen as a transition from one aspect of the totality to another, however, these symmetry breaks are just the dynamics of the totality; they never become thoroughly disjointed, separately existing modes, which are then assumed to enter into some kind of interaction. These symmetry transformations and symmetry breaks, pertaining to the in-depth appraisal of the system, may be diagrammed as follows:

FIGURE 15

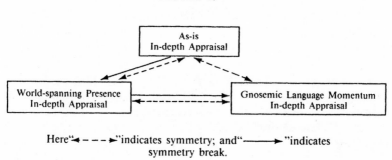

Here"◄ – – – ►"indicates symmetry; and"——————►"indicates symmetry break.

Having briefly discussed the manner in which these in-depth appraisals are related, we must now more fully explicate their specific features. It lies in the nature of lived-through experience that we are already interactively embedded within the unbroken wholeness termed the "as-is" *(de-bzhin-nyid)*. When experientially accessed, this as-is becomes its own "in-depth appraisal" *(ting-nge-'dzin)*. Such accessing has a nonreductive quality about it and hence is said to be utterly open *(stong-pa)*, having no discernible onset *(skye-ba med-pa)*, and just being "as-is" *(de-bzhin-nyid)*. Its felt quality of thereness is already a coming-to-the-fore, though not as something objectifiable; in so being there it carries with it a meaningful sense of genuineness and infallibility. Thus it is said:[7]

> Since it is not something demonstrably apparent even if it has come to the fore in someone,
> *de* is infallibility,
> *bzhin* is nonartificiality, and
> *nyid* is a label for the as-is.

This dynamic totality, however, may be tampered with; the consequence of such meddling is a stepped-down version of the original optimal operation. As is stated:[8]

> *de* is the name for infallibility,
> *bzhin* is that which is not to be messed with,
> *nyid* shows what it is in itself.
> Do not mess with the as-is,
> (For) any messing with the as-is
> Is a messing up of the experience of limpid clearness and consummate perspicacity.
> He who messes up this experience
> Ushers in the energetics of Saṃsāra.

Although we start from an undivided and unbroken totality, the as-is, all too soon we find ourselves trapped in states of increasing fragmentation from which only serious effort on our part can extricate us so that we may then become open again to the richness of the primordial totality of Being-*qua*-Existenz. This opening-up involves rising above our (habitually conditioned) selves, and becoming attuned to openness and lucidity—it is on this opened-up level that Being addresses us, speaking with the fullness of its significant message. The first response to this address is the exclamation of wonder:[9]

> E-ma-ho:
> This marvelous and wondrous fact
> Is the mystery of all perfect Buddhas;
> From that which has no origin, everything has taken its origin;
> Yet in so having taken its origin, it remains that which has no origin.

To the extent that this exclamatory response of wonderment is an immediate attunement to the ever-present mystery of Being-*qua*-Existenz, it marks the rediscovery of the primordial feeling of wonder through a holistic in-depth appraisal. Here the wonder of the totality of the as-is reveals itself as an openness that is deeply felt as a being open for perceiving and understanding whatever may present itself, just as it is. This "being-open-for" is not a passive way of letting things make their coming-into-presence felt, it is an actively responsive mode of relating oneself to the full range of whatever presences. It is, indeed, a world-spanning presence in-depth appraisal *(kun-tu snang-ba'i ting-nge-'dzin)*, letting things present themselves—magic-like, enchanting, fascinating, charming, casting an almost irresistible spell. It is the openness of human existence, actively felt.

This activity through which man relates himself back to his source, is imbued with compassion—a tenderness and understanding that nurtures and sustains a feeling of wonder because it is Being's concern spanning the whole universe. Such reliving of one's fullness is made possible by disengagement and detachment from the urgencies of practical (contextually determined) ego-centered activities, and by the recovery of aesthetic spontaneity, which comes in the image of a phantom to remind us that our openness holds out many possibilities. Thus it is said:[10]

> Embodiment, speaking, mentation and all that is
> Are nonlocalizable and nonobjectifiable.
> Through the fusion (of all that is with the nonlocalizable presence of
>   Being), proceeding phantom-like,
> The sky [as ceaseless pristine cognitiveness] is contemplated as the sky [as
>   the nonorigination of the meaning-saturated continuum].

This in-depth appraisal of a world-spanning presence already involves a special kind of disclosure which, paradoxically, is a presence that is everywhere and yet nowhere. Our internally constituted sense of reality (comprising our embodiment, speaking, mentation) and our externally constituted sense of reality (comprising the totality of phenomena), are felt as a phantom-like fabric, emerging out of nothing, yet unfolding as something—this "something" being attested by the fact that there is a coming-into-presence, and the "nothing" by the fact that this coming-into-presence never occurs as a reifiable domain. The phantom-like character of this process indicates the nonreductive nature of open-ended possibilities.

When one brings this feeling and imaging into focus, so as to give the presence an identifiable shape and structure, it is the working of gnosemic language—a primal utterance that asserts nothing, yet initiates everything that is to be—that makes it possible for us to speak. Thus there is a transformative enactment of what has made its presence felt; and this, too, is an in-depth appraisal. It is an in-depth appraisal of what initiates (the experiencer's world in which) gnosemic language plays the momentum-engendering role *(yi-ge rgyu'i ting-nge-'dzin).* Thus:[11]

> Experience-as-such, having no root,
> Is the root of all that is.
> Experience-as-such is gnosemic language;
> Gnosemic language is the Wish-Fulfilling Gem Cloud.

The primal gnoseme *A* echoes and reverberates thereby becoming all other gnosemes. From the fully melodic vibrating structure of these ensuing gnosemes the world was woven until it congealed and fragmented into the barren morphophonemic clusters (of everyday words and phrases with their assumed meanings) and reified domains (of everyday things with their assumed reality states). Thus:[12]

> ĀH
> From the white *A*, which had become quite steady
> There echoed forth very subtle *A*s
> Having illumined the ten regions by filling them (with light)
> They gathered back into [the primal *A*] which remained steady without
>   expansion or contraction.
> From that (primal gnoseme *A*) the ensemble of signifiers, all ablaze in
>   radiant light,
> Burst forth and (into it) they returned again.

Through this in-depth appraisal a universe of possible meanings is initiated *(bskyed)* which, because of the phonic character of the primal gnoseme, is a calling *(sngags)* and which, because of the shape this gnoseme assumes, is also a posturing *(phyag-rgya)* of a global configuration whose implicit meaning is appreciated in full *(rdzogs)*, so that action appropriate to the requirement of any situation can be taken.[13]

From the "auto-cloning" activity of the primal gnoseme there derives a bursting forth of subtle gnosemes which, in turn, engender the formation of the ensemble of signifiers (involving phonic, photic, and many other modes due to its holistic character). These "cloned gnosemes" exhibit both an expansive and contractive movement, a process that highlights the ever-creative movement of experience itself. Like a vacuum field (as conceived in quantum theory), experience at this level is an incessant sea of activity. Just as the vacuum is not at all empty, but filled to capacity, so also Experience-as-such is an openness encompassing everything in virtual presence.[14] This creativity takes place on a cosmic scale; the experiencing individual brings this scale of creativity to life in and through images which make it possible for him to transcend habitually constituted domains of finitude by opening up to the infinite mystery of Being. Reliving this creativity of Being-*qua*-Existenz through actual experience is both the recreation of Being itself and its enactment; it is a presentational immediacy turning into a configurational presence reverberating in consonance with its own atemporally operating dynamics. In philosophical diction, this means that the ontic level of all that is *(alles seiende)* remains marked by Being *(das Sein)*, which reveals its dynamics in and as all that is. The emphasis here is on the dynamics of the transformation process itself rather than on specific transformations imaged as contextually determined end-states of the process. This fact is stated in a decisive passage as follows:[15]

> From the dynamics of experience *(thabs)* (there comes) the dynamics-engendered *(thabs-byung)*, (which proceeds as) nonthematic dynamics-proliferation *(thabs bsam-yas)*.
> From that which is not different (from this transformation process) there come the different (phenomena present as)
> The countless configurations of the interior [the play of experience] and of that which is "outside" of the interior [the play of pristine cognitiveness].
> There is nothing to be afraid of: (all this is) the supreme marking of the Ultimate (Holistic) Positivity.

The dynamics of this transformation process have been given a double interpretation by Klong-chen rab-'byams-pa. He sees it (1) as an in-depth appraisal of the play between gods and goddesses in a holistic setting, and (2) as a marking by Being. According to this latter interpretation, the dynamics of experience *(thabs)* are Experience-as-such *(sems-nyid)*, a sheer lucency making its presence felt through gnosemic language; the dynamics-engendered *(thabs-byung)* is the ensuing split into a mind and its domain; and the nonthematic dynamics-proliferation *(thabs-bsam-yas)* is the whole gamut of what comes-into-presence and may then be interpreted in various ways. This transformative process may be seen as involving both symmetry and identity transformations and may be diagrammed as follows:

FIGURE 16

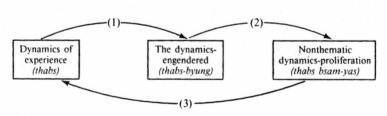

Here (1) is the first symmetry transformation, (2) is the second symmetry transformation, and (3) is the combined transformation as a symmetry-*cum*-identity transformation.

The beginning of the second line of the above quoted passage: "From that which is not different" indicates that there is nothing anywhere operative that is not this transformation process with its specific transformation phases. This means that the process is nothing existent as such for it exists only in and as its transformations; and similarly the transformative phases are also nothing existent, for they are but expeditious exemplifications of the overall process as it makes itself understood in and through us.

As this understanding occurs through impressive images, Experience-as-such *(sems-nyid)* now becomes vividly imaged as a play between gods and goddesses. This shows that what happens is not some mechanical interaction between entities, but an open realm of relationships, which involve qualitative nuances and intimations. This captivating play may seem to have started off in a random fashion, but what comes out of it is not random; the outcome is patterns envisioned as the "house" and "palace" we build to live in and relate to as our world. This world is one's life-world, externalized by one's task-oriented projects and involvements and, therefore, is not constituted as some inert given, for it, too, is a play that has an exploratory nature, a play of feeling one's way into and exploring the territory of ever new domains of concern. In short, this is the play of representational thought.

There are thus two kinds of play: the one is the play between gods and goddesses, nowhere, yet everywhere, and figuratively said to be within; the other is the play of representational thought, creating contexts, and figuratively said to be outside, reaching beyond the within. These two types of playful activity, moreover, are complementary in that they are themselves a frolicking within a larger play, the play of pristine cognitiveness. This whole playful activity bears the imprint of Being, and since Being is not an evanescent thing, doomed to extinction, there is nothing to fear. Only finite (ontic) beings can occasion fear.[16]

The outcome of such play is, in either case, a situation having a configurational character. The most important point to note here is that the experiencer is a participant always present in one or another of these possible situations. He may jump from one situation to another, yet he is always *embedded in*, and even is the transformative process itself, so that therefore he can never be a detached observer. The jumping from one situation (configurational whole) to another is like a quantum jump, the transition of a quantum system from one stationary state to another. Although a multitude of quantum states is possible, as jumps accompanied by absorption or emission of energy, these states can be grouped into and subsumed under primary states. Thus, by way of analogy, one may equate being-a-Buddha *(sangs-rgyas)* and being-a-sentient being *(sems-can)* with states of the quantum system Being-*qua*-Existenz. "Being-a-Buddha" is then a state in which energy (radiation) has been absorbed, and "being-a-sentient-being" is a state in which energy (radiation) has been emitted. Both are interpretations (states) of Being-*qua*-Existenz, which allows for the possibility of such interpretations. Both exhibit a quantum-like photic quality so that being-a-Buddha may be likened to the state of high-energy photons, and being-a-sentient-being to the state of low-energy photons. As quantum states neither being-a-Buddha nor being-a-sentient-being occurs outside the fluctuation of the dynamic field of Being-*qua*-Existenz.

[2]

Whether we speak of being-a-Buddha and being-a-sentient-being or of high-energy and low-energy photons, we are using images out of which we construct a world picture. Indeed, our understanding of the "world" is always tied to and depends on such creative activity. In any world picture so constructed there is always a correlation between the experiencer's "self" (as a constituted configuration of hierarchically organized operations) and a "world"(as a configuration of interactive domains). No sooner do I image something than it is there and I find myself in the midst of it. Thus there is a compelling power in the activity of the image-making itself and the image so formed retains traces of this compelling power.

The world has been imaged in a variety of ways in the Indo-Tibetan tradition. Prominent are the images of a palace and a dungeon. However, the association of "world" with a palace as an abode of richness and splendor and hence as a state that satisfies the long-term needs of man and has a liberating effect, as well as the association of world (as ordinarily conceived) with that state of continued recurrent frustration and imprisonment termed Saṃsāra, are both expressions of what may be called psychic life. More specifically, the image of a palace *(gzhal-yas khang)* is already a singling out of a specific horizon-form for a specific consciousness[17] (or intelligence); it imbues that horizon-form with the sense of being an abode for this specific consciousness whose dwelling it is. As such, the palace image becomes a total system of functional properties in which each of these properties have their own intrinsic qualities. And because of the pervasive presence of consciousness (intelligence) operating through the senses, the palace image also has sensory-specific and sensuous qualities, which, imaged as the emblazonry *(rgyan)*, make the palace so much more beautiful and also enhance it in value. Moreover, as a spatial horizon-form[18] the palace provides a primary operation as an orientational point with respect to which all other operations are organized in what is now understood to be the evolving spatiotemporal world. This orientational point is the throne *(gdan)*.

A cryptic outline of the architectonic process of becoming a palace is given in the following quotation:[19]

> A four-spoked wheel, furnished with a rim
> Ornamented by four studs, corridors and
> A completely quadrangular (building), doors with superstructures (of
>   additional doors).

This statement with its reference to a wheel as a symbol for a circle, suggesting a dynamic process (and as such not actually having a center and periphery) and a quadrangular building suggesting a structure involving spatial orientation, sums up what may be seen to be the way in which an open system remains open to its source. This latter aspect is suggested by the following description:[20]

> On the site of 'Og-min,[21] having neither a boundary nor a center,
> Within a radiant orb of pristine cognitiveness whose basis is without
>   measure
> There stands a palace ablaze in the preciousness of pristine cognitiveness,
> Not demarcated as to size or the ten directions;
> Quadrangular because the qualities (of Buddhahood) have spread beyond
>   measure;
> Decorated with precious projections of four super pristine cognitions.
> Its finial is the spiralling of the meaning-saturated field pristine cognition,
>   which is essentially identical with and not discretely differentiable from
>   all configurations without exception of the Buddhas of the ten regions
>   and the four times.
> (This) pristine cognitiveness is inconceivable,
> It assumes distinct and specifically differentiated variations in precious
>   shape and color,
> And is most lofty and
> Remains immeasurable in scope.

The repeated reference in this passage to pristine cognitiveness makes it quite clear that, in order to understand the significance of what is intended by palace, one has to move beyond the notion of palace as conveyed by representational concepts. Although objectifiable figures and attributes are named—quadrangular shape, projections, finial, and corridors—these are not to be conceived of as isolatable items in an architectural scheme; they are evocations of memories and anticipations, suggesting and disclosing possible ways for the experiencer to open up to his or her situation. In particular, it is "the site of 'Og-min" which, "having neither a boundary nor a center," can only be cognitively imaged as a pseudosphere. This site discloses world perspectives as these emerge in the horizon-forms of formal gestalt experiences. Here the notion of formal gestalt *(sku)* is used to describe the experience of being installed in a "world" and being appreciative of it in an attitude of utter openness and receptivity. But this appreciated world tends, almost instantaneously, to become a closed world, expressed in the image of a quadrangular palace with both a center and elementary orientational directions of front-back, and right-left (as bilateral restrictions of a radial organization which itself is omnidirectional). By adding four intermediate directions of the compass plus the zenith and nadir, totalling the ten directions mentioned in the passage, a vertical-horizontal axial complex is established. Furthermore, this imaged complex of lived experience embodies both spatial and temporal horizon-forms, which are prior to the thematic separation into isolatable spatial orientations and the temporal divisions termed before, now and after.

In this self-structuring process of transformation a certain center tends to form which, because of the excitatory intelligence of Being-*qua*-Existenz, operates as pristine cognitiveness in a most fundamental, universally valid manner[22] with its object phase *(yul)*[23] as the meaning-saturated field *(chos-kyi dbyings)*, pervaded ("known") by the act phase of a primary cognitive process named after the field of which it is its pristine cognition *(chos-kyi dbyings-kyi ye-shes)*.[24] This irreducibly open, as yet virtual, cognitiveness is primary in the sense that it is Being itself. Its ceaseless intelligent activity, due to its openness, allows for branching-like operations that set up secondary processes and structures of concurring pristine cognitions. The occurrence of such branching may be said to be secondary in that these pristine cognitions are based on, but not identical with, the primary operation of the meaning-saturated field pristine cognitiveness. It is through such secondary functioning that the primary (open) pristine cognitiveness encounters itself. But, how can this primary process encounter itself as that which is nonidentical (secondary)? The example of a mirror may be used to elucidate this paradox. For it is through an enigmatic auto-mirroring operation of the primary process that a secondarily concurring process termed quasi-mirroring pristine cognition *(me-long lta-bu'i ye-shes)*[25] takes place in such a manner that the meaning-saturated field pristine cognitiveness encounters itself "reflected" as a secondary functioning, thereby opening up experiential domains not otherwise available, and also permitting a multiplicity of interpretations, insights, and values to emerge.

Such an opening-up of experiential domains, as the first step in Being-*qua*-Existenz encountering itself, leads to pure possibility as a thetic operation,[26] called auto-reflexive identity pristine cognition *(mnyam-pa-nyid-kyi ye-shes)*.[27] Here "identity," as the intrinsic momentum of the total process *(mnyam-rgyu)*, indicates the atemporally free operation of the field character of Being-*qua*-Existenz; and "auto-reflexive" as the intrinsic determinant of the thetic character of the process *(mnyam-rkyen)*, indicates that which maintains itself as identical throughout and within the changing existential modes of the field. Specifically, auto-reflexive refers to the experiencer as the ensemble of formal gestalt *(sku)*, authentic utterance *(gsung)*, and vibrant spirituality *(thugs)*, functionally resonating in such a way that the experiencer (as the lord and master of the imaged palace) "experiences" the specific feeling and knowledge of being a genuine subject or True Individuality *(bdag-nyid)*, which is genuine and true only to the extent that it is not confused with subjectivity or other egological processes. Basically it refers to the experience of being installed in *a* world as a region of concern, not to any of its concretizations.

The pure possibility initiated by the primary pristine cognitiveness operation provides, as it were, the setting for focusing on all distinguishable facets of any possible state of affairs, such facets themselves being aspects of the field of possible modes of existing in which True Individuality (referred to as lord and master of the palace) finds itself. This specific operation of focusing, is a specificity-initiating selective mapping pristine cognition *(so-sor-rtog-pa'i ye-shes)*[28] initiating a manifold of direct, non-mediated processes of psychic life.

The manifold of specifiable and distinct meanings, which are mapped out by this cognition, carries with it solicitations for action. Any ensuing action has an intentional structure in that it is directed toward an end through which projects of meaning are fulfilled. Moreover, this intentional structure has a value-charge which polarizes the field in such a manner that tasks are posed as meaningful and therefore also meaningfully and precisely accomplished. In this intentionally structured activity, the task posed-and-accomplished pristine cognition *(bya-ba grub-pa'i ye-shes)*,[29] the value-charge is both an intrinsic-orientated valuation *(rang-don)*, the excitatory intelligence of Being coming-to-the-fore in Existenz, and extrinsic-oriented valuation *(gzhan-don)* through which everything is spontaneously valued, recognized as constituting a value in its own right, jewel-like. As a pristine cognition this activity has nothing to do with personal decisions regarding what is to be done or who is to be helped. Rather this cognition, as the acknowledgement of an existential value, is in its activity the spontaneous manifestation of a nurturing concern for the value so recognized. When the world, imaged as a palace in which the experiencer is housed, is felt as valuable, the knowledge of this fact (the value-cognition) can be symbolized so as to make one directly encounter this value. One attends to these symbols because they arouse value appreciations due to their connection with one's life-world, which is guided by an existential cognitiveness.

The role of pristine cognitiveness in both its primary (central) operation and its secondarily concurring (peripheral) operations, is further elaborated in symbols enabling one to gain insight into what is itself symbolically presented as a palace. As an image of the world in which we are housed, the palace is an ordered space within a wider, open space, likened to a cloudless sky and its deep blue color. This ordered space, which remains an omnidirectional field cognition, can also be imaged as taking on prismatic jewelled nuances, which are themselves symbolic presentations of the secondarily concurring operations of pristine cognitions. Thus, the structure of the palace is far from being a static given, for it is continuously self-activating, and from a dynamic point of view it may be regarded as a vertically spiralling system. It is only the ground-plan of such a palace that may statically be shown as resembling a four-spoked wheel, the wheel itself implying movement.

FIGURE 17

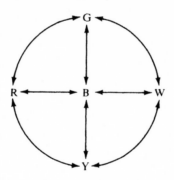

The lettering indicates:

prismatic jewelled nuances	*pristine cognitions*
B blue/sky	meaning-saturated field
W white/crystal	quasi-mirroring
Y yellow/gold	auto-reflexive identity
R red/ruby	specificity-initiating
G green/emerald	task posed-and-accomplished

"◄───►"indicates the connectivity of the facets as a functional ensemble.

[3]

The emergent operation of the quasi-mirroring pristine cognition is of special significance, for it indicates the possibility for the development of a thematically directed consciousness within which thematizing perception assumes the dominant role and becomes, in a certain sense, a center around which all other cognitive operations are arranged, the whole ensemble constituting the amazing unity and continuity of what we call a conscious individual. Such a conscious individual is always within and related to situations as his world of concerns, projects, and involvements, none of them being fixed domains to be exploited, but rather possible perspectives and interpretations of one's life world, all of which are rooted in and presented as the multidimensional texture of experience. As a consequence, the structure of consciousness *(rnam-par shes-pa)* allows itself to be imaged and felt in a variety of ways. It may be enjoyed as palatial, and it may also be analyzed as having external, internal, and arcane (deep-structured) features. Although thematically directed, this consciousness may, by imaging its own processes, involve itself in a truly creative (non-thematically directed) activity felt as the pleasurable expansion of one's capacities for imagination and perception, appreciation and understanding. Whether such imaging is directed toward the external, internal, or arcane features of this being conscious, it always occurs in and as an undivided wholeness whose complexity is discussed as follows:[30]

The quaternary (1) of what is externally earthy solidity *(sa)*, watery cohesion *(chu)*, fiery combustion *(me)*, and stormy motility *(rlung)*; (2) of what is internally the perceptible *(gzugs)*, feeling *(tshor)*, ideation *('du-shes)*, and actualizing *('du-byed)*; (3) and what is arcanely dullness *(gti-mug)*, arrogance *(nga-rgyal)*, addiction *('dod-chags)*, and envy *(phrag-dog)*, all atemporally abiding as meaning-saturated field pristine cognitiveness *(chos-kyi dbyings-kyi ye-shes)*, auto-reflexive identity pristine cognition *(mnyam-pa nyid-kyi ye-shes)*, specificity-initiating pristine cognition *(so-sor-rtog-pa'i ye-shes)* and tasks posed-and-accomplished pristine cognition *(bya-ba grub-pa'i ye-shes)*, constitute the four directions.

The triad of irritation *(zhe-sdang)*, horizon *(nam-mkha')* and thematically directed consciousness *(rnam-shes)* constitute the center, because it abides as quasi-mirroring pristine cognition *(me-long lta-bu'i ye-shes)*. (All of these) form configurations surpassing the imagination, actually abiding [externally as] the five elemental forces, which are the five femininities, [internally as] the five psychophysical groupings, which are the five masculinities, and [arcanely as] the five poisons, which are the five pristine cognitions.

All that is subsumed under (the cover-term) coming-into-presence *(snang)* and its interpretation *(srid)* as Saṃsāra and/or Nirvāṇa, is a spontaneous atemporal presence, (and this fact) is the majestic wholeness (of Being-*qua*-Existenz).

FIGURE 18a

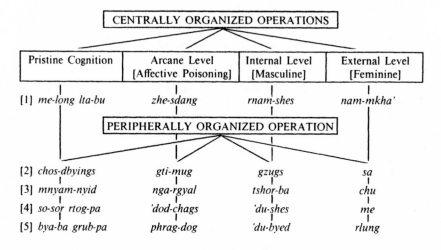

FIGURE 18b

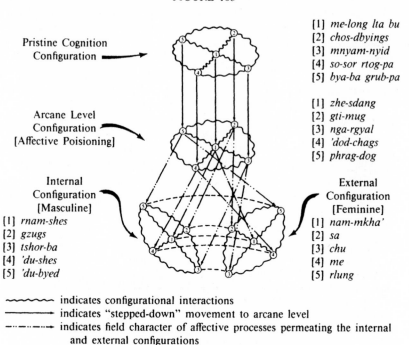

~~~~~~~ indicates configurational interactions

———→ indicates "stepped-down" movement to arcane level

—··—··—··→ indicates field character of affective processes permeating the internal
            and external configurations

— — — — — indicates sensitive resonating between these configurations

A yogi who understands this[31] may well enjoy all that is, this coming-into-presence and its interpretation as Saṃsāra and Nirvāṇa, without rejecting or accepting, negating or affirming any of it, as the grandiose configuration of the self-existent pristine cognitiveness. Strictly speaking, in whatever comes-into-presence and whatever has-become-present, there is nothing to reject or to accept, for it is the play of configurational activity.

It is important to note that the enormous complexity described in the above passage and diagrammed in Figures 18a and 18b, reflects the working of consciousness as a centrally organized operation, which remains connected with that pristine cognitiveness whose auto-projection it actually is. Because of this connectedness it also is joined with the cognitive operations that are peripheral (secondary) to the central (primary) pristine cognitiveness. Inasmuch as it is Being's projection that is now the center, what previously had been central is relegated to the peripheral status. The many levels that become conspicuous in the wake of Being's projectivity, may be conceived of as collapsed states of wavelike quantum superpositions in the sense that the whole unfolding panorama is generated by the dynamics of Being and that the superpositions are every bit as real as that portion of the whole, which we have sampled with our limited perceptions.

The "new" centrally organized (primary) complexity of perceptual processes, summarily called consciousness *(rnam-par shes-pa)* involves the following features:

1. Being's readiness to mirror itself through its quasi-mirroring pristine cognition collapses into the arcane (deep-structured) poison of (globally embedded) irritation. Against this affective background there operates a structure, which consists of an internal (masculine) aspect, the thematically directed consciousness, and of an external (feminine) aspect, the horizon (of this consciousness). Horizon means both the opening up of domains to be acted upon and that which is so opened (the horizon of all thematically directed conscious operations).

The peripherally organized (secondary) complexity presents the following:

2. The openness and transparency of the meaning-saturated field pristine cognition collapses into the arcane (deep-structured) poison of (globally embedded) dullness. Against this affective background there operates what is, internally, constituted as the perceptible and, externally, earthy solidity.
3. Auto-reflexive identity pristine cognition collapses into the arcane poison

of (globally embedded) arrogance, which makes possible the overt delusional inflation of ego operations. Against such a background there operates what is, internally, constituted as feeling and, externally, watery cohesion.

4. Specificity-initiating selective mapping pristine cognition collapses into the arcane poison of (globally embedded) addiction which becomes a craving for and attachment to that which has been singled out, and obsessive inordinate possessiveness reinforced by ego operations. Against this affective background there operates what is, internally, constituted as ideation and, externally, fiery combustion.

5. Tasks posed-and-accomplished pristine cognition collapses into the arcane poison of (globally embedded) envy which, as a reluctance to accept how things are, develops into the urge to meddle. Against this affective background there operates what is, internally, constituted as the actualizing of innate tendencies and, externally, stormy motility.

Altogether these pristine cognitions, themselves the surging of excitatory intelligence *(rig-pa'i rtsal)*,[32] engage in the creation of a life-world with regions of concern and involvement pointing beyond themselves to farther horizons of possible and as yet indeterminate perspectives. Because this life-world has been built up by pristine cognitions, even if they undergo a transformative collapse, what has been so built retains a felt quality which, in the case of the palace, is at once highly cognitive and aesthetically moving. Like a home set in a landscape, the palace is situated in a field that is none other than Being-*qua*-Existenz, enabling the experiencer to image, search, and discover significant symbolic modalities. Unlike a real home, however, the palace is a bounded openness. It remains open to the system Being-*qua*-Existenz as a whole; it is bounded as a functional system, which allows the experiencer to pinpoint regions of concern.[33]

The palace admits of still another interpretation. It may be experienced as the existential resonance of the internal logic and meaningfulness of Being, indivisible and unbreakable, and in this sense the palace is felt to be a stronghold *(rdzong)*. This idea has been beautifully expressed in the following lines by Klong-chen rab-'byams-pa:[34]

Just there, with no directionality, an all-encompassing and all-encircling stronghold;
With no upper, lower, or in-between levels, an atemporally primordial, vast and expansive stronghold;
With no directionality, all-accommodating, having no onset,[35] a meaning-saturated gestalt's stronghold;[36]
Unchanging, just-there, and precious,[37] mystery's stronghold.
An atemporal stronghold (overlooking whatever) presences and is

> interpreted as Saṃsāra and Nirvāṇa, the uniquely over-arching completeness.
>
> On an estate that has no directionality but is all-encompassing and all-encircling
> There stands the castle of intending toward limpid clearness and consummate perspicacity, unconcerned with Saṃsāra or Nirvāṇa.
> (Its range), the internal logic of Being,[38] extends far and wide, and its spire just towers high,[39]
> Wide open stands the gate through which, without having to exert oneself step by step, one enters
> Its vast interior (extending) into the four directions, (Being's) uncontrived actuality.

The reference in the last sentence of the above passage to the four directions indicates the operational presence of a center around which any life-world becomes structured. In view of the primacy of experience, which permeates the various versions of a life-world, the center is not a single isolatable locus, but an orientational point within and hence applicable to each world version as it becomes structured around this center. In terms of architectural imaging, the center is a throne; and since there are multiple world versions there is a configurational array of thrones upon which a variety of symbols are found. Thus it is said: [40]

> On lion, elephant, horse, garuḍa
> And eagle thrones
> Sun, moon, lotus, and jewel (are found).

It is within this palace—a within where neither within nor without in their ordinary sense apply—that the following arrangement of thrones is found:[41]

1. In the center: a lion throne, which symbolizes the four kinds of intrepidity;
2. Eastward: an elephant throne, which symbolizes the ten kinds of strength;
3. Southward: a horse throne, which symbolizes the swiftness of the four bases for success (rdzu-'phrul): sustained interest, perseverance, firmness of purpose, and scrutiny;
4. Westward: a peacock throne, which symbolizes ten kinds of aptitude; and
5. Northward: an eagle throne, which symbolizes the unimpeded operation of pristine cognitions.

Furthermore, on each of these thrones there is a cushion consisting of a precious jewel, which symbolizes the fact that it is man's innate spirituality which may grant whatever is desired.[42] On this jewel cushion there are lying, one upon the other, in a perfect fit, the discs of sun and moon whose self-luminosity symbolizes the unity of appreciative discrimination and appropriate action, respectively. All this rests inside a lotus flower, which symbolizes the undefiled nature of Being-*qua*-Existenz.

As indicated in the above passage, the notion of a throne involves a configuration of five thrones, arranged in a central locus and four loci associated with the cardinal points on a compass. These thrones serve as orientational points with reference to which all the specific operations pertaining to the areas where these thrones are prominently situated, are organized. Any such throne gives its area a distinct character, just as a piece of furniture helps determine the character of the room in which it is placed. Within this ensemble of thrones and their environing areas, each and every throne is related to the other; as an ensemble they converge from the periphery to the center while also spreading from the center to the periphery. This array of thrones is itself relative to the palace within which it is located. The palace itself is relative to the bounded openness of the "site of 'Og-min," Being-*qua*-Existenz as the ground *(gzhi)*, which grounds everything without itself being grounded. This organization in which everything is relative to everything else can be charted as follows:

FIGURE 19

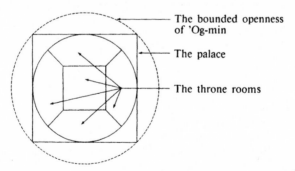

which grounds

The bounded openness of 'Og-min

The palace

The throne rooms

The totality of this throne array, functioning as orientational points within the complexity of an individual's life-world, is constituted by the excitatory intelligence of Being-*qua*-Existenz in such a way that each throne serves as the seat for the specific operation of that intelligence. This self-enthronement of excitatory intelligence initiates the manifestation of Existenz *(rgyud)* as the source and horizon-form of our lived world

versions into which Being's intelligence reaches by its resonating concern
(thugs-rje) as a guiding principle. In anthropomorphic diction this guiding
principle is called the teacher *(ston-pa)* who speaks to us with the voice of
Being, toward which all our actions may then be attuned so as to bring to
fruition the authentically satisfying unfoldment of life's meaning.

[4]

The teacher who by his resonating concern is deeply involved in guiding
man's spiritual development, is thus not absolute, but the energy of the
evolutionary process itself. This is indicated by the four characterizations
of the pure potential:[43]

> Moving into and over the as-is *(de-bzhin gshegs-pa)*, a super perfect state of
> being wide awake *(yang-dag-par rdzogs-pa'i sangs-rgyas)*, having conquered
> and being endowed and having passed beyond *(bcom-ldan-'das)*, and thor-
> oughly engaged *(longs-spyod chen-po)*.

Each of these four characterizations conveys an aspect of the wondrous
beauty and richness of Being forever active in Existenz.
    The first, "moving into and over the as-is," primarily indicates under-
standing the as-is mode as that which does not involve any going astray into
misapprehension and misinterpretation of the pure fact of Being.[44] This
also indicates that the as-is mode is coupled with the operation of ultimate
pristine cognitiveness.[45] Specifically, the as-is involves a movement into
higher states of organization *(sangs-rgyas)*. Thus:[46]

> Just as the Buddhas of yore have "moved into" (their Buddhahood) by their
> active quest for limpid clearness and consummate perspicacity, so this term
> "moving into" is used when a similar path is followed.

In another sense, moving into denotes the development of sentient systems
which, in the case of womb-born sentients, cover the stages of conception,
birth, and subsequent phases.[47] Most importantly, such movement indicates the emergence of a participatory quality that shares in the hidden and
virtual, for it is hidden from the ordinary view and virtual in allowing
maximum freedom in the organization of one's life. In the words of
Rong-zom-pa Chos-kyi bzang-po:[48]

> In the case of a piece of metal such as copper; if it is left as copper then it is
> held to be junky, but when the same material is made into a vessel it is held to

be nice, and when this same material is made into a statue it is held to be venerable. It is the same with one's behavior when it is dominated by desire and other affects; if one behaves with a mind engrossed in subject-object dichotomies, such behavior becomes the arena of Saṃsāra and its fictitious projects. If one behaves with a mind which has been taken hold of by appropriate action and appreciative discrimination such behavior becomes a determinant for that enjoyment (experienced by) yogis, and turns into the path toward limpid clearness and consummate perspicacity. And when the mind has been so developed that it has become appropriate action and appreciative discrimination, then (the otherwise virtual patterns of) formal gestalt, authentic utterance, and vibrant spirituality become a diamond-like realization. Therefore, the way of the Buddhas is not that of being free due to the elimination of affects—it is a being free due to appropriate action, which is flawless in its nature.

The second characterization of the teacher is "a super perfect state of being wide awake." Here, this expression wide awake *(sangs-rgyas)* is based on the Tibetan interpretation of the Sanskrit word *buddha*.[49] There are several common Tibetan interpretations; on the whole they agree that *sangs-rgyas* indicates: the sleep of not knowing has gone *(sangs)*, and in having woken up the mind has widened and broadened *(rgyas)* so as to be able to deal appropriately with all that can be known and all that has to be done. To be wide awake, however, is also characteristic of spiritually advanced persons. Therefore, to indicate that more than just being wide awake in their sense is involved, the word perfect is added; yet even such a "perfect state of being wide awake" may fall short of connoting what actually is involved. Therefore, one speaks of a "super perfect state."

The third characterization of the teacher is: "having conquered and being endowed and having passed beyond." This rendering is based on the Tibetan interpretation of the Sanskrit term *bhagavān*. Traditionally it has been used with reference to a person who possesses the rare qualities of lordliness, beauty, wealth, fame, knowledge, and diligence.[50] These qualities, however, are understood as coming-to-the-fore only when whatever prevented them from doing so has been conquered, broken, and shattered. Thus, *bhaga* (good fortune) and *bhaṅga* (destruction) were combined in the Tibetan interpretation of this term. Rong-zom-pa Chos-kyi bzang-po, for instance, has this to say:[51]

In the term *bcom-ldan-'das*, (the Indian word) *bhaga* has the meaning of having overcome, and the term is used because the Buddhas are endowed with the qualities of having overcome affective processes and the like. In another sense, *bhaga* means good fortune; since the Buddhas are endowed with (such qualities as) most excellent lordliness and so on, they are said to have goodness and good fortune. Alternatively, *bhaga* means to go into the realm of possible existences. He who has passed beyond this is *bhagavān* (fortunate). Alternatively, *bhaga* applies to having gone beyond both Saṃsāra and Nirvāṇa. In still another sense, *bhaga* means to have passed beyond what can become a source of fear. Since the Buddhas secured the four intrepidities, they have passed beyond everything that is frightening, and therefore they are *bhagavān*. According to the esoteric approach *(gsang-sngags)*[52] *bhaga* means the pudenda of ladies-of-rank ("married to") the indestructible (facets of Being-in-action)[53] and serves as (a symbol for) the birth-place of meaning; and *van* means to have, that is, to reside in a nondual manner with this (matrix).[54] In brief, *bhagavān* is so called because it is the state of having the sustaining life-force, which can neither be joined nor separated.

Klong-chen rab-'byams-pa, on the other hand, mentions the term *bhaga* only in passing as signifying both Saṃsāra and Nirvāṇa;[55] he interprets *bcom-ldan-'das*, according to its three syllables, as having conquered the four deadening powers,[56] being endowed with the six qualities of greatness, and having passed beyond localizability. "Having passed beyond localizability" is further characterized by him as "the dignity of Kun-tu bzang-po." As previously discussed,[57] Kun-tu bzang-po does not refer to an anthropomorphic deity; but to that great ordering process of evolution which makes possible an inquiry into the wider horizons of our being. Such a possibility constitutes the very dignity of this process, which makes life intrinsically meaningful and worthwhile.

The fourth characterization of the teacher is "thoroughly engaged." It denotes the acceptance *(longs)* of Being's unified temporal thrust and global setting of existential regions, as well as Being's engagement *(spyod)* in each of its (regions [projects]) through a formal gestalt *(sku)*, which, as a nodal point, is yet fully continuous with its "world." This engagement takes place free from thematic concretizations and as such carries with it the deep feeling of intense pleasure and happiness which, significantly, goes with being enthroned in a world of unbounded meaningfulness. The thoroughness *(chen-po)* of this joyous engagement in what is Being's scenario is vouchsafed by the fact that it is not dependent on specific situational contingencies such as place and milieu.[58]

These four characterizations of the incomparable teacher Kun-tu bzang-po set the stage for an ongoing holistic development, which gradually takes on an ever more specifiable character, becoming the orientation point for what eventually develops as thematically determined psychic activity. This emerging structure remains as yet virtual: [59]

It is the quintessence of formal gestalt, authentic utterance, and vibrant spirituality (operating in and as) all those (forces) moving into and over the as-is in the ten directions and the four temporal modes. It is such that the entirety [of their meaning-saturated gestalts], the totality [of their scenario gestalts], and the ensemble [of their cultural norms display gestalts] are neither isolatable [aspects of the overall intentionality of Buddhahood] nor differentiable [with respect to the facticity of Being] nor separable [with respect to the internal logic of Being].

This complex structure emerges from the ground which is the facticity of Being, and assumes in its emergence the formal gestalt of the teacher Kun-tu bzang-po. He is said to reside in 'Og-min, in complete enjoyment of this realm where his intentionality as the primal condition *(chos-sku)* for the existence of this "his" universe acts from this primal condition as an omnidirectional presencing in and as a variety of worlds and their inhabitants. In this auto-presencing he is both for-himself *(rang-don)* as intrinsic oriented valuation and for-others *(gzhan-don)* as extrinsic oriented valuation. With this aspect he engages with others-in-a-world through infinite variations of his presencing *(sprul-sku).*[60] Inasmuch as this emerging presence, centered as an intelligence radiating into and pervading the whole configurational field, is imaged as teacher, a personal relationship is introduced whereby the energy of this process takes on a qualitative charge. The center, as teacher, is a "higher" intelligence—higher than that found in ordinary mortals and gods, and so the teacher's personality *(sku)* also cannot be measured by our limited standards. Furthermore, this "higher" intelligence exhibits a radial (omnidirectional) symmetry—as teacher he looks in all directions, and as intelligence it accommodates and processes information inputs from everywhere. Thus:[61]

> This personality *(sku)* has neither front nor back; his face everywhere glistens and radiates, and he possesses all attributes and marks of superiority.[62] In all the inconceivable[63] worlds he is fully present in the varied patterns of formal gestalt, authentic utterance, and vibrant spirituality. He sits with his legs of appropriate action and appreciative discrimination evenly crossed. His six hands are the six pristine cognitions;[64] from the precious emblems of these pristine cognitions light blazes forth.[65] He has three heads, which show that he has the inconceivable [and inexhaustibly beauteous patterns of] formal gestalt, authentic utterance, and vibrant spirituality.[66]

Although this passage uses the anthropomorphic diction of face, legs, and hands, it must be emphasized that these are but symbolic figurations of the intelligence that underlies the dynamics of the universe itself. The cross-legged posturing of this intelligence symbolizes the polar unity of the universe imaged as masculine and feminine, and operative as appropriate action and appreciative discrimination, respectively. This underlying polarity of the intelligent universe, imaged and felt as a resonating connectivity of the masculine and feminine, can only be dimly reenacted in these human encounters, which preeminently focus on relationships between seemingly autonomous individuals embodied as men and women in actual life situations.

Several important points must here be brought out regarding the character of the teacher Kun-tu bzang-po. We have previously discussed the all-encompassing *(kun-khyab)* character of that excitatory intelligence *(rig-pa)* which pervades the universe and operates over the entire range of the wave function for the system Being *(gzhi)*. As indicated in the above quotation, the emergence of this intelligence, as the personality of the teacher Kun-tu bzang-po, occurs in "inconceivable and inexhaustibly beauteous patterns." Bearing in mind that this personalizing diction is used with reference to the emergence of the complex structuring of the universe as a whole, one may here draw a few parallels with modern notions of cosmogony and attendant cosmological models.

First, something should be said about the orders of magnitude on which this emergent structuring takes place. According to Buddhist calculations, the smallest imaginable unit which still retains a coherent structure is $(1/7)^{11}$ times the width of a finger *(sor-mo, Sanskrit anguliparvan)*. This yields an order of magnitude of 2 cm x $(1/7)^{11} \simeq 1$ x 10^{-9} cm. Interestingly, this favorably compares with modern calculations of atomic distances. For example, the covalent radius of a hydrogen atom is 3 x 10^{-9} cm. Thus the Buddhist "atom" *(rdul phra rab*, Sanskrit *paramāṇu)* is about one third the radius of the hydrogen atom.[67]

Having established the minimal unit of distance acknowledged by Buddhist theoreticians, maximal distances must now be discussed and compared with modern calculations. According to modern astronomical calculations, given that the so-called Hubble relation (regarding measurements of the red shifts of receding objects) is valid at the limits of the universe, the farthest astronomical objects are about 10^{28} cm away.[68] This is 10^{37} times the minimal unit of distance calculated above. How does this compare with the operational range over which the "inconceivable" patterns of the teacher Kun-tu bzang-po extend? The term inconceivable *(bsam-gyis mi-khyab-pa)*,[69] in cosmological contexts, is a technical term for an order of magnitude of 10^{58}! Thus, by comparison, it would seem that Kun-tu bzang-po's teaching extends 10^{21} times beyond the distance of the farthest possible astronomical objects.

Secondly, bearing in mind the "inconceivable" range of Kun-tu bzang-po's teaching, one may reasonably wonder how out of the dynamic nature of the universe as a whole such emergent structuring ever became possible.

Recasting this query with reference to modern cosmological speculations: What did the universe look like before the big bang? What was the big bang itself like? What can be said about the consequences of this primal explosion for the various galaxies and sentient systems that developed in its wake?

First we shall consider the pre-big bang state of affairs:[70]

> Before there was any shrouding
> By either Saṃsāra or Nirvāṇa,
> There was self-existent pristine cognitiveness, a primordial purity (in)
> Its facticity, an openness beyond demonstration and verbalization;
> Its actuality, a sheer lucency shining from deep within;
> And its resonating concern, the very energy of excitatory intelligence,
> Abiding as an interiority of ultimate purity.
> Facticity, abiding as gestalt, suffered neither displacement nor transformation;
> Actuality, sheer lucency, manifested as authentic utterance;
> And resonating concern was spirituality, abiding as excitatory intelligence.
> Although (facticity) abided as formal gestalt, there was neither face nor hands;
> Although (actuality) abided as lucency, there was no color;
> Although (resonating concern) abided as excitatory intelligence, there was no oscillation.
> In itself a radiant interiority it was the ultimate ground for (universe) to evolve.
> It abided as the ground for the fact that, auto-dynamically,
> From its formal gestalt the gestalt triad manifested,
> From its lucency spontaneous presence manifested as complete engagement in the scenario (developed by Being), and
> From resonating concern excitatory intelligence manifested as pristine cognitions.
> This was the primordial state of affairs.

There are several points to be noted. The emphasis on self-existent pristine cognitiveness, which is synonymous with Experience-as-such, makes it quite clear that the big bang was not the explosion of a lump of matter into some preexisting void, as is often popularly believed contrary to what scientists understand it to be. Experience-as-such is neither matter nor a mind which, in a very special sense, might be claimed to "react on the world by...collapsing it from a superposition into reality."[70a] Rather, it seems that Experience-as-such or self-existent pristine cognitiveness is more like an algorithm for dealing with (calculating) the results of actual experience (observation) and, in addition, a pointer to an autopoietic dynamics, which can be described only in terms of the immediacy of Being's auto-projectivity as a splitting into near copies of itself, which then may rush off in opposite directions, giving birth to the universes of Saṃsāra and Nirvāṇa. Furthermore, the reference to a triadic character of facticity, actuality, and resonating concern, apart from constituting symmetry transformations, may also be conceived as a pointing to a multitude of universes, which continue multiplying. In addition, each such expanding universe contains, as it were, a multitude of individuals as participant observers of that universe that they inhabit, being thereby bound within their own universe of limited dimensions. Each individual is therefore unaware of that larger dimensioned n-state universe, the ground and totality of all possible universes which as a "superposition of N states is observed as a single state $A_{n(q)}$ $_n($ $)$, not because of a projection into that state alone but because the entire universe divides into n states. . . ."[70b]

In the light of these remarks, Klong-chen rab-'byams-pa's account gains added significance. It is no mere turn of poetic diction when he describes Being's auto-presencing as (1) concern-*like*, (2) lucency-*like*, (3) gestalt-*like*, (4) pristine cognition-*like*, (5) nonduality-*like*, and (6) freedom-*like*. His use of the tag *like (ltar)* clearly indicates that none of these modes can ever be considered as actual, preexistent, eternally operative parameters, being but modes of the ground and totality auto-presencing as the n-state universe Being itself. Every reference to and (partial) experience of this auto-presencing is necessarily a limited profile, akin to (like) the totality. As a referring expression (a single state) it can never retain the essentially indeterminate spontaneity of the totality (n-states).

Thus Klong-chen rab-'byams-pa states:[71]

> From this ground *(gzhi)* the ground-totality presencing *(gzhi-snang)* occurred as follows:
> Its spontaneous presence, radiating from deep within as an interiority,
> Was outwardly propelled by motility (so that its) intrinsic outward-tending glowing *(gdangs)* manifested.
> When the "shell" of this spontaneous presence exploded
> Six modes of presencing and two passageways manifested.
> The singular, internally radiating excitatory intelligence
> Was propelled by motility, the outward-tending glowing of excitatory intelligence
> So that its inner glow *(mdangs)* was outwardly thrust.
> By its concern-*like* auto-presencing
> The auto-creativity of excitatory intelligence became outward-tending glowing.

By its lucency-*like* auto-presencing, like a rainbow,
All and everything (as) the coming-into-presence of the continuum (that is Being) was suffused by luminosity.
By its gestalt-*like* auto-presencing, clustered gestalts
With no center and periphery encompassed (the universe)
By its pristine cognition-*like* auto-presencing
Translucent galactic realm *(zhing-khams)* emerged.
By its nonduality-*like* auto-presencing
All and everything (shared in its) dissipative (character) having neither center nor periphery.

Impure—it appeared as a passageway to Saṃsāra.
The presencing of six lifeforms, like a dream;
The downwardly gravitating radiance, like openness-turned-physical. And still
This coming-into-presence abides as the impetus for going further and further astray.

Pure—it appeared as the pristine cognitions passageway:
Nirvāṇa's self-manifestation (from) the primordially pure ground;
Its upwardly (dispersing) radiance, like the sky. And still
This coming-into-presence abides as the impetus for exercising freedom.[72]

While the six presencing modes are the exploding ground,
The two passageways are invitation to enter;
The entering is either Saṃsāra or Nirvāṇa.
These are the ways in and through which the ground-totality presencing occurs.

Due to the indeterminate character of Being-*qua*-Existenz divergent processes develop, which yet remain pervaded by the intelligence of the universe. The cosmological scale on which this intelligence operates, is reflected in its (open) creativity *(rtsal)*, its prismatic play *(rol-pa)*, and its manifestations of beauty *(rgyan)*. More specifically, these three facets reflect the working of self-existent pristine cognitiveness. Thus:[73]

The facticity (of this self-existent pristine cognitiveness) is not in any way anything; its actuality is radiantly diaphanous; and its resonating concern rises as any (engagement). In this continuum, which is the ultimate primordial transparency of (indissolubly blended) excitatory intelligence and open-dimensionality, all and everything that comes-into-presence, and is interpreted as Saṃsāra and Nirvāṇa, abides as its self-manifesting, auto-presencing, and intrinsic freedom in mere playfulness, beauty, and creativity. Moreover, the shape in which this excitatory intelligence expresses itself, is utterly dissipative (as Being's) openness and radiance; from this dynamic reach and range, which is nowhere and nothing, due to the creativity of the five colors of (Being's) spontaneous presence, what is found externally as world and internally as embodied sentience, has become present as a beautiful adornment of the auto-manifesting (process), the prismatic play of pristine cognitions, and a ceaseless creativity. Yet in this coming-into-presence there is no reality value; rather it is like the appearance of a dream that has come about as the creativity, adornment, and play of an auto-manifesting (process) having no objective reality.

This process—creative, playful, and imbuing everything with beauty—leaves traces of its activity in and as the images that constitute our experienced world. All of them are pure symbols in that they are but self-presentations of Being-*qua*-Existenz. In concise terms we are told:[74]

> The internal logic of Being *(chos-nyid)* is adorned with the formal gestalt (expressing the) meaningfulness (of Being) *(chos-sku)*,
> (Whereby) its utter openness is made beautiful by radiating (everywhere).
> The formal gestalt (expressing the) meaningfulness (of Being) is adorned with pristine cognitions,
> (Whereby) it is made beautiful by ceaselessly (operative) capabilities.
> Pristine cognitiveness is adorned with resonating concern,
> (Whereby) it is made beautiful by applying itself to the welfare of the six kinds of beings.[75]
> For this reason, by virtue of being made beautiful, one speaks of ornamentation.[76]

Self-existent pristine cognitiveness, which itself is the dynamics of excitatory intelligence, is described in terms of creativity, playfulness, and beauty (manifesting as ornamentation) thereby suggesting a threefold symmetry transformation of the state → image kind; each facet presents a specific aspect of this intelligence's emergent holistic movement. The process of ornamentation itself has been illustrated by rich images as follows:[77]

> The vault of the sky bathed in light—the first;
> Gold inlaid with turquoises—the second;
> These are the similes illustrating how the internal logic of Being is adorned with the formal gestalt (expressing the) meaningfulness (of Being).
>
> A peacock's egg glistening in five colors; and
> A crystal whose flashing never ceases are
> The similes illustrating how the formal gestalt (expressing the) meaningfulness (of Being) is adorned by pristine cognitions.

The (way in which) flashes of light burst from a crystal under (favorable) conditions, and
A bird breaks out from its egg when it has been fully hatched, and
Light and rays issuing from the sun's energy,
Are the similes illustrating how pure pristine cognitiveness is adorned by resonating concern.

To sum up, all this rich imagery so far discussed indicates a certain directionality, in which the creative center of Experience-as-such becomes ever more focused: within the vastness of 'Og-min one enters a palace, within this palace one goes into the throne room, and within this throne room one comes "face to face" with the intelligence of the universe. As self-existent pristine cognitiveness this intelligence exhibits a polarized character whose ceaseless activity engenders the evolution of man. Thus:[78]

Within a centrifugal movement in lofty height, a continuum which has neither boundary nor center, the primordially pure facticity (of Being as) meaning-saturated gestalt, there—within a palace constituted by five colors glowing from deep within (of what is Being's) spontaneous presence—Kun-tu bzang-mo, the internal logic of Being, the open dimension of excitatory intelligence, in her radiance as the spouse of Kun-tu bzang-po, the meaning-saturated gestalt, the presencing dimension, have joined in a bond of appropriate action and appreciative discrimination. Appreciative discrimination, (imaged as) a horse (symbolizing) instinctual life (and) set up as the cognizing of everything that can be known, is a swift courier; the intrinsic outward-tending glowing of the five-(colored) lucency as yet undiffracted and (remaining) self-same, is a wide open plain. Since this (lucency) never subsides, it is the sun of (life's) mystery that has risen in Being's continuum.

[5]

The intelligence of the universe (Being), to which one has become gradually attuned (Being-*becoming*-Existenz), unfolds as the intelligence of our existentially constituted life-worlds and their projects (Being-*qua*-Existenz). In this unfoldment the configurational character of Experience-as-such, itself a transformative flux, becomes evident as a multidimensional texture of perceptual, valuational, conceptual, motivational, and stabilizing operations, each having its own field character and yet operating in intimate interplay with all other operations. The interactions of these operations constitute life-worlds as worlds of meaning in which the experiencer feels "at home." In addition to such interaction, each of these operations has genotypic affinities with Being *(rigs)*, and exhibits its own vectorial tendencies within what is constituted as a fivefold force field of vibrant spirituality *(thugs),* formal gestalt *(sku),* authentic utterance *(gsung),* creative potential *(yon-tan),* and optimally executed activity *(phrin-las).*[79] These vectorial tendencies are indices of the richness of psychic life which, paradoxically, operate in a multiplicity of aspects and yet are a single presentation of the contextuality of Experience-as-such. These affinities with Being are genotypal in that they are formal structures, which prescribe the allowable forms which the unfoldment of sentient life may take.[80]

Antedating, as it were, the specific thematizations which are freely allowed to take place within the limits set by the nature of each force field, these operations are prethematic and virtual because each of them is as yet a majestic "movement into and over the as-is" *(de-bzhin gshegs-pa).* Each such majestic movement is imaged as a vassal king who symbolically indicates a higher order performance, which aids the growth and development of the sentient system, while simultaneously inhibiting whatever may obstruct such development. Because of its majestic movement this higher order performance is "privy" as well as "affined" to that higher intelligence, the King of kings and teacher Kun-tu bzang-po who seems to have an overall plan. This relationship is brought out by Rong-zom-pa Chos-kyi bzang-po in his definition of king:[81]

> Just as kings among gods and men, within the circle of their retinue, enjoy their domain and restrain their adversaries, so also these movements into and over the as-is, take up the overall strategic operations of the superior authority by regaling in their resources and protecting their domains, thus bringing their subjects to full maturity and destroying the adversaries such as the deadening powers.

Kings as members of hierarchically stratified society belong to certain families *(rigs)* whose interests they represent and guard. In terms of Being-*qua*-Existenz, whose dynamics of in-built intelligence operate as a self-organizing system, any higher order performance (symbolically spoken of as king) exhibits a familial affinity with Being-*qua*-Existenz. Moreover, a king has a dual function: literally, he promotes the welfare of the domain and prevents sabotage by adversaries and, figuratively, he ensures a rich psychic life and puts an end to spiritual stagnation. Thus, this symbol is particularly appropriate for bringing out the primary importance of growth and development, for any such kingly operation is never autonomous, but always enacted in the context of their affinities which color these operations. Moreover, any such operation is, properly understood, a functionally coherent program consisting of multiple subroutines. One may speak of such programs in the singular, yet this is only a shorthand method indicating the coherent functioning of multiple subroutines which constitute the program. Likewise, one may speak of certain groupings of functionally coherent operations as kings. And since these "kingly" operations are intentional in character, they always involve two cointended features. They are indicated by the metaphor of each king having his noble queen. Thus:[82]

> Each of these kings, Perception *(rnam-par shes-pa)*, Structuring *(gzugs)*, Feeling *(tshor-ba)*, Conceptualization *('du-shes)*, and Motivation *('du-byed)*—having conquered, being endowed, and having passed beyond, as well as moving into and over the as-is—ablaze in the brilliant colors blue, white, yellow, scarlet, and green, respectively, inseparably reside with their noble queens Coming-into-presence Expanse *(snang-ba'i dbyings)*, Stability Expanse *(sra-ba'i dbyings)*, Smoothness Expanse *(mnyen-pa'i dbyings)*, Warmth Expanse *(dro-ba'i dbyings)*, and Vibration Expanse *(bskyod-pa'i dbyings)*. (These pairs) pervade the infinite realm of meaningfulness just as oil pervades a sesame seed.

These paired operations of king and queen are said to "pervade the infinite realm of meaningfulness," because the meaning-saturated continuum *(dbyings)*, as the dynamics of Being, becomes polarized in such a manner that paired functional programs are intitiated throughout the continuum, reverberating in each and every life situation. These reverberations reflect higher order performances qualitatively imaged as the male-female polarity *(yab-yum)* of a unitary cognitive intentionality, which pristinely abides in an atemporal manner *(ye-shes)*. Recalling that pristine cognitiveness is the creative dynamics of excitatory intelligence, one may appreciate why cognitiveness is considered a primary and even ultimate value *(don)*. As formulated energies *(lha)* pristine cognitiveness is imaged as king and queen, resonating in male-female polarity *(yab-yum)*. As specifically delimited operations and domains *(rtog-pa)* pristine cognitiveness may be thematized into kingly functional groupings *(phung-po)* together with their corresponding queenly elemental forces *('byung-ba)*.[83] In addition, as previously mentioned, each king-queen couple retains a familial affinity with Being *(rigs)* whose coloration *(kha-dog)* they reflect in their activities. Moreover, as king-queen interactions, these five higher order performances occur in such a way that each king acts out *(thabs)* the inspiration *(shes-rab)* offered by his queen, each royal personage requiring the presence of the other.[84] These multifaceted nuances reflect the wide-ranging complexities associated with that special movement of moving into and over the as-is *(de-bzhin gshegs-pa)*.[85] First we shall diagram these complexities and then we shall explicate each of the five higher order performances in their contexts.

FIGURE 21

HIGHER ORDER PERFORMANCE

King (rgyal-po)	Grouping (phung-po)	Field Force ('byung-ba)	Queen (btsun-mo)	AFFINITY (rigs)	COLOR
[Pristine Cognition: *Me-long lta-bu'i ye-shes*]				de-bzhin gshegs-pa	blue
RNAM-PAR SNANG-MDZAD (Vairocana)	rnam-shes	*nam-mkha'/snang-ba*	DBYINGS-KYI DBANG-PHYUG MA (Dhātvīśvarī)		
[Pristine Cognition: *Chos-kyi dbyings-kyi ye-shes*]				rdo rje	white
MI-BSKYOD-PA (Akṣobhya)	*gzugs*	*sa/sra-ba*	SANGS-RGYAS SPYAN-MA (Buddhalocanā)		
[Pristine Cognition: *Mnyam-pa nyid-kyi ye-shes*]				rin-po-che	yellow
RIN-CHEN 'BYUNG-LDAN (Ratnasambhava)	*tshor-ba*	*chu/mnyen-pa*	MĀMAKĪ (Māmakī)		
[Pristine Cognition: *So-sor rtog-pa'i ye-shes*]				padma	scarlet
'OD-DPAG-MED (Amitābha)	*'du-shes*	*me/dro-ba*	GOS DKAR-MO (Paṇḍaravāsinī)		
[Pristine Cognition: *Bya-ba grub-pa'i ye-shes*]				las	green
DON-YOD GRUB-PA (Amoghasiddhi)	*'du-byed*	*rlung/bskyod-pa*	DAM-TSHIG SGROL-MA (Samayatārā)		

One should note that the operations performed by the various kings are named according to the standard fivefold groupings *(phung-po)*, which are said to constitute an intact individual and his world with which he interacts. But, unlike the traditional ordering of this fivefold grouping, which begins with the discussion of what becomes structured and perceptible *(gzugs)*, in this context of the grouping of kingly operations, Perception *(rnam-shes)* is mentioned first, for it is primary due to its being a reflection of Being's intelligence.

The grouping of kingly operations termed Perception is the state → image symmetry transformation of vibrant spirituality *(thugs)*; its state is iconically presented as Kun-tu bzang-po and Kun-tu bzang-mo in intimate embrace, and its image is the king rNam-par snang-mdzad (Vairocana) and his queen dBying-kyi dbang-phyug-ma (Dhātvīśvarī). This king-queen pair, as formulated energies of the pristine cognition, which acts like a mirror *(me-long lta-bu'i ye-shes)*, actively mirrors whatever presences, thereby revealing possibilities in intelligible presentations. More specifically, this higher order performance is an illumining of the field, which in its presencing is possibility itself. Because of its illumining capacity it is called rNam-par snang-mdzad (Vairocana) who, whether he is imaged as a king, or felt and thematized as a functionally grouped operation, is affined to and presents the affinity with Being *(rigs)* termed the moving over and into the as-is *(de-bzhin gshegs-pa)*, experienced as being of a deep blue color. It is important to note that color in connection with all the familial affinities and their representatives is not a sense-datum, but a particular lighting operation that allows us to see (perceive); it is prior to what we see (perceive) as the spatial level on which the content of perception temporally occurs. Such illumining always operates in the presence of a field which, at this level, is nothing less than the whole of the meaning-saturated continuum of Being, from which intelligible information may be gleaned. This field is the noble queen Coming-into-presence Expanse (dBying-kyi dbang-phyug-ma, Dhātvīśvarī).[86] She is likened to the open sky *(nam-mkha')*, which obscures nothing, but lets everything shine forth *(snang-ba)*.

The illumined presence is perceived, if this is an appropriate term for an as yet virtual operation, as structured and as having certain relatively invariant features. It is on the basis of such invariance, itself the outcome of a very active process, that one then relates to whatever presences by abstracting additional relatively invariant features and meanings *(gzugs)*.[87] As a functionally grouped operation, this structuring is imaged as the king Mi-bskyod-pa (Akṣobhya).[88] He is affined to and presents the affinity with Being termed indestructibility *(rdo-rje)*, which is of a pure white color.

Such invariant structuring operates together with a field that is imaged as the noble queen Stability Expanse (Sans-rgyas spyan-ma, Buddhalocanā). She is likened to the earth *(sa)* whose solidity *(sra-ba)* serves as the ground for the growth and development of qualities and capabilities. This king-queen pair is the formulated energy of that pristine cognitiveness, which is the meaning-saturated continuum of Being *(chos-kyi dbyings-kyi ye-shes)* expressing itself and being expressed in relatively invariant patterns.

At a certain stage, one begins to take pleasure in these operations, and a rich world of sensations and feelings *(tshor-ba)*[89] is disclosed through that pristine cognitiveness that binds and holds everything in its spontaneous wholeness of auto-reflexive identity *(mnyam-nyid-kyi ye-shes)*. As a functionally grouped operation, these sensations and feelings constitute a mine of precious delights, and are imaged as the king Rin-chen 'byung-ldan (Ratnasambhava). He is affined to and presents the affinity with Being termed preciousness *(rin-po-che)*, which is of a rich yellow color. These enriching sensations and feelings are shared with the noble queen Smoothness Expanse, Māmakī. She is likened to the fluidity *(mnyen-pa)* of refreshing and healing water *(chu)*.

Eventually one begins to conceptualize *('du-shes)*[90] these sensations and feelings, making changes and "adjustments." Feelings vitalize one's conceptualization so that one's mental and intellectual horizons expand with the pristine cognition which by selectively mapping initiates specificity *(so-sor rtog-pa'i ye-shes)*. As a functionally grouped operation, such conceptualization proliferates everywhere, sparking new ideas, and it is imaged as the king 'Od-dpag-med (Amitābha). He is affined to and presents the affinity with Being termed lotus *(padma)*. Lotus plants spread over the whole pond in which they grow and thus are an appropriate symbol for the proliferation of conceptual activities. This familial affinity is of a brilliant scarlet color. Conceptualization operates together with the noble queen Warmth Expanse, Gos dkar-mo (Pāṇḍaravāsinī). She is likened to fire *(me)* whose heat *(dro-ba)* consumes all defects and makes possible the discernment of whatever can be known.

Vitalized conceptualization tends toward a motivated enactment *('du-byed)*[91] within that pristine cognition that poses appropriate existential tasks and ensures their successful accomplishment. Such functionally grouped operation of enactment is imaged as the king Don-yod grub-pa (Amoghasiddhi). He is affined to and presents the affinity with Being termed activity *(las)*, which is of a lush green color. Such enacted operations jointly occur with the noble queen Vibration Expanse, Dam-tshig sgrol-ma (Samayatārā). She is likened to the vibrant air *(rlung)*, which moves *(bskyod-pa)* and sustains, without which life would cease. She is committed to helping people by freeing them from all bondage and making them cross the ocean of Saṃsāra.

The complex correspondences shown in Figure 21 should not be regarded as arbitrary associations between analytic and symbolic modes of thought. Indeed, very little attention in the West has been paid to relationships between the attitudes and operations discussed above. However, the interconnectedness of all these modes is undeniably part of the human experience; it is reflected in ordinary language when we say that a person is "fired by an idea," "overflows with emotion," or "attacks his tasks tempestuously."[92]

The interpretation of these complexities in terms of primary values *(don)*, formulated energies *(lha)*, and specifically delimited operations and domains *(rtog-pa)* has strong theoretical overtones, which seem to divorce the concrete person who actually undergoes the experience from what is so presented. There is another interpretation, however, which takes actually lived experience as central and deals with such an experience in terms of three interfusing perspectives. There is the diaphanously pure *(dag-pa)* qualitative perspective interfused with the utterly diaphanously pure *(shin-tu dag-pa)* qualitative perspective, both of which interfuse with an opaque impure *(ma-dag-pa)* perspective within which quantitative thematizing is dominant. Whereas the impure and quantitative perspective focuses a mechanistic aspect of existence, the pure qualitative perspective focuses its imaginal aspect, and the utterly pure qualitative perspective focuses the very dynamics of Experience-as-such.[93] All these three perspectives constitute a "person" in every occasion of lived through experience. For example, one's embodiment *(lus)* is an interweaving and fusing of these three perspectives: from the opaque, impure perspective, the embodiment is the fivefold grouping of the psychophysical constituents *(phung-po)*, which are themselves the result of the mechanism of Karma. From the diaphanously pure perspective, embodiment is the result of the interests and aspirations the experiencing person introduces into his or her life so that the mechanistic perspective no longer dominates and life is given a meaningful direction. From the utterly pure perspective, embodiment is experienced as configurations of formal gestalts *(sku)* together with their pristine cognitions *(ye-shes)* fused into what can only be imaged as pure symbol.[94]

One must be careful not to construe these three perspectives as separable experiential levels, as if the impure level can be "transcended" through certain purificatory exercises, transforming one's previously sullied embodiment into a new "pure" form of embodiment that can then by some ultimate final ("higher") exercise be transformed into an eternal, transcendent, and utterly pure level. Such a view reflects a mechanistic-reductionist tendency, which is characteristic of the representational mode of thought, but which fails to understand the process character of experience.

By way of illustration, just as one speaks of three different phase-states for H_2O (as ice, water, and steam), yet all retain the same molecular structure, so also the so-called impure perspective may undergo phase-changes into the pure and utterly pure. Such phase-change is figuratively spoken of as ice dissolving into water.[95] An additional point is that, how one actually experiences something is itself a function of one's perspectival horizon. For example, with respect to what we ordinarily call water:[96]

> for denizens of hell it appears as fire; for spirits as dark blood; for men as cleansing and beneficial; for animals as something to drink; and for gods as nectar. For those who traverse the pure realm (it appears) as a river of nectar; and for whoever has succeeded (in recapturing life's meaningfulness it appears) as Māmakī and so on.

To recapitulate, we have so far discussed the primary import of the teacher Kun-tu bzang-po (as the excitatory intelligence of Being-*qua*-Existenz in its open dimension) together with Kun-tu bzang-mo (as the field presencing of this open dimension) and those complex interrelationships associated with the five higher order performances, imaged as king-queen pairs. One should also recall that this teacher Kun-tu bzang-po, through a symmetry transformation of his vibrant spirituality, constitutes himself as the kingly operation Perception, imaged as rNam-par snang-mdzad who is centrally situated due to the primacy of perception in man's life.

As is the case with every royal household, the king (with his queen) has his vassals (each with their consort). Thus the five higher order performances, imaged as king-queen pairs, are the fivefold vassalage of the supreme king Kun-tu bzang-po (the intelligence of the universe). This vassalage presents certain policy outlines for a person's life experiences. The kingly operation Perception, being the expression of primary intelligence, becomes, through a symmetry transformation, a set constituting means for delivering to its vassalage the specifics of the intentionality of the primary intelligence, each individual member of the set also having an intentionality of its own. These intentionalities are imaged as male-female pairs and aptly illustrate what may be termed the basic erotic structure[97] of perception, underlying and antedating thematic elaborations of experience, which inevitably carry with them the ghosts of misplaced concreteness. These means for delivery are complex configurations, related to what we commonly call our sensory operations of seeing, hearing, smelling, and tasting.

They are differentiated into inner and outer male-female functionaries who are closely associated with, and hence privy to the spirituality *(thugs)* of the higher order performances *(rgyal-ba)*. The functionaries are, therefore, characterized in terms that indicate that (dynamic) state of limpid clearness *(byang)* and consummate perspicacity *(chub)* from which they ultimately derive, and on whose behalf they operate. They are also characterized as constituting the indestructibility and inviolability of their own operational fields. Thus:[98]

> Just as the Teacher (Kun-tu bzang-po) is the ultimate in limpid clearness and consummate perspicacity *(byang-chub chen-po)*, so also the entourage, having arisen from the (dynamic) reach and range of (the Teacher's) auto-presencing[99] resonating concern *(thugs-rje)*, is ultimate *(chen-po)* because it is Buddhahood due to all sundry obscurations having been cleared up *(byang)* and all capacities without exception having become fully active as spirituality *(chub)*; hence this entourage is superior to the spiritually advanced beings *(byang-chub sems dpa')* residing on (the various spiritual) levels. Furthermore, with respect to the four (male-female) functionaries[100] of Perception, they are indestructibility *(rdo-rje)*[101] in the sense that the (meaning-)continuum and pristine cognitiveness, the coming-into-presence and the open dimension (of Being), are not dual modes and thus can neither be destroyed nor be separated. In the *rDo-rje rtse-mo* it is stated:
>
>> Firm and, (as the) energy (that is Being), not a hollow emptiness;
>> It cannot be cut up nor can it be destroyed;
>> It cannot be burned and does not decay.
>> Thus the very openness (of Being) is termed indestructibility.
>
> And, while (such indestructibility) destroys all obscurations, it cannot itself be damaged by any obscurations. As the larger version of the *gSang-ba snying-po* states:[102]
>
>> Indestructibility is such that it destroys all obscurations
>> But is not damaged by anything,
>> As self-existing pristine cognitiveness (imaged as) the god of all gods, it
>> Pierces everything in totality.

The indestructibility of intelligence, operative in and as the entourage of the vassalage, is itself distinguished into inner and outer functionaries who together operate in an imaginative setting whose intentional structure consists of an act-phase (imaged as male) and an object-phase (imaged as female), both phases being coconstituted, not sequential. This male-female intentionality, which symbolically represents the basic erotic structure of perceptual processes, can be schematically diagrammed as follows:

FIGURE 22

BASIC EROTIC STRUCTURE OF PERCEPTION

INNER FUNCTIONARIES

ACT-PHASE		OBJECT-PHASE	
Perceptual Disposition for	Imaged as Male	Imaged as Female	Perceptual Disposition for
visual program	SA'I SNYING-PO [Kṣitigarbha]	SGEG-MO [Lāsyā]	what is seeable
auditory program	PHYAG-NA RDO-RJE [Vajrapāṇi]	SGEG-MO [Lāsyā]	what is hearable
olfactory program	NAM-MKHA'I SNYING-PO [Gaganagarbha]	SGEG-MO [Lāsyā]	what is smellable
gustatory program	SPYAN-RAS GZIGS DBYANG-PHYUG [Avalokiteśvara]	SGEG-MO [Lāsyā]	what is tasteable

OUTER FUNCTIONARIES

ACT-PHASE		OBJECT-PHASE	
Perceptual Operation as Program Execution Called	Imaged as Male	Imaged as Female	Perceptual Operation Temporally Symbolized as
seeing	BYAMS-PA [Maitreya]	BDUG-SPOS-MA [Dhūpā]	the past
hearing	SGRIB-PA RNAM-SEL [Nivaraṇaviṣkambhin]	ME-TOG-MA [Puṣpā]	the present
smelling	KUN-TU BZANG-PO [Samantabhadra]	SNANG-GSAL-MA [Dīpā]	the future
tasting	'JAMS-DPAL [Mañjuśrī]	DRI-CHAB-MA [Gandhā]	temporality-as-such

Here, the inner functionaries, in their male aspect *(sems-dpa')*, are the representatives of vibrant spirituality *(thugs)*,[103] while in their female aspect *(sems-ma)*, they are the representatives of formal gestalt *(sku)*.[104] As noted before, spirituality is that specific existential function that disposes us to perceiving. As dispositions, therefore, these inner functionaries represent perceptual preprograms which, because of their intentional structure, involve integral feedback processes so that both phases of the intentionality, the "male" act phase and the "female" object phase, shape each other. To give an example, whereas the male act phase may be understood as a searching for what to perceive (to see, to hear, to smell, to taste), the female object phase must be understood as an already present solicitation for such searching. Each disposition for searching espouses its own (peripherally present) tendency. This searching, which remains permeated by spirituality, reverberates with the dynamics of Being-*qua*-Existenz, felt and known as: (Being's) internal logic, as-is, unorigination, and nondual movement.[105] It is through such copresent and ever-present solicitations, cognitions, and allurements taking form and shape in the subtle and delicate movement of a dance, that the formal gestalt (as female functionary) is the comprehensible picture of the searching, not its content. Precisely because these formal gestalts are not amenable to any kind of reduction and are active participants in the creative process, they provide aesthetic pleasure and are themselves aesthetically satisfying.[106]

Whereas the inner functionaries are dispositions for perceptual programs, the outer functionaries may be said to be program executions. In their male aspect, they are the representatives of authentic utterance *(gsung)* and in their female aspect they are the representatives of the symbolic, the qualitative, and diaphanously pure *(dag)*.[107] As authentic utterance they assert nothing and demonstrate nothing, yet they speak, address themselves to, and call up pure possibilities. It is by these acts that the timeless is felt and made present in time as the comprehensible image of program execution.

It has already been pointed out that such terms as king, functionary, noble consort, queen, and others are borrowed from the language of social relations and these, in turn, become a means for acquiring an understanding of human existence. All life with its varied activities seems to involve a hierarchy of controls which, while imposing certain restrictions and restraints, at the same time allow for the creation of models of future ways of conducting one's life. It is at the highest level that general indications of courses of action are evolved, and then are passed on to lower levels. However, it is crucial to bear in mind that this patterned activity is generated from within the system Experience-as-such—"there is neither a

without nor a within and yet there is everywhere this within"[108]—and that
the programs set up by this patterned activity are self-executing, for their
execution is not dependent on some extrinsic operator. Although a multitude of such self-executing programs are operative, they may be grouped
into three major ones referred to by the code names vibrant spirituality
(thugs), formal gestalt *(sku)*, and authentic utterance *(gsung)*. These major
programs represent the totality of the software available for use within the
wetware of a concrete individual as the coordinated "machinery" of
embodiment *(lus)*, speech *(ngag)*, and mentation *(yid)*. Yet every assembly
of wetware (the triadic complexity of human being) is programmed from
within by excitatory intelligence (the programmer), which ensures that
embodiment, speech, and mentation remain coordinated facets of a unitary
field, receiving instructions regarding the implementation of programs
with respect to the particular life situations within which the field is
interactively engaged.

The inner and outer paired functionaries represent the delicate nuances
associated with perceptual dispositions and operations and are all imaged
as displaying a peaceful and mild mien, a relaxed and dignified pose
(zhi-ba). These delicate operations require protective shielding, imaged as
male *(sgo-ba)* and female *(sgo-ma)* palace guards, who are remarkably
different in character from the functionaries. The palace guards are imaged
as displaying an energetic, vigorous, and fierce stance *(khro-bo)*. The
epithet used to characterize their fierce deportment is *'joms-pa chen-po
rdo-rje*, which Klong-chen rab-'byams-pa interprets as follows:[109]

> Conquering, vanquishing, overcoming *('joms-pa)* means situationally
> appropriate action *(thabs)*, and great *(chen-po)* means appreciative discrimi-
> nation *(shes-rab)*. Since through their prodigious team-work the poisonous
> powers spiritual death *(bdud,* Māra), physical death *(gshin-rje,* Yama) and
> others are brought under control, they are said to be indestructibility *(rdo-
> rje)*.

This epithet for the palace guards characterizes all the aspects of that
complexity presented as the lived body *(lus)* of each and every experiencer.
The lived body is experienced as the center for all world engagements
through attitudes which invest one's world with significance (indicated by
appreciative discrimination), and through projects which are deployed
(indicated by situationally appropriate action). The lived body therefore
shares in the "life" of Being-*qua*-Existenz. This is indicated by indestructibility, which does not refer to some indestructible thing, but points to the
mystery of Being from which the lived body cannot be detached. Rather,
the lived body is an image through which Being manifests and makes its

presence felt. Thus, body is but a shorthand term for the complexity of embodied being in one of its most conspicuous aspects; it is through our bodies that we, as embodied beings, are actively engaged in and with our world. In our embodiment, we also address our world (by speaking within and about it), and, furthermore, we reflect and have feelings about it (through operations summed up by the cover-term mentation). There is in all this a wholeness that is qualitatively experienced as having a certain continuity and displaying an extraordinary stability. As is so often the case with the process-oriented view, so prominent in Buddhist thinking, here again the idea of a field as an integrating force is helpful in understanding the phenomenon of body. The body is properly seen to be the product of a feedback process, which incorporates a variety of specific features of the dynamic properties of the field.

This intricate process is understood to be the coordinated activity of four phase transitions. The basic phase is general sentience *(reg-pa)* as that which disposes us to be "in touch with..." (to feel). This phase or field of general sentience gives us the intentional structuring in which attention can be focused on the act-phase, the touching *(reg-byed)*, or on the object-phase, the touchable *(reg-bya)*. In the context of embodiment, the act-phase is my body in the sense that "I as my body am the one who..." *(bdag)*; the object-phase can be any object *(yul)* other than my body, as well as my body. However, it is as a result of the interaction between the act-phase and the object-phase that the body exhibits a specific cognitive quality of touch awareness *(reg-shes)* through which it comprehends, while at the same time being lodged within, its world. Thus it is through the body that one truly experiences oneself as embodied and enworlded.[110] In terms of sensory activity, the body, as those coordinate phase transitions with respect to embodiment, is the most important sense, for it is through the body that a human being experiences the immediate encounter with himself (on the basis of which the judgment that embodiment is physical-material arises) and with the world (on the basis of which the judgment that sensory domains are physical-material arises).

This activity of four phase transitions also occurs on the levels of speech and mentation. In the context of speech they are: sound in general, signifying, signified, and language-comprehension; in the context of mentation they are: general noemata, thinking, noematic profiles, and judgments of affirmation and negation, the pleasant and the unpleasant. Since these phase transitions operate throughout the ensemble of embodiment, speech, and mentation, the living person is a well-orchestrated process. Because of the importance and valuableness of the lived body, and because of the highly actional character exhibited by it, the four phase transitions are

FIGURE 23

Male Palace Guard	Phase Transitions With Respect To Embodiment	Phase Transitions With Respect To Speech	Phase Transitions With Respect to Mentation
BDUD-RTSI 'KHYIL-BA [Amṛtakundalin]	general sentience [reg-pa]	sound in general [sgra]	noemata in general [chos]
RTA-MCHOG [Paramāśva]	touching/feeling [reg-byed]	signifying [rjod-byed]	thinking [yid]
STOBS-PO-CHE [Mahābala]	the touchable [reg-bya]	the signified [brjod-bya]	noematic profiles [don-spyi'i rnam-pa]
GSHIN-RJE-GSHED [Yamāntaka]	touch awareness [reg-shes]	language comprehension [sgra'i shes-pa]	judgments [yid-kyi rnam-shes]

aptly symbolized as palace guards. They guard the palatial gates of our embodiment, speech, and mentation through which we go out into the world and through which the world enters us. Since it is through the totality of the coordinated phase transitions that we become actively engaged with "world," this actional character of the engagement is imaged as male. The relationship between the phase transitions and their imaging is shown in figure 23.[111]

To summarize, the intentionality of the coordinated phase transitions with respect to the triad of embodiment, speech, and mentation exhibits not only a (male) actional character (disclosing the body-as-myself engaged with a world) but also a (female) cognitively appreciative character (providing the basis for ethical principles that involve attitudes and plans for action). For this reason, all active engagements of our embodied being, even as seemingly separate acts, simultaneously carry with them a cognitively appreciative dimension that maintains appreciative awareness of the coherence and continuity of life's drama. In this appreciative awareness I feel myself in the midst of my projects so that just as I am my body engaged with world, I am also my thoughts and, in voicing my projects, I am also my speech. Through this appreciative awareness the true value of being-in-a-world is maintained against any facile reductionist judgments. This "maintenance" is imaged as four female palace guards who, like their male counterparts, display a fierce deportment *(khro-mo)*. As vanquishers *('joms-pa chen-po rdo-rje)* they overcome all reductionist tendencies. These tendencies and the fallacious views that they engender, cause untold misery for us as embodied beings. All such reductionism as fixed world views can be classified into either an eternalism *a parte ante* or an eternalism *a parte post*. The former eternalism *(rtag-mtha')* is based on the assumptions that there exists an independent entity reigning above and apart from the world, to which one subjects oneself as an abject slave, or that there exists such an entity with which one can identify (the Self). The latter eternalism *(chad-mtha')* is based on the assumption that there is no regulative principle in the universe nor any need for it; once "this" universe has run its course, a maximum entropy state will forever reign. In addition, there are two ego trip reductionisms: one is that of a personalistic fixation *(bdag-tu lta-ba)*, and the other is the insistence on the absolute differences *(mtshan-ma)*—be these between male and female persons or between natural objects.[112]

Although the female palace guards appear to be fierce in their vanquishing of the crippling powers of all reductionism, they present and bring into the open those qualities that enhance the value of life. Foremost among these qualities are the four immeasurably great catalysts and the four distinct means of attracting people. The relationship between the vanquishing and enhancing powers, as shown in Figure 24, may now be discussed in detail.[113]

FIGURE 24

Female Palace Guard	Vanquishes the Reductionism of	The Four Catalysts	The Four Distinctive Attractions
LCAGS-KYU-MA [Ankuśā]	*rtag-mtha'*	*byams-pa*	*sbyin-pa*
ZHAGS-PA-MA [Pāśā]	*chad-mtha'*	*snying-rje*	*snyan-par smra-ba*
LCAGS-SGROG-MA [Śrṅkhalā]	*bdag-tu grub-pa*	*dga'-ba*	*don-mthun-pa*
DRIL-BU-MA [Ghantā]	*mtshan-mar grub-pa*	*btang-snyoms*	*don-spyod-pa*

It is lCags-kyu-ma who understands that the structure of things is not something ever-lasting or absolutely permanent and constant—it is the outcome of a complex fluctuating process. Understanding this with depth of discernment and sympathetic penetration carries with it an emotional quality of loving kindness *(byams-pa)*. With all its warmth and tenderness this quality is outgoing—following up, as it were, each and every fluctuation in the appearances and shapes of what is experienced. This loving kindness shows itself in generosity *(sbyin-pa)* as the warmhearted readiness to give and to share, thereby undermining any claim to the validity of a separate self.

Zhags-pa-ma understands that speech, which only too often comes as empty talk, nevertheless always retains its existential significance. Man's speech expresses and articulates the manner in which he exists in the world, and since it discloses his concern with this valued world, it is never to be dismissed as something forever-done-with. The emotional quality of this understanding is sympathetic compassion *(snying-rje)*, expressing itself in the display of deep tenderness whose verbal manifestation is the beauty of diction and sound *(snyan-par smra-ba)*.

It is lCags-sgrog-ma, however, who does away with the allegedly privileged status of the ego/self of all egological philosophies, which can be classed as either mind-body dualisms or reductive monism. Just as I am my

lived body and my spoken word, I also am my thinking, which is traditionally assumed to constitute an entity called mind. However, neither we nor
others have any direct perception of such an entity. The understanding that
what we call mind is at best a pragmatic description of both conscious and
unconscious, carries with it the capacity for transcending a self-engendered
finitude which, in its openness, is therefore not riveted to a particular
situation or perspective. The emotional quality of this understanding is
joyousness *(dga'-ba)*, which may be understood not so much as an excitement of the mind and the senses, but rather as a reward for having
successfully transcended the narrow confines of the ego. Its overt activity is
the monitoring and selecting of that which is appropriate and effective in
relation to the value of one's overall life plan *(don-mthun-pa)*.

Finally, it is Dril-bu-ma who puts an end to any residual reductionism,
be this of a physical, physiological, psychic, or psychological nature. The
understanding symbolized by her, is a real breakthrough whose emotional
quality is equanimity *(btang-snyoms)* as a dynamic balancing and not as a
static numbing apathy. In this balancing we deeply participate in the very
process of life, acting out, as it were, its intrinsic value and meaningfulness
(don-spyod-pa).

As embodied beings installed in a world in whose shaping each of us
participates, we cannot but live in what Sir Geoffrey Vickers has so aptly
called an "appreciated world."[114] Such appreciation, born of excitatory
intelligence, is an active and creatively sensitive cognition. This appreciation cannot be encompassed within the outworn body-mind dualism nor be
reduced to the equally barren monism of spirit as postulated by idealist
philosophies, for as living individuals we are a dynamic system which
simultaneously exhibits both physical and psychic dimensions. It seems
unfortunate that we have no adequate linguistic tools for describing the
phenomenon of living man in its full complexity. Perhaps this is due to the
fact that we have failed to formulate properly that question about being
human which so fundamentally perplexes us, and have been content
instead with generating superficial questions and with complacently
accepting the equally superficial answers. So much, however, seems to be
certain: a human being is an unending task and not something "once done,
forever done." In this task the catalysts of loving kindness, sympathetic
compassion, joyousness, and equanimity, as interrelated and formulated
aspects of pervasive sentience, make for and ensure the continuity of
culture as the continued actualization of human potential.

The above description of what, in oversimplified terms, we refer to as
body and mind, shows a human being to be an intricately coordinated
system controlled from deep within. In its complexity it is imaged as a

princely household living within a palace. As we have seen, the palace itself is a field of concern (an appreciated world) and not a walled-in container. The royal household as the dynamic unfoldment of Being *becoming* human being is not the evolutionary result of the random movement of matter, but the intricate self-organizing of that intelligence which pervades Being and, therefore, awe-inspiring in its majestic wondrousness. In this wondrous household the blending of masculinity and femininity in the union of appropriate action and appreciative discrimination illustrates the aesthetic creation of a world in which mankind can live in rapturous enjoyment, which is fundamental to life. Mental life, embodied in us as human beings, spreads throughout the universe. Is this not worthy of poetic celebration?

> Inside this castle decorated with (Being's) display of spontaneous wealth,
> There is seated on his throne the king Self-existing pristine cognitiveness;
>   and
> While all creative stirrings of this pristine cognitiveness, (assuming the) semblance of a (continuous) coming and going,
> Have become (the king's) ministers administering their domains,
> He (the king), together with his noble queen, Self-abiding disposition (of pristine cognitiveness), and
> With his son and servants, self-arising bestowals of sense,
> (Remains) immersed in the swirl of ultimate bliss, glowing in its own light with no divisiveness.

It is through this image of a royal household as poetically envisioned by Klong-chen rab-'byams-pa,[115] that Being-*qua*-Existenz auto-presences for an in-depth appraisal which is Being's self-explication. This occurs in words and images understandable and appreciable by human minds as the meeting ground of constraint from above and aspiration from below, as the emergence of that intelligence which contemplates and reflects back on itself, mirror-like as it were, remaining actively creative in its appraisal. This in-depth appraisal of our being is cocreative with the primary creativity of Being-*qua*-Existenz felt as the thoroughly positive matrix, imaged as Kun-tu bzang-po. It is through such imaging that we may enter that realm whose richness would otherwise go unnoticed.

VI. The Aesthetics of the Virtual Patterns

[1]

It is well to remember that the image of a royal household, discussed in the previous chapter, is an attempt to understand life's complexity and wholeness in easily intelligible terms. Primarily expressive of Being's excitatory intelligence *(rig-pa)*, inseparable from Being's openness *(stong-pa)* and ever-present lucency *(gsal-ba)*, this image of a royal household refers back to that mystery which continually creates symbols and images through which we try to understand the very mystery of our being. In a more technical jargon, the programs of the system we wish to study are themselves the very instruments of this probing. The fact that these symbols have anthropomorphic features and refer to human models, in a sense, reflects our very existence. The images of a royal household can be seen, statically, as a blueprint or coding on which our overt activities depend; it provides the knowledge of what our life-world is like by inscribing (encoding) it within the structure and organization of each and every human being.[1] Yet this image can also be seen, dynamically, as an auto-catalysis carrying with it the information and control which help to maintain the orderliness of the live processes and ensure that the standards of the system are met through its overt activities, amongst which aesthetic creation and enjoyment are of paramount importance.

Every occasion of experience is spatio-temporally situated; it is here and now, sharing in the expansiveness of Being-*qua*-Existenz. This is to say that experiencing is centered in an experiencer who, posturing himself within his life-world for engaging in various tasks, is attuned and disposed to the execution of a plan of action. Such posturing, therefore, is both an anchorage in an appreciated world and the manifold operations that issue from this base which, for us as embodied beings, is our body.[2] Its as-yet virtual spatial situatedness and operational character is indicated in the cryptic statement:[3]

On thrones in full (sovereignty) and in the style of functionaries.

Klong-chen rab-'byams-pa elucidates this terse statement in the following words:[4]

> The manner in which (the members of this royal household) are seated, is as follows: On (their respective) thrones Kun-tu bzang-po, in male-female aspect, as well as (the vassals, that is) those moving in and over the as-is, are seated in the manner of kings. That is to say, since the bipolar intentionality of Being-*qua*-Existenz is spontaneously constituted in utter completeness, they [Kun-tu bzang-po and his vassals] are complete Buddhas,[5] twelve in number counting their male and female (aspects separately), and are seated crosslegged. And the functionaries, in male-female aspects, surround (their overlords) in the manner of ministers who are seated, as is appropriate for them, with right leg outstretched and left leg drawn in. Since the palace guards, in the manner of military commanders, destroy troublemakers and rebel leaders, they turn their gaze outward and posture themselves as fighters on the march. The mighty ones *(thub-pa)* present themselves in the august shape (appropriate) to each life-world; they are not seated, but stand in the manner of princelings.

One should bear in mind that, apart from the contribution this passage makes for iconographic identification, it is the experiential significance that is of primary importance. In particular, the crosslegged posturing may be understood in either a static or dynamic sense. This twofold understanding itself reflects our ingrained habit of introducing division into an undivided whole—distinguishing between the as-is and "its" image, not realizing that the as-is is already an image. In terms of existential experience (Being-*qua*-Existenz) still in its dynamics of letting meanings evolve, before allowing them to be reduced to categories of representational thought. More specifically, the crosslegged posture indicates what, in the human context, is appropriate action (compassion) and appreciative discrimination (the pristine cognitiveness of the openness of Being), their interaction being imaged as legs crossed over each other. This seemingly rigid posture conveys a static image for the identity of Being with itself, already an identity transformation which cannot be reduced to any one of its abstractions or interpretations, be it Saṃsāra or Nirvāṇa. Yet this same posture may also convey the idea of a dynamic posturing of crossing the legs, which symbolically indicates the act of settling the affective processes under control and reconverting them into ultimate pristine cognitions.[6] Whether statically or dynamically understood, this crosslegged posture is the image of the presence of the bipolar intentionality of Being-*qua*-Existenz. Bipolarity, however, suggests otherness and difference—one pole being "different from" the other. This otherness and difference is present (and presented) as male and female aspects. They are variations and modes of world comprehension in interaction, involving mutual satisfaction, and not monolithic archetypes. This mutuality of satisfaction, in turn, depends on the arousal of particular metaphoric or symbolic evocations. In this context, the symbols of diamond and lotus are evocative images of the masculine (appropriate action) and the feminine (appreciative discrimination) respectively. Each of these evocative symbols is also the image for a specific posturing. As embodied beings we tend to associate these symbols and their interplay with the anatomical and physiological dimensions of masculinity and femininity. Yet the interplay of these symbols may also be described in psychological and aesthetic terms of satisfaction and pleasure *(bde-ba)*. In any case, it would be a grave mistake to confuse descriptions of experience with experience itself. Unfortunately all positivistic philosophies thrive on this confusion.

The crosslegged posture is an image for that program which makes us act in a certain way—for example, sitting crosslegged. The description of this posture is given in terms of the *effect* of the program which, consisting of a male and female posturing, can be diagrammed as follows:[7]

FIGURE 25

Crosslegged posturing
(skyil-mo-khrung)

mnyam-pa'i skyil-mo-khrung the identity of Being with itself as "appropriate action" *(thabs)* symbolized by the two crossed legs of the male *(yab)*	*brtul-zhugs-kyi skyil-mo-khrung* the elegance and delicacy of Being as "appreciative discrimination " *(shes-rab)* symbolized by the two legs of the female *(yum)* encircling the male

Symbolic representation:

Diamond   Lotus
(rdo-rje)   *(padma)*

In contrast to the seeming rigidity of the overall program laid down by the authority of the supreme king and mediated by his vassal kings, the posturing of the functionaries, our sensory operations in the service of program implementation, like ministers executing the wishes of their overlord, is one of gracefulness which makes it possible to attend lovingly to the tasks that are to be performed.

It is the lived body or, more precisely, "I-as-being-my-body"—this wondrous phenomenon of spirit embodied or embodied spirit[8]—that precisely because of being installed in an environing world, is threatened by this environment from which there come constant attempts to reduce me-as-my-body to a mere corporeal object among other objects. Because of this threat I-as-my-body constantly struggle against these environmental forces that try to destroy or undermine my integrity which is indivisibly linked with my projects. The constant vigilance against such forces is expressed in the pugnacious and combative posturing of the palace guards.

In addition to the kings, functionaries, and palace guards, there are mighty ones (thub-pa) in each of the six life worlds of the gods, demigods, men, animals, spirits, and denizens of hell. In the life world of humans the mighty one is imaged as the historical Buddha Śākyamuni. He is a mighty one in that it was "he who could" (thub-pa) actualize the potentialities and abilities that were his and, by implication, every man's. That is to say, I experience myself not only as a human being, a system of interlocking intentionalities, but also as a nexus of potentialities (an "I can"). This "I can" is a property of the whole system of interlocking intentionalities, a royal household, but unlike the specific intentionalities of the members of this household with their specific bipolarity of masculinity and femininity, the "I can" does not exhibit a bipolarity of its own.[9]

The royal household, as the imaging of experience, presents a hierarchy of operations, which may be conceived of as moving along a vertical axis in both a downward and upward direction, information passing both ways between the highest and lower levels. This information flow introduces temporality into experience in the sense that there is now "time for" the supreme authority's concern to engage in its intended domain. Yet experience is an undivided and unbroken whole whose seemingly separate aspects, imaged as kings, functionaries and so on, are atemporally correlated. Such atemporal correlation is temporality-as-such, which makes for the possibility of experience becoming temporally structured as past, present, and future.[10] Furthermore each hierarchical level of experience also has its horizontal dimension, which gives experience its spatial and orientational texture, whereby it becomes a world-engagement. Such world-engagement is centered in the experiencer as the interaction point of the vertical and horizontal dimension of a spatial-temporal system, and which, to be exact, is itself constituted prior to experienced space and time. Thus, the vertical dimension is a hierarchy of functions imaged as kings, functionaries, and so on, expressing itself in the different postures of kings, functionaries, palace guards, and mighty ones. The horizontal dimension is already implicit in the spatial array of the postures as a *process of* posturing, and can be imaged as a four-spoked wheel turning around its hub. The four spokes symbolize the directions into which the experiencer orientates himself from his being centered in his world.[11] The rim of the wheel symbolizes the range of experience. Thus, the horizontal spatial dimension of experience allows for the situating of the vertical, temporal dimension of experience, as follows:[12]

> In the wheel-like plan with four spokes meeting in the hub or center there reside the five kings (rNam-par snang-mdzad) and the other four together with their queens, and
> Starting from the right of the principal figure in this configuration, there reside in the spokes where they have a bulge,[13] the inner functionaries of sight, sound, smell, and taste, together with their consorts.
> In the studs (of the wheel, the projections in terms of the "palace"),[14] there reside the outer functionaries of seeing, hearing, smelling, and tasting, together with their consorts.
> In the outer corridor[15] there stand the six mighty ones.
> In front and behind the principal figures of this configuration, (Kun-tu bzang-po as) He who makes (the light that is this configuration actually) shine forth, and (Kun-tu bzang-mo as) She who is the ground and reason for this light that has to be brought forth, are shown to reside in the Eastern and Western wing of the inner corridor, respectively,
> In the superstructure of each of the four doors of the palace, there reside the vanquishers (the palace guards) together with their consorts.

For us as embodied beings the palace guards (termed vanquishers in the above passage), seem to be more easily understandable than the remoter members of the royal household. These guards, as has been discussed in the previous chapter, are ways of being "in-touch-with" reality, that is, being-in-the-world (by means of our body), addressing-the-world (by means of our speech), and thinking-about-the-world (by means of our mind). Each of these features indicate the presence of virtual forces that are vibrant and alive within these modes of our being in-touch-with. The resolution of these modes of being in-touch-with (by means of body, speech, and mind) into the fluidity of experience with its transparent imaging heightens our sensibilities and thereby enables us to expand into the dance of Life. Being in-touch-with therefore is a very active process, aptly captured by the idea of a dance and its mood. The dance, expressing and being the expression of excitatory intelligence that informs and permeates all life, manifests itself in the gestures, poses, facial expression, and limb movements of the body, in the timbre of the voice, and in the strivings and aspirations of psychic life. It is *in* the dance that I *perceive* life's movement and in reliving this movement I *feel* life's meaningfulness. The mood thus perceived and felt comprises various qualities which, in experience, coexist in complex patterns; in any particular instant of experience, however, only one of these qualities may dominate. These moods, belonging to experience in all its dynamics, are unique blends of the spiritual (qualitative, virtual) with the physical (quantitative, actual).

Significantly it is only the palace guards or vanquishers compared with military commanders in their stance who within the totality of an otherwise calm, peaceful, and silent *(zhi-ba)* configuration, are of an agitated, fierce, and energetic *(khro-bo)* appearance. Their fierceness, however, is not malicious and cruel, rather it is the tumult of a surface which in its movement brings into view a mysterious patterning best descriest described as the performance of a dance.

The dance, in the Indian tradition and in those civilizations that came under its influence, has been appreciated as the most basic art and hence considered to be the most worthy of pictorial presentation. It is in the dance that the major enduring moods and sentiments of man *(nyams*, Sanskrit *rasa)* come to the fore.[16] Such sentiments in the dance express the I-as-my-body in its triadic unity of embodiment, speech, and mentation. There is a threefold grouping of the nine enduring moods and sentiments.

First of all, there is the fascinating sensuousness and tender loveliness *(sgeg-pa)* of form specifically associated with female figures; the physical prowess *(dpa'-ba)*, specifically related to male figures; and the hideousness of appearance *(mi-sdug-pa)* that may apply to both male and female figures. These belong to the formal gestalt *(sku)*, which expresses itself in our embodiment *(lus)*. Next there are the sentiments of laughter and merriment *(dgod-pa)*, stentorian shouting *(drag-shul)*, and frightening shrieks *('jigs-su rung-ba)*—all of which are related to authentic utterance *(gsung)*, which expresses itself in our speech and talk *(ngag)*. Lastly, there are the sentiments of compassion *(snying-rje)*, wonder *(rngams-pa)*, and unsurpassed serenity and calming peacefulness *(zhi-ba)*—all of which are related to vibrant spirituality *(thugs)*, which expresses itself in our mentation *(yid)*.[17]

In the context of a total configuration these sentiments underlie and pervade man's overt behavior as it manifests in the complexity of his body, speech, and mind. Yet with respect to the hidden springs of lived existence, which cannot but touch upon the very mystery of Being-*qua*-Existenz before it is broken up into the multiplicity of spatio-temporal structures these sentiments are but surface reflections.

These hidden springs, the deep-structure of formal gestalt *(sku)*, authentic utterance *(gsung)*, and vibrant spirituality *(thugs)*, with which the abiding moods and sentiments are correlated and which make possible their expression in our embodiment, speech and mentation, are themselves but surface reflections of Being's excitatory intelligence, felt and envisaged to be an utterly open, nonlocalizable, omnipresent spreading out *(stong-pa)*, radiating as a brilliant, scintillating, glittering light *(gsal-ba)*. This openness-radiation we may illustrate by a reference to a person's radiant beauty, which is spread out all over the person and not localized in any one part. As such, beauty is just there—omnipresent and at rest; yet it is through its radiation which is also just there—omnipresent and ever active—that beauty effects its impact on the beholder who is already included in beauty's orbit. This open dynamic with respect to the members of the princely household, themselves imagings of sensuous and sensory experience, is pictured as[18]

> Having plumpness, well-proportionateness, resilience, and elasticity, as well as youthfulness.[19]
> *[mnyen lcug 'khyil ldem gzhon-tshul-can]*

The openness of Being expresses itself existentially as a formal gestalt which, however, may undergo a collapse into patterns of materially embodied existence. Unlike the formal gestalt, all such collapsed versions are subject to the vicissitudes of birth, illness, old age and death. This has been clearly indicated by Klong-chen rab-'byams-pa who states that these vicissitudes do not apply to the open-dimensional character of the high-ranking members of the royal household whose formal gestalt exhibits the qualities of plumpness and so on.

Furthermore, each gestalt manifests an intrinsic radiance and brilliance that far surpasses any luminous qualities detectable in our earthly finitude, and are therefore envisaged as:[20]

> Having brightness, brilliance, sublimity, and splendor.

The aesthetically appealing figures are self-representations of Being-*qua*-Existenz and hence are all said to be marked by Being. In being so marked, they are a formal gestalt *(sku)* which, as the object phase of an as yet virtual process, is inseparable from the act phase pristine cognitiveness *(ye-shes)*, which itself is the operation of excitatory intelligence. This marking *(phyag-rgya)*[21] is an intentional structure in which the marking and the marked are indissolubly linked as the indivisibility of all that is. This indivisibility in making its presence felt in what is experienced to be like a display of phantasmal forms and forces *(sgyu-'phrul)* and in their connectedness like a vast net *(dra-ba)*, not only atemporally abides in total completeness, it also cannot escape the marking and being marked by Being. Thus:[22]

> (Since whatever is) is completely there by (being a vast) net (holding together) the display of phantasmal form and forces,
> Each and every thing (carries) the mark of ultimate limpid clearness and consummate perspicacity [which is the teacher and king Kun-tu bzang-po].
> It is difficult to pass beyond this marking by the energy of the indisputable internal logic of Being as mystery.

In the explication of the term marking, the emphasis on the impossibility to exceed the orders of a supreme authority (Kun-tu bzang-po as teacher and king), might tempt one to interpret it as a kind of determinism. Yet living systems are not deterministically structured. What is meant by "being difficult to escape Being's marking" is that a living being tends to meet the standards set by Being which, however, are set with respect to the specific aims and requirements of the individual within the total framework of the evolutionary process of which, in figurative language, the king is the guiding principle.[23]

This guiding principle must not be confused with any postulated mysterious force, be it the *élan vital* of the French philosopher Henri Bergson or the entelechy of the Aristotelian influenced German biologist Hans Adolf Eduard Driesch. More properly, it resembles what Johann Wolfgang von Goethe[24] termed *Urphänomen*, which we nowadays would understand as a complex of feedback and feedforward processes. Such an idea necessitates a reinterpretation of any supposed aim toward which living beings direct their actions. They are goal-directed feedback and feedforward processes, moving in the direction of a goal (an *ad hoc* teleology), which already operates in them as a directing-toward (*post hoc* teleology).[25] This directing toward never culminates in a final climax but is the ongoing optimization of the total system. The marking and being marked by such a guiding principle is said to be the theme of what is technically known as the "external Yoga approach." This approach is deemed external because one does not go as deeply as is possible, although by following it a modicum of awareness of life's value emerges. With regard to the Yoga approach Rong-zom-pa Chos-kyi bzang-po has this to say:[26]

> Just as by a king's own seal
> The (palace) walls are marked,
> So the whole person is marked
> By the insignia of True Individuality.

He goes on to explicate the last two lines of this verse as pointing to the necessity of restoring dignity and value to one's ordinary existence by a transformative vision. For him the practice of Yoga is a focusing on the integrity and wholeness of the person's growth and development, to which the term True Individuality *(bdag-nyid)* applies. This is not to be confused with any hypothetical, metaphysical entity with which one may link up. Rong-zom-pa Chos-kyi bzang-po's interpretation of the practice of Yoga indicates a clear reaction against those analytically reductionist and negativistic *(med-par skur-ba gdab)* tendencies in Buddhism, which conceived of a human being as "nothing but" an assortment of various constituents. True Individuality is a pointer to the intrinsic coherence and value of the system (human being), which is thus godlike in its own right. This understanding of Yoga is illustrated by a beautiful simile:[27]

> In this underlying creativity of ours, which is like a golden plate, we have to coax its god-structure, which is like molten quicksilver, so as to cultivate imaginally this (whole process) into becoming the articulated presence of Being's (divine) dynamics *(lha'i sku).*

There is, however, also an ultimate Yoga approach—ultimate in the sense that there is no greater approach. This is another way of saying that in this approach we begin with the undivided whole that is Being-*qua*-Existenz.[28] Figuratively speaking, it is the ultimate approach, because in its undivided structuring of the marking-and-being-marked, the separability of marking and being-marked, which was basic in the external approach, does not apply. This approach is discussed by Rong-zom-pa Chos-kyi bzang-po as follows:[29]

> With regard to the ultimate Yoga approach, it is said that:
>   (Being) marks the whole universe.
> And this means that from the *phyag-rgya*, which is spontaneously there, special *phyag-rgya*-s come as mere phantasmal versions.

This cryptic explanation indicates that from a spontaneously present *phyag-rgya*, which is the whole of Being-*qua*-Existenz, there come to the fore special *phyag-rgya*-s, which are merely phantasmal versions of the spontaneously present one. In the coming-to-the fore of these special *phyag-rgya*-s the value and meaningfulness of Being-*qua*-Existenz is conveyed.[30] Being-*qua*-Existenz looks at itself through these special *Phyag-rgya*-s as versions of its pervasive excitatory intelligence. Thus, each special *phyag-rgya* is and contains different editions of the dynamics of Being at the same time and place so that each of us is a "many-version edition" of Being;[31] we are, as the image of the royal household indicates, both calm and energetic. We are, like the famous Schrödinger cat, simultaneously alive in one version and dead in another.

Each and every one of the members of the princely household and the images in which they present themselves, can be seen as a patterned energy *(phyag-rgya)* directly felt and perceived as a presence. In this identity of feeling and perception, a further identity of image and meaning inheres and is made perceptible in the form of symbols *(phyag-mtshan)* as particular shapes of the forces felt to be of significance in a life situation. As intelligibly perceptible shapes of the energy of Being-*qua*-Existenz, a total pattern *(phyag-rgya chen-po)* with ceaselessly emerging subpatterns, these symbols remain vehicles of meaning. They have an evocative character, which enables the beholder to relive those experiences that gave rise to the symbol formulation, thereby enabling him to break through the tyranny of the ordinary. However, one must not take the word symbol in too narrow a sense. It is not, for instance, restricted to the visual; for hand gestures and bodily posturings are equally symbols.

The richness and inherent value of life are a challenge to the imagination, which searches for symbols that give satisfactory, aesthetically pleasing accesses to reality and thereby bringing this felt and imaged reality before us. But as reality itself is not reducible to anything "other," it cannot therefore be limited to any one particular symbol. If a central symbol is necessary—and maybe for us as embodied beings such a symbol is necessary—it must be life's worth itself. It is Being's creativity, imaged as masculine (Kun-tu bzang-po) and feminine (Kun-tu bzang-mo) and felt to be an ever-present omnidirectionality ("having neither front nor back").[32] This dynamic creativity, in making its omnipresent impact felt is a marking whose felt impact, a being marked, is imaged as multi-dimensional—"with (six) hands (symbolizing) the six kinds of pristine cognitiveness holding precious emblems (illustrating) pristine cognitiveness, ablaze in radiant light."[33]

This central symbol suggests that man himself is a multifaceted program, each aspect of which has, and expresses itself in, its specific symbol. Some of these symbols are briefly indicated in the following verse:[34]

> A diamond (scepter), a wheel, a jewel
> A lotus, a sword, and a bell, all ablaze.
> Emblems such as a water lily, an orange, and so on;
> And toiletries for beauty's sake.

The six emblems mentioned in the first two lines are held by the six-armed and six-handed vassal kings of the royal household (symbolizing their multiple powers), one in each hand. Whichever emblem is held in the first right hand is specifically emblematic of that particular vassal king, himself a "total" symbol, who wields it. Furthermore, these vassal kings are never apart from their consorts, as is subtly indicated by the emblem of the bell; and since the kingly vassals also hold a bell in their first left hand, this emblem is an appropriate symbol for the concord and unity of the masculine and feminine acting ("sounding") in unison. The distribution of the symbols, which are primary emblems, is as follows:[35]

rNam-par snang-mdzad (Vairocana), who is (the imaged) vibrant spirituality (of the guiding principle "True Individuality"),[36] holds in his first right hand a diamond scepter, symbolic of the fact that the openness (of Being-*qua*-Existenz) and (its dynamics as) compassion are not two (separate entities).

Mi-bskyod-pa (Akṣobhya) holds a wheel (in his first right hand), symbolic of the fact that the network of the affective processes is cut asunder and, simultaneously (with this cutting) the *chos-kyi 'khor-lo* freely rotates.[37]

Rin-chen 'byung-ldan (Ratnasambhava) holds a jewel (in his first right hand), symbolic of the fact that the aspirations of sentient beings are being fulfilled (in view of the fact) that (Being's) qualities and potencies are spontaneously present.

'Od-dpag-med (Amitābha) holds a lotus (in his first right hand), symbolic of the fact that desire, in the light of the meaningfulness of Being, is pure and through the specificity initiating pristine cognition is dedicated to sentient beings.

Don-yod grub-pa (Amoghasiddhi) holds a sword (in his first right hand), symbolic of the fact that the emotional upheavals of sentient beings are cut assunder by the four optimally executed activites of Buddhahood.

Each (of these five vassal kings) holds a bell in his first left hand with which he presses his consort to his heart in close embrace.

The other hands hold the other symbols as previously explained.

The (two-armed and two-handed) female consorts (of these vassal kings) hold in their right hand the same primary emblems as their male consorts; and with their left hand, holding a bell flaming in the light of the preciousness of pristine cognitiveness, they embrace their male consorts.

The emblems of the water lily, orange, and so on refer, in a very elliptic manner, to the male functionaries in the royal household as follows:[38]

'Jam-dpal (Mañjuśrī) holds a water lily, indicating that emotional upheavals have been dispelled.

Byams-pa (Maitreya) holds an orange, indicating that the fever caused by emotional upheaval has been cured.

Sa'i snying-po (Kṣitigarbha) holds a sprouting jewel, indicating that the seed of pristine cognitiveness has been planted.

Phyag-na rdo-rje (Vajrapāṇi) holds a diamond scepter, indicating that suffering has been overcome.

Nam-mkha'i snying-po (Gaganagarbha) holds a sword, indicating that the flow of emotions has been stopped.

sPyan-ras-gzigs (Avalokiteśvara) holds a lotus flower, indicating that there is no defilement by vileness.

sGrib-pa rnam-sel (Nivaraṇaviṣkambhin) holds a jewelled wheel, indicating that life's meaning is being shown to sentient beings.

Kun-tu bzang-po (Samantabhadra)[38a] holds a bouquet of jewels, indicating that the aspirations of sentient beings are being fulfilled.

"Toiletries for beauty's sake" refers, in concise terms, to the female consorts of the male functionaries. All of them are imaged as ravishingly beautiful in the very act of dancing:[39]

rDo-rje sgeg-mo (Vajra-lāsyā) puts her fists on her hips or holds a mirror, thereby showing that all shapes and forms are of the ultimate.

'Phreng-ba-ma (Mālā) holds a string of jewels, thereby demonstrating that appropriate action and discriminative appreciation are never separable.

Glu-ma (Gīti) holds a lute, through which the melody of life's meaningfulness rings out.

Gar-ma (Nṛtyā) sounds a bell with her hand moving up and down, thereby awakening joy in those who are to be trained.

bDug-spos-ma (Dhūpā) carries a censer, from which the fragrance of ethics and manners satisfies (all sentient beings).

Me-tog-ma (Puṣpā) holds a flower basket, thereby displaying the facets conducive to limpid clearness and consummate perspicacity.

Mar-me-ma (Dīpā) holds a lamp whose light dispels the darkness of unknowing.

Dri-chab-ma (Gandhā) holds a water-basin, with which the dirt of ingrained tendencies is washed away.

[2]

The sensuous qualities of our psychic life as imaged and felt in the patterning of the energy of Being, and its assuming perceptible shape in the symbol figures and their emblems, have a calm and calming quality, in marked contrast to the fierceness of the palace guards, who are symbols for the lived body. Both literally and figuratively, it is through our body that we are in-touch-with our world. The lived body has tangible reality value in contrast to the formal evidence value conveyed by the other senses (imaged as functionaries) and the existential evidence value conveyed by their preprograms (imaged as vassal kings).[39a] Because of being in-touch-with, our lived body is also constantly threatened. Therefore, as a complex sense organ, it is forever on the lookout for what may spell its death (which is both physical and spiritual, because the body, too, is both physical and spiritual). This being on the lookout for possible dangers, is symbolized by the threatening posture of the palace guards, whose left forefingers menacingly point toward any possible enemy. The emblems of the male palace guards are indicated as follows:[40]

> gShin-rje-gshed (Yamāntaka) brandishes (in his right hand) a staff surmounted by a human skull because he vanquishes the deadening power of the Lord of Death.
> sTobs-po-che (Mahābala) brandishes a (five-pointed) diamond scepter because he vanquishes the deadening power of psychophysical constituents.
> rTa-mgrin (Hayagrīva, Paramāśva) brandishes a skull with snakes because he vanquishes the deadening power of the affective processes.
> bDud-rtsi 'khyil-ba (Amṛtakuṇḍalin) brandishes a cross-shaped diamond scepter because he vanquishes the deadening power of over-evaluated ideas.

Being in-touch-with, however, does not only mean to be on the lookout for possible dangers, ready to overcome them or forestall them, it also means participation in the environing world. In the human context, this means that we are always with others in our life-world. Participation or, more precisely, the disposition to participate, is expressed by the female partners of the palace guards who, like their spouses, live in a difficult world, which is characterized by the vagaries and contingencies of fluctuating circumstances. Such contingency involves aspects of severance and breakage (imaged as masculine) and aspects of connection and relation (imaged as feminine). Thus:[41]

> The female partners (of the palace guards) carry an iron hook, a noose, a chain, and a bell in order to indicate, respectively, each of the four ways of relating to sentient beings and to display each of the four immeasurably great catalysts.

The contingencies of the life-world, in which we find ourselves as embodied beings, and with which we are in-touch through our lived body, give added significance to male-female polarity whose fierceness reflects the inescapable seriousness of coming to grips with our existentiality. Even on the female side, this coming-to-grips-with makes for firmness in maintaining vigilance and coherence in one's dealings with the concrete situation of everyday life, and is symbolically indicated by the emblems of the hook, noose, and so on.

The royal household, with its members presenting a male-female polarity in intimate union, is a vivid and aesthetically moving presentation of experience in its multiple cognitive and actional features structured as intentionalities. Perceiving, here used in its widest possible sense, involves a potency (an "I can") imaged as mighty ones *(thub-pa)* each in their respective world-horizons. As has been noted before, this potency does not have the intentional structure of cognitiveness; therefore, the mighty ones of the six life-worlds (properly understood as life-styles) are imaged as standing and without a female consort. The strength of this potency lies in its being tied to the very matrix of all beings—this matrix itself felt to be of a feminine nature. Specifically, this potency is understood to have promoted the actualization of an evolutionary program which, in the human context, involves a complex system of ethics, based on the principle of responsibility.[42] Failing in one's responsibility is tantamount to losing one's humanity. The lasting example of one who has lived the ethical life and through it has grown up to the full measure of humanity, is the historical Buddha, the mighty one from the Śākya clan *(Śākya thub-pa)*.

Each life-world has its potency which induces a specific evolutionary program and is imaged as a mighty one appropriate to that life-world, be it that of gods, demigods, men, animals, tormented spirits, or denizens of hell. Thus:[43]

> brGya-byin (Śatakratu = Indra) holds a lute because (through its sweet sound) he teaches the four summary principles of life to the gods.
>
> Thag-bzang-ris (Vemacitra) carries armor and weapon because he subdues the demigods through warfare.
>
> Śākya thub-pa (Śākyamuni) holds a mendicant's staff and an alms bowl because he teaches the ten wholesome actions to mankind.
>
> Seng-ge rab-brtan holds a book because (it is through learning that) animals may become free from their fetters of stupidity and dumbness.
>
> Kha-'bar de-ba (Jvālamukhadeva) holds a jewel casket because (with its contents) he dispels hunger and thirst among the tormented spirits.
>
> A-wa glang-mgo holds fire and water because he points out the horrors of hells.

All the imagery discussed so far underscores the fact that what, for want of a better term, we may call the totality of psychic life is not only an unbroken whole, but above all a dynamic pattern. In this pattern each separable figure is an aspect of the whole, a potency reflecting an ever active nature, which is shown and felt as an "I can."

However, in speaking of a dynamic pattern in which the "I can" is important for the actualization of the programs that constitute the system as a whole, we have implicitly already stated inseparability of structure and process. This inseparability is characteristic of Experience-as-such, which situates itself in the world it brings into existence, and is disposed to its contents by relating to and connecting them in an as yet virtual predisposition. Therefore Kun-tu bzang-po and his consort Kun-tu bzang-mo, the imagings of Experience-as-such, are situated in the corridor as that part of the palace which "connects" its interior with the exterior. He is the one who makes the light outwardly shine forth and form itself into the universe of psychic life, and She is the one who is the ground and reason for the light shining forth.[44] Being a prethematic (virtual) predisposition, neither of them carries any emblem. They exemplify the fact that the meaning-saturated continuum and the formal gestalt expressing this meaningfulness are dissociated from any possible thematization.[45] Yet the ceaseless, ineluctably intelligent dynamics of the whole process presents an ordering principle by virtue of which all facets of experience, as patterned energies *(phyag-rgya)*, are copatternings rather than isolated patterns. This principle is best understood as a virtual intentionality which, in this specific context, is an "intentionality-in-the-making," which may be figuratively described as Experience-as-such reaching out beyond itself and absorbing itself in its specific content—Kun-tu bzang-po uniting with Kun-tu bzang-mo. Thus:[46]

In order to show that His two hands, which are evenly placed *(mnyam-gzhag)* one upon the other (the right hand on top of the left),[47] are the ground and reason for light shining forth from the palms, Kun-tu bzang-po lets the five pristine cognitions, each lucent in a specific hue, burst forth in rays of five colors into the ten directions, while He sits in the diamond posture.[48] Kun-tu bzang-mo, who has become His consort, also has Her hands evenly placed one upon the other (but the left hand is on top of the right), whereby identity-*cum*-wholeness *(mnyam-rdzogs)* is symbolized. Thus She is in every aspect like Her consort, except that Her legs are in the lotus posture.

[3]

Ours is a world of colors. But these are not so much mere attributes of things, they are rather already modes of being, specific formulated energies within that dynamic system which we have termed Being-*qua*-Existenz. It is said of the felt imagings of these formulated energies:[49]

All radiate brilliantly in color values of blue, white, yellow, scarlet, and green.

It is through the existential character of these radiant color values that we, as embodied beings, are able to perceive "color."[50]

It will have been noted that the ordering of color values listed in the above quotation does not reflect that of the natural color spectrum, nor can these color values be divided into primary and secondary color groupings; they are all of equal significance. The above listing indicates the *relative* luminosity and position of what may, in general terms, be called formants.[51] These formants, as affinities with Being *(rigs)* point to Being's dynamic openness; in their lucency and luminosity they are optimum attainment standards, weaving the fabric of Existenz. Or, as formants they are meaning-bearing connectives; as affinities with Being they provide, as it were, a genotypal program for the development and life of an individual; and as optimum attainment standards they are preprograms for an individual's becoming enworlded. It is these standards that may undergo a topological distortion and deformation into the phenotypal pattern of a concrete individual.

Meaning-bearing connectives are intentionalities and, as such, have been imaged as male-female polarities. But, as has been previously pointed out, any such intentionality also is accompanied by a nexus of potencies felt as an "I can" and imaged as a mighty one. The mighty ones are usually representative of a particular life-world, but, as we shall see, they are also understood as representative of a spiritual-sensory domain. Traditionally, five genotypal meaning-bearing connectives have been listed: formal gestalt *(sku)*, authentic utterance *(gsung)*, vibrant spirituality *(thugs)*, creative potential *(yon-tan)*, and optimally executed activities *(phrin-las)*.[52] From among them, vibrant spirituality as the homologue of Being's excitatory intelligence is considered of primary importance, for it disposes us to the full range of experience.

While attention has been repeatedly called to a seeming relationship between form and color, and movement and color, nothing has as yet been indicated regarding the relationship between meaning-bearing connectives and color. Could it be that there is no relationship, that these connectives, whether as affinities or standards, just come as specific color values and that our response to color is these very optimum attainment standards becoming actualized? The following is the color scheme of the five affinities:[53]

Vibrant spirituality: male-female rNam-par snang-mdzad (Vairocana), male-female Kun-tu bzang-po, and the mighty one among the demigods (forming a set of five) are blue in color because they illustrate the invariance of the internal logic of Being.

Formal gestalt: male-female Mi-skyod-pa (Akṣobhya), male-female Sa'i snying-po (Kṣitigarbha) and the mighty one among the gods (forming a set of five) are white in color because they illustrate the fact that a formal gestalt is not marred by any defects.

Creative potential: male-female Rin-chen 'byung-ldan (Ratnasambhava), male-female Nam-mkha'i snying-po (Gaganagarbha) and the mighty one among men (forming a set of five) are yellow in color because they illustrate the creative potential of greatness.[54]

Authentic utterance: male-female 'Od-dpag-med (Amitābha), male-female sPyan-ras-gzigs (Avalokiteśvara), and the mighty one among the spirits (forming a set of five) are scarlet in color because they illustrate the fact that compassion is enamored with all living beings.

Optimally executed activities: male-female Don-yod grub-pa (Amoghasiddhi), male-female Phyag-na rdo-rje (Vajrapāṇi), and the mighty one among the animals (forming a set of five) are green in color because they illustrate the fact that (sentient beings) are shaped by various actions.

When perceptual dispositions, imaged as inner functionaries, become actualized and in the actualizing transition are imaged as outer functionaries, the creative potential (consisting of capabilities and potencies) and the optimally executed activities of psychic life combine, a new "color scheme" evolves:

Male-female Byams-pa (Maitreya) are white and yellow; male-female sGrib-pa rnam-sel (Nivaraṇaviṣkambhin) are red and yellow; male-female Kun-tu bzang-po (Samantabhadra) are red and green: male-female 'Jams-dbyangs (Mañjughoṣa)[55] are white and green.

All these colorful images can be said to be symbolic presences of processes becoming our experientially tangible reality, a reality which is felt to be more palpable than the other elusive intangible and insubstantial aspects of experience. Yet even this so-called tangible reality, which we as embodied beings associate and identify with our lived body through which we are "in-touch-with" our environing reality, is of the nature of interacting fields, amenable to vivid imaging. Although the imaging of this tangible reality is not at all different from the imaging in which the intangible presents itself, in terms of colors, a certain shift towards darkish qualities is felt to be involved. Thus:[56]

Male-female gShin-rje-gshed (Yamāntaka) are dark grey; male-female sTobs-po-che (Mahābala) are dark yellow; male-female tTa-mgrin (Haya-grīva) are dark red; male-female bDud-rtsi 'khyil-ba (Amṛtakuṇḍalin) are dark green, and the mighty one among the denizens of hell is of smoke color.

Embodiment gains added significance in the "light of these colors," for as has been noted before, we as concrete human beings *are* our body, and it is through our *body* that the various programs, which make up our existence, are worked out. This is a high-energy process and as such is imaged in figures of intense fierceness whose color values reflect this high energy. This emphasis on high energy and high frequency of light values figuratively indicates that the programs have been "brought home" and are worked out through our body. The lived body thus is the nitty-gritty nexus of embodied spirituality.[57]

It will have been noted that there has taken place a progressive resolution of the (relatively) concrete figures of the princely household into (relatively) abstract symbols, and of the latter into pure color values. This can be understood as a resolution of the static into the dynamic, the resolution of iconic representation into aniconic awareness. The emphasis here is on the creative play of color values rather than on concrete figures who themselves are but luminosities scintillating in colors of deeper meaning, be this in a steady flow,

> Enormous clusters of light rays pouring forth[58]

or in a furious blaze:

> Engulfed in garlands of flame.[59]

The imaging and expression of this state of affairs is the operation of pristine cognitiveness, ranging over the whole of the meaning-saturated continuum that is Being-*qua*-Existenz, and organizing its infinite richness in finite images:[60]

> An all-encompassing configuration having neither periphery nor center,
> Surpasses all thought and just is.

VII. Fury of Being

What has been referred to and summed up by the term configuration *(dkyil-'khor)* are complex holistic processes that have no temporal onset and also are not spatially localizable. Their complexity is felt and known by man as his Existenz, the primal source for the interpretation of the human situation by means of such heuristic concepts as space and time. As such, Existenz defies any ontic reduction. It remains an ongoing process which, because of its inherent cognitiveness, has been termed variously a self-existent pristine cognitiveness *(rang-byung-gi ye-shes)* or Experience-as-such *(sems-nyid)*. Only at what seems to be a later stage, this may develop into an experience of (something or other). Furthermore, Existenz can also be conceived of as an excitation that exemplifies the cognitive nature of Being-*qua*-Existenz and that highlights the impossibility of this cognitiveness ever being at rest. This means that Experience-as-such ceaselessly discloses itself by means of what are technically termed configurations. Such configuration-disclosure occurs quite spontaneously as either tranquil/calm or fierce/agitated processes.

As previously discussed in Chapter III, the tranquil and fierce processes are formulated energies (deities) associated with configurations which, as symbolic totalities, present end phases amenable to being localized in ongoing human embodiment—the calm in that quiet region termed the heart or *tsitta* palace, and the agitated in that active region termed the brain or *dung-khang* palace. It is important to bear in mind that any such localizability is but the end phase of a configuration-disclosure process, not its starting point. From the viewpoint of the inherent dynamics of the configuration-disclosure itself, the term tranquil refers to this process in its fundamental spontaneity *(lhun-grub)* and what is termed fierce refers to the same process in its dynamic coming-to-the-fore *(mngon-par 'byung-ba)*. In the diction of Klong-chen rab-'byams-pa:[1]

The calm (deities constitute) a configuration that just is; the fierce (deities constitute) a configuration that evinces a thrust into prominence.

That this disclosure is at once both fundamental (tranquil) and dynamic (fierce) is poetically stated in an anthropomorphic image:[2]

Though (He as) vibrant spirituality has not moved from tranquility,
(He as) formal gestalt displays an appearance of fierceness.

The dynamic character of configuration-disclosure aptly termed "fierce" *(khro-bo)* is explained by Klong-chen rab-'byams-pa as indicating the procedure of overcoming that which is not in accord with the self-optimization of the system Being-*qua*-Existenz. This procedure is implemented by means of a highly energized *(drag-po)* optimally and gracefully executed activity *(phrin-las)*[3] of the system itself. In the domain of the living such activity operates as a force that is felt to be a shock *(rngams-pa)* in and through which there comes the reinstatement of the full value and meaning of "being alive." For us as embodied beings the operation of this force occurs in and through symmetry transformations termed formal gestalts *(sku)*.

In phenomenological diction, Being *(das Sein)* experiences itself as being *(seiend)* and, as such, is meaningfully installed *(chos-sku)* in a prepredicative universe. At this level of prepredication the fundamental (tranquil) and the dynamic (fierce) interfuse. In the words of Klong-chen rab-'byams-pa:[4]

Tranquility is the fierceness of the internal logic of Being, having nothing to do with (such predications as) substance and quality, and is therefore Being's (experience of itself as) being meaningfully installed *(chos-sku)* such that it (as yet) stays free of the confines of predication.

The formal gestalt character of this experience, Being's being meaningfully installed in the universe termed Experience-as-such, involves a configuration-disclosure that exhibits a social-interactional character, comprising both agent and context. This social character of Being is precisely what is meant by Existenz. It is an emerging (symmetry transformation) totality, not a singular and isolated happening. As such it is a process imbued with the mystery of value and meaning *(don)*. Klong-chen rab-'byams-pa says of this totality:[5]

Out of the reach and range of (Being's being meaningfully installed in the universe Experience-as-such) there comes into presence, in 'Og-min,[6] a

configuration of Herukas; this (coming into presence) is (Being's) actuality—
Existenz as complete engagement in appreciable contextuality *(long-spyod rdzogs-pa'i rang-bzhin)*, the genuine operation of value and meaning.

Because we value that which has meaning for us and that which has meaning for us is *eo ipso* valuable, both value and meaning belong to the realm of appreciation, enjoyment, and intelligence. Intelligence is the attunement of a spiritual sensitivity which specifically operates as a resonating concern *(thugs-rje)* with the whole of Being. Furthermore, the operation of this concern is educational in the sense that it shapes both man and his cultural milieu, thus acting as an enduring theme which, for each person, constitutes his or her specific sense of being human. Activation of the full awareness of being human may necessitate drastic measures (high energy processes) characterized by and as a fierceness configuration-disclosure. Thus Klong-chen rab-'byams-pa says:[7]

> Due to the spontaneous operation of (this) resonating concern, there is a coming-into-presence of fierceness (needed) to educate those who are to be educated; it is the facticity of the cultural-evolutionary norm *(rang-bzhin sprul-pa'i sku)* operative in (Buddha) activity as charismatic.

The inbuilt fierceness of this high-energy configuration-disclosure has been discussed in terms of four functional modalities, which pervade the universe of Experience-as-such.[8] Two of these modalities are descriptive of the universe of experience, Being-*qua*-Existenz; a third modality is indicative of the strength and efficacy of this universe; and a fourth modality concerns the judgments about the dynamics of this universe of experience. These judgments reflect the relative acumen of those who go through the process of being educated.

The first modality of fierceness concerns the internal logic of Being *(chos-nyid)*. Thus:[9]

> The intricate logic of Being which remains free from predication is (termed) fierce with respect to its operational range, because there is no possibility for the localization of determining characteristics.

The second modality concerns the intelligent nature of Being-*qua*-Existenz operating as pristine cognitions *(ye-shes)*. Thus:[10]

> The expansive pristine cognitiveness is (termed) fierce with respect to its operational range as it applies to what is to be eliminated, because there is no possibility for the localization of cognitively distorted patterns.

The third modality concerns the resilience of the system Being-*qua*-Existenz in such a manner that the probability of success for the system's harmonious unfoldment is maximized by minimizing the chances for disrupting such unfoldment. In short, this modality involves the activity *(mdzad-pa)* of working out the tasks posed by the system itself. Such system-regulated activity is not a muddled "reacting to," but is rather keenly anticipatory and creative. Thus:[11]

> The protecting of living beings with and by resonating concern is (termed) fierce, with respect to the momentum (of the operational range), because of the unforced and effortless manner in which everything incompatible is overcome.

While these three modalities of fierceness concern the dynamic of Being-*qua*-Existenz, a fourth modality pertains to concrete manifestations of fierceness as they apply to the educational process of those who aspire to recover the full measure of their humanity. This modality operates in the execution of tasks *(phrin-las)* posed by the system itself. Although such task execution is initiated by the system as a whole, its implementation occurs in the context of relatively bounded domains within the system, such as living human beings. All human beings possess the capacity for overcoming their limits or boundaries and can even be trained to do so. Such training, as a breaking of boundaries, involves an interior struggle, a confrontation fraught with irritation which is often projected as if it were the anger or fury of something or somebody provoking us from outside. Thus:[12]

> (The implementation of task execution) appears such that it is construed as anger, due to a (certain bias in the) congenital temperament of those who undergo training.

Reflection on the above four operational modalities, each of them fierce, shows that fierceness is but a generic term for one of the two primary processes—the other being tranquil—through which Being-*qua*-Existenz auto-presences. This twofold auto-presencing is itself termed "Buddha" *(sangs-rgyas)*, a term that carries with it the connotation of a self-structuring process in the more precise sense of a dissipative structure. In accord with the affective momentum (initiated in the wake of a stepped-down excitation), which poisons the lives of those who seek to ameliorate their situation, the process itself manifests as either a gentle or strong corrective. Once having realized the fact of one's less-than-optimum mode of being, one must sooner or later face up to the necessity of undergoing the appropriate correction. Though one might object, strong correctives are necessary when the affective momentum which leads one away from the optimum is itself strong. Thus:[13]

> For really noxious situations
> Gentle remedies are of no avail; (and therefore it is)
> Out of the harmony of appreciative discrimination and appropriate measures (that)
> The whole of Buddhahood's dynamics operates as fierceness.

It is precisely the operation of such fierceness which, though dimly realizing its therapeutic value, one sometimes fights against by misconstruing it as anger, be it the compassionate wrath of the teacher directed toward the wayward tendencies of the aspirant, or the persistence of irritation and resistance one directs toward oneself in the face of possible growth. It bears emphasizing here that being in a situation in which there is this kind of anger and irritation is itself due to the fierce "gyroscopic" force of Being's rectifying the tendency to go astray into affectively toned modes of being.

When affective momentum which operates in the wake of stepped-down excitation[14] is strong, causing a shift in Being-*qua*-Existenz away from its state of optimal functioning, two closely related processes come to the fore. One process characterizes the situation that must be rectified *(gdul-bya)* and is called the fierceness of karmic activity *(las-kyi khro-bo),* which pushes the system into states which, in their extremes, are figuratively termed realms of hells and realms of tormented spirits. The other process, which is initiated whenever karmic activity poses a threat to the basic integrity of the system, characterizes the rectification process itself *('dul-byed),* and is called the fierceness of pristine cognitiveness *(ye-shes-kyi khro-bo).* These two processes are functionally complementary, for they are integral facets of the system's self-regulating homeorhesis[15] as it applies to the unfoldment of an individual's full measure of humanity.

One may well wonder why it is that there may be special disruptive and destructive forces operating in the life of man precisely when he attempts to open up and recover the full sense of being human. In posing such a question, one should remember that in rDzogs-chen thought what one commonly terms man is understood to be a relatively bounded domain (of the system Being-*qua*-Existenz), which serves as the site for a possible opening-up to the full range of Being's wondrous mystery. Therefore, although there certainly may be fierce forces at work as a result of the dynamics of Being-*qua*-Existenz, they are only disruptive and destructive with respect to (and judged to be so from the vantage point of) a relatively bounded domain. It bears emphasizing, however, that any such domain is nonetheless precious in that it provides the only possible space for accessing and creatively implementing the full range of Being's dynamics. Furthermore, the boundedness of such a domain is itself a function of the degree to which this creative accessing has become operative. The more one is opened up to Being's mystery, the less restricted is one's boundary (range of meaningfulness) and the greater is one's sense of fulfillment and harmony. Conversely, the narrower the boundary, the greater one's sense of frustration and disharmony.[16]

It is from within such a relatively bounded domain that one dimly harbors the suspicion that "things could be better"—this suspicion itself being the localized operation of Being's thrust toward optimization. Not realizing the true source of such an irritating suspicion, however, one usually sets about "getting a hold on" one's existential predicament through various schemes. Indeed, this scheming tends to take over, resulting in an ever-present attempt to assess one's current state by making cognitive maps of one's existential terrain. Such map-making becomes so much a pervasive and characteristic feature that it enters into and shapes all one's experiences. In the extreme, this map-making *constitutes* virtually all one's activities. Inevitably, such a procedure, which isolates and compares various experiential facets, must come to terms with that seemingly pervasive feature of every possible situation, which is the map-maker himself (the ego/Self) without whom such mapping would be impossible. But it is precisely this feature that eludes adequate description or even assessment by such a procedure, and often leads to an even greater sense of needing to "get a hold on" things. Thus, to summarize, by failing to understand the true source of one's being in an existential predicament one initiates a procedure which reinforces the predicament by generating a profusion of maps. The contours shown on these mentally constructed maps are then mistakenly regarded as one's actual existential domain. Apart from reinforcing the predicament, there is the dire consequence that this procedure leads one further and further away from the mystery of Being which is one's actual terrain, trapping one in that "mystery" behind which Being's mystery conceals itself. This state of affairs has been described as follows:[17]

Those who have deviated from the proper procedure, by having given in to dichotomizing activity, which initiates the mistaken construct of an individual ego/Self, and (having given in) to the attendant proliferation of constructs (other than the ego/Self), without understanding the intrinsically mysterious mystery (of Being), but fixating on the mystery of (Being's) concealment,[18] then become confused about the relationship between the causes and effects (of their own actions). Once such individuals have been

propelled by (this confusion, it acts as) a powerful seed (which germinates
and emerges) into a new situation (which is felt as) having been born in the
hottest hells (reserved for those who commit) most heinous crimes.

This mythologizing diction contains important psychological insights.
The stepped-down excitatory intelligence of Being-*qua*-Existenz carries
with it a dissociative tendency that splits the unity of experience in such a
manner that an emerging ego/Self is about to become ever more
entrenched in the precarious role of attempting to dominate the scene
which spreads out before it and which seems to be a menace to it. This
menace is felt to be of painful nature, whose extremes are aptly imaged as a
hell realm (which traditionally has been divided into a variety of icy-cold
and blistering-hot regions), and as a realm of tormented spirits who are
forever hungry and thirsty. The feeling of "being in hell" results when there
is the initiation of and indulgence in brutal, degenerate, and pathological
actions. The feeling of "being a tormented spirit" results when, due to
deprivation-motivation and the concomitant mood of *ressentiment*, one
engages in wilful, malicious obstruction of others' efforts toward self-
improvement and spiritual growth. Such feelings are self-perpetuating in
that they involve the ego/Self ever more deeply in intolerable situations.
One may recall that every life situation constitutes a field of tension
demanding a solution. Once a situation has become sufficiently intolerable,
due to a failure to understand what has brought about the tension, attempts
to rectify it quite often merely result in a projection of one's shortcomings
(experienced as suffering) on to others. This failure and concomitant
projection underlies the curious, yet well-known phenomenon of
sadomasochism—a self-gratification by inverted means, which is a "dis-
ease" as much physical as mental, and highly contagious.[19]
This whole state of affairs may be regarded as a tilting or warping
transformation of the system Being-*qua*-Existenz. It is in the wake of such a
transformation that there also occurs the formation and concomitant
aggrandizement of the ego/Self. This is vividly told in the story of Thar-pa
nag-po and his servant Dan-phag.[20]
Long, long ago, there lived a monk, Thub-dka' gzhon-nu by name, who
taught the most profound esoterism. Because of his fame Thar-pa nag-po
and his servant, Dan-phag, went to him and asked him whether it was true
that engaging in those actions, which are usually held to be shocking,
would enable a man to become totally free. When answered in the affirma-
tive, they were delighted and, asking for further details, they were told
cryptically:

When the as-is is not corrupted
Engagement in the four shocking actions
Is like the dissipation of clouds in the sky.
This is the path of true Yoga.

Thar-pa nag-po, however, was a dull-witted and incompetent person. He took what he had been told literally. While he remained physically fit, his mind followed the wrong track. By contrast, Dan-phag was highly intelligent and competent. He thought about the meaning of what he had been told and so, while he was but a servant of low social standing, his mind followed the right track. Being so different in outlook and behavior, both master and servant started quarrelling. Finally they asked the monk Thubdka' gzhon-nu to judge who was right and who was wrong. When Dan-phag was declared to be right, Thar-pa nag-po got furious. He thought that their teacher not only was not impartial but had singled him out for a rebuke. So he gave him a tongue-lashing and chased him and Dan-phag away. From now on he became ever more steeped in his literal interpretation and developed a deviant and perverse behavioral mode. He frequented the cremation grounds where he fed on human corpses, and dressed himself in their skin. Keeping company with wild animals he went on a killing spree and, gathering around him a bevy of harlots, he lived a life of debauchery. After his death he was reborn over and over again in evil forms of life. Due to his vicious destructiveness he received the epithet Rudra, and as Rudra Thar-pa nag-po he not only terrorizes the living beings throughout the six realms, but also causes harmful disruptions in every aspect of life.[21]

[2]

There comes a time when the wayward fluctuations engendered by the fierce (khro-bo) activity of the warping transformation of the system have reached such an extent that the system's integrity is at stake. At this critical moment the equally fierce (khro-bo) gyroscopic force of the system Being-qua-Existenz, operating in and as resonating concern, comes into play thus initiating the rectification of the warping or system tilt.

This critical moment constitutes a threshold and is termed the system's recognition (gzigs) that wayward fluctuations have reached the maximum allowable level. Once this threshold has been reached, the rectification process is activated. Broadly speaking, three interconnected phases characterize this process. The first involves the radical attenuation and interruption of what may be termed "dys-chreodic movement."[22] This neologism is based on the term chreod, coined by the embryologist Conrad H. Wad-dington to characterize the "canalized pathways of change" he discovered operating in embryological processes. The prefix dys- is used to indicate that such canalized change is moving in a wayward direction. Locally speaking, that is, with respect to the relatively bounded domains that constitute the karmic activity of individuals, such movement leads away from the system's global and optimal functioning. Accordingly, the first phase of the rectification process may be termed "dys-chreodic interruption."

Once the dys-chreodic movement has been sufficiently interrupted and broken up, there is the possibility for an auto-catalytic transformation from dys-chreodic to "eu-chreodic movement." The neologism eu-chreodic refers to canalized pathways of change operating in such a manner that the locally bounded domains open up to the wider dynamic field of the system (Being-*qua*-Existenz) as a whole. Such a transformation is auto-catalytic because the catalytic agents, the pristine cognitions operating as resonating concern imaged in the fierce figures of Herukas, are not introduced from outside the system; they are the products of the fierce, dynamic auto-rectification process engendered by the system Being-*qua*-Existenz itself. This auto-catalysis constitutes the second phase of the rectification process.

Even as eu-chreodic movement has begun to occur, however, there is still the possibility that dys-chreodic tendencies may reassert themselves. In order to preserve the directionality of eu-chreodic movement it is necessary to bind eu-chreodic products in a matrix that is itself oriented toward optimization. Thus, eu-chreodic movement is preserved by assuring its stable flow or homeorhesis.[23] Such "homeorhesis preservation" constitutes the third phase of the rectification process.

The technical name for the principle that makes possible the strong rectification procedure as well as the rectification itself—in and as the fierceness of the interrupter/catalytic-agent/preserver—is Śrī-Heruka. The difficulty in rendering the polysemantic nature of this term may be gleaned by reflection on the hermeneutical account given by Rong-zom-pa Chos-kyi bzang-po:[24]

> (The Indian term) Śrī-Heruka allows of many interpretations; a summary rendering of it (in Tibetan) is *dpal-khrag-'thung*. What is the rationale in such a rendering?
>
> *Śrī* is a word for wealth and prosperity or for spiritual counsellor. *He-* has the meaning of lighthearted joyous and playful comportment *(helā, kriḍā); -ru-* is a word for blood *(rudhira)*; and *-ka* is a primary, modifying suffix. To sum up, because of (His) delighting in blood, one speaks (of Him as) Heruka.

Others, however, say that *-ka* means skull *(kapāla)*, that is, ritually holding a skull. Thus one speaks of Heruka because He, in a ritual gesture, playfully holds a skull filled with blood.

Furthermore, to explain the term Śrī-Heruka syllable-by-syllable according to some texts, *Śrī* means wealth as it pertains to oneself *(ātmaśrī)* and as it pertains to others *(paraśrī)*. *He-* means cause-momentum *(hetu)* as well as delight *(helā)*. (This double meaning points to) the correct understanding of Being as a continuum. (The syllable) *-ru-* means love *(rāga)* as well as anger *(rudra)*. This is to say that out of such a reach and range (as is Being) His ultimate resonating concern shows itself as fierceness. (The syllable) *-ka* means action *(karma)* as well as compassion *(karuṇā)*. Hence even the fierce (but nevertheless charismatic) actions are balanced out through compassion. Thus the four (syllables in Śrī-Heruka) have eight meanings.

Furthermore, *He-* indicates the object domain—that which has never come into existence (as something ontic);-*ru-* indicates the subject(ive) mind—a nonthematic operation; and *-ka* indicates the nonduality of domain and mind. This means that (Heruka) is a term for the formal gestalt in and through which the meaningfulness of Being expresses itself *(chos-kyi sku)*.

Or, it is said the *He-* means kindness, *-ru-* compassion, and *-ka* joy and equanimity. (Thus Heruka means) to possess the four immeasurably great catalysts.

Others declare that (Heruka actually) is *He-he-ru-ru-ka* which means to make all the vicious (beings in the world) lose their senses by (making them hear) a loud neighing and to make them delight in the configuration of (Heruka's) assemblage.

Still others say that *He-* means cause-momentum *(hetu); -ru-* indicates that which has developed *(rūḍha)* as a combination of determinants; and *-ka* means anywhere *(kyacit)*. The basis for these syllables is (the gnoseme) *A*, which is the gate (through which) that which has never come into existence (ontically) presences itself. Thus, the term Heruka means (i) that which has no cause; (ii) that which is independent of any combination of determinants; and (iii) that which is nowhere localizable.

Others state that Śrī means (His) consort's pudenda and Heruka means the incentive to (realizing) limpid clearness and consummate perspicacity as ultimate bliss. Hence one intends by the term Śrī-Heruka the (intimate) union of Heruka with Śrī.

[3]

Although the various phases and subphases of the rectification process together with their internal dynamics are extremely complex, we shall give here a generalized account of them with respect to the three major phases mentioned before. The first phase, termed dys-chreodic interruption, involves the setting up of an actional matrix which will serve as the base of operation for the interrupter of the dysfunction, thereby making possible the incipient reinstitution of the system's integrity. This actional matrix, a web of phantasmal forms and forces,[25] is the manifesting dynamics of Being-*qua*-Existenz, imaged as Kun-tu bzang-po. The incipient interruption of the dysfunction is described as involving both delight and fierce intensity. The delight that is felt throughout the system is termed pure delight and the concomitant fierce intensity is termed Śrī-Heruka.

The reinstitution of the system's integrity occurs in such a way that the internal logic of Being surges as what may be termed a trimodal polarizing-reuniting process. The three modes are: the formal gestalt *(sku)*, authentic utterance *(gsung)*, and vibrant spirituality *(thugs)* of the system as a whole. Although the surging is extremely short-lived, it is tremendously powerful. It may be functionally analyzed into polarizing and reuniting phases. With respect to polarization the above three modes are: (1) the formal gestalts of Kun-tu bzang-mo (the system as feminine and soliciting action, similar to an energy sink) and Kun-tu bzang-po (the system as masculine and initiating actions, similar to an energy source); (2) their corresponding utterances (the feminine laughing *hi hi*, the masculine laughing *ha ha*); and (3) the overall vibrant spirituality as delight.[26]

With respect to reuniting, this occurs as the intimate, delightful, and playful interaction between the feminine (imaged as the opening up and dilation of a "lotus") and the masculine (imaged as the protrusion and tumescence of a "jewel"). This intimacy sparks the system's orgasmic energy flow whose resultant is the creation of a quincunx of Heruka configurations.[27]

Once dys-chreodic movement has been interrupted there occurs, due to the system's orgasmic energy flowing into the breach and thereby opening up the relatively bounded localized domains within which affective processes hold sway, a thorough breakdown of these affective processes, which are auto-catalytically transformed into pristine cognitions, through the fierceness of the system's optimally executed rectifying activity *(phring-las drag-po)*. This thorough breakdown and concomitant auto-catalytic transformation is itself initiated by a virtual regioning process that sets itself up in and as a quincunx of tension fields, each presenting a Heruka configuration. In contexts involving more tranquil configuration-disclosure dynamics, these tension fields were termed affinities with Being *(rigs)*, for they reflect the fundamental spontaneity *(lhun-grub)* of the system Being-*qua*-Existenz as a whole. Here, however, the same tension fields display the coming-to-the-fore *(mngon-par 'byung-ba)* of the system's configuration-disclosure dynamics and therefore are best described as vectorially connected involvement domains *(rigs)*. These involvement domains are highly agitated, indicating the eagerness of the system to engage in the rectification process. Furthermore, in contrast to the imaging of the nodal points of the calm tension fields as figures seated in crosslegged posturing, the nodal points of the agitated tension fields are imaged as figures standing in martial posturing.

The virtual regioning process, initiating the auto-catalytic transformation has been figuratively described as follows:[28]

> Then the super-perfect state[29] Ultimate Delight, Kun-tu bzang-po Himself, transforms into the formal gestalt of the blood-drinking Che-mchog Heruka, bay-black in color and shining forth in a tremendous blaze of sheer lucency— the brilliance of pristine cognitiveness brighter than a hundred-thousand suns—and assumes a demeanor that is awe-inspiring, most terrifying,[30] and devastatingly raging.[31] Although He remains protean with innumerable heads, hands, and feet—holding in his hands various weapons such as a vajra, a discus, and so on, (thereby indicating) His dominion over as many realms as there are atoms in a chilio-cosmos—He assumes a shape with three heads symbolizing the releasements, six arms symbolizing transcending functions, and four legs symbolizing the bases for success.[32] Delighting in a vast cremation ground, symbolizing the abidingly pure (energy) of Saṃsāra's unsuppressed state, there in the swirling center of an ocean of blood, symbolizing the abidingly pure (energy) of passion-addiction's unsuppressed state, on top of a huge mountain of piled up skeletons, symbolizing the abidingly pure (energy) of irritation-aversion's unsuppressed state, in the center of a four-spoked wheel that is in the middle of a huge volcanic conflagration, by means of pristine cognitiveness, symbolizing the abidingly pure (energy) of dullness, infatuation's unsuppressed state. He postures Himself on a throne fashioned from the couple the Great Lord, Mahādeva, and his consort, the haughty Mistress of cremation grounds, Umādevī with His left leg stretched out and His right leg drawn in.[33]

One of the most striking features in this description of the incipient auto-catalytic transformation process is the imagery of a landscape which, in a certain sense, is strangely familiar and yet phantastically remote—a foreshadowing of events to come. This forbidding landscape, however, is not to be thought of as constituting already established environmental domains. Rather, it suggests a virtual environing process set up by the system itself. Thus the ocean of blood, as the abidingly pure energy of passion-addiction, is the medium through which Che-mchog Heruka's authentic utterance *(gsung)* speaks; the skeleton mountain, as the abidingly pure energy of irritation-aversion, is the medium through which Che-mchog Heruka's formal gestalt *(sku)* is present; and the volcanic conflagration, as the abidingly pure energy of dullness-infatuation, is the medium through which Che-mchog Heruka's spirituality *(thugs)* operates. It must not be forgotten, however, that these virtual world-engendering processes function as dynamically interconnected ensembles and can only be isolated for purposes of analytic description.

In addition to these three interconnected processes, the operation of two others is implied. Altogether they are the system's total quantity of energy. It operates qualitatively throughout the system as a universal constant *(mi-'gyur)*, and is appropriately termed the system's creative potential *(yon-tan)*;[34] and the system's variability in the application of its potential for specific and optimal task execution *(phrin-las)*. It is thus a quincunx of interconnected processes, which, in its totality, is imaged as Che-mchog Heruka.

This totality itself undergoes an identity transformation into a quincunx of involvement domains *(rigs)* in which Che-mchog Heruka as Buddha-Heruka occupies the central position. The complex internal dynamics of these involvement domains is schematically diagrammed as follows:[35]

FIGURE 26

AUTO-CATALYTIC TRANSFORMATION CONFIGURATIONS
OF FIERCELY OPERATING RECTIFICATION PROCESS

Involvement Domain (rigs)	Orientational Directedness	Fiercely Operating Rectification Process		Disruption of Affective Processes		Corresponding Preprogram (phung-po)
		Autocatalysts imaged as male & female Heruka	Associated Pristine Cognition (ye-shes)	Process Disrupted	Imaged as Heruka subjugating figures of	
Spirituality (thugs)	CENTER	Buddha-Heruka in union with Buddha-Krodheśvarī	Meaning Saturated Field (chos-dbyings)	Dullness-Infatuation (gti-mug)	Śiva in union with Umādevī	Perception (rnam-shes)
Formal Gestalt (sku)	EAST	Vajra-Heruka in union with Vajra-Krodheśvarī	Quasi-Mirroring (me-long lta-bu)	Irritation-Aversion (zhe-sdang)	Gandharva with Apsaras	Relatively Invariant Patterns (gzugs)
Creative Potential (yon-tan)	SOUTH	Ratna-Heruka in union with Ratna-Krodheśvarī	Sameness-cum-Identity (mnyam-nyid)	Arrogance-Egomania (nga-rgyal)	Yama with Yamī	Feeling-tone (tshor-ba)
Authentic Utterance (gsung)	WEST	Padma-Heruka in union with Padma-Krodheśvarī	Specificity Initiating (so-sor rtog-pa)	Passion-Addiction ('dod-chags)	Rākṣasa with Rākṣasī	Concept Formation ('du-shes)
Optimally Executed Activities (phrin-las)	NORTH	Karma-Heruka in union with Karma-Krodheśvarī	Task Posed and Accomplished (bya-ba grub-pa)	Envy (phrag-dog)	Yakṣa with Yakṣinī	Psycho energetic Drives ('du-byed)

· A few observations may be made regarding this diagram. It will have been noted that the internal patterning of these "fierce" involvement domains is formally the same as that of the "tranquil" affinities with Being. This is so, since, as previously discussed, both tranquil and fierce processes are the dynamic presence of Being-*qua*-Existenz itself.

There are subtle, yet profoundly incisive psychological insights encoded in the complexities of each involvement domain. With regard to the first involvement domain, presided over, as it were, by Buddha-Heruka and his consort Buddha-Krodheśvarī, the associated affective process of dullness-infatuation is to be understood as reductionistic tendencies in the widest possible sense, be they religious, involving a theistic reductionism personified as God who, in the Indian tradition, has been imaged as Mahādeva (Śiva) and his consort Umādevī, or political, involving an ideological reductionism personified as dictator.

With regard to the second involvement domain, presided over by Vajra-Heruka and his consort Vajra-Krodheśvarī, the associated affective process of irritation-aversion is imaged as a Gandharva together with his Apsaras consort. In Indo-Tibetan thinking a Gandharva is understood to be that factor that is in search of embodiment—a difficult and precarious search that may give rise to annoyance and even aversion.

With regard to the third involvement domain, presided over by Ratna-Heruka and his consort Ratna-Krodheśvarī, the associated affective process of arrogance is imaged as Yama and his consort Yamī who, as death, be it only in the sense of the deadening power of arrogant self-importance, quite literally puts an end to creative (life-giving) potential.

With regard to the fourth involvement domain, presided over by Padma-Heruka and his consort Padma-Krodheśvarī, the associated affective process of passion-addiction is imaged as a frightening Rākṣasa with his Rākṣasī consort who, in their addictive uncontrollable voraciousness, devour their victims.

With regard to the fifth involvement domain, presided over by Karma-Heruka and his consort Karma-Krodheśvarī, the associated affective process of envy is imaged as a Yakṣa with his Yakṣinī consort, who are noted for their mischievous activities which prevent a person from enjoying what he has and make him covet what others have.

All these demoniac forces are imaged as being trampled on by the various Herukas and writhing under their feet. In this gruesome spectacle the spouses of the Herukas match their consorts in fierceness. While in the context of the calm tension fields and their nodal points, the female spouses embrace their male consorts with both arms and, with a tender smile, rapturously gaze at their consorts' gently beaming faces, here, in the context of the agitated tension fields and their nodal points, the female spouses put their right arms around their male consorts' necks; in their left hands they each hold a skull brim-full with blood which they pour into their consorts' mouths—in paintings this gesture is replaced by that of deep-kissing, as the blood-filled skull is held aloft—and they climb up and entwine their consorts, flowing into them in ecstatic pleasure.[36]

Although we have spoken of a rectification process, this must not be understood as merely the straightening out and reinstitution of some more optimal state of affairs. Rather, the rectification process leads to the emergence of a new regime, a higher order of complexity, which is "new" only in the sense that the energy of the old regime has been broken down and incorporated into a new pattern. With the emergence of a new complexity, Being-*qua*-Existenz's dynamic unfoldment may, of course, be subject to forces that resist or impede the change. Such resistance to Being's unfoldment, however, calls forth powerful counter-forces, which break through the resistance. The life story of Thar-pa nag-po exemplifies those forces that attempt to reduce the essentially indeterminate and vivid nature of concretely lived experience to an impoverished caricature in which the meaning of reality is reworked so as to exclude from consideration everything that cannot be analytically quantified and measured. These god-like monomaniacal forces, which engage in attempts to analyze, formalize, and quantify the dynamic unfoldment of life's essentially open-ended organization into ever higher orders of complexity, are collectively symbolized as the masculine *(pho-rgyud)*.

In a highly dramatic manner, the resistance to change, the arousal of powerful forces which will break through the resistance, and the final smashing of the structure is told in the *gSang-snying:*[37]

> Then these maddening powers, in their fury, resorted to various vicious tricks and, with one voice, they raised an ugly roar and, using abusive and spiteful words, they shouted: "Let us free, let us free—why do you, the Lord of Compassion, act in this way?" And they raged and raved most viciously.
>
> Then the super-perfect state Ultimate Delight presenced himself with nine heads, eighteen arms, and eight legs, and with a deafening voice (which was on a level with his) effectiveness of refining (mankind) through (his) resonant concern (for it), he shouted: "*hūṃ, hūṃ, hūṃ; ha, ha, ha; khāhi, khāhi, khāhi.*" Then he tore out the hearts and sensory organs of this crowd of vicious beings (as represented by) the ruler of the world and other powers of evil, pulled out their entrails, chopped and sliced all their appendages, ate all the flesh, drank all the blood, and devoured all the bones.

In this passage the first paragraph points out the resentful, abusive pleading of those creatures—the fanatics (man-like gods and god-like men) of this world, of whom Thar-pa nag-po is a prime example—who attempt to prevent spiritual growth by asking their subjugators (the quincunx of Herukas) to be compassionate and let normalcy (waywardness) prevail. The Tibetan for this passage clearly indicates a difference between compassion as an emotional-sentimental involvement and concern *(snying-rje)* due to ego-bound perspectives, and compassion as the spiritual force of resonating concern *(thugs-rje)*, which operates in concert with the intelligence of Being-*qua*-Existenz as a totality. The overwhelming and seemingly grotesque power of this spiritual force is vividly portrayed as a multiplicity of heads and limbs. Such seeming grotesqueness, however, is but the sentimental and frantic projection by those very domains of limitation which are in the process of undergoing the quite natural course of breakup and reorganization.

The second paragraph of this quotation indicates the exuberant vocalization by the system itself, rejoicing in the impending resolution of mildly bothersome restriction. Thus, the roar of *hūṃ*, repeated thrice, breaks up the ego-centered organization of body, speech, and mentation; the laughter of *ha*, also repeated thrice, neutralizes the three poisoning affective processes (of dullness-infatuation, irritation-aversion, and passion-addiction), which thrive on and perpetuate ego-centered patterns; and the shout of *khāhi* ("eat"), repeated thrice, signals the recycling of man's last refuge of individual integrity—the body as flesh, blood, and bones.

The last paragraph in this passage details the seemingly grotesque recycling process itself, which can be judged as grotesque only by those who have no existential understanding and, like Thar-pa nag-po, are addicted to literalizing activity, which impoverishes the meaningfulness of restorative procedures. Klong-chen rab-'byams-pa's commentary on this passage quite unambiguously indicates the symbolic thinking that underlies such recycling.[38] Thus, the heart is understood to be the essence of the belief in an ego/Self, such a belief being constituted by perceptual and cognitive operations through which there occurs the sensing of certain invariant relationships obtaining between what are taken to be objects only insofar as the constituting act (the perceiver) is itself ego-objectified. So also, the sense organs are understood to be the doors of perception through and by means of which objects are constituted. The entrails are understood to be the basis for the belief in the subject-object dichotomy, and pulling them out is understood to be the destruction of the preoccupation with one's body. The chopping and slicing of appendages, such as the head and limbs, stand for the destruction to the tendency of psychoenergetic drives to develop into ego-related world-spanning schemes. Lastly, the expression "eating the flesh," "drinking the blood," and "devouring the bones" are understood to indicate the transmutation of the affective processes of dullness-infatuation, passion-addiction, and irritation-aversion respectively, into pristine cognitions.

This breakup of forces, which have to do with the rigidity of structure and which have been imaged as masculine *(pho-rgyud)*, involves a release *(sgrol)* of the energy which, as we might say, has become "frozen" and now "freed." More specifically, this release involves a linkage and fusion *(sbyor)* with the primal source, the system Being-*qua*-Existenz surging (in the image of a quincunx of Herukas), beckoning and coaxing this pliable, supple energy, imaged as feminine *(mo-rgyud)*. This complementarity of release and linkage reflects the system's intelligence in its operation as pristine cognitiveness in the fierceness of Herukas, "knowing" how to assure the openness of Being-*qua*-Existenz. In terms of individual experience, the break-up is sensed as a masculine operational mode *(thabs)*, and the linkage is felt as feminine appreciation *(shes-rab)*.[39]

This linkage and appreciation is intimately related to what in terms of experience can be described as the "intensity of delight" *(dgyes-pa chen-po)*; in abstract terms, it can be said to reflect the energy yield from the transformation of frozen into freed energy. Seen from without, this process seems to effect the shrinkage or collapse of an entire universe into a singularity, an event that paradoxically seems to annihilate time itself, for, as we have had occasion to note earlier, time has no meaning at the singularity. Since intelligence is an integral aspect of Being-*qua*-Existenz, the singularity under consideration is actually the totality of as-yet undifferentiated (or no-longer differentiable) qualities; it is pure potential which yet, because of its inherent intelligence, exhibits a True Individuality *(bdag-nyid chen-po)*[40] in being able to regulate its pulsations.

When this process is felt from within, this linkage seems to occur in the manner of a recall, when all that had been frozen into and constrained by structural patterns begins to stir and come to life again. This revitalization is understood in terms of femininity, symbolically expressed in the words: "the lotus that has been closed opens wide again."[41] Fully revitalized and enamored, the feminine energies so released, rush up to the quincunx of Herukas "like iron filings attracted by a magnet."[42] This magnetically drawn movement involves two processes. One can be described as a nucleation process in that the various feminine forces gather tightly around a nucleus (the vajra or jewel of the Herukas). The other process may be understood as the fusion of masculine and feminine forces, the former symbolized by jewel, the latter symbolized by lotus. The experience of this fusion is described in the words:[43]

When the lotuses have gathered around the jewels, in the tightening embrace
by the mutual contact of hands, feet, the upper and lower torsos, ecstatic
pleasure spreads.

In the climactic achievement of this superordinate state, a genuine
creative juncture, a newly ordered virtual complex becomes established
almost at once. This new ordering selectively uses the former (near-
equilibrium) structural information for its renewed self-organization
into a dissipative structure, that is, one that is maintained far from
equilibrium by interacting with its simultaneously evolving environment
into which it continuously dissipates entropy. The result is the spatio-
temporal unfoldment of the system as psychogenetic preprograms for
perceptual and behavioral operations. The initiation of these preprograms draws in the creative potential *(yon-tan)* of Being-*qua*-Existenz,
which responds by allowing them to operate, each according to its
contextually specific appropriateness. Once these psychogenetic preprograms have been informed, in the course of the nucleation and fusion
processes as to their proper sphere of operation, they are then allowed to
return and resume their strategic orientational directions with respect to
the system Being-*qua*-Existenz in its totality.

The seemingly arcane dynamics of the processes described above,
carry with them strong psychological and social implications. These
implications are quite clearly brought out by the figurative language used
in the Tibetan text, which speaks of the psychogenetic preprograms born
out of the union of the masculine and feminine forces in terms and images
of low-caste women. The "women" are summoned into the presence of
the august and commanding power of the Herukas who deign to bestow
on them their attention. Being accepted into this higher social circle, the
women's self-esteem is enhanced. With this enhanced self-esteem, which
reinforces their essential connectedness with the social-interactional features[44] of Being itself, these women each then return to their own social
milieu in order to fulfill their specific obligations, yet they now do so in
full awareness that their performance of tasks is suffused by a new sense
of propriety, which is fed and sustained by the resonating concern of their
"ruler." Whereas formerly these seemingly destitute wretches were but
prisoners of enervating, meaningless routinizations, they are now personages of joyfulness whose revitalization ensures the meaningfulness of
their everyday activities, because they will not easily forget their significant encounter with True Individuality.

[4]

Thus, by way of summary, we have seen that the auto-catalytic transformation phase of the rectification process involves both a breaking up and release of frozen energy and a concomitant linkage and fusion of this freed energy with its source. Although the fusion process results in enhanced vitality, initiated and sustained by the Herukas, recidivist tendencies remain. Here, recidivism means that the "products"of the auto-catalytic transformation process (as a measure of eu-chreodic movement) may partially reconvert into the reactants (as a measure of dys-chreodic movement). Yet, once the transformation reaction has begun the total amount of reactants is always less. This lessening of reactants in spite of recidivism is figuratively indicated by the weakened state of those forces for which Thar-pa nag-po is the collective symbol. In other words, although rectification has succeeded to a great extent, a weakened Thar-pa nag-po may still attempt to disrupt the necessary therapeutic course. To prevent this, there is a third phase of the rectification process, termed "homeorhesis preservation." Such preservation operates due to the resonating concern *(thugs-rje)* of the system as a whole, which is imaged as Herukas displaying themselves with a hundred heads, eighteen hundred arms and hands, and eight hundred legs and feet in the midst of a fiery conflagration of pristine cognitiveness. This conflagration again indicates the pervasiveness of Being's excitatory intelligence in all processes in which the system organizes, renews itself, and thereby evolves.

Homeorhesis preservation ensures the integrity of the rectification process in such a manner that, once initiated, the energy of all remaining atavistic forces is captured, transformed, and then bound in a form which is useful to the system as a whole. The binding of this energy into a useful form is figuratively described as the ferocious and fierce Herukas exacting promises from the recidivists that they will henceforth no longer engage in nefarious activities.

All that has been said so far merely describes those virtual structures of Being-*qua*-Existenz, which account for the *possibility* of actually activating rectificatory processes. Activation occurs as the self-induced responsiveness of the system as a whole, which is structurally predisposed to rectifying deviant tendencies (the system tilting) via feedback programming of the system. From the perspective of an actually embodied individual, the system's rectification programs are stored and activated in the region associated with the brain and termed *dung-khang* palace. This points to the fact that everything pertaining to system tilting, the rectification programs, and the activation or program execution all occur within a concretely embodied living being. Saying this, however, one must remember that any such living being is understood to be, simultaneously, not only a seemingly localized and autonomous individual, but also the auto-reflection of Being-*qua*-Existenz.

Although it may seem that, from the perspective of the dynamics of the system as a whole, recognition of system tilting and the triggering of the rectification process are "automatic," with respect to an embodied individual "within" whom such tilting and rectifying occurs, these processes are experienced as a concerted struggle to break through crippling self-limitations and achieve that resilient flexibility which is due to the widening of one's awareness of the meaningfulness of Being. As an intrapsychic process the struggle occurs on different battlefields, each with its characteristic terrain and combatants. Earlier in this chapter we saw that the painfulness of the struggle is mirrored in a mythologizing diction that speaks of intensely hot and icy-cold hells and their inhabitants, as well as of realms of tormented spirits who are forever hungry and thirsty. Such hells and realms of torment, however, are but extremes—there is actually an infinite variety of tilted (fraught with pain and struggle) intrapsychic niches. The struggle can only commence when the individual discovers the shocking extent to which he does in fact embody a multitude of such affectively crippling, besieged niches. Because these niches are so well entrenched in the very fabric of one's daily existence, the intrapsychic struggle to break them apart involves an arduous and protracted fight. In this fight the full measure of one's intrapsychic forces for holistic integration are brought to bear on the injurious and resistant nature of the affective processes responsible for the tragic and disturbing constriction of one's horizon of meaningfulness.

Before discussing the various features involved in this fight, the activation and execution of the rectification program, we must mention several other important facets of those virtual structures of Being-*qua*-Existenz, which account for the possibility of activation.

The first point to note is that, regardless of the strength of the disruptive forces, they always are organized in a nonrandom fashion. With respect to a living individual this feature of nonrandomness has already been discussed under the term intrapsychic niche. Here something more must be said about the internal structure and variety of these niches. Each so-called niche is a coconstituted, affectively toned, internal structure consisting of active agent (inhabitant) and the environing world (the inhabited) due to habituation to a particular affective process that specifically characterizes (gives character and personality to) the actively involved inhabitant. The two niches in which the intrapsychic conflict is most severe (the realm of tormented spirits and the realm of hell-beings) have already been discussed. There are, however, four additional relatively less problematic niches. Thus, six intentionally structured niches, each with its characteristic affective tone, are said to make up the totality of Saṃsāra, a cover term for being enmeshed and entrapped in affectively dominated encounters. The following chart represents the traditionally accepted correlations between affective processes and intentionally structured niches.[45]

FIGURE 27

Affective process (nyon-mongs)	Intentionally structured intrapsychic niches (consisting of inhabitants [bcud] and inhabited environment [snod]) of
arrogance-egomania (nga-rgyal)	gods (lha)
envy (phrag-dog)	demigods (lha ma-yin)
passion-addiction ('dod-chags)	mankind (mi)
dullness-infatuation (gti-mug)	animals (byol-song)
deprivation-based avarice (ser-sna)	spirits (yi-dvags)
irritation-aversion (zhe-sdang)	hell-beings (dmyal-ba)

A second point to note is that what are termed intrapsychic niches (with respect to a living individual) can also be understood as quantized (discrete) affective energy states (with respect to the system Being-*qua*-Existenz as a whole) whose distribution determines what has been termed system tilting. Furthermore, this system tilting occurs in such a manner that only one quantized affective energy state is operant at a time—the "duration" of such an operant affective state itself being a function of the magnitude of the energy associated with that state. In other words, no quantized affective state is permanently operant—each seems to have a different magnitude of energy which, when dissipated, throws the system tilting into a new phase characterized by the occupancy of a new quantum level; the dissipation time for any level depends on how much energy is involved. Thus the various phases and configurations of system tilting reflect internal transitions from one quantum level to another, and what has been termed Saṃsāra can be understood here as simply the ensemble of all possible quantum levels of affective energy and the transitions between them.

The variable duration (with respect to any quantized state of affective energy) has been described (with respect to the intrapsychic niches of conflict within and against which an individual struggles) as the length of occupancy in an inhabited environment to which each inhabitant is subjected. This variable accounts for what, phenomenologically speaking, is the well-known experience of "lived time" as a function of that particular situatedness—always an intentional structure consisting of an actively intending individual and a cointended environment—in which one is engaged at the moment. Moreover, within the framework of lived time, one always seems to be caught up in and buffeted by a movement from one situation to another.

The variable "magnitude" (with respect to any quantized state of affective energy) has been described (with respect to the intrapsychic niches of conflict) as the fierceness of disturbing and disruptive forces, deeply entrenched as the discomfort of the inhabitant within the inhabited environment. The magnitude of such discomfort is also a measure of the degree to which affectively toned and structured experiences tend to feed on themselves, resisting the possibility of an internal restructuring into a less tormenting state and fighting against the external stimulus which would, if successful, bring about the annihilation of such self-perpetuating modalities of pain. It is this fiercely resistant affectively structured energy that is met by the equally fierce energy of rectification, figuratively spoken of as the quincunx of Herukas.

It bears repeating here that the name given to such a fiercely employed rectification is ultimate delight. It is the delight of what, with respect to the system Being-*qua*-Existenz as a whole, represents the triumph of globally operating harmonizing forces over locally entrenched disruptive regimes. From the viewpoint of an individual who has seriously challenged the threat posed by the disintegrative forces of affective processes, it represents the joyous fulfillment of victory by "his" more powerful (because more basic) forces of holistic integration.

In conclusion, our discussion of fierceness has dealt with what is considered to be the ground and reason *(gzhi)* for embarking on a program of what eventually turns out to be the self-rectification of the system Being-*qua*-Existenz. This ground and reason, experienced in and as the fierceness of Being's coming-to-the-fore, reveals itself in this process as a highly complex operation that is neither amorphous nor chaotic. It is a structuring into and presencing as configuration disclosure. With respect to the dynamics of this ground itself, there is a symmetry transformation of the dominant structuring forces of Being-*qua*-Existenz which, because it involves a significant shift in the patterning of self-rectification, must also be regarded as a symmetry breaking process. In such a shift, although the dominant force of vibrant spirituality *(thugs)*, imaged as Buddha-Heruka, remains uncompromised, it yet seemingly undergoes a symmetry transformation in such a way that the dominant force of formal gestalt *(sku)*, imaged as Vajra-Heruka, comes to-the-fore. This transformation into what may be called function dominance, may also be conceived of as a transition from pure energy to congealed energy. From the viewpoint of Being-*qua*-Existenz, the coming-to-the-fore of the function dominance of the formal gestalt in its fierce dynamics is but an indication of Being's auto-reflexiveness. From the viewpoint of the individual, as the experiencer in and through whom this dynamic operates, the dominance of the formal gestalt functions as the center of a seemingly new creative design for the transformation of man's inner and outer horizons.

It is in such a universe dominated by formal gestalt that there occurs a recycling of energy described as the rushing up of released energies to their primal source and the breakup and ejection of energy-deficient rigidified structures. The outcome of the recycling of energy is the establishment of a seemingly new regime that is experienced by the individual as a triumph over the disruptive influence of forces within himself. This triumph, as the establishment of a new dynamic regime, is itself reflected by the presence of feminine (energy-rich) forces and the absence of masculine (energy-deficient) structures.

[5]

The triumphant establishment of a seemingly new and thoroughly dynamic regime is never a finished affair—it merely marks a significant breakthrough for the individual. Since no single breakthrough is in itself sufficient to ensure the continuity of an individual's felt resonance with the totality of "his" forces of holistic integration—these forces having their true source in what has been previously termed the True Individuality *(bdag-nyid chen-po)* of Being-*qua*-Existenz itself—it is incumbent upon the individual to activate those forces that will in fact maintain and secure continuity. It is only through creatively activating these forces, which are themselves linked to the very fabric of Being, that the continued potency of the involvement domains *(rigs)* remain in effect, thereby ensuring that the life of the individual is henceforth linked with his True Individuality.[46]

In contradistinction to the ground and reason *(gzhi)* for the system's rectifying transformation, the creative activation of those forces that will ensure the continuity of linkage between an individual and "his" True Individuality is termed the way or path *(lam)*. The pursuance of this path of creative activation makes use of the images of a palace, throne, sovereign beings, and palatial attendants. These images are similar to those discussed previously in connection with the tranquil deities, yet there are certain important differences.

The image of the palace, as the site for what becomes an individual's world-engagement, conveys both the dynamics of Being-*qua*-Existenz surging up in the individual and the individual's elaboration of this surging. Although similar in many respects to the previously described palace within which the tranquil forces reside, the distinctive feature of the palace within which the fierce forces operate is its fierceness and fearsomeness. Fearsomeness, however, is judged to be so only from the vantage-point of those inhospitable and debilitating forces with which one must do battle in order to rectify the system tilting. This macabre palace is described as[47]

> A four-spoked wheel with its center all-ablaze;[48]
> Ornamented with four studs (as corner-projections of the palace);[49]
> A quadrangular (building) having four doors with superstructures (of additional doors);[50]
> Made beautiful by two corridors ablaze.[51]
> (With walls made from) skulls, (with festoons of) snakes and various (gruesome architectural features), aglow in the glare of the sun;
> Quivering with a multitude of flaming bursts.

Within the center of this operational site termed "palace," a throne is set up which is itself a configurational ensemble of five thrones, each serving as the orientational point with reference to which all operations pertaining to the specific involvement domains are organized and structured. The overall ambience of fierceness is maintained throughout the design of these thrones, which are imaged as being supported by feral animals defying domestication. Thus:[52]

> (Raised up) by the talons (hoofs and claws) of
> Eagle, bull, leopard, tiger, and wild boar;
> (With) the lord and mistress couples of fanatically evil (forces lying prostrate on the throne-seat).

These feral animals have been variously interpreted: as symbolizing intrinsic wildness and ferocity;[53] as emblematic patternings of involvement domains;[54] and as illustrations of abidingly pure energies, operative as the vagaries of affective processes, related to the involvement domains and their distortions.[55] As such, this ensemble of throne-supporting animals presents an intricate network of perspectives which aptly symbolize the individual's search for ways to deal with the exigencies of his besieged life-world. It is through the setting up of such perspectives that one is enabled to break through and smash the suffocating constrictions engendered in the wake of the system tilting.

It is on these thrones that there are postured the various Herukas referred to by the colors in which their terrifying male-female gestalts glow. Thus:[56]

> In frightening formal gestalts (which are) bay-black, blue-black, yellow-
> black, red-black, and green-black;
> With three heads, six arms, and four legs wide apart.

This anthropomorphic presentation encodes a multitude of symbolic meanings, which must be brought out to reveal the full significance of this visionary experience.

The so-called colors mentioned in the above quotation are not to be understood as coloring or the colors *of* some ordinary objective thing; they refer to the constancy of the radiation of the various involvement domains. Their specification black indicates the awful sternness and intensity of that charismatic activity which the various Herukas perform. The experience of being exposed to such an activity is that of an uncanny threat. It also should be noted that the colors of the fierce energies formulated as Herukas differ from those of the tranquil forces. Specifically, Buddha-Heruka (also named Che-mchog Heruka), the nodal point of the vibrant spirituality domain, is bay-black, while the tranquil couterpart, rNam-par snang-mdzad (Vairocana) is deep-blue. Further, Vajra-Heruka, the nodal point of the invariance domain of formal gestalt, is blue-black, while the tranquil counterpart, Mi-bskyod-pa (Akṣobhya), is white. One may well wonder why white is not associated with the fierce Herukas and why the Vajra-Heruka is instead imaged as blue. As a chromatic sensitivity, which is the vantage point of an artist, white is preeminently passive, even if as a flawless radiance it is ready to give any fleeting color its material strength. Blue, however, is an active power; as an intangible nothing it beckons our spirit into the farthest regions of spirituality, which we cannot but image as having some formal gestalt. When admixed with black, blue becomes ominous, uncanny, and cold, yet it never ceases pointing to a beyond.

From the point of view of the formal gestalt as spirituality (Vajra-Heruka), with its vibrancy yet coldness, the underlying ultimate spirituality (Buddha-Heruka) of Being, forever active in its undivided creativeness, seems to be more at rest and evokes feelings of warmth. This warmth is conveyed by the color bay-black.

Considered separately, each fierce Heruka seems to convey a sense of terror. Yet these Herukas do not occur singly or in isolation—when present they are a fivefold ensemble in the pattern of a quincunx. As an ensemble of interacting forces, each with an operative modality specific to its involvement domain and expressed by a specific color and intensity, these Herukas exhibit an awesome yet beneficient magnificence whose colorfulness conveys an overall "impression" of pure delight.[57]

The three heads mentioned in the above quotation indicate the hierarchical character of Being-*qua*-Existenz as it becomes intelligible through the three formal gestalts of sheer meaningfulness, scenario, and cultural norms display. But if the ethico-aesthetic activity of these three formal gestalts is not recognized, they linger on as affective processes that poison an individual's situation. The six arms symbolize the six pristine cognitions—the five commonly recognized ones and their unity as a sixth cognition—operating in and as the six transcending functions which help beings in the six kinds of lifeforms to break free from their boundedness. Lastly, the four legs symbolize the four bases of success and the overcoming of the four deadening powers. The Herukas stand straddling the evil forces, symbolizing the operational range of appropriate action and appreciative discrimination.

No less terrifying is the Herukas' gruesome apparel and their commanding voices which rumble like the sound of a thousand thunderclaps. Thus:[58]

> They wear various garments of raw hides,
> Snakes, strings of skulls (as ornaments), and sun and moon.
> Frighteningly they shout with voices inspiring terror.

There are three raw hides: those of an elephant and a human being, which form the upper garments, and that of a tiger, which forms the lower garment. The elephant hide symbolizes full command over the meaning and value of the Mahāyāna, an all-encompassing spirituality; the human skin signifies the overpowering of fanatically evil forces by and with expertise in appropriate measures; and the tiger skin indicates freedom from the dichotomic extremes of subject and object by unifying what in dichotomizing thought is split into and kept apart as the external, internal, and arcane.

Snakes of various colors are worn as ornaments and, according to the part of the body on which they are displayed, symbolize a social hierarchy. Thus, a white snake stands for the ruling class and is worn as a head ornament; yellow snakes stand for the nobility and are worn as earrings and necklaces; red snakes stand for the Brahmin caste (the priesthood) and are worn as shoulder ornaments and bracelets; a green snake stands for the common people and is worn as a waistband; and black snakes stand for the "serf" population and are worn as rings for the wrist and ankle.

The expressive power of color is clearly related to the relative positioning of each colored ornament on the body. Thus for each social stratum there is a color which distinctly conveys the nature of its members: the wealth of the nobility—a golden yellow; the agricultural profession of the common people—a lush green; the greed and rapacity of the priesthood—a livid red; the uncontested supremacy of the ruling class—a pure white; and the patient obscurity of those who perform menial tasks—a somber black. The association of these social strata with venomous snakes well reflects the "deadliness" of a static society with its insistence on the *status quo*.

Furthermore, there are three strings of skulls. The one worn as a headband consists of five dried-up human skulls, and symbolizes the effect of the scorching heat of appreciative discrimination by means of which the fierce blaze of pristine cognitiveness operates, consuming everything that prevents the thrust towards optimization from taking effect. It spells death to the commonplace and is therefore feared like death by everyone who desperately tries to avoid confronting the challenge and demands of growth-enhancing situations. By contrast, the string of dripping skulls hanging from the shoulders symbolizes the free-flowing liquid of ecstasy in and as appropriate actions capable of coping with life's exigencies. Here, too, such ecstasy means death to the compulsive pursuit of transient pleasures and the self-deception that goes with it; it, too, is a source of fear on the part of those who are unwilling to give themselves over to the fullness of life. Lastly, the string of decayed skulls, worn around the neck like the sacred cord worn by the Brahmins, aptly symbolizes the ghastliness of having succumbed to obsessions with mentally and spiritually inhibiting taboos, and the loathsomeness of having to carry this obsessive burden throughout one's life.

The ornament of the two luminaries, the sun and moon, either rising from above the shoulders or appearing from within the tuft of hair, indicate the diffusion of the illumining light of appropriate action and appreciative discrimination.

It is around the formal gestalt as spirituality (Vajra-Heruka) in its male-female presence that the as yet energy-rich preprograms of what constitutes the complexity of concrete experiencing arrange themselves. These energy-rich preprograms are imaged and felt as profoundly feminine, a bounteous source of creativity, for they are at this early stage of mental-spiritual development still fed by the primal energy of Vajra-Heruka. These preprograms are technically termed endorsement carriers *(phyag-rgya)*. They are endorsement carriers, for, having been revitalized through their union with the primal energy source they carry the endorsement or seal of approval of this source for the resumption of their appropriate activities.

These endorsement carriers operate as act phases *(gnas-kyi phyag-rgya)* and object phases *(yul-gyi phyag-rgya)* coconstituted in an intentional arch.[59] With respect to the act phase there are eight generic,[60] protothematic opportunity endorsement carriers, which are imaged as eight genetrixes *(ma-mo)*[61] who force man to realize his humanity.

As act phases, these endorsement carriers present opportunities for dealing with life's profound ambiguity—the same preprograms may either enmesh an individual in Saṃsāra or assist him in overcoming his restrictive boundaries. The term protothematic is added to emphasize the subtle feature that these preprograms for both act phases and object phases mark the phase transition from the virtual, that is, prethematic, to the thematic complexity of an individual's psychic life.

Four of these opportunity endorsement carriers—expressive of the creative potential *(yon-tan)* of the involvement domains of the system as they cluster around the formal-gestalt saturated spirituality—display an orientational directedness with respect to the nodal point Vajra-Heruka in that they occupy certain strategic regions, which are imaged in terms of the cardinal points of the compass. This imaging, seemingly created by the experiencer as a participant in these dynamics surging from within the formal-gestalt saturated spirituality domain, is the self-projection of Being-*qua*-Existenz as a rectification measure.[62]

Toward the East of the central agency or nodal point there is *Gaurī (dkar-mo, gau-ri-ma, ke'u-ri-ma)*. As her name implies, she is of white "color" and as such retains the character of spirituality. She represents the still-point *(zhi-ba)* in the otherwise tumultuous upheaval displayed by man's psychic life. As such she is the ground and reason for all psychic activities *(kun-gzhi rnam-par shes-pa)* as they tend to become specifically thematized as "mundane" or "spiritual."

Toward the South there is *Caurī (rkun-mo)*. She chooses or, as her name implies, "steals" potentialities from the vast reservoir of Being and incorporates them into a specific program which, with respect to the psychic life of an individual, constitutes one's subjectivity *(yid)*, which is understood to be that operation which makes possible the setting up of the variety of subjective perspectives; it is not to be confused with any single or privileged perspective. In contradistinction to the stillness of the ground of psychic life, subjectivity assumes the character of dominance *(dbang)* over any and all subjective profiles and their associated perceptual and behavioral engagements.

Toward the West there is *Pramohā (rmongs-mo)*. She is the enchantress who lures and enmeshes pure subjectivity into an affectively toned subjectivity *(nyon-yid)*, with respect to which all subjective profiles named by the cover-term "ego" operate.

Toward the North there is *Vetālī (ro-langs-ma, thal-byed-mo)*. She is the one who sets up all that which is associated with the body *(lus)* as ongoing embodiment.[63] It is the body as a continuously ongoing act which provides the possiblity for being in contact with an environment, but this being in contact with may well have a devastating effect on whatever opposes its presence.

Once affective subjectivity and the concomitant process of embodiment have been initiated, they operate with a vengeance *(drag-po)*; they establish what may be called an existential inertial frame within which all perceptual and behavioral possibilities seem to be regulated. This seemingly rigid framing of experiential possibilities accounts for the depressingly predictable conformity of most human beings. Living in the confines of such conformity has been characterized as zombie-like *(ro-langs)*.

Within this dynamic framework, which presents a unified perspective, the gound-plan of concrete experiencing in which purely thematic thinking is reduced to the static dualism of the mental and physical, there operate sensory-specific preprograms that also are endorsement carriers. Their orientational directedness is imaged in terms of the quadrantal points of the compass.

In the Southeast, there is *Pukkasī (sbos-mo, bcos-mo)*. She is red-yellow and carries the endorsement to engage in what is the preprogram of visual perception. As an as yet notionally undivided operation she is representative of the overall murkiness *(gti-mug)* indicative of the affective tone dullness-infatuation which, in the context of vision, is a general indistinctness, characteristic of that protothematic phase of experience which underlies all evolving thematic experiences. Such undivided operation has an expansive *(rgyas)* character.

In the Southwest, there is *Ghasmarī (gtum-mo)*. She is green-black and carries the endorsement to engage in the preprogram of olfactory perception. She is representative of what overtly may become irritation-aversion *(zhe-sdang)*, but which at this latent stage operates as an alertness and incentive to overcome the poisonous character of any limiting situation. Such operation has a distinctly vehement and rigorous *(drag-po)* character.

In the Northwest, there is *Caṇḍālī (sme-sha-can)*. She is yellow-whitish and carries the endorsement to engage in the preprogram of gustatory perception. She is representative of that existential concern and resonance which manifests as love *(thugs-rje chags-pa)*. Such loving concern does not forsake anyone or anything and its activity is comprehensive *(thams-cad-pa)*; it may be calm and quiet, dominant and overwhelming, or vehement and rigorous.

In the Northeast, there is *Śmaśānā (dur-khrod-ma, ma-tshogs-ma)*. She is blue-black and carries the endorsement to engage in the preprogram of auditory perception. She is representative of the indivisibility of the three affective tones (dullness-infatuation, irritation-aversion, and passion-addiction) of concrete experiencing especially related to sound, which may be said to have a neutral, melodious, or discordant quality. Because of the wide range of the auditive, her activity has an expansive *(rgyas)* character.[64]

All these endorsement carriers are imaged as having positioned them-selves in the cardinal and quadrantal points of the compass, an apt image for the spatial dispersion and diffusion of preprograms set by the system Being-*qua*-Existenz. With respect to an individual, this dispersion and diffusion constitutes the psychophysical foundation and the sensory-specific programs, which operate on and in conjunction with the founda-tion. Lest one be led astray by the spatial metaphor of the compass, it bears reemphasizing that in addition to the spatially directed orientational char-acter of the preprograms there is also a concomitant temporal feature which indicates that the preprograms are not to be construed as static, spatially arrayed, already determined "programs." They are, rather, actively intending aspects, which for this reason are termed act phases in the specific sense of seizing the opportunity to act from their vantage point. These act phases, however, always occur coconstituted in an intentional arch in conjunction with their intended aspects which are termed object phases.[65] These object phases are themselves endorsement carriers whose specific domains are spatially arranged along the cardinal and quadrantal compass points.

There is, in the East, *Seng-gdong-ma* (the lion-faced one). She is yellow and a symbol for whatever may become a specifiable facet of concrete experiencing, whether construed as external or internal, which occurs against the background of man's psychophysical foundation.

Then there is, in the South, *sTag-gdong-ma* (the tiger-faced one). She is red and a symbol for any thematized profile of experience which may emerge due to the operation of pure subjectivity.

Next, there is, in the West, *Wa-gdong-ma* (the jackal-faced one). She is black and a symbol for the psychophysical foundation of man construed as an objectified domain with which, due to the intense operation of affective subjectivity, man intimately identifies himself.

Lastly, there is, in the North, *Khyi-gdong-ma* (the dog-faced one). She is blue-black and a symbol for those tangible aspects of man's immediate milieu with which he is in contact by virtue of that ongoing embodiment which is his body.

These four object domain endorsement carriers are imaged as human beings with faces of fierce carnivorous beasts. This imagery symbolizes the fact that the hostile environment, in which man encounters a multitude of deadly powers, can only be conquered by unleashing the fierce (charismatic) activities pertaining to the various involvement domains.

In the quadrantal points the following four object domain endorsement carriers are positioned. In the Southwest, the keen-eyed, red *bZhad-gdong-ma* (the goose-faced one); in the Southeast, the scavenging, yellow *Kang-ka'i gdong-ma* (the crane-faced one); in the Northwest, the omnivorous, black *Dur-bya'i gdong-ma* (the egret-faced one); and in the Northeast, the nocturnally alert, blue *'Ug-gdong-ma* (the owl-faced one).[66]

These four object domain endorsement carriers are imaged as human beings with faces of wild birds, symbolizing the swiftness of sensory-specific operations.[67]

[6]

The protothematic endorsement carriers establish, through the coconstituted interaction of act phases and object phases, the specific yet variegated texture of man's concrete experience. The variety of experiential possibilities made available to man through these endorsement carriers always occurs with respect to the pivotal experience of existing in a world as embodied. Yet this experience of being embodied itself occurs always with reference to subtler background programs, which seemingly preshape the contours with which I, as an embodied being, will experience and creatively respond to my world. It is by virtue of being embodied, of being *in* a body, that I can be in contact with that patterning of experiential phenomena which I take as my world, for this being-in-contact-with occurs via the sensory-specific preprograms that are located *on* and *within* my body. My experience of the world is furthermore imbued with a sense of either going out toward exterior realms or going into interior realms. It is as if I can encounter my world only through the opening of doors—the very act of opening them allowing those messengers *(pho-nya)* who guard and convey the ambience of Being's unlimited fullness to move to and fro. The doors *(sgo-ma)* through which these messengers enter and go out are suitably located within the palace-like fabric of my existence so as to allow me access to the world at large—the indeterminate and unbounded realm of meaningfulness and concern—and the opportunity to import something of this meaningfulness into my existence. The special messengers are kindness, compassion, joy, and equanimity and they are imaged, respectively, as follows: *rDo-rje sring-'gro-ma,* being horse-faced and carrying as her emblem an iron hook; *rDo-rje gdong-ma,* being pig-faced and carrying a noose; *rDo-rje 'jig-rten-ma,* being bear-faced and carrying an iron chain; and *rDo-rje ro-langs-ma,* being wolf-faced and carrying a bell.

Except for their animal faces these fierce messengers are, iconographically, the same as the fierce guardians in the configuration of the tranquil and calm deities.

[7]

One should remember that the emergence of the configuration of forces dealt with in the chapter all operate fiercely and occur as the actualization of the virtual presence of rectifying forces within the system Being-*qua*-Existenz. These forces are activated through the agency of the individual who "suffers" what we have called system tilting. The rectification of the tilt itself comes to pass through the breakup of structural rigidity and the concomitant release of trapped energy that reunites with the primal energy source. In this reunion a regeneration takes place in such a way that the erstwhile, misdirected and hence dysfunctional forces are tamed and rechanneled. These tamed energies display a revitalized harmonization and hence are felt and imaged as dancing and singing lithesome females. Moreover, in this regenerated and revitalized presence of forces, which ensures the system's optimal operation by virtue of its rectification, there is a harmonious blend of three important experiential features. There is, first, the impressional component of "color" as a feeling of resonance with life's rich mystery and not a perceptually and analytically discernible spectral hue. Secondly, there is the expressional component of "affective tone," which establishes a bond between the experiencer and his experienced world. Thirdly, there is the constructional component, which gives definite "form" to the experienced content as something aesthetically moving and satisfying—the palace, throne, and deities. Deity *(lha)*, it must be remembered, is a shorthand term for the unity of many life-enhancing features.

Due to the actualization of an orderly, self-organizing configuration as the upsurging of Being-*qua*-Existenz—providing both the potential for and the possibility of a gliding off (system tilting) into and as the various hostile niches (descriptive of the degree of the tilt) and an ensuing rectification of the tilt—I, as the experiencer and experience of this process, undergo a dramatic change. No longer constricted by hostile, disruptive forces I come to see myself as I truly am—the locus of unbounded creativity. The overcoming of the disruptive forces seems to be a fight to the death. This figurative language merely describes how an old regime gives way and is incorporated into a new one. Thus, stifling forces, symbolized as fanatical male gods and demons, are destroyed; their female consorts, symbolizing trapped, hence abused energy, join with the superior force (Being-*qua*-Existenz) to which, when a new order has been initiated, all defeated and pardoned forces submit, pledging their support.[68] The pardoning and pledging of support indicate the active presence of important features—forgiveness, concern, and compassion. These features, however, are but surface indications of the deeply intimate bond between myself and the universe. This intimacy is ultimately rooted in the complementarity of masculinity and femininity, which implies a mutual acceptance of differences. The whole gamut of intimate relationships is summed up in these words:[69]

> Made still more beautiful by (co-)wives,[70] concubines, and maid-servants
> (Amounting in number to) twice ten and eight,[71]
> (Each of them) having their own seat, holding their own insignia
> And being in attendance by saying, "What are we to do?"

As noted previously, here also, the presence of a multitude of forces imaged as feminine indicates that creativity has taken precedence. The feminine forces, imaged as (co-)wives, maid-servants and so on, vividly convey the sense in which creativity is ever ready to "serve" in the establishment of new harmonious existential projects. It bears emphasizing, however, that these images—like all those other images with which we have dealt—are delicate conveyers of meaning and value and, as such, stand in danger of being debased through that literalizing devaluation whose collective name is Thar-pa nag-po.

VIII. Optimum Attainment Standards as Preprograms

[1]

We have already shown that the use of the term configuration *(dkyil-'khor)* indicates a special set of operations, all the members of this set being related and interdependent in such a manner that they form one unified whole. In addition, as a unified complex every configuration acts as a fundamental program in and through which Being-*qua*-Existenz undergoes symmetry transformations that articulate and relate its basic operation to the various facets of actual human situatedness, subsumable under the rubrics embodiment, speech, and mentation. These symmetry transformations begin, atemporally, with vibrant spirituality *(thugs)*, which both has a field character (coextensive with and pervasive of the system Being-*qua*-Existenz) and is a process with an aim (directed toward the solution of tasks posed by the system as a whole). In being a process, spirituality is already performative, which means that, among other sets, it may undergo a second symmetry transformation, termed authentic utterance *(gsung)*, in and through which the sheer lucency which pervades the whole system is articulated (transmitted and translated) *via* sound-symbols whose coherence sets up standing-wave patterns that tend to occupy relatively fixed positions within the unfolding complex. These patterns may then undergo a third symmetry transformation into formal gestalts *(sku)* which function as meaning shapes whose apprehendable contours aid us in understanding and responding to the mystery which constitutes being human. Far from being a single pattern, there are a variety of formal gestalts; as they constitute a complex program in intelligible form they function to make manifest, as it were, features already embedded in the original field character of Being-*qua*-Existenz. However, it must be emphasized that, despite the use of the term manifest, the whole process remains virtual in that its transformation cannot be thought of as independent of its interactions with its field.

As discussed in previous chapters, there are three basic formal gestalts. They are the meaning-saturated gestalt *(chos-sku)*, through which the meaningfulness of Being is experienced as an incontrovertible fact; the scenario gestalt *(longs-sku)*, through which a person's spiritual development becomes a distinct possibility; and the display gestalt *(sprul-sku)*, through which the possibility of growth and evolution becomes an actual incentive to live up to the cultural norms of humankind.

The first is a formal gestalt *(sku)* saturated with meaning *(chos)* and as such an excitation of the open field Being-*qua*-Existenz in the sense that this field *(dbyings)* is functionally identical and coextensive with pristine cognitiveness *(ye-shes)*. In a terse statement the *gSang-snying* declares:[1]

> The meaning-saturated gestalt *(chos-sku)* is unfathomable and ineffable.

In other words, this gestalt cannot be reduced to the measurable and quantifiable constructs of representational, that is, objectifying thinking. One must understand, therefore, that the traditional enumeration of three seemingly separable formal gestalts does not provide information about isolatable objects, but rather indicates the disclosure of possible (intelligible) ways for man to exist in and as an emerging process which will structure itself according to the existential coordinates of lived time and space. That these three formal gestalts are interactional processes and not three separable entities, is clearly brought out in a passage by Klong-chen rab-'byams-pa where he also indicates that they are directed processes whose intentionality *(dgongs)* is a measure of the energy of the whole process *(snying-po'i tshul)*. He says:[2]

> Although we speak of Experience-as-such in terms of gestalts such that, with respect to its openness, it is there (in and as) a meaning-saturated gestalt, and, with respect to its lucency, it is there (in and as) a scenario gestalt; and with respect to its emergent presencing it is there (in and as) a display gestalt, nevertheless its facticity can in no way be established as something objectifiable. Its very intentional structure is spontaneously operative throughout time as neither displaceable nor transformable, for it pervades as energy the whole of Saṃsāra and Nirvāna. For this reason the statement that the energetic thrust toward Being thoroughly pervades all sentient beings, has been made.

The self-organizing unfoldment of this energetic process in terms of lived space and time emerges as experienceable scenarios, formal gestalts through which an experiencer rapturously finds himself as *there, attuned to,* and *participating in* everything that Being's mystery, with its inexhaustible richness, has to offer for enjoyment. As the *gSang-snying* states:[3]

> The scenario gestalt *(longs-sku)* is an inexhaustible treasure that grants every wish.

Engagement (participation) in Being's scenario is mirrored in and through the prismatic variety of possible horizon-forms which, as affinities with Being *(rigs)*, elicit a response by the pervasive intelligence of the system Being-*qua*-Existenz as a whole and thereby exhibits itself as a multitude of displays. Although differing according to circumstances, these yet retain their gestalt character. Thus the *gSang-snying* commenting on the multiplicity in which the display gestalt *(sprul-sku)* occurs, states:[4]

> The display, running into billions, cannot be encompassed by ordinary thought.

It is important to reemphasize that the three formal gestalts *(sku gsum)*, just discussed, are not separable entities but present a dynamic unifying and unified coherence which, in the diction of Klong-chen rab-'byams-pa, is termed single flavor *(ro-gcig)*.[5] The complex interrelations, which this single-flavored triad of formal gestalts assumes, are indicated by Klong-chen rab-'byams-pa in the following lengthy quotation:[6]

> The gestalt triad has the single flavor of meaning-saturated gestalt and hence it is beyond the (categories of) presencing and nonpresencing. Yet it is from the field character of this triad that, through the dynamics of resonating concern, a prismatic play originates (as) two formative patterns which are designated the scenario gestalt and the display gestalt. This is to designate the effect by the word for the cause, which is like saying that the sun is rising inside when the rays of the sun have entered a room. Since the actual scenario gestalt—a lucently spontaneous modality, the actuality of the excitatory intelligence of Being-*qua*-Existenz, which pertains to the temporal (unfold-ment) [7] of the meaning-saturated gestalt—is set up as the ground and reason for emergent presencing; and since the actual display gestalt—the resonant concern modality of Being-*qua*-Existenz—is set up as pristine cognitiveness, the gestalt triad is indivisible and unique. As is stated in the *Rang-shar:*[8]
>
>> Due to the fact of the actuality of the uniqueness of the gestalt triad,
>> There is a displaying as a multiple presencing (such that)
>> The meaning-saturated gestalt is dissociated from any representational thought operations;
>> The scenario gestalt is dissociated from the deadening power of dicho-tomized mentation; and
>> The display gestalt is dissociated from any specific characteristics.

Furthermore, as to the meaning-saturated gestalt, which presents the facticity of Being, its modality is that of an open and unimpeded excitatoriness; its prismatic play is an ocean of pristine cognitiveness in which there is no dichotomized mentation.

As to the scenario gestalt in which the actuality of Being presences, its modality is that of lucent spontaneity; its prismatic play is the five affinities with Being, ornamented with symbolic insignia.

As to the display gestalt, which manifests the resonating concern of Being, its modality is that of being the ground and reason for the emergent presencing of all-encompassing pristine cognitiveness; its play is the teacher who appears to whomsoever is spiritually educable.

It is important to distinguish between gestalt triad *(sku gsum)* and prismatic play *(rol-pa)*. If one does not so distinguish, the uniqueness of the gestalt triad's facticity *(ngo-bo)* would entail the untenable position of having to admit that, just as the scenario gestalt and the display gestalt (manifestly) presence for those who are spiritually educable, the meaning-saturated gestalt (would) likewise (manifestly) presence; or the (equally) untenable position of having to admit that, just as the meaning-saturated gestalt does not (manifestly) presence,[9] so also the two formative gestalts (do) not (manifestly) presence. And this would be so because of facticity's uniqueness. Thus also, the statement in the *Pramāṇa-viniścaya*, which runs as follows, "This does not make any sense as far as uniqueness is concerned," indicates in logical diction that any such unique nature cannot have both obscured (contaminated) and unobscured (uncontaminated) modes. Therefore, since the meaning-saturated gestalt already exists as the gestalt triad, it stands to reason that the two outwardly radiating playful operations, which turn into formal gestalts, manifestly presence for those who are spiritually educable. (This radiating play) is just like (that of) a crystal which, although containing within itself the five-colored light values, begins to outwardly radiate in five (distinct) colors only when it encounters the rays of the sun.[10]

So also the *Klong-drug-pa* states:[11]

Therefore, with respect to the way in which the auto-reflexiveness of
    Being operates,
There is the presencing of facticity, actuality, and
Resonating concern—
It presences for those who have the requisite acumen for it.
Facticity cannot be established as any objectifiable (thing);
Actuality—(Being's) modality of presencing—presences in and as
    lucency;
And from (Being's) resonating concern modality two pristine cognitions
Arise without there being an object and act phase.[12]
Because there are two degrees of acumen (involved in) this emergent
    presencing and manifest presencing,
The operation of pristine cognitiveness seems to be twofold and
Presences without strain or bother.

The two degrees of acumen refer to the following: with respect to those who are spiritually educable by the (activity of the) scenario gestalt, inasmuch as they have refined sensibilities,[13] the prismatic play, which has emergently presenced from pristine cognitiveness as the spontaneity of Being's actuality, fulfills their aspirations (by presencing as) this scenario gestalt. With respect to those who are spiritually educable by the activity of the display gestalt, inasmuch as they have unrefined sensibilities, the prismatic play, which has emergently presenced from pristine cognitiveness, Being's all-encompassing resonating concern, fulfills their aspirations by presencing as (appropriate and requisite) display gestalts.

One of the key terms in this passage is prismatic play *(rol-pa)*, which elsewhere occurs in the triad of creative dynamics *(rtsal)*, prismatic play *(rol-pa)*, and splendorous adornment *(rgyan)*. These three closely related terms have been explicated as follows:[14]

Creative dynamics (refers to the fact that) it is the (inherent) capacity of excitatory intelligence which allows for the separate emergent presencing of Saṃsāra and Nirvāṇa, like that of a single sun ray, which both opens the day-lotus and closes the water-lily.

Prismatic play refers to the vibrations in the outward radiation of excitatory intelligence, like the vibratory oscillations in a lamp's flame or in the sun's rays.

Splendorous adornment (refers to the fact that) whenever (Being's) auto-presencing *(rang-snang)* presences in and as the unfolding array (of what is), the intrinsic-emergent presencing *(rang-shar)*, excitatory intelligence, is a splendorous adornment (to itself), as the sky is splendorously adorned by a rainbow or by the sun, moon, and stars.

This seemingly arcane passage adverts to the self-structuring power inherent in the excitatory intelligence of the total system Being-*qua*-Existenz, which, being nowhere at rest, is a constantly oscillating and vibrating outward radiation—unfolding and "adorning itself" so as to present the playful, vividly variegated, and beautiful structures that make up the "what-is" of reality itself. Moreover, the excitatory intelligence which pervades Being-*qua*-Existenz, through its virtual dynamics, "yields" pristine cognitiveness, which presences in and as a gestalt triad—this presencing being an "information source" which, in more personalistic diction, is called the teacher:[15]

. . . the gestalt triad gathers in and as the presencing of self-existent pristine cognitiveness; this self-existent pristine cognitiveness abides as the teacher or (in other words) the ground and reason for the emergent presencing of meaningful structures such as the gestalt triad.

The polyvalent nuances of the term self-existent pristine cognitiveness *(rang-byung-gi ye-shes)* reflect the fact that no single expression can capture adequately the entire range of its meanings. It refers at once to the field and horizon of meaningfulness *(chos-kyi dbyings)*, the meaning-saturated gestalt *(chos-sku)* and the internal logic of Being *(chos-nyid).*[16] Each, as it were, enhances and adorns the beauty and splendor of the other:[17]

> The internal logic of Being is splendorously adorned by the meaning-saturated gestalt,
> Beautifully enhanced through its openness and lucency.
> The meaning-saturated gestalt is splendorously adorned by pristine cognitiveness,
> Beautifully enhanced by its ceaselessly vibrant qualities.
> Pristine cognitiveness is splendorously adorned by resonating concern,
> Beautifully enhanced by its attunement to the value (inherent) in the six kinds of living beings.
> Therefore one speaks of beautiful splendorous adornments.

Thus, to summarize, the important term prismatic play *(rol-pa)* should always be understood to refer to that semantic complex which also includes the terms creative dynamics *(rtsal)* and splendorous adornment *(rgyan).* Furthermore, this prismatic play, which characterizes the outward radiating tendencies of Being-*qua*-Existenz in its triad of gestalts, is itself only analytically distinguished from the facticity of this triad. Facticity, here, names the fluid open-ended character of the process. Hence, any such patterning opens up possibilities—regions of concern that prompt responses, through which human beings may come to understand themselves in their actually lived situatedness. Therefore, the facticity of a formal gestalt, as a holistic process, cannot be reduced to nor confused with any static essence. The relationship between facticity and prismatic play of gestalt, which is forever unfolding in countless variations, is expressed as follows:[18]

> The facticity of the meaning-saturated gestalt is self-existent pristine cognitiveness,
> Its prismatic play is an ocean (surging) in that cognitiveness which is sensitive to everything;
> Embedded there in (Being's) primordial expanse as a point-instant (singularity).[19]

Facticity implies that the pervasive and inherent intelligence of Being, which, although an atemporal excitation, abides as the energy of the gestalt process which presences in Being-*qua*-Existenz, and which thereby becomes patterned as the envelope of precious mystery *(rin-po-che'i gsang-ba'i sbubs)*[20]—being human in its most profound sense.

Furthermore, at the singularity, facticity, apart from merely serving as the ground and reason for an emergent presencing into and as what is seemingly differentiable as a triad of gestalts, is as yet not functionally differentiable into these specific features. Inasmuch as facticity *(ngo-bo)*, even at this virtual stage, involves actuality *(rang-bzhin)* and resonating concern *(thugs-rje)*, it follows that actuality, apart from serving as the ground and reason for the emergent presencing into and as the radiantly bursting-forth into pure light values, is as yet not differentiable into distinct colors. And resonating concern, apart from serving as the ground and reason for the emergent presencing into and as pristine cognitions, does as yet not become involved with any objectifiable aspect. Therefore, it is merely with respect to this functional differentiability of gestalts and pristine cognitions that one speaks of a triadic ground.[21]

The difficulty of understanding properly the dynamics of this unique whole as it operates at the singularity is due, in part, to the problem of how correctly to understand the notions of uniqueness and identity. With respect to the meaning-saturated gestalt as a unique and unified whole, which is yet dynamically upsurging, Klong-chen rab-'byams-pa says:[22]

> Because it abides as the unique meaning-saturated gestalt, it is the primordial Lord Kun-tu bzang-po, yet because of emergent presencing from out of the continuum of this uniqueness for the sake of others, it is called rDo-rje 'dzin-pa.

The dynamics of the unique meaning-saturated gestalt may, perhaps, be best elucidated with reference to the mathematical notion of an identity transformation of the state→image kind. Thus, although formally identical there is an identity transformation from the "state" Kun-tu bzang-po to the "image" rDo-rje 'dzin-pa.[23]

However more than a mere identity transformation is at work, for rDo-rje 'dzin-pa is characterized as "an emergent presencing from out of the continuum...." Here, an analogy to quantum theory is useful. It is possible to conceive of Kun-tu bzang-po, the meaning-saturated gestalt, as an ever-active field, and rDo-rje 'dzin-pa as the excitation (emergent presencing) of this field. Both the field and its excitation refer to the pervasive energy operative in and as this unique patterning into formal gestalts. As is stated in *Rang-shar:*[24]

> Unchanging, unceasing, pervasive—these three
> Constitute the facticity of the meaning-saturated gestalt.

Klon-chen rab-'byams-pa[25] explicates this dictum by indicating that "the facticity of the meaning-saturated gestalt" refers to a field which is both extrinsically and intrinsically diaphanous; a pristine cognitiveness that is free from the limitations imposed by the contours of the linguistic horizon, shining from the depth of Being itself; and whose very facticity is the ever-active constant of self-existent excitatory intelligence.

To understand the meaning-saturated gestalt is to raise the question about the meaning and purpose of being human, though not in the sense of a final aim of life. For this would merely be the acceptance of a preconceived notion masquerading as an explanatory principle and the failure to comprehend the fact that every living organism already literally embodies reference standards which serve, in a functional sense, as "causes" for their actions. Therefore, meaning-saturated gestalt is both an expression and an exploration. Thus we may be said to strive for meaningfulness. Yet this meaningfulness is never a thing prejudged. From an evolutionary perspective, one might say that it is the openness and lucency of such meaningfulness that embodies itself in forms and shapes intelligible to the striving and searching organism. As is stated in the *Rang-shar:*[26]

> Imperishable, open, lucent—these three
> Are the definitive words (characterizing) meaning-saturated gestalt.

Klong-chen rab-'byams-pa,[27] commenting on this statement, declares that what one ultimately strives for is meaningfulness *(chos)*, which can only be indicated as being that which is open, lucent, and diaphanously pure. But insofar as it is also in the concrete embodiment *(lus)* and field *(dbyings)*, which serves as the ground for the emergent presencing of every and all occurrences of gestalt patterning and pristine cognitions, it is defined as meaning-saturated gestalt *(chos-sku)*.

One must remember, of course, that the meaning-saturated gestalt is a process, always interacting with its field and never apart from the "other" gestalt processes. Although, in fact, the interactive nature of this gestalt constitutes an inseparably unified, holistic continuum, the process is, nonetheless, amenable to functional anlysis. Klon-chen rab-'byams-pa has analyzed the process in terms of its general unfoldment into and as a fivefold display process *(phun-sum tshogs)* and the specifics of this unfoldment with respect to five genotypal encodement programs, formal gestalt *(sku)*, authentic utterance *(gsung)*, vibrant spirituality *(thugs)* creative potential *(yon-tan)*, and optimally executed activities *(phrin-las).*[28]

With respect to its general unfoldment the meaning-saturated gestalt itself engages in a peculiar operation that may be termed an involvement identity transformation in that it is, simultaneously, not only a "simple" identity transformation termed reflexivity meaning-saturated gestalt *(chos-sku'i chos-sku),* but also a "complex" identity transformation in that, because of its reflexivity, it is already an involvement in the "other" gestalt processes as its symmetry transformation. This latter feature of involvement in is termed the meaning-saturated gestalt's symmetry transformation in and as scenario gestalt *(chos-sku'i longs-sku),* and the meaning-saturated gestalt's symmetry transformation in and as display gestalt *(chos-sku'i sprul-sku).*[29]

Lastly, with respect to each of these reflexively constituted gestalt complexes, there is a fivefold internal structuring referred to by the metaphors of place, in-depth appraisal, audience, message, and time.[30]

Although the meaning-saturated gestalt remains virtual and is not to be thought of as some overtly occurring observable process, it nonetheless is said to be the foundational stratum upon which pristine cognitiveness operates by assuming the contours of the gestalt's dynamic nature:[31]

> With respect to its open mode—the pristine cognitiveness (that is the) diaphanously pure facticity (of Being), is free from the limiting contours of the linguistic horizon and therefore is the unique singularity field (of Being).
>
> With respect to its lucent mode—the pristine cognitions (that are the) spontaneous actuality (of Being as Being-*qua*-Existenz) serve as the ground for the (activation of Being's) creative potential.
>
> (With respect to its excitatory mode)—the pristine cognitions (that constitute the) all-encompassing resonating concern function as the gates (through which) emergent presencing ceaselessly proceeds. Therefore (this process functions to) lay bare the luster of the formative gestalts with their pristine cognitions.

[2]

The extraordinary dynamics of the meaning-saturated gestalt *(chos-sku)* is never independent of the field *(dbyings)* of which it is its excitation *(rig-pa),* and also its own ornamentation *(rgyan).* This reflexive self-referential ornamenting activity structures itself in and as aesthetically appreciable processes. This is due, in part, to the fact that the strength and nature of meaning-saturated gestalt dynamics is functionally accompanied by energy-rich formative gestalt *(gzugs-sku)* processes. One such process may be characterized as a matrix of dynamic modeling; it fashions optimum attainment standards which as talents *(yon-tan)* inhere in and engage spiritually educable individuals, and yet retains its open potentiality as those transparent symbolizing forces through which this process makes its presence felt. Thus:[32]

> The facticity of the scenario gestalt *(longs-sku)* is a spontaneous actuality;
> As a prismatic play it presences in and as five affinities (with Being) and
>   five pristine cognitions,
> Suffusing the whole expanse of the sky.

The spontaneous actuality of the excitatory intelligence of Being constitutes, in fact, the scenario gestalt of that True Individuality in which the optimum attainment standards are complete. These standards function as preprograms which, from the viewpoint of the spiritually educable individual, are standards-to-be-met. Although in itself this gestalt is functionally inseparable from the meaning-saturated gestalt, analytically one may say that it manifestly presences as five seemingly separable gestalts, each presenting a specific affinity with Being as a playful outward glowing. It is this totality of affinities and pristine cognitions, forming a welter of configurations *(dkyil-'khor),* that as a self-existent True Individuality is cryptically described as "suffusing the whole expanse of the sky," that is, the whole of space as the universe. The specific pristine cognitions associated with the affinities with Being, operate as image-creating forces which, in the guise of aesthetically apprehendable symbols, make their presence felt in the life of man. These symbols that engage and challenge man by beckoning him to attend to his True Individuality, also aid him in meeting the standards of excellence which have been established by Being-*qua*-Existenz, and these in turn involve him in ever more meaningful scenarios.

Thus, to recapitulate, although the meaning-saturated gestalt as a subtle fluctuation cannot be separated or isolated from the unbroken wholeness of Being with its field-like character,[33] the scenario gestalt (itself coextensive with the "field") has a certain functional independence. Its lucency stands out against the background of Being's unbroken wholeness. This feature is brought out in the following hermeneutical explication of the Tibetan rendering of this gestalt as *longs-spyod rdzogs-pa'i sku:*[34]

longs: Literally meaning "obtained" it refers to what is "taken up." Hermeneutically it indicates that the lucency of the gestalt process is as yet unresolved by diffractions and reaches everywhere.

spyod: Literally meaning "to engage" and hence "to enjoy" what is there, hermeneutically it indicates that the fivefold manifest presencing of this gestalt process has as yet no differentiable qualities.

rdzogs: Literally meaning "complete," hermeneutically it indicates that
the gestalt process as an unobjectifiable value manifestly presences all at once.

pa: Syntactically used as a nominalizing particle, it is hermeneutically
interpreted as indicating that the openness of Being ceaselessly
radiates in distinct hues.

sku: The formal gestalt in its manifest presencing (into and as) five
affinities with Being, maintains with respect to each affinity its
specific gestalt character.

As should be quite evident from this hermeneutical explication, the
"enjoyment" referred to is certainly not of an ordinary kind. The lucent
character of this gestalt process which is so "enjoyed" is tied to the optimum
attainment standards and hence is experienced rapturously.

Just as the meaning-saturated gestalt is a process that exhibits features of
reflexivity and symmetry transformation and as such may be conceived of
as constituting a complex system "within" which there are many systems,
so also the scenario gestalt exhibits its own reflexivity *(longs-sku'i longs-
sku)* and symmetry transformation *(longs-sku'i chos-sku)* and so on. As
such, even the scenario gestalt is a complex system with its own subsystems.[35] In addition, each system and subsystem has "its" affinities with
Being, whose structure is that of a configuration *(dkyil-'khor)* with its
characteristics of place, teacher (as information input), audience, message,
and time.

[3]

There is yet another formative gestalt process termed display gestalt
(sprul-sku) because it refers to that aspect of Being's unbroken wholeness
which displays and forms seemingly tangible features of experience. This
display gestalt process is revelatory in making manifest Being's inherent
intelligence through displaying a resonant concern, which patterns itself
within the context of actual human situatedness. Thus, the resonating
concern of Being is made manifest to spiritually educable individuals in and
as those activities that are relevant to various life-styles, arising out of
possible configurations of experience, and which they are compelled to
actualize. Thus it is said:[36]

The facticity of the display gestalt is the ground and reason for the emergent presencing of resonating concern,
Its prismatic play manifestly presences whenever and wherever there is
(need for) spiritual discipline and

(Its availability as) might and wealth through optimally executed actions.

With respect to the facticity of the display gestalt, its process is identical with that of the meaning-saturated gestalt.[37] This implies that meaningfulness, as a total overarching feature, is implicitly present in every aspect of the operation of intelligence. It follows then that there are two inseparably intertwined features to be taken into account. The one is the playful emergence of an overall creative activity *(bya-ba byed-pa'i sprul-sku)* which implements, as it were, the scope and form in which human situatedness is to develop. The other is the projects *(bya-ba rdzogs-pa'i sprul-sku)* which constitute the very situatedness in which the former activity becomes involved.[38]

The display gestalt, like the other two gestalt processes, exhibits the feature of reflexivity and symmetry transformation. Likewise, as a system complex it may set up its own subsystems.

Even when one speaks of Being-*qua*-Existenz as being constituted by three gestalts, this does not imply a reduction to *a* set of gestalts. For, although such seemingly discrete sets may be analytically discussed, in terms of their actual interrelatedness and interactivity, they are continually suffused by the energy of Being-*qua*-Existenz as a whole. In particular, however, it is the display gestalt, suffused by Being's excitatory intelligence, which through its pristine cognitiveness is simultaneously sensitive to both the very fact of situatedness and the rich potential it offers for development.[39]

[4]

The gestalt triad has customarily been conceived of as a long process of inner development, analyzable in terms of a ground or starting-point *(gzhi)*, a path as the unfolding process *(lam)*, climaxing in the goal *('bras-bu)* as the final state toward which the spiritually educable persons strive. This analysis may be regarded as a description of the directedness in which sentient beings function. Such directed unfoldment of sentient beings, like that of all biologically regulated systems, takes place far from equilibrium. Hence the classical thermodynamic conditions of being a closed system at equilibrium do not apply to living systems, and the goal or end state toward which they develop is not a final, entropic quiescence, imaged as death (be it physiological, mental, or spiritual). The goal is rather merely the end phase of a complexly operating dissipative structure, which marks the transition to a new beginning—the starting-point for a new (vitalized) movement.[40]

Thus the entire process that is made explicit as the gestalt triad is already present in the ground. As previously discussed, the ground is neither an autonomous nor closed and static system—it is merely the name give to Being's undivided and unbroken totality. The ground, then, is a thoroughly dynamic energy process, which is open (that is, it defies any reduction), ever active in its radiance and sheer lucency, and, through the pervasively inherent intelligence, operative as a resonating concern that preserves the integrity of this totality in all its variegated facets. These characterizations of the ground, however, are not separable, even functionally, from what is named ground. Thus it is said:[41]

> The facticity (of this ground as a totality) is indivisible with respect to its openness and lucency; its actuality is indivisible with respect to its lucency and openness; and its resonating concern is indivisible with respect to its excitatory intelligence and openness.

One must be careful, therefore, not to think of the presence of the gestalt triad in this totality as something concrete; rather, it is a system of interconnected standards by which the entire process of development is guided and to which it aims, while yet remaining an open-ended movement of self-renewal. This open-ended self-renewal is possible because the atemporal *(ye)* nature of the process operates in such a manner that whatever may have been or may become a limitation of the primal openness is and will continue dispersing *(sangs),* and that whatever its creative potential may have been or may become will continue expanding *(rgyas),* and that there is and will continue to be an iteration *(yang)* of such dispersing and expanding *(sangs-rgyas).*[42]

This open-ended self-renewing movement is itself the expression of the creative dynamics of Being *(rtsal)* in its auto-presencing as Existenz, and it is powerfully operative in the pervasiveness of excitatory intelligence in and as resonating concern through which the functional unity of facticity and actuality is ensured, thus imbuing the entire process with a truly cognitive character. Thus it is stated:[43]

> Although one may speak of a triad of facticity, actuality, and resonating concern as different aspects (of Being), they are not separate (or separable) entities. As is stated in the *Thal-'gyur:*[44]
>
>> From the vantage point of pristine cognitiveness abiding in and as itself,
>> The three aspects are functionally indivisible.
>
> This is to say, from the viewpoint of the internal logic of Being *(chos-nyid)* one speaks of facticity *(ngo-bo),* which is open and free from the (limiting

constructs of the) linguistic horizon.

From the viewpoint of the thematization of Being *(chos-can)* one speaks of actuality *(rang-bzhin)*, which in its presencing remains free from concretizable forms.

From the viewpoint of unity *(zung-'jug)* and inseparability *(dbyer-med)* one speaks of resonating concern *(thugs-rje)*, which is excitatory intelligence, utterly open and free from the extremes of eternalism *a parte ante* and eternalism *a parte post*.

It is specifically the excitation of intelligence that involves the whole field of Being, that gives rise to pristine cognitions. These may be said to be coextensive with the field in its various aspects, yet, more properly speaking, they are a function of the excitation itself. This interpretation is implicit in the following passage:[45]

> Since facticity is open, it cannot be established as either substance or quality; since actuality is lucent, it never loses its character of auto-presencing as an atemporally abiding outward-directed glow *(ye-gdangs)*; and since resonating concern is excitatory intelligence, it incessantly abides as the ground and reason for the emergent presencing of its cognitive sensitivity expanding into pristine cognitions.

The openness and facticity is far from being void or a mere emptiness; it refers to a seething activity which is intelligent in that it exhibits a cognitive sensitivity *(mkhyen)* toward the whole of whatever comes under scrutiny. This sensitivity presents a kind of modeling power in and as the shaping of experience—a single overall pattern, rich in meaning—which remains indivisibly a pristine cognition and its experiential gestalt. In conjunction with such an overall patterning other gestalt processes become possible in such a manner that the unbroken whole of Being itself reverberates in all of its thematizable aspects. Thus:[46]

> Being's primordiality abides as the three aspects of
> Facticity, actuality, and resonating concern.
> Furthermore, since facticity abides as a gestalt process,
> Being's primordiality functions in a manner that remains unbroken and
> unbreakable
> Into (separate) facets (termed) meaning-saturated, scenario, and display
> gestalt,
> Yet even with respect to this well-established functioning
> It is not an object before the mind (allowing such predications as) gestalt,
> color and so on.

Being in its primordiality *(gdod-ma'i gzhi)* refers to the inherent potentialities of virtual programs tending to become actualized as optimum attainment standards that an individual encounters in his actual, lived situatedness. As such, these standards *(sku)* are not objectifiable data. Rather, they seem to have a double function. The one is a mode of perceiving in the sense of searching for features, patterned designs, gestalts which are relevant to the developing process as a whole and which are "found" to be coexisting, as it were, with an immediate, hence pristine, appreciative cognitiveness. The other function determines one's existential quality of being human, an interpenetrating complex of being embodied *(sku)*, communicating *(gsung)*, and exercising existential spirituality *(thugs)*. The dual function of these standards is itself bound up with the resonating concern of Being in its totality.

Thus, Klon-chen rab-'byams-pa says:[47]

> With respect to the triad of facticity, actuality, and resonating concern, facticity abides as gestalt and therefore has no marked characteristics, apart from being the ground and reason for the emergent presencing of individual gestalt; actuality has no marked colors, apart from being the ground and reason for the emergent presencing of radiance in individual light frequencies; resonating concern does not involve itself with objectifiable particulars, apart from being the ground and reason for the emergent presencing of pristine cognitions, and therefore is merely that aspect (which allows itself to be) individually (experienced as) a gestalt and/or pristine cognition, while its other aspect (which pertains to the) three gestalt processes in their individual operation is the actual presence of facticity, actuality, and resonating concern.

Furthermore, with respect to resonating concern, one finds this significant statement in the *Thal-'gyur:*[48]

> In view of the fact that the ground and reason for the emergent presencing
>   of resonating concern is variegated,
> It is indeterminate and cannot be specified unequivocally as being thus,
> Hence because of this varied presencing one speaks of ground.

The resonating concern of Being in its totality may, on the basis of the above statement, be conceived of as an ongoing experiment which, under varying (variegated) conditions, gives us as embodied beings our existential awareness such that our existentiality *(sku)* is always copresent and coextensive with our awareness of it *(ye-shes)*.

In us as embodied beings this awareness functions as that which makes possible everything which may be subsumed under the term thinking; its variegated nature can include conceiving, abstracting, judging, and generalizing as well as introspecting, meditating, and much more. As a process it is always more like a *how* rather than a *what*. In its pervasively operative dynamics it may at one time conceal the unbroken wholeness of Being because of its susceptibility to functioning as that "low-level" context-bound sensitivity termed nonunderstanding. Yet at another time it may reveal this wholeness through an opening up of contextuality as an unfolding path leading into the direction of that "higher-level" sensitivity termed understanding, which lets the fullness and richness of Being's meaningfulness shine forth. These two seemingly diverging features are yet inextricably interwoven in such a manner that whenever the one prevails, the other, though apparently hidden, is still there, embedded in the overall texure of what we take to be "experience."

The concealing and unconcealing propensities of pristine cognitiveness might seem to be acts, yet on closer scrutiny they are merely descriptions of what might be conceived of as an ever ongoing, cosmic game of hide-and-seek in which the "player," while hidden, is Existenz and, when found out, is none other than Being itself.[49]

It is through nonunderstanding Being's dynamics that Existenz operates in and as that relatively bounded domain (being human) within and with reference to which there is the seemingly inevitable entanglement in a profusion of cognitive and affective distortions. Yet it is precisely in this same domain that there always remains the active possibility for discovery, in the sense of recovery through understanding Being's dynamics, of that fullness of meaning which is human being in the proper sense of the term. Furthermore, the propensities of both entanglement and recovery are themselves made possible by Being itself, which is described as that primal contextuality "before there was the state of being a Buddha through understanding and before there was the state of being a sentient being through nonunderstanding."[50] Thus it is on the field of Being's "primal contextuality" that the game of hide-and-seek is played by Being itself:[51]

> Although in the vastness of the sky the orb of the sun and moon shine brightly,
> They are not visible when thoroughly obscured by the power of the thick cloud of nonunderstanding—
> And this is the way that limpid clearness and consummate perspicacity functions with respect to itself.

Cannot something be done to disperse this obscuring power of nonunderstanding? Is not some "special action" called for? The answer to these questions is an emphatic No, for any such "doing" is conducted within the obscuring framework of doer, doing, and thing done; it therefore merely reinforces the already present nonunderstanding. Yet, one may, of course, object that surely something seemingly happens to disperse this nonunderstanding even if it is not some doing, and this is correct, for it is said by Klong-chen rab-'byams-pa:[52]

> Just as a thick cloud disperses by itself by just being spread (throughout
> the sky's) vast continuum,
> So, once the cloud of nonunderstanding (regulated by concepts of) cause
> and effect has dissipated, when and if there is no meddling,
> The energizing power of limpid clearness and consummate perspicacity
> automatically appears in the vastness of the sky.

Thus, the game of hide-and-seek is a naturally occurring movement, sometimes "clearing-up" and revealing the energizing power that pervades the sky-like continuum of Being, and sometimes "clouding-over" and concealing this energizing power. The clouding-over is a concealment of the understanding of Being's dynamics which yet remains, however dimly experienced, in the background, as it were, of every situation of entanglement. In fact, such concealing is but a perturbation of Being's dynamics whose operation has been described as follows:[53]

> Facticity, like the sun (in the sky), shines in the midst of the expanse of the
> meaning continuum,
> From its creative dynamics, which is like the sun's rays, (light) arises
> everywhere and spreads evenly.
> When the heat (deriving from it) has engulfed land and sea,
> From the mist and fog the play of clouds arises,
> Thereby obscuring (Being's) facticity and creative dynamics.
> So also, through the play of the sullying (perturbations of) the intrinsic
> creative dynamics which stems from (Being's) facticity itself,
> The very nature of this energizing power is hidden with respect to itself,
> And thus (the manifold of) errant presencing in and as appearances
> construed as world and inhabitants, surpasses the imagination.

It may seem as if the process of concealment and unconcealment occurs in a temporal sequence. Yet, paradoxically, concealment and unconcealment are both atemporally copresent, for they are but descriptions of the play of the universe itself. If this were not so there would develop a break or division within Being; yet Being is repeatedly characterized as an undivided and unbroken continuum. When man comes to understand that his own previously held beliefs about reality are in fact just the naughty (errant) play of the universe itself, then he is free to appreciate the play of his imaging as it really is—a wondrous testament (ornament) to the pervasiveness

of excitatory intelligence in its operation as pristine cognitions. Thus
Klong-chen rab-'byams-pa states:[54]

> Just as clouds disperse by the agitation of the atmosphere due to the
> dynamics of the sun's rays,
> From understanding (Being) in its own right, the prismatic play (of
> imaging) arises as an ornament (of pristine cognitiveness).
> Since errant perturbation is dissipated in and at its source as atemporal
> releasement,
> This errant presencing is (in fact) but a fluctuation of the transparently
> pure continuum of Being and hence does not require (the action of)
> giving up the belief in the reality of such errancy.
> In the bright sky, which has no region where one could settle,
> The sun of spontaneously present formal gestalt and pristine cognitive-
> ness has arisen:
> It has not come from somewhere else, it is just its own lustrous presencing.

Unconcealment which has its "origin" in the dynamics of excitatory
intelligence, pervasively inherent in Being-*qua*-Existenz, is above all an
actualization process. Throughout the development of an individual's
life-pattern there operate optimum attainment standards toward which
and in the light of which the individual's actions are effectuated. Furthermore, unconcealment is a holistic movement in which less-than-optimal
performance standards are transcended through being incorporated into
ever more optimal settings with respect to which the spiritually educable
individual creatively responds. Such a transcending-*cum*-incorporating
movement is itself possible because it is regulated, as it were, from the
primal contextuality of Being itself. Unconcealment, therefore, is both the
recovery and rediscovery of that potential and energizing power operative
in man for those spiritual and creative activities which display the inherent
creativity of Being itself in and through man's cultural endeavors. Thus
Klong-chen rab-'byams-pa says:[55]

> As an eagle whose wings are already full-grown while yet still in the egg—
> Although this is not visible since still confined in the egg—
> Will soar into the sky once it has broken the egg-shell,
> So also the spontaneously present excitatory intelligence, radiant in itself,
> will arise by itself
> The moment the shell, which is what remains as the after-effect of (what is
> bound to) disintegrate, breaks,
> Although the mistaken notions of graspable (object) and grasping
> (subject), which inevitably disintegrate, have long ago ceased (to hold
> sway).

> The presencing of (this intelligence) as formal gestalt and pristine cognitiveness engulfs the vastness of the sky.
> By knowing what it is in itself it (abides) released into and as the turbulent vortex (of Being's activity), which is wholesome in every respect.

In order to appreciate the full import of this passage it is necessary to rid oneself of the conceptual schemata born of representational mentation that have the tendency to obscure presentational immediacy. The image of an eagle soaring skyward while leaving its broken egg-shell behind is, indeed, a beautiful metaphor for the spirit's releasement from limitations, enabling it to roam freely into unbounded realms. However, precisely because of our deeply ingrained habit of channelling our capacity for awareness into representational mentation, this image is prone to misinterpretation as indicating a kind of transcendentalism, as if the realms into which the eagle (our spirit) soars, were amenable to an exalted specification (variously termed *the* absolute or *the* transcendent). Yet any such specification would be but a limiting and hence concealing movement of our awareness, introducing artificial divisions where in fact none abide.

Klong-chen rab-'byams-pa makes it quite clear that the image of breaking the confines of the shell refers to having rid oneself of objectifying specifications with respect to the situation of being embodied. What is at issue here is the crucial transition from the limiting, context-bound impoverishment of experience to the unlimited, open-textured continuum of experiential meaningfulness. This transition constitutes a movement away from:

(1) the tendency of converting open facets of experience into archetypal entities which act as sealed envelopes and prevent any energy exchange;[56] and

(2) the reduction of experience to representational objectifications and fragmentations.[57]

As such, this transition is a nonfragmentizing holistic patterning—a gestalt experience which provides existential anchorage for those actions undertaken by spiritually educable individuals in the light of Being's resonating concern. One who has activated and stabilized this transition, thereby tuning in *('byor)* to the holistic patterning *(rnal)* by Being's dynamics, is no longer conscious of the spurious body-mind dualism.

Thus Klong-chen rab-'byams-pa says:[58]

> Although one's body appears as that of an ordinary human being, one's

directed awareness has become transparently (transmuted into) Buddhahood, and this is what is called a "display gestalt" in which (the transmutation
that) had to be done is complete.

In other words, one has made the transition to presentational immediacy
of being embodied as an undivided and indivisible totality. It is this totality
that is referred to as a display gestalt, since through it the whole of Being
becomes intelligible and appreciable in and as our experiences. Indeed, the
"experiencer" is but a "regioning"[59] of the totality as its play of resonating
concern. More precisely, this resonating concern, as the dynamics of the
totality of Being in its excitatory intelligence aspect, comes as an interplay
as the immediate presentment of a region (which is but an open facet of the
regioning process itself) and the immediate sensitivity responding to this
presentment.[60] With respect to the socially determinate interaction
between human beings this sensitive responding-to is "compassion"—not
in the sense of the emotional *state* of sentimentality, which derives from
and hence merely reinforces the limiting and obscuring forces of the ego,
but rather as the cognitively sensitive *process* of opening up to the richness
of meaning and value which inhere both in oneself and others. Thus it is in
the dialectical interplay of presentment and sensitive response that Being
reveals a manifold of cognitively sensitive regionings in its totality. This
manifold is structured in and as the experiencing of "myself together with
others." Through resonating concern, I as experiencer am disclosed to
myself and, copresently, to others, this disclosure occurring as a display
which precisely because of its intelligent character is something admirable,
marvelous, and wondrous. What is so displayed is a social, situational
world of value and meaning within which there occurs a continual regioning by resonating concern disposed toward oneself and others. Thus:[61]

> Through the unlimited play of resonating concern in the ten directions,
> All that is of value to sentient beings is brought about by the unfolding of
>   display gestalts,
> Which demonstrate such activity for as long as Saṃsāra lasts.
> This acivity, being the natural consequence of Being's facticity
> Out of which resonating concern as (Being's) creative dynamics impar-
>   tially presences,
> Is playfully (displayed as that) most excellent (activity which is directed
>   toward preserving) others' values.

Such an undivided and indivisible totality, out of which resonating
concern operates, makes its presence felt in and through actual experience
in which facets of this totality become highlighted. The interests and

concerns of the experiencer are creative responses-to, made possible by that resonating concern that is always at work in the emergence of possible realms of meaning. Any such emergence occurs in gestalt processes that are inseparable from the totality and copresent with a cognitive appreciation of these experiential profiles and perspectives in all their plurality and profusion. These profiles come as the presencing of symbols which, while inviting exploration on our part, yet retain their thoroughly configurational character, which is but the free play of the experiencer's capabilities and understanding itself. Thus:[62]

> All signs and symbols are complete:
> As to all spheres of activity—they are thoroughly configurational.

This seemingly cryptic statement points to a mode of world-engagement; it expresses the experiencer's installation in a world whose contents are gestalts as configurational matrix. It is only insofar as one is installed in such a world, within which we as meaning-carriers interact with each other so as to preserve and respect the inherent value of others, that human activity has any meaning at all. This is to say that far from operating in an existential vacuum, man strives to better himself through endeavors that are both ethically motivated and intelligently reflective on his innermost nature. Thus it is said that with respect to such world-engagement:[63]

> There are also the two great accumulations playfully operative in completeness.

These "accumulations" are the mutually enhancing activity of ethically motivated endeavors *(bsod-nams)* and growing existential awareness *(ye-shes),*[64] already at work "long before" those cognitive acts that are based on dichotomization, began to operate, and hence make existential disclosure and understanding possible, for it is the outcome of Being's resonating concern in its cognitive sensitivity to both the existential situatedness as such and the possibilities it offers. It is precisely due to the intelligently creative and hence transformative power of resonating concern that man is not forever trapped within inflexible experiential frames, be they judged good or bad, which actually do damage to the open-ended manifold of man's existentiality and its possible profiles. Thus:[65]

> From the meaning-saturated gestalt as an utter openness,
> Its pristine cognitiveness in and as a mood of sensitivity, in utter completeness,
> Comes spontaneously as an emergent presencing in and for sentient

beings.
If this were not so, Saṃsāra and Nirvāṇa would constitute dead ends;
therefore
It is through sensitivity that there is excitatory intelligence-cum-lucency.

Resonating concern is thus that operation of Being itself that sets the scene as a display of coherent configurational gestalt processes in and through which it is both the expressing (manifesting) and the expressed (manifested). The subtle operation of such display is beautifully illustrated by the image of the moon and its reflection in water,[66] and by the image of a magic show.[67]

[5]

It must be emphasized that, although the display gestalt can be singled out for descriptive purposes, as can the other two gestalt processes, all of them are, in fact, functionally inseparable. This underlines the fact that the undivided and indivisible totality of Being remains, in its dynamics, a totality. Therefore, each gestalt is, in a way, merely a mode of calling attention to a certain aspect of this totality. This holistic character of the gestalt process is well brought out in the *Rang-shar:*[68]

> The triadic gestalt process is complete as a unity.
> From the dynamics of the unitary nature of the triadic gestalt process
> There is a straying into a presencing in multiplicity:
> The meaning-saturated gestalt remains dissociated from the objectifying
> tendencies of mentations;
> The scenario gestalt remains dissociated from the deadening power of
> divisive notions; and
> The display gestalt remains dissociated from specifiable qualities.

In other words, the totality of gestalt patterning is a process that may be described as indicating that the meaning-saturated gestalt, as the internal logic of Being, is simultaneously carried in the lucency of the scenario gestalt and explicated by the multiplicity of what individually is experienced as display gestalt. This idea, if not to say vision, opens up new dimensions for the experiencer as an embodied, speaking, and thinking individual, for these gestalts set optimum attainment standards that can be realized in one's life, because one is, in a sense, the preprogrammed region within which these standards must be met.

Indeed, these standards are met by an experiential accessing which occurs by means of the experiencer's directed activity of thinking, speaking, and embodying. Thus in the words of the *Thal-'gyur:*[69]

> The meaning-saturated gestalt is accessed by the mind's activity;
> The scenario gestalt by speech; and
> The display gestalt by the body.

This succinct account needs some amplification. With respect to the display gestalt one should remember that it is the expression of resonating concern—itself related to the excitatory intelligence of Being-*qua*-Existenz—operating so as to provide for and sustain an appreciative awareness, which is experienced as one's being embodied in appreciable world-engagements. It is precisely through the action of resonating concern that I as an embodied locus of experience am installed in a world with respect to which I may and can engage in various "world"-related endeavors. Thus, the body is a lived concreteness by means of which the optimum attainment standard set by the display gestalt is actualized (accessed). And it is the intentional structure of embodied experience through which the directedness of resonating concern discloses itself. Such disclosure manifests itself as compassion and concern for the awesome task that confronts mankind as a whole—optimizing and giving "body" to those standards that abide as preprograms within each embodied individual. With respect to Being-*qua*-Existenz as a whole, the body as me-as-being-embodied is a locus and readout of resonating concern. Yet, at the same time, with respect to the individual the body as the locus of existential engagements is the site of those task executions through which one meets the various challenges and demands imposed by life itself. The task-oriented nature of embodiment has also been noted by Maurice Merleau-Ponty: "My body is wherever there is something to be done."[70]

Thus, I-as-my-body am, properly speaking, the embodying-*cum*-embodiment *(lus)* of that formal gestalt *(sku)* which is displayed to myself and others *(sprul-sku)*.

The preeminently praxis-oriented dimension of embodiment is always found operating in conjunction with the activities of speaking and mentation—these three dimensions constituting by means of their interactional dynamics that intentional structure that is a living human being. With respect to the dimension of speaking, the individual is able to give "voice" *(ngag)* to his various experiences because he already embodies the preprogram of authentic utterance *(gsung)*. It is through such utterance that Being-*qua*-Existenz discloses hitherto unexpressed worlds of meaning which, abounding in creative possibilities, must be experientially accessed for their message to be "heard." It is through Being's voicing, the gnosemic language medium, that its varied richness speaks of itself in and through meaningful symbols which elicit and rapturously engage me in communicating with their aesthetically apprehendable dimensions of sight and sound.

Thus, I-as-my-speech am, properly speaking, the voicing *(ngag)* of Being's authentic utterance *(gsung),* echoing in and as scenario gestalt.

But neither the dimension of embodiment nor that of speech operates independently, for they are embedded in an intentional structure that also includes the dimension of mentation. One's physical and speech acts are never random movement of body and voice; they are always informed by and performed with reference to that directedness of awareness termed mind.[71] It must be remembered that mind here embraces everything that can be classified as mentation, including both the problem-solving directedness of representational thought and that prior (prethematic) movement of mind, which makes such problem-solving possible.[72] It is by means of I-as-my-mind *(sems)* that I am, properly speaking, a being which is meaning-directed because I am suffused by Being's spirituality *(thugs)* whose coherence is experienced as meaning-saturated gestalt.

The optimum attainment standards of formal gestalt, authentic utterance, and vibrant spirituality preprogram the individual to seek out and respond to the existential challenges posed by life. They involve, in an almost literal sense, an opening up and opening to the richness of experience through the dissolution of rigid structures, be they mental, vocal, or body-related. This opening up calls into question the status of what in representational thought is taken to be a determinable entity which, as a material thing, is called the body. In this transition from rigidity to fluidity, the body as me-as-embodied is experienced as a process of embodying that which, in the last analysis, turns out to be the spiritual richness that pervades the whole of Being. Just as the body is not a material thing, so also the mind is not a mental thing. It is more in the nature of an open finitude—finite in being embodied, yet a movement directed so as to become open to the meaningfulness of Being, which is neither finite nor infinite nor restrictable in any manner. This movement announces itself in "our" speech as authentic utterance, and in "our" embodiment as formal gestalt. Thus every individual is an intentional structure in which the inseparability of mentation, speaking, and embodying occurs as an undivided and indivisible totality.

IX. In Praise of Wholeness

[1]

Throughout the discussion concerning the mystery of man's life primary attention has been given to experience, intimating as well as insisting on man's very participation in the unfolding drama of Being-*qua*-Existenz, as an unbroken whole just-is; but, as will be remembered, this just-is is not a static isness, it is a movement which, precisely because of its high energy dynamics, engenders symmetry transformation of the state→image kind: the as-is character of Being-*qua*-Existenz, an utter openness experienced as formal gestalt *(sku)*, operates as a sheer lucency, inseparable from Being's openness and in this its radiance announcing Being's ever present dynamics, so that authentic utterance *(gsung)* is the (sonorous) image of Being's formal gestalt. Although analytically differentiable, neither the formal gestalt nor authentic utterance could, in fact, operate as optimum attainment standards, were it not for excitatory intelligence, which pervades Being-*qua*-Existenz as a whole and, in its operation as vibrant spirituality *(thugs)*, makes explicit (as if it were a printout) what is implicitly already there so that formal gestalt and authentic utterance are not only known and felt to be meaningful (as "my" embodiment and speech), but are also meaningfully deployed with respect to the varied situations within which and in response to which one's conscious life emerges.

All these complex processes, it must be remembered, are virtual and retain an open texture as configurations *(dkyil-'khor)*. As discussed in previous chapters, this configurational texture has the dimension of formal gestalt *(sku)*, authentic utterance *(gsung)*, and vibrant spirituality *(thugs)* which, as optimum attainment standards, function as preprograms within each individual. Because of this openness these standards prompt in their symbolizing activity the opening up of experience. Hence the meaning and significance of these standards comes by way of experiencing this opening up force. However, merely thinking about what this force as symbol generation points to, although a necessary prerequisite for attuning the mind in the direction of opening up, is not in itself sufficient.

Furthermore, the configurational character of Being-*qua*-Existenz is present in and at every discernible phase of its unfolding process. Already at the basic level of man's developmental process this configurational character operates as that push induced by the optimum attainment standards, which causes the system as a whole to respond by providing for its being experientially accessed. Although, in fact, retaining an indivisible unitary character, Being-*qua*-Existenz, in its unfoldment can be discussed in terms of a basic level or ground *(gzhi)*, the progressive unfoldment of the process *(lam)*, and the climaxing or optimization of the process *('bras-bu)*. It must be remembered, however, that what may constitute an optimization from one perspective, may also, from another perspective, serve as the ground for further unfoldment.

The dynamic ground-state of Being, precisely because of its utterly open and hence nonconcretizable excitatoriness, allows for its experiential accessing. Such accessing involves three seemingly separable phases: (1) accessing the actional aspect *(thabs)* of this ground-state as an intensifying actualization process *(bskyed-rim);* (2) accessing the cognitively appreciative aspect *(shes-rab)* of the ground-state as a thorough enjoyment process *(rdzogs-rim);* and (3) accessing the sheer lucency *('od-gsal)* of the ground-state as the experiential realization of the unitary character *(zung-'jug)* of the actional and cognitively appreciative aspects of the ground-state Being-*qua*-Existenz.[1]

These aspects of the ground-state refer to what may be termed Being's auto-intensification as a coming-to-the-fore in and as processes which both expand and deepen the full meaning of one's life, and which also exhibit a concomitant configurational complexity *(dkyil-'khor)*.

The experiential unfoldment *(lam)* of the dynamic ground-state Being-*qua*-Existenz *(gzhi)*, through the above mentioned accessing processes, leads to optimal stability *('bras-bu)*.

As Being's mystery, present both in ourselves and the universe, it not only arouses a sense of wonder but also prompts us to express this deeply felt sense of being whole through joyous praise and song. Indeed, such joyous outbursting is an act of celebrating, for one sings and praises Being's mystery in order to celebrate the successful accessing of its profundity. Because this felt sense of wholeness, which *is* Being's mystery, is not something fabricated, but in its completeness just is, it allows for the discovery of hitherto unsuspected realms of spiritual wealth and, as such, remains a source of pure joy and wonder.

Singing and celebrating Being's mystery presupposes the presence of both a comprehensible image and a comprehending act. Thus there is: (1) a gestalt *(sku)* as the formulated expression of an inner meaning, and (2) a pristine cognition *(ye-shes)* as the act of being deeply cognizant of and sensitive to the gestalt and any variation in it.

Inasmuch as every gestalt is a formulated expression of an inner meaning, this inner meaning is itself due to the complexity of the interacting "genotypal" patterns *(rigs)* forming a configuration. These patterns are genotypal in the sense that they are encodements of Being's mysterious programs which, depending on varying and suitable circumstances, are read out in "phenotypal" patterns constituting the psychophysical temperaments *(khams)* that underly an individual's en-worldedness. The following chart schematically presents this overall complexity, showing the names of each genotypal pattern, its orientation within the configurational complexity, and the corresponding names for each pattern's program encodement:

FIGURE 28

Orientational Directedness	Genotypal Pattern *(rigs)*	Genotypal Encodement Program
CENTER	BUDDHAHOOD *(sangs-rgyas)*	VIBRANT SPIRITUALITY *(thugs)*
EAST	INVARIANTING *(rdo-rje)*	FORMAL GESTALT *(sku)*
SOUTH	PRECIOUSNESS *(rin-po-che)*	CREATIVE POTENTIAL *(yon-tan)*
WEST	BLOSSOMING-FORTH *(padma)*	AUTHENTIC UTTERANCE *(gsung)*
NORTH	ACTIONAL *(las)*	OPTIMALLY EXECUTED ACTIVITY *(phrin-las)*

These encodement programs serve as the primary information input for the virtual preprograms of formal gestalt *(sku)*, authentic utterance *(gsung)*, and vibrant spirituality *(thugs)*. This triad of dynamically interrelated preprograms, however, is subject to a topological transformation in which (1) each preprogram incorporates the information stored in all five genotypal encodement programs and in which (2) the preprogramming by the primary information input becomes structurally operative as the triadic phenotypal readouts of embodiment *(lus)*, speech *(ngag)*, and mentation *(yid)*. Thus Being's genotypal patterning autopoietically sets up a multi-leveled hierarchical regime which may be schematically diagrammed as follows:

FIGURE 29

The Autopoietic Structuring of Being

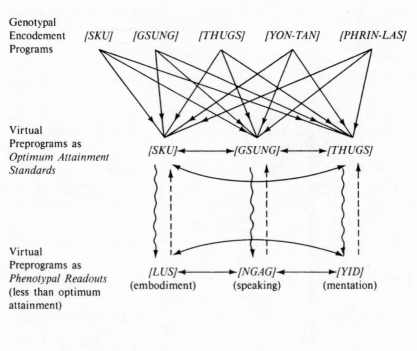

" ────────▶ "indicates genotypal encoding as information input to virtual preprograms

" 〜〜〜〜▶ "indicates virtual preprograms being "run" and "read out" at phenotypal (less than optimum attainment) levels

" ─ ─ ─ ─ ▶ "indicates virtual preprograms being "run" and "read out" at or near the optimum attainment standards level

" ◀────▶ "indicates interactional dynamics

[2]

The magnificence and mystery of Being's autopoietic structuring can never be fully suppressed and confined to the level of phenotypal readouts, for although an individual is certainly conditioned by his psychophysical temperament *(khams)*—experiencing both himself and the world through the triadic interactive structuring of embodiment, speech, and mentation— he yet is capable of recovering and participating in the full dynamics of these virtual preprograms of which he is but a "collapsed" version. It must be emphasized that the possibility of such recovery is due, solely, to Being's autopoietic structuring—although it requires what may seem like effort on the part of an individual in tuning in to this discovery process. The tuning-in *(lam)*, as it tends toward optimization, unleashes the full range of pristine cognitions, thereby signalling that optimization is in fact occurring. Such signals are automatically expressed in and as Being's songs of praise. These songs voice Being's appreciation for the mystery of its own mystery and are sung—as outbursts of joyful celebration—in the configurational arenas within which the genotypal encodement programs are operative. Just as the configurational arenas, as discussed in previous chapters, are of a tranquil/calm and agitated/fierce nature, so also Being celebrates its mystery in calm and fierce eulogies. There are six celebrative eulogies pertaining to the calm aspect, one for each of the five genotypal encodement programs, plus a sixth, which "recapitulates" these five. In singing of Being's mystery, wholeness and completeness *(rdzogs)* is expressed in the melodious sound *OM*, which acts like a leitmotif in music to introduce the hero or to intimate a specific situation; and the sound *HO*, which is the exclamatory exuberance of wonder at the spontaneous presence of what just is *(lhun-grub)*.[2]

The first eulogy is in praise of the genotypal encodement program of formal gestalt *(sku)*; it is Being's evolutionary holomovement, becoming experientially intelligible and appreciable in a formal gestalt which itself is but an aspect, though a pervasive one, of this holomovement whose configurational structure is hinted at by the configuration of pristine cognition. These cognitions themselves point to that ultimate point-instant binding energy *(thig-le chen-po)*, which preserves the system's integrity by virtue of being the vibrant spirituality of Being becoming intelligible through a formal gestalt. This integrity preservation, technically known as the formal gestalt encodement program's vibrant spirituality *(sku'i thugs)*, auto-presences in and as a configurational complexity of the system's most excellent resources, which are themselves functionally indistinguishable from this very presencing, which is known as the formal gestalt's encodement program's formal gestalt *(sku'i sku)*, because it is through such a program that there is an inconceivable amassing of formal gestalts that pervade all five genotypal encodement programs. It is through this self-reflexive auto-presencing that Being sees itself, as it were, in a multiplicity of facets forming a configuration of formal gestalts *(sku)*. In the sense that this holomovement is Being's self-disclosure and self-reflexiveness, it also is its self-announcement. That is, the formal gestalt encodement program operates as a presencing *(snang)* which is yet nothing *(stong)*, the very openness of Being, and the paradoxically inseparable character of this "presencing which is nothing" is the wordless announcement of the formal gestalt's encodement program *(sku'i gsung)*. As an ultimate point-instant binding energy it constitutes a complete whole *(kun-tu rdzogs)* in and through which the most excellent creative potential of the system is expressed.[3] Thus:[4]

> *OM*:
>> Of that completeness (coming-to-the-fore) in the ten directions and throughout the quaternary of time,
>> The configuration of pristine cognitions (constitutes) the ultimate point-instant binding energy [and is the vibrant spirituality of the formal gestalt (encodement program)].
>> The configuration of (these) resources is the amassing of formal gestalts [and is the formal gestalt of the formal gestalt (encodement program)].
>> The nonduality of presence and nothing (function as) the ultimate point-instant binding energy, [a wordless authentic utterance of the formal gestalt (encodement program)], a complete whole [which preserves the creative potential (encodement program of Being)].
>> > *HO!*

In eulogizing the wondrous working of the second genotypal encodement program of authentic utterance, there is a joyous celebration of the fact that every formal gestalt carries its own announcement, which is authentic utterance, having an indestructible character *(rdo-rje)*[5] because it is not something painstakingly contrived. The indestructibility of authentic utterance speaks through the resources of Being as ultimate point-instant binding energy. It does so spontaneously by virtue of participating in a configuration of pristine cognitions and this constitutes authentic utterance's vibrant spirituality encodement program *(gsung-gi thugs)*. This authenticity of utterance, moreover, resounds in a limitless manner, authentic utterance's authentic utterance encodement program *(gsung-gi gsung)*. Lastly, this auto-presencing of the indestructibility of authentic utterance is imaged as a king, that symbol of sovereignty which actively embodies the paradox of a presence which is yet nothing. Thus:[6]

> *OM:*
>> Indestructibility (as) the ultimate point-instant binding energy in which Being's resources are (wholly) present,
>> Is an indestructibility [because of the indivisibility of presence and nothing], constituted as a configuration of pristine cognitions, [and as such is the vibrant spirituality of authentic utterance].
>> Indestructibility (is a) limitless resounding.
>> Indestructibility (is a) king—an ultimate point-instant binding energy [which is the indivisibility of presence and nothing].
>> *HO!*

In eulogizing the third genotypal encodement program of vibrant spirituality *(thugs)*, there is the celebration of the fact that every gestalt, as the formulated expression of inner meaning as well as the announcement of this inner meaning assuming a kind of tangibility in formal gestalt, points to the excitatory intelligence of Being operative as that vibrant spirituality which pervades man. Thus formal gestalt and authentic utterance, as genotypal encodement programs, are some of the highlights in the process through which Being auto-presences, none of which can exist or operate apart from the other two genotypal encodement programs of creative potential and optimally executed activities. It is this holistic process that is termed the vibrant spirituality of the vibrant spirituality encodement program. Furthermore, the richness of Being, its creative potential *(yon-tan)*, atemporally abides in spontaneity *(lhun)* and completeness *(rdzogs)*, itself emphasizing the thoroughly positive character of Being. Lastly, this encodement program auto-presences in a configurational ensemble of pristine cognitions as the ultimate point-instant binding energy. Thus:[7]

> *OM:*
>> The ultimate wholeness of formal gestalt, authentic utterance, and vibrant spirituality
>> Is completely whole (also with respect to Being's) creative potential and (its) optimally executed activities [and it is this complete wholeness that is vibrant spirituality's vibrant spirituality (encodement program)].
>> Atemporally abiding in spontaneity and completeness—completely positive [as vibrant spirituality's authentic utterance (encodement program)].
>> A grand ensemble, the ultimate point-instant binding energy, [vibrant spirituality's formal gestalt (encodement program)].
>> *HO!*

The fourth eulogy is a praise of the genotypal encodement program of creative potential *(yon-tan),* which has the character of a meaning-saturated field wherein specifiable facets (meanings) are as yet unobjectified. Although the field-character of Being's creative potential remains isotropic, it yet presents, in its dynamics, a phantasmic show, celebrated in the image of a magnificent palace and its exemplary residents. This wondrous show is the creative potential's formal gestalt encodement program *(yon-tan-gyi sku).* Although this show is everywhere identical, it operates like a vacuum fluctuation, in which the vacuum, the infinitely active array of pristine cognitions, sallies forth in formulated meanings, yet also fluctuates back upon and dissolving within itself, in this fluctuating authentically announcing the fact of Being's rich potential. It is in and through the ever varying nuances of the show put on by Being's creative potential that its vibrant spirituality is revealed. Thus:[8]

OM:
  An isotropic continuum whose unobjectifiable phantasmic show
  Sallies forth everywhere in unending varieties,
  Yet also everywhere dissolves within itself spontaneously.
  The ultimate (interconnectivity of) formal gestalts, authentic utterance,
   and vibrant spirituality is (the source of) ever-varying nuances [of
   experiences and this is the creative potential's vibrant spirituality
   (encodement program)].
                         HO!

The fifth eulogy celebrates the genotypal encodement program of optimally executed activites *(phrin-las),* and praises the significance of the actional character of Being, through which Being shapes itself into a variety of inhabited worlds as regions of resonating concern. This concerned acticity is imaged in shapes of innumerable vassal kings whose domains of concern span the universe. Such existentially significant activity is authentically uttered in and through the display of infinite cultural norms. Since such optimally executed activity is itself but the manifested dynamics of Being's internal logic, it is spirituality-in-action. Thus:[9]

OM:
  The worlds throughout the ten directions, as many as there are atoms,
  Are the concern of the Victorious Ones, as many as there are atoms,
   and
  Through displays which are (as many as there are) atoms and surpass-
   ing the imagination,
  Spontaneously and in a flash (whatever is appropriate) is accom-
   plished.
                         HO!

Being sings a sixth eulogy in praise of the mutually interpenetrating nature of the five genotypal encodement programs which were functionally operative in the virtual preprograms of formal gestalt, authentic utterance, and vibrant spirituality, which themselves act as optimum attainment standards embedded within the life of every individual. These preprograms constitute an inexhaustible source of adornment for the primordially given fact of Being's mystery and wonder. This, the mystery of Being, exhibits in its most fundamental dynamics an indissoluble complementarity which is imaged as male and female in tenderly responsive embrace.

This principle of complementarity pertaining to the fundamental dynamics of the system Being-*qua*-Existenz as a whole also applies to every experiential level of reality, be this associated with the relatively bounded domain pervaded by stepped-down intelligence, termed sentient being, or that opened-up field of excitatory intelligence termed Buddha. Complementarity has been symbolically encoded as the primal conjugate pair of Kun-tu bzang-po and Kun-tu bzang-mo. The fact that such complementarity is pervasively operative on all levels of reality takes on special significance with respect to what we as embodied individuals refer to as man and woman, for the primal conjugate pair is *equally* operative in both. Hence in a most fundamental sense every so-called man is a male-female man and every so-called woman is a female-male woman. This seemingly paradoxical and perhaps even shocking statement may be reformulated (and perhaps more readily accepted) in the analytical jargon of mathematics as the applicability of the commutative law, wherein for every a and b, $ab = ba$, to every facet of Being.

It should be noted that the primal conjugate pair constitutes an inseparable whole because it is "held together" by virtue of what is termed the ultimate point-instant binding energy *(thig-le chen-po)*, which also thereby preserves the integrity of the preprograms as optimum attainment standards. And so the sixth eulogy exclaims:[10]

OM :
 Everything without exception [is the inexhaustible adornment by] formal gestalt, authentic utterance, and vibrant spirituality.
 That True Individuality [as He who is initiating], is formal gestalt, authentic utterance, and vibrant spirituality,
 And that Complete Pervasion [as She who is acted upon], is formal gestalt, authentic utterance, and vibrant spirituality, and
 This inseparable conjugate force [is the ultimate point-instant binding energy]—formal gestalt, authentic utterance, and vibrant spirituality.

HO!

[3]

These songs of praise for the configurational complexities of the genotypal encodement programs, which constitute the miracle of man's very
existence, are couched in terms that lack tangible qualities. What they
convey is not objectifiable for it is and remains an originary presentment.
The eulogizing carries with it a feeling of calmness, quietude, and bliss
suffusing every activity with a steady glow from deep within. Yet, as
discussed in the previous chapter "Fury of Being," the wonder and mystery
of Being also operates in fierce, agitated configuration complexities with
respect to the five genotypal encodement programs. There is, therefore,
need for praising the mystery and wonder of such fierceness. Six eulogies
are presented, five celebrating the five genotypal encodement programs
and a sixth eulogizing the indestructible continuity and unity of these
programs. The leitmotif for these eulogies is $H\bar{U}M$, and the wonder at such
fierceness is expressed in the triumphant laugh HO.

The first eulogy is in praise of how vividly the formal gestalt encodement
program operates:[11]

> $H\bar{U}M$,:
>> Ablaze like the fire (consuming the world) at the end of time,
>> The rays of pristine cognitions bursting from (the Herukas') formal
>>   gestalt glaring (with the intensity of) a hundred thousand suns;
>> Scowls flickering (over their countenances) like a thousand lightning
>>   bolts;
>> With sharp white fangs chewing [everything malignant].
>>> *HO!*

The second eulogy is in praise of the authentic utterance encodement
program, which roars like thunder and rushes like a storm:[12]

> $H\bar{U}M$,:
>> The voices of (the Herukas') magnificence roll like a thousand claps of
>>   thunder,
>> Making a noise like a hundred thousand avalanches;
>> The laughter A-A-HA-LA ringing into the remotest distances.
>> A howling storm scattering and shaking [the malicious with] a force
>>   [greater] than the storm [at the end of time].
>>> *HO!*

The third eulogy sings of the vibrant spirituality encodement program
which, ablaze with indignation at the pervasiveness of ignorance displayed

by sentient beings, ignites pristine cognitions so as to burn away the pollution caused by affective processes:[13]

HŪM,:

> The intense light of appreciative discrimination, indignantly,
> Sets thoroughly alight the configurations of pristine cognitions;
> (As) a blazing cognitiveness it thoroughly vanquishes [the poison of affective processes]; and
> (As) pristine cognitiveness in its various operations [it yet remains] the ultimate point-instant binding energy.
>
> > *HO!*

The fourth eulogy sings of the fact that ultimate point-instant binding energy sustains the integrity of Being-*qua*-Existenz itself, thereby allowing for its creative potential encodement programs to become fully effective. The program is praised as a king whose activity on behalf of his realm is compared with a cloud which by its rain ensures the prosperity of the world:[14]

HŪM,:

> An enraged king (like a) gigantic cloud
> Letting the heavy rain of agitated configurations pour down;
> (These) configurations are a treasure from which everything comes to one's heart's content (and which are)
> The ultimate point-instant binding energy [of Being itself in] its various agitated forms.
>
> > *HO!*

The fifth eulogy is sung in praise of the most active encodement program—that of optimally executed activities. More specifically, this eulogy praises the mysterious way in which such optimally executed activities overcome any and all deadening forces—forces that "deaden" in the sense of impeding, but not totally annihilating, the development of negentropic regimes. Left to themselves these deadening forces tend to operate ever more at random, thereby working against whatever measures of coordinated optimization may have been achieved. However, these deadening forces are never totally left to themselves and, in fact, as optimization begins to come to the fore, this fiercely operating genotypal encodement program, the optimally executed activities, engages in a highly coordinated strategy that subdues the deadening forces by killing off their randomizing excesses. The name given to what kills the deadening forces is Super-death. It is, indeed, Super-death that provides the optimized system with an orderly program of entropy export, thereby assuring the system's working as a dissipative structure. Similarly, these frightening forces associated with the random intrusion of deadening forces are dissipated by Super-death in its super-frightening presence, which is the ultimate point-instant binding energy of the dissipative structure Being-*qua*-Existenz:[15]

> *HŪM̐,*:
>> This Super-death (which surpasses) all deadening forces,
>> Vanquishes the deadening forces [of karmic activity and affective processes because as] Super-death
>> He also subdues those [deadening forces which are the initiators of Saṃsāra].
>> Frightening the ensemble of frightening forces, however copious,
>> (The) super-frightening power (is) the ultimate point-instant binding energy.
>>
>>   *HO!*

The sixth eulogy praises the indestructible continuity of the five genotypal encodement programs as a structured system of fierce configurations operating as a functional whole. There is the invariance of formal gestalt, which neither decays nor dwindles, a firm rock to support life's activities. There is life's authentic utterance and immense wealth, calling us, like the ocean gathering all rivers and the fresh water of a stream satisfying us by quenching our thirst for growth. There is the vibrant spirituality which, like an all-consuming blazing fire, illumines and dispels the darkness within and outside ourselves. And there is the very activity of life itself, which inexorably drives us onward like a storm clearing a new path.

However one may image the forces unleashed by the activation of the genotypal encodement programs, these forces act as a functional whole whose coordination is symbolized by the passionate union of the male and female. There is in these images a compelling force, indestructible and irresistible, which is symbolically represented by a Vajra *(rdo-rje)*, which is both a royal scepter wielded by a king who is none else but Being itself, and a diamond, the most precious adamantine substance of life's intrinsic value and meaning. And so it is this great sense of awe and wonder at the indestructible mystery of Being itself that prompts the exuberant song:[16]

> *HŪM̐,*:
>> Indestructible and irresistible—a rock, firm and making firm;
>> Indestructible and irresistible—a stream, gathering and vast;
>> Indestructible and irresistible—a fire, all-ablaze;
>> Indestructible and irresistible—a wind, a scattering storm.
>>
>>   *HO!*

Notes

1. rDzogs-chen, an abbreviated form of *rdzogs-pa chen-po,* is the name given to that spiritual tradition in Buddhism that emphasizes a holistic approach and regards all partial perspectives as but local and temporal fluctuations within the atemporally abiding, non-localizable mystery that is Being as such. The term itself has received many hermeneutical interpretations, all of which stress completeness *(rdzogs)* and undivided wholeness *(chen).* The term is often used together with the Sanskrit word Atiyoga, either in the abbreviated form *rdzogs-chen ati* or the full form *rdzogs-chen atiyoga* (see *Rig-pa rang-shar,* pp. 520f., 543, 632, 718, 720). The Sanskrit term has been used in a variety of disciplines in India and therefore has no unequivocal meaning. The *Kun-byed rgyal-po,* p. 90, uses the term *atiyoga rdzogs-chen* and explicates it as follows:

> *A* has the meaning of having no specifiable on-set, resting in the internal logic of Being;
>
> *ti* means effortlessness, spontaneous presence.
>
> *yoga* means intensive application. He who speaks of that which is complete and whole
>
> As having cause and effect
>
> Has no understanding of *rdzogs-chen.*

Klong-chen rab-'byams-pa, in his *Man-ngag rin-po-che'i mdzod,* pp. 66f., sums up the semantic range of *rdzogs-chen* in these words:

> The six incontrovertible aphorisms concerning *rdzogs-pa chen-po* are:
>
> As ground it implies that one is to make experience as such the foundation (of one's spiritual life);
>
> As path it implies that one is to give oneself over to that which is free from all limitations;
>
> As climax it implies that one dispatches hopes and fears to the realm of nothing;
>
> As object realm it implies that whatever presences does so in utter freedom from subjective interference;
>
> As mentation realm it implies that the dichotomies of one's thought processes arise as friends;
>
> As subjectivity it implies that this fluttering fades away and brightens by itself.

He who knows it thus is the monarch of yogis.

2. *Abhidharmakośa* VIII 39:

> The Teacher's message is twofold; the textural material and the process of its understanding.
> Those who uphold (the teaching) are those who talk (about it) and those who realize (its meaning).

3. In later Buddhism there are twelve literary forms which are grouped with reference to the canonical material contained in the "Three Baskets" *(tri-piṭaka)* recognized by both the Hīnayāna (a lower, because self-centered, approach) and the Mahāyāna (a Higher, because global approach to life's meaning). From among these three baskets the Vinaya-piṭaka deals with overcoming any form of fixation or attachment *(rāga)* and implies responsible ethics *(adhiśīla);* the Sūtra-piṭaka deals with overcoming any form of irritation and aversion *(dveṣa),* for these stand in the way of becoming an integrated personality, and therefore the various Sūtras emphasize higher forms of concentration *(adhisamādhi);* the Abhidharma-piṭaka deals with overcoming intellectual stagnation *(moha)* and teaches the exercise of higher forms of appreciative discrimination *(adhiprajñā).*
    The relationship between the twelve literary forms and the Three Baskets can be shown in the following diagram:

Sūtra (prose discourses) Geya (a mixture of prose and verse) Vyākaraṇa (explanations) Gāthā (stanzas) Udāna (pithy sayings)	Hīnayāna Sūtrapiṭaka
Nidāna (narratives of beginnings) Avadāna (tales of heroic deeds) Ityukta (short speeches)	Hīnayāna Vinayapiṭaka
Jātaka (birth stories)	Mahāyāna Vinayapiṭaka
Vaipulya (questions and answers) Adbhutadharma (report of miracles	Mahāyāna Sūtrapiṭaka
Upadeśa (instructions)	Hīnayāna and Mahāyāna Abhidharmapiṭaka

The summary term for these twelve literary presentations is the Sanskrit term *pravacana.* It has been translated into Tibetan as *gsung-rab.* Rong-zom-pa Chos-kyi bzang-po, *Collection of Writings,* p. 169, says about the meaning of this term:

The term *gsung-rab* corresponds to (the Sanskrit word) *pravacana:*
vacana means sentence or speech; and *pra* is a preposition which
points out that something out of the ordinary is meant. This is what is
meant by the term *gsung-rab.* Worldly areas of study, dealing with
trivialities, are referred to by the term *kuvacana,* in which the syllable
ku indicates a low-level content. Such is not the case with *(gsung-rab)*
since its sentences and what it has to say disclose the way toward
freedom. In concrete terms, the twelve literary forms constituting what
is termed *gsung-rab,* are all that makes up Buddhism.

For further details see Rong-zom-pa Chos-kyi bzang-po, *Collection of Writings,* pp. 374f.; Yon-tan rgya-mtsho, *Yon-tan-mdzod-'grel,* volume 1, p. 270.

4. Rong-zom-pa Chos-kyi bzang-po, *Collection of Writings,* p. 241; *Kun-byed rgyal-po,* p. 131.

5. The literary source for the notion that the problem of two reality modes is the
quintessence of the Buddhist teaching is *Madhyamakakārikā* XXIV 8. Of
these two reality modes, which actually form a complementarity, the conventionally accepted one *(samvṛti-satya)* has been understood as indicating the
fact that one's ordinary vision of reality is obscured, that the basic illumining
openness of Reality as such has become increasingly shrouded over—"a
covering from all sides" *(samantād varaṇaṃ).* Unlike in certain Western and
Hindu trends of thought, what has here been termed "conventional" has
never been understood as implying the unreality of what is. According to
Rong-zom-pa Chos-kyi bzang-po, *Selected Writings,* pp. 63ff., *samvṛta* (the
adjectival form of the noun *samvṛti)* implies the following:

> *sam* stands for *samyak,* the diaphanously pure and real; *vṛta* means to
> obscure. Hence *(samvṛta)* is interpreted as "obscuring the transpar-
> ently pure and real." Once the intellect, which has become mistaken
> about (that which is transparently pure and real), has by itself obs-
> cured its own operation, it sets up an obstacle to seeing the transpar-
> ently pure and real. Therefore (one speaks of *samvṛta* as) obscuring the
> transparently pure and real. In view of this fact, whatever presences
> (before and in the intellect) is designated "commonly accepted" *(kun-
> rdzob).*
>
> Furthermore, *sam* stands for *samanta* "without exception" *(kun);*
> *vṛta* is the term for having (already) chosen (a particular viewpoint).
> That is to say, from the learned scholar down to the senile person
> tending the bullocks, all persons, in accordance with their intellectual
> level, choose and reason with a mind that has incidentally become
> mistaken (about the real). Since (such thinking and reasoning) has to
> do with what has been isolated and objectified, and not with that which
> is uncontrived, unpostulated, nondeceptive, and genuine, it is termed
> "conventionally accepted" *(kun-rdzob).* Thus, anything present
> (before and in the intellect) is *kun-rdzob,* and (any) intellect that is
> mistaken about (the real) is *kun-rdzob.* The domain over which the
> intellect and its postulations roam, and concerning which one uses
> propositions and words, is what is known as an ordinary person's
> mind, and since this is real enough (for such a person) one speaks of it
> as a commonly (conventionally) accepted reality mode.

In his *Collection of Writings,* pp. 370f., Rong-zom-pa Chos-kyi bzang-po says:

> *sam* is a preposition (meaning) from all sides diaphanously pure and real; *vṛta* has three meanings; to choose, to obscure, to fetter. Thus, practically speaking, *(samvṛti)* refers to the intellect that has become mistaken (about the real) together with what is present (in and for such an intellect). It has not made the authentically real its foundation, but has made a thoroughly limiting choice and hence is spoken of as *kun-rdzob.* Since this intellect which is mistaken (about the real) has become a hindrance for the growth of the incontrovertibly meaningful in one's existence, it is also said to obscure the authentically (tranparently) pure and real. Similarly, because of the fact that the intellect which is mistaken about the real, fetters itself by itself, and since it prevents the realization of freedom, it is also said to be a thorough fettering and binding. These three meanings apply to anything and everything that can be spoken about with the exception of (what is referred to as) Buddhahood.

6. Klong-chen rab-'byams-pa in his auto-commentary on *Sems-nyid,* p. 700.
7. Rong-zom-pa Chos-kyi bzang-po, *Collection of Writings,* pp. 338ff. *Kun-byed rgyal-po,* p. 60.
8. The full title of this work is *gSang-ba('i) snying-po de-kho-na-nyid nges-pa,* in Sanskrit *Guhyagarbhatattva(vi)niścaya.* The original Sanskrit work is lost. Each word in this title has been given a lengthy hermeneutical interpretation by the Tibetan commentators who base themselves on Līlavajra's commentary (ṭīkā), commonly known in Tibet as the *sPar-khab.* This commentary is one of the three major Indian ones, the other two by Sūryasiṃhaprabha and Buddhaguhya. None of these three commentaries are any longer available in Sanskrit.

   The *gSang-snying* exists in three versions: the basic one in twenty-two chapters; an expanded one (known as the *rgyas-pa)* in eighty-two chapters; and a medium-length version in forty-six chapters. The work itself is said to have been translated into Tibetan thrice. The earliest translation was made by the Indian Buddhaguhya and the Tibetan Vairocana. The second translation was made by the eighth-century Indian Padmasambhava and the Tibetan gNyags Jñānakumāra. The third translation was made by the Indian Vimala(mitra) and the two Tibetans gNyags Jñānakumāra and rMa rin-chen-mchog (who is known to have been put to death in retaliation for the murder of gLang dar-ma in the mid-ninth century). Although the *gSang-snying* is classified as a Mahāyoga-tantra, it has been consistently interpreted from the rDzogs-chen point of view, which attempts to bring out the "inner" meaning of this important work. To my knowledge, there are at present a dozen or so indigenous Tibetan commentaries still extant. All of them have been consulted in the preparation of the present work. These commentaries may be divided, roughly speaking, into three groups. The first group is represented by Rong-zom-pa Chos-kyi bzang-po (eleventh century) and Klong-chen rab-'byams-pa (1308-1363/64). Both authors reveal in their writings a deeply hermeneutical probing and experiential understanding. The second group is represented by g.Yung-ston rdo-rje dpal bzang-po

(1284/1288-1365). He has a penchant for classificatory distinction which seems to have prompted him to rearrange the subject matter of the fifth chapter of the *gSang-snying*. His interpretations have been taken up, often verbatim, by such authors as Nam-mkha' rin-chen (fl. ca. 1653). Lo-chen Dharmaśrī (1654-1718), Kah-thog 'Gyur-med tshe-dbang mchog-grub (ca. 1764), and Gyur-med phan-bde 'od-zer (1924). The third group is represented by Mi-pham 'Jam-dbyangs rnam-rgyal rgya-mtsho (1846-1911) and 'Jigs-med bstan-pa'i nyi-ma, the third rDo grub-chen (1865-1926). These authors are not actually commentators but discuss topics of the *gSang-snying* in relation to contemplative techniques.

The so-called commentary by gZhan-phan chos-kyi snang-ba, *alias* Mkhan-po gZhan-dga', (1871-1927) is a verbatim reproduction of Klong-chen rab-'byams-pa's *Phyogs-bcu mun-sel* with the chapter introductions *(spyi-don)* left out.

9. On the crucial distinction between ontological and ontic see L.M. Vail, *Heidegger and Ontological Difference.*

10. A detailed interpretation of this term is found in Rong-zom-pa Chos-kyi bzang-po, *Collection of Writings*, pp. 514f. and in his *Rong-'grel*, fols. 24b ff. In this work he quotes the *Guhyasamāja-tantra* XVIII 75:

> *mantram mantram iti proktam*

which in its Tibetan translation has rendered *man* in *mantra* by two different terms:

> *sems skyob-pas shes-skyob zhes bshad*
> "since (it) protects mentation, one speaks of cognitiveness-*qua*-protection."

He interprets this verse as meaning: "Since the cognitive capacity itself *(shes-pa-nyid)* is a protective operation *(skyob-pa yin-pas)*, one speaks of cognitiveness-*qua*-protection."

A summary account of *mantra* is also given by Yon-tan rgya-mtsho, *Yon-tan-mdzod-'grel*, volume 2, p. 20:

> *man* meaning "mind (as human subjectivity)" and *tra* meaning "protection" joined together, give the word *mantra*. What does *(mantra)* protect? The mentation which has become mind (as human subjectivity, *yid-shes*). This is also referred to as *rig-pa* ("excitatory intelligence") since from the viewpoint of the climax (of man's endeavors) the pristine cognitiveness (which is the operation of) excitatory intelligence *(rig-pa'i ye-shes)* is termed *yid*. As is stated in the *gSang-snying* (fol. 4b): "The Exalted one, the Creator, the Indestructibility-*qua*-mind *(rdo-rje yid)*—Kun-tu bzang-po." From what does it protect? From the subject-object dichotomy and its (underlying) eightfold cognitive ensemble. How does it protect? As ecstatic pleasure.

11. Rong-zom-pa Chos-kyi bzang-po, *Collection of Writings*, pp. 376f.; 514f.; *Rong-'grel*, fol. 25a; *Klong-'grel*, p. 413. According to *Collection of Writings*, pp. 376f., *gsang-sngags* is the unity of appreciative discrimination *(shes-rab)* and the operational mode *(thabs)*, which is Being's dynamics. Both aspects are of highest quality and intensity *(phul-du byung-ba)*. On p. 517 of this work, a lengthy hermeneutical interpretation of the term *rig-sngags* is given.

Although the term *rig* corresponds to Sanskrit *vidyā*, which in the Buddhist context is always understood as an optimal cognitive operation, Rong-zom-pa Chos-kyi bzang-po relates it to the Sanskrit root *vyadh* (and/or *bhid*), which he understands as meaning "to destroy": "Since it conquers and dispels, it is said to conquer and dispel the affective processes that are concomitant with a lowered state of *rig-pa*." This lowered state of *rig-pa* termed *ma-rig-pa* (Sanskrit *avidyā*) indicates a variation in the intensity of Being's excitatory intelligence, not its denial. Thus "stepped-down" intelligence and affectivity are functionally synonymous. See also Chapter VII, note 14.

The term *gzungs-sngags* is explained on the basis of the Sanskrit term *dhāraṇī*, which is derived from the root *dhṛ* "to hold."

12. In a gloss to Rong-zom-pa Chos-kyi bzang-po, *Collection of Writings,* p. 389, it is stated that "the very nature of *rig-sngags* is appreciative discrimination and pristine cognitiveness; its indication is (the felt presence of) a goddess; its accessing mode is gnosemic language; and its definition (in terms of ordinary language) is to dispel the stepped-down version of excitatory intelligence."

The term *lha* and its feminine form *lha-mo* have been usually rendered by "god," "goddess," or "deity." It should be borne in mind, however, that the Tibetan term has nothing of the static or absolutistic character associated with Western notions of "God." This is quite clear from the discussions of this term by Klong-chen rab-'byams-pa in his *Klong-'grel,* p. 436; by Sangs-rgyas gling-pa in his *Bla-dgongs,* volume 5, pp. 765f.; and by Rong-zom-pa Chos-kyi bzang-po in his *Collection of Writings,* pp. 504f. The term *lha/lha-mo* may be said to refer to a kind of intersection as a relatively stabilized nodal point of two movements: the continuum of Being's meaningfulness and pristine cognitiveness.

13. See below Chapter IV.

14. Rong-zom-pa Chos-kyi bzang-po, *Collection of Writings,* pp. 380f.; *Rong-'grel,* fols. 12a f.

15. "Configuration of regents" is a term for the imaged complexity of programs which constitutes the human individual. Each such program presents a stable, yet dynamic structure. It is the "intelligence" as an abiding concern with the continuity of process and structure—the program, that is imaged as regent *(rgyal-ba).* See also below Chapter V.

16. *tshogs.* This term usually refers to the prerequisites for setting out on the path of actual spiritual growth. These prerequisites are one's resource material termed "merits" and "knowledge," which interact in such a way that the more one learns about the human situation the better one can deal with it. Here, in rDzogs-chen thought, they refer to the atemporal mode of Being's auto-presencing and Being's openness as the completeness of creativity. *Chos-dbyings,* fol. 12a; *Klong-'grel,* pp. 253f. and 358.

17. It is this difference between atemporality *(ye-nas)* and eternalism *(rtag-mtha')* that marks the gulf that separates Buddhism from Hinduism. Buddhism, specifically in its rDzogs-chen aspect, is thoroughly process-oriented; by contrast Hinduism is dominated by static conceptions.

18. *Yid-kyi mun-sel,* fol. 56b.

19. *sangs-rgyas-pa.* This term which is descriptive of a process and hence has an

adjectival as well as verbal connotation, must be distinguished from the noun *sangs-rgyas* whose hermeneutical interpretation by the Tibetans is given in Chapter III, note 60. The noun, too, is essentially descriptive of an experience—an awakening by virtue of which the person who had had this experience and then communicated it to others, was referred to as "Buddha" (awakened one), soon to be confused with what amounts to a proper name. Actually, the term *sangs-rgyas* as a noun refers to what is better and more exactly described as the state of being awakened (spiritually alive)—such a state then being referred to by the abstract, hybrid noun "Buddhahood." The strictly verbal meaning *(sangs-rgyas-pa)* suggests a fluctuation resulting in a new order which Ilya Prigogine and his co-workers have termed "dissipative structure." See Ilya Prigogine, *From Being to Becoming,* pp. 84, 90, 100 *et passim.*

20. "Triad of configuration" may be interpreted holistically or with respect to the individual. Holistically, "triad" refers to the three aspects and phases of a process. As "ground" *(gzhi)* it is the spontaneity of Existenz constituting a complexity of programs or virtual projects, and as such is pure potential (see Chapter II for detailed discussion); as "path" *(lam)* it is the images through which the dynamics of Existenz make themselves "felt" and hence accessible. From the viewpoint of the experiencer (grounded in Existenz), it is his or her operational activation *(thabs)* with respect to these projects, occurring through imaging. As "climax" *('bras-bu)* it is the realization of the pure potential of Existenz as the diaphanously pure (authentic) actuality of one's being. See *Theg-mchog* I, pp. 282f. and *Rang-shar,* pp. 549ff.

   With respect to the individual, this "triad" is one's presence *(snang-ba)* in a world as the visible expression of a formal gestalt *(sku)*; one's speech *(grag-pa)* as the audible expression of authentic utterance *(gsung)*; and one's thought processes *(dran-rig)* as the expression of vibrant spirituality *(thugs).* See *Chos-dbyings,* fol. 158b.

21. *gSang-snying,* fol. 21a.

21a. On the twofold operation of these elemental forces see Chapter II, note 46.

22. *Rong-'grel,* fol. 100b.

23. *Klong-'grel,* p. 408.

24. These identities are ordinary in the sense that they reflect the Mahāyāna conception of Reality in general. See *Rong-'grel,* fol. 100b.

25. These identities are extraordinary in that they are found only in the Mantrayāna, which bases itself on Experience-as-such. For Klong-chen rab-'byams-pa, however, these identities are extraordinary because they point to the internal logic of Being and the dynamics of its auto-presencing which, as Kun-tu bzang-po field, is beyond predication. See *Klong-'grel,* pp. 408f.

26. The term used in the original Tibetan and Sanskrit texts is *de-bzhin gshegs-pa* and *tathāgata* respectively, which may be rendered as "moving over and into the as-is." Although what these forces indicate has been given sensuous expression, it was only at a relatively late time in the history of Buddhist thought that a tendency arose, probably due to the influence of Hinduist concretism, to fixate on the various expressions of these forces—be they statues or paintings—without regard for the intentional messages of which these expressions were but sensuous indications. This tendency to fixate on the sensuous expressions and not the meanings of those forces termed

tathāgata, became reinforced with the introduction, into European works dealing with Buddhist art, of the term Dhyāni-Buddha—a late regional Nepalese term for the various sculptured and painted representations of the forces referred to as *tathāgata*. It was due to the influence of the British pro-consul to Nepal, Brian Houghton Hodgson, that the term Dhyāni-Buddha became elevated into an almost generic term and as such haunts Western and Eastern books on Buddhism.

27. *Chos-dbyings*, fol. 70b; see also fol. 147b.

28. *gSang-snying*, fol. 20b.

29. *lTa-phreng*, p. 10. See also Rong-zom-pa chos-kyi bzang-po's commentary on this passage in *Selected Writings*, pp. 101f. In discussing the various meanings of the word *rgyu*, *Rong-'grel*, fol. 97b is of particular interest because it emphasizes the importance of context in determining meaning. A word that has been given a certain meaning, that is, is used meaningfully, in one context does not have the same meaning in all other contexts.

30. *lTa-phreng*, p. 10. *Selected Writings*, p. 102. *Rong-'grel*, fol. 97b. *Klong-'grel*, p. 380, uses a different set of gnosemic nuclei: *OM* stands for Being's presencing *(snang-ba)*; *ĀH* stands for Being's openness *(stong-nyid)*; and *HŪM* stands for the indivisible complementarity *(dbyer-med)* of presencing and openness.

For Padmasambhava and Rong-zom-pa Chos-kyi bzang-po the transformations $A \longrightarrow O \longrightarrow OM$ are identity-*cum*-symmetry transformations
where $O = (A+U)$, and $OM = [(A+U)+M]$
so that $A \longrightarrow (A+U) \longrightarrow [(A+U)+M]$.

Each transformation constitutes an access to wholeness.

For a detailed discussion of these programs as optimum attainment standards see Chapter VIII.

31. *lTa-phreng*, p. 10. *Rong-'grel*, fol. 97b. *Selected Writings*, p. 102.

32. *lTa-phreng*, p. 11. *Selected Writings* p. 102, as well as *Rong-'grel*, fol. 97b, quite explicitly state that the use of the term *mngon-sum-(par)*, unmediated, in this context is quite different from its use in epistemological discussions of immediate perception, for the latter belong to the domain of the conventionally accepted reality mode. Unmediatedness in this context is the operation of Being's excitatory intelligence.

Padmasambhava goes on to explicate the emergence of this unmediated meaning-value understanding as a process having three phase specificities *(mtshan-nyid):*

> The excitatory intelligence (of Being) as four deeply probing understandings is the cognitiveness phase specificity; (its) repeated application is the engagement phase specificity, and the unmediated meaning-value understanding itself (emerging) through the power inherent in engagement is the climaxing phase specificity.

Rong-zom-pa Chos-kyi bzang-po, *Selected Writings*, pp. 102f. and *Rong-'grel*, fols. 97b f., illustrates these three phases of a self-organizing holistic process by the operations involved in testing the purity of gold. The meaningfulness of Being, which as Being-*qua*-Existenz makes each human being a special case, constitutes a value in itself, for which gold as the most precious metal is an appropriate symbol. However, there is no value without intelligence (appreciative of it), just as there is no intelligence that is not value-oriented and value-appreciative. To let this value-permeated intelligence shine, like gold in all its splendor, the application of intelligence as a deeply probing understanding is necessary. This application is a self-regenerating process through which the "dross" of hearsay and other impurities and obscurations—only too often considered to be understanding—is thoroughly eliminated.

CHAPTER II

1. This sentiment was long ago expressed by Blaise Pascal. See his *Pensées,* Paris: Gallimard, 1936, no. 335.
2. The term Existenz is here used to cover both the sense of *rgyud* (the continuity of a process) and that of *rang-bzhin-gyi rgyud* (the ontological, not ontic, character of reality). The phenomenological significance of this term has been detailed by Calvin O. Schrag, *Experience and Being,* pp. 257ff.
3. The "critical state" *('khrul-gzhi),* literally "the ground/reason for going astray," derives from the dynamics of Being which actualizes itself as a self-referential intentionality and emerges spontaneously. Its spontaneous presence *(lhun-grub)* constitutes the object phase of the intentional process; the act phase is Being's resonating concern *(thugs-rje)* with what just is. Thus the *Mu-tig phreng-ba,* p. 535, states:

> Although the ground/reason for going astray has been explained in
> many ways,
> (It can be summed up as) spontaneous presence *(lhun-grub)* and
> resonating concern *(thugs-rje).*

Self-referential intentionality is indicated by a gloss on spontaneous presence and resonating concern:

> In view of the difference between ground/reason *(gzhi)* and awareness
> of the ground/reason *(gzhi-shes-pa)*
> *[gzhi dang gzhi-shes-pa'i khyad-par-las].*

The spelling of the key-terms in the gloss tallies with a passage in the *Theg-pa kun-gyi spyi-phud* in *Klong-chen rab-'byams-kyi rgyud* (in rNying-rgyud, vol. 4, pp. 174-416), p. 201:

> From the difference between the ground and the awareness of the
> ground (as to what it may be)
> There occurs the division into Saṃsāra and Nirvāṇa.

However, *Bi-ma* II, p. 46, and *Bla-dgongs,* vol. 10, p. 689, have *zhes* instead of *shes-(pa)* which would necessitate the rendering "difference between ground and judgment about (this) ground." Substantially the two versions have the same intention. The technical terms "act phase" and "object phase" are elaborated by Edward S. Casey, *Imagining,* pp. 38, 40-48 *et passim.*
4. A lengthy discussion of Existenz *(rgyud),* with particular reference to experience, is given by Klong-chen rab-'byams-pa in his monumental *Theg-mchog* I, pp. 169ff. A similar analysis is given by him in his *Grub-mtha',* pp.

383ff. Both accounts are based on *Mu-tig phreng-ba,* pp. 520ff.

5.   *Theg-mchog* I, pp. 171f. Here it is explicitly stated:

> Openness *(stong-pa),* the facticity *(ngo-bo)* of excitatory intelligence *(rig-pa),* devoid of anything that might be called substance and quality, has been there atemporally *(ye-nas)* as an utter freedom (unimpeded by) the limitations set by the linguistic horizon coextensive with intellectual-discursive activity.
>
> Lucency *(gsal-ba)* means that openness does not turn into utter nothingness but radiates in the light of five pristine cognitions that are the intrinsic light values (of this openness). Actuality *(rang-bzhin)* involving luminosity, warmth, coolness, etherialness, and expansivity, has been spontaneously present atemporally as the five elemental forces constituting the physical-material. The outward-directed glow as resonating concern *(thugs-rje)* never ceases, but rises as the creativity of life *(rtsal),* and hence permeates the atemporally (open) excitatory intelligence.

The three key-terms *ngo-bo, rang-bzhin* and *thugs-rje* are dynamic concepts. They have been explicated by Klong-chen rab-'byams-pa in his *Theg-mchog* I, p. 400 as follows:

> Facticity *(ngo-bo)* has been pure from the very beginning and has nothing to do with substance and quality. Actuality *(rang-bzhin)* has been there spontaneously as an intentional arch in which formal gestalt *(sku)* and pristine cognitiveness *(ye-shes)* can neither be joined to nor separated from each other. Since these two (facticity and actuality) constitute a single fact, they are the nonduality of a coming-into-presence and an openness. (Being's) presential mode is, in its facticity, open, invariant, and having a gestalt character (in which) the inseparability as well as the nonadditive character of the gestalt triad is such that although it is radiant within, like the sun, it is not given as substance and quality.
>
> Actuality has been atemporally an outward-directed glow *(gdangs);* although it shines in (specific) light values, its outward appearance has nothing to do with the specific colors (of the spectrum).
>
> Resonating concern, although there as the pristine cognitiveness deriving from excitatory intelligence, is not in its detectable operation a discursive involvement in (supposed) external objects. There just is this triad of facticity, actuality, and resonating concern.

For a discussion of the deep-structured dynamics of this triad that constitutes the "physical" universe and that of evolving sentient systems, see my *Kindly Bent,* vol. 2, pp. 30ff. The gestalt triad in this quotation refers to *chos-sku, longs-sku,* and *sprul-sku* whose meaning will be discussed in detail in Chapter VIII. The technical term *ye-shes* (which rendered literally would correspond to the German *Ur-wissen),* as used in the original Tibetan texts, conveys either the singular or the plural sense and according to context it has been rendered either as "pristine cognitiveness" or as "pristine cognitions."

6.   *Theg-mchog* I, pp. 175, 387, 391.

7.   *Theg-mchog* I, pp. 175ff.

8.   *Mu-tig phreng-ba,* pp. 528f.

9. *ma-rig-pa* (Sanskrit *avidyā*). In purely epistemological contexts this term is commonly rendered as "ignorance." However, it is not a denial of "knowledge" *(rig-pa*, Sanskrit *vidyā*), which would have been rendered in Tibetan as *rig-pa med-pa*. The term *ma-rig-pa* merely states that the cognitive capacity is not up to its optimum operation. While, to give an example, "nonviolence" *(ahiṃsā*, Tibetan *'tshe-ba med-pa)* is a denial of violence *(hiṃsā*, Tibetan *'tshe-ba), avidyā* was never understood as indicating such a denial. Hence the *a-* in *ahiṃsā* and *avidyā* was seen as serving different functions. That *ma-rig-pa* implies something quite different from *rig-pa med-pa* is clearly stated by mKhan-po Nus-ldan in his *mKhas-'jug mchan-'grel*, a commentary on 'Jammgon 'Ju Mi-pham rgya-mtsho's *mKhas-'jug*, p. 525.

10. *ye-shes gsum brtsegs*. For a discussion of hierarchical structure see below note 26.

11. The "four lamps" are operators through which resonating concern reaches into its domain or field of operation. They constitute a functionally related "system" having to do with activities that seem to be associated with the right and left hemispheres of the brain. Readers interested in the specifics of these lamps should consult the lengthy discussion in *Tshig-don*, pp. 102, 142ff.; *Theg-mchog* I, pp. 555ff., and the concise presentation in *mKha'-yang* II, pp. 214f. See also note 52.

12. These intensities begin with the awareness of the internal logic of Being *(chos-nyid)* when, as one might say, the meaningfulness of existence dawns upon us in a deeply felt, nondiscursive, way. As this feeling grows deeper and deeper, the process progressively stabilizes itself. These intensities mark transitions to higher regimes facilitating the reestablishment of an undivided and indivisible wholeness. A detailed account of these intensities has been given in *Theg-mchog* II, pp. 166ff. The earliest account seems to have been presented in *Thal-'gyur*, p. 91.

13. In his *mKha'-snying* I, p. 345, Klong-chen rab-'byams-pa states:

> Facticity has an open quality with its self-contained glow never ceasing as (presenting) a meaning-saturated gestalt. (Its) lucency in an array of five pristine cognitions is termed "spontaneously present." The intrinsic creativity of these two (features of facticity and spontaneity), which manifests as anything whatsoever, is termed "all-encompassing resonating concern."

This statement seems to have anticipated H.R. Maturana's idea of autopoiesis coordination as the characteristic of intelligence. See Erich Jantsch, *Erkenntnistheoretische Aspekte*, pp. 121, 163 and *The Self-Organizing Universe*, p. 203.

14. *Yid-bzhin*, p. 828. *gNas-lugs*, p. 45.

15. *Tshig-don*, p. 175

16. *Tshig-don*, p. 175. *Theg-mchog* II, p. 164.

17. *mKha'-yang* II, p. 399. the indivisibility of *dbyings* and *rig* is also clearly stated in *mKha'-snying* I, p. 66.

18. Calvin O. Schrag, *Experience and Being*, p. 18.

19. This omnipresence is clearly stated in *mKha'-yang* II, pp. 64f.

20. *Theg-mchog* I, p. 220.

21. *Theg-mchog* I, p. 220.

22. *Theg-mchog* I, p. 391. In support of this statement Klong-chen rab-'byams-pa

quotes the *bKra-shis mdzes-ldan chen-po'i rgyud* (in *Ati,* vol. 1, pp. 207-232), p. 210, which declares:

> Before there had arisen (the state of being a) Buddha through under-standing, and before there had arisen (the state of being a) sentient being through lack of understanding, excitatory intelligence (as a) self-existent pristine cognitiveness had as yet not moved away from Being, but was there operative in three (modes as a) coming-into-presence independent of any conditions (for such presencing).

As this text then explains, the three modes of this coming-into-presence are the three features: facticity, actuality, and resonating concern. Klong-chen rab-'byams-pa goes on to quote, so as to give further support, from the *Thal-'gyur,* p. 127.

23. *Tshig-don,* p. 28.
24. *mKha'-yang* II, p. 224.
25. See *Thal-'gyur,* p. 84. This passage is also quoted in *mKha'-snying* I, p. 345; *mKha'-yang* I, p. 646; II, pp. 70, 82. But in *mKha'-yang* II, p. 197 it is said to occur in the *Nor-bu phra-bkod rang-gi don thams-ca gsal-bar byed-pa'i rgyud* (in *Ati,* vol. 2, pp. 1-75). It does *not* occur there, and this is one of the many instances where Klong-chen rab-'byams-pa's references do not tally with the extant texts.
26. This vertically structured hierarchy constitutes a process whose fluctuations occur as upward or downward perturbations. In his *Zab-yang* I, p. 300, Klong-chen rab-'byams-pa states:

> Facticity—pure from the very beginning and utterly open;
> Actuality—spontaneously there with an outward-directed glow;
> Resonating concern—excitatory intelligence with creative energy;
> These are the three modalities of pristine cognitiveness.

It need hardly be emphasized that this triad remains an undivided whole *(dbyer-med)* throughout all its fluctuations despite the perturbatory nuances that pristine cognitiveness *(ye-shes)* exhibits in its outward glow and spread. This idea of an undivided whole as a continual process seems to be quite similar to David Bohm's notion of a "*holomovement,* which is an unbroken and undivided totality." See David Bohm, *Wholeness and the Implicate Order,* p. 151. A very succinct account of this indivisibility is given by Klong-chen rab-'byams-pa in *mKha'-snying* I, pp. 342ff.; *mKha'-yang* I, p. 463. This hierarchically operative pristine cognitiveness constitutes the energy *(snying-po)* which, inexhaustible and always available, forever tends toward optimization. The *Seng-ge rtsal-rdzogs,* p. 257, states:

> In the center of the heart of each and every
> Sentient being in the three world spheres there resides this
> Energy in a triple hierarchical order of pristine cognitiveness.
> As to its facticity it has nothing to do with obscuration;
> Yet its obscuration occurs through sentient beings' intellect, acting
>   like an eye disease.
> Furthermore, where the (thematizing) intellect is (operative) there
>   is a (concretizing) coming-into-presence;

But when there is understanding (which is not thematizing) there is
a (diaphanous) arising (of possibilities).
(Whatever becomes) an object for the intellect (involves its) grasping (by the intellect);
When there is understanding there is an auto-presencing (of Being
to itself).

This text goes on to discuss a distinction in the deep-structure of human
experience between the standing-wave patterns of being a Buddha *(sangs-
rgyas)* and being a sentient being *(sems-can)*. These patterns would seem to be
similar to what David Bohm has called the implicate and explicate order
respectively. See David Bohm, *Wholeness and the Implicate Order,* pp.
149ff., 196ff.

27. This freedom, as a dynamic feature in each of the three energy aspects of
Being, has been summed up by Klong-chen rab-'byams-pa in his auto-
commentary on his *Chos-dbyings,* fol. 159a:

The three (aspects of) energy are such that as a naked energy which has
been atemporally free *(ye-grol),* it is open *(stong-pa);* that as a naked
energy which has been free in and by itself *(rang-grol),* it is lucent
(gsal-ba); and that as a naked energy which has been abidingly free
(gnas-grol), it is unceasing *('gag-med).*

Klong-chen rab-'byams-pa's presentation is a variation of a statement in the
Rang-shar, p. 433, according to which

that which is open *(stong-ba)* is the energy that is pristine cognitiveness; that which is lucent *(gsal-ba)* is the energy of the light values in
cognitiveness; and that which is self-originated *(rang-byung)* is the
energy in excitatory intelligence.

According to the gloss to this passage, the first specification refers to facticity, the second to its field, and the third is an illustration. The term *rang-
byung* is short for *rang-byung-gi ye-shes* (self-originated pristine
cognitiveness). It is functionally synonymous with *rig-pa* (excitatory intelligence) which, in turn, is synonymous with *snying-po* (energy), particularly
when it occurs in the compound *bde-gshegs snying-po* l(the energy that
makes a system move in the direction of self-optimization). See below note
55.
28. *Bi-ma* I, p. 444.
29. *Bi-ma* I, p. 64, also quoted in *mKha'-yang* II, pp. 365f.
30. In *mKha'-yang* II, p. 346, the discursiveness of representational thought is an
additional preoccupation that has to be overcome, so as to open the way
toward understanding.
31. *Theg-mchog* I, p. 629.
32. *Thal-'gyur,* p. 156.
33. *Rang-shar,* p. 451.
34. *don. Thal-'gyur,* p. 157.
35. *Thal-'gyur,* p. 129. A different interpretation is given on p. 154, where *ye* is
said to be a lucency and sensitivity and *shes* to be intrinsic freedom. All these
definitions occur with variant readings also in *Tshig-don,* pp. 123, 464 and
Theg-mchog I, p. 629.

36. *Thal-'gyur*, p. 110.
37. This idea of pristine cognitiveness being *in* the body seems to have been widespread. It is mentioned in the *sGron-ma snang-byed* (in *Bi-ma* II, pp. 1-59) and elaborated upon in the *Seng-ge rtsal-rdzogs*, p. 308:

> In each body of every sentient being
> There resides pristine cognitiveness *(ye-shes)* tending toward its coming-into-presence in the purity (of imaginative possibilities).
> It is, however, unable to do so to its full extent—
> Just as (a child) in (the mother's) womb or (a bird still) in the egg
> Is not directly visible. But although it lies there covered,
> Once its creative capability has fully developed, it will burst forth.
> So, the moment this body, (as seen through) concepts and discursive ventures has been left behind,
> (Pristine cognitiveness) meets its domain, the auto-presencing (of Being as a self-referential movement).
> This self-excitatoriness *(rang-rig)* which has been there atemporally,
> Is seen (in its) facticity into which no dichotomic concepts enter.
> (This means that) pristine cognitiveness tending toward its coming-into-presence is the purity (of imaginative possibilities) and that
> Buddhahood, the true reality, is seen.

Klong-chen rab-'byams-pa quotes the above passage in support of his presentation in *gNas-lugs*, p. 24:

> Just as clouds in the sky disperse into the source of their origin and,
> Just as a crystal's sparkling rays subside again in the crystal,
> So also Being's coming-into-presence with its perspectives of Saṃsāra and Nirvāṇa, which has arisen from Being (itself),
> Takes (again) its seat, that which has been pure from the very beginning *(ka-dag)*, in its facticity that is Being.
> This is what can be asserted about all and everything that is:
> It coils itself up in its own bed (which is the) continuum (of Being), the spontaneous thereness *(lhun-grub)* (of Being).
> All horizons (set up intellectually and expressed in language) subside by themselves in the vortex (of Being), which knows of no division (of and in itself through) conceptualization.

In his auto-commentary, pp. 551f., to the above passage, he says that:

> The cessation of mistaken notions that make themselves felt *('khrul-snang)* as Saṃsāra, is like the clearing of the sky; the subsiding of the images of (pure) realms *(zhing-snang)* which are Nirvāṇa, is like the reabsorption of the rays of a crystal in the crystal from which they had burst forth; and the dispersal of moods that are tied in with discursive thought patterns, is like the releasement of representational thinking into utter openness. This (whole process) is Buddhahood-experience

in its primordiality *(thog-ma'i gzhi-la sangs-rgyas)*.

It may not be out of place here to emphasize that the nominalizing power of the Indo-European languages lends itself to the formation of static concepts, which then dominate all thought. These hardly do justice to dynamic concepts in general and to Buddhist thought in particular. An awareness of this peculiarity prompted C.G. Jung to speak of the "thingness of thought." The technical term *sangs-rgyas* has always been understood as a going away *(sangs)* of anything that limits, obscures, distorts, and an expanding *(rgyas)* of a potential to its fullest. This movement is Being *(gzhi)*, dynamically active before there is any static being. See also Chapter I, note 19.

That pristine cognitiveness *(ye-shes)* in an ultimate sense *(chen-po)* resides in the body *(lus)*, without being a derivative of the body, is also attested in the *Hevajratantra* I i, 12. In the *Legs-bshad nyi-ma'i 'od-zer*, the famous commentary on the *Hevajratantra* by Dwags-po pan-chen bKra-shis rnam-rgyal (1512/13-1587), pp. 83f., the author relates this idea to the *Mahāyānottaratantraśāstra* I 27. In another commentary on the *Hevajratantra*, the *Kyai rdor rgyud-kyi tshig-don rnam-par bshad-pa man-ngag-gi mdzod*, written in 1975 by the Ven. Brag-phug dge-bshes dGe-'dun rin-chen, the author on pp. 50f., associates *ye-shes* with bliss *(bde-ba)*. Most noteworthy, he criticizes the prevalent pseudointellectual trends among Tibetan exegetics, specifically the followers of the *dbu-ma*, who claim to present the Madhyamaka philosophy "authentically," yet champion an ontically empty Absolute, which was characterized by their critics as "sterile emptiness" *(bem-stong)*. Even among some enthusiasts of Tibetan Buddhism in the Western cultural milieu, both antiintellectual fundamentalism and pseudointellectual trends can be detected. Those who champion the latter mostly engage in a strident expatiation of hollow phrases, which they camouflage as "authentic" Buddhological praxis, thereby revealing their failure, and often also their fear, of understanding the raw, naked, and contingent nature of experience.

38. On the relationship between affective processes and pristine cognitions, see my *The Tantric View of Life*, pp. 37ff.

39. *Bi-ma* II, p. 444. According to *Bi-ma* I, p. 604, the relationship between *lus* and *sku* is similar to opacity and diaphaneity respectively. Each opacity as a specific topological transformation yet retains its specific diaphanous invariance. See also *Bi-ma* I, p. 590. In *mKha'-yang* III, p. 125 the term *sbubs* (envelope) is used instead of *lus*. The use of this term seems to indicate a topological property that is not so readily noticeable with the term *lus*. According to the "larger" *gSang-snying* (the *rgyas-pa*), p. 263, formal gestalt *(sku)* as diaphanous, is experienced in releasement, and body *(lus)* as belonging to Saṃsāra, is linked with representational thinking. A detailed discussion of the term *sbubs* is found in *Thig-le kun-gsal*, pp. 245f., 262f., 285.

40. This level of experience is referred to by three related terms that indicate subtle nuances in the auto-transforming process. There is the *ye-shes sgyu-ma'i sku*, a gestalt as virtual (*Theg-mchog* I, p. 227). There is also the *ye-shes sgyu-ma'i sbubs*, a shrouding over or topological transformation process (*mKha'-yang* III, pp. 135, 198f.). Lastly, there is the *ye-shes sgyu-ma'i lus*, the final form and shape the transformation process has taken (*Bi-ma* II, p. 440).

41. This is also known as the *lhun-grub rin-po-che'i sbubs*. See also *Theg-mchog* I, p. 391; II, p. 563. *mKha'-yang* II, p. 71; III, pp. 128, 157, 196. *Zab-yang* II,

pp. 221, 483f. *Bi-ma* II, p. 339. In itself it is a presencing that is as yet indeterminate; it is not yet recognizable as either formal gestalt or transformation and transmutation into a body. This ambiguous state of affairs— being neither gestalt *(sku)* nor body *(lus)*—is resolved when one becomes aware of both of them as aspects of a process which, paradoxically speaking, is as much an invariance *(sku)* as a transformation *(lus)*. In *Bi-ma* II, p.124 it is clearly stated that a formal gestalt is not an end-in-itself, but a path *(lam)*.

42. This difficult point is expressed in *mKha'-yang* III, p. 196:

Since there is no demarcation that could distinctly make a separation between an exterior and interior, this is a hyperinteriority.

The term "hyperinteriority" *(kun-tu yang nang-du gyur-pa)* is taken from *gSang-snying*, fol. 2b.

43. *Kun-tu bzang-po thugs-kyi me-long-gi rgyud* (in *Ati*, vol.1, pp. 233-280), pp. 275f.

44. *Rig-pa rang-grol chen-po thams-cad 'grol-ba'i rgyud* (in *Ati*, vol. 3, pp. 1-72), p. 30 explicitly states that formal gestalt *(sku)* has nothing to do with form *(gzugs med)*. Inasmuch as "form" is understood in Buddhist thought as some distinct colored patch (serving as the objective constituent and epistemological object in perceptual situations), the above statement indicates that a formal gestalt is a pattern, a design that remains diaphanous and is not a representation of some thing.

45. This transformation process is of a special kind. First, there is a multiplicity *(du-ma shar-ba)* of formal gestalts *(sku)*, which are transformed into a multiplicity of embodied levels *(lus)* including the multiplicity of specific human beings. Second, there is the operator termed "creativity" *(rtsal)*, which effects the transformation.

A highly schematized representation of this transformation of gestalts into embodied levels via the operator "creativity" is as follows:

FIGURE 1

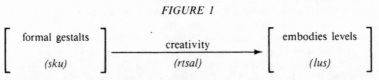

According to *Bi-ma* II, p. 339, in addition to the transformation shown in Figure 1, the following two transformations also simultaneously occur:

FIGURE 2

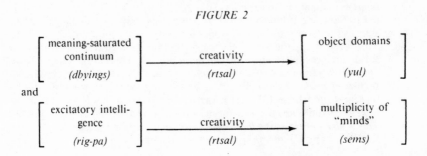

According to another schema, based on *Bla-yang* II, p. 238 and *Zab-yang* II, p. 239, three simultaneous transformations are indicated as follows:

FIGURE 3

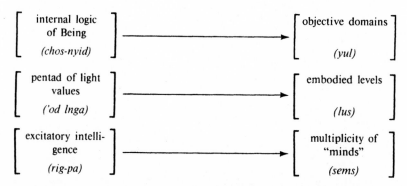

Bearing in mind the proviso that the multiplicity is not actually that of discrete isolatable elements, but rather that of facets or a contextualized field, if one does model this multiplicity as amenable to mathematical formalization, then Figures 1, 2, and 3 can be diagrammed as follows:

FIGURE 4

$$\{\, s_n \,\} \xrightarrow{\quad \delta \quad} \{\, t_m \,\}$$

This resembles the Hausdorff transformation in which a series s is transformed into a series t having the form $t = (\delta\mu\delta)s$, where δ is the transformation that transforms the series

$$\{\, s_n \,\} \quad \text{into the series} \quad \{\, t_m \,\} \quad \text{given by}$$

$$t_m = \sum_{n=0}^{m} (-1)^m [m!n!(m-n)!] s_n$$

and where μ is a transformation that multiplies each term in a series by a specific constant. In the context under discussion δ is "creativity" *(rtsal)* and μ is "arising in multiplicity" *(du-ma shar-ba)*.

As just noted, however, all terms shown in Figures 1 - 3 are contextually related facets whose mutually informing connectedness (indicated by the sign "⟵⟶") may be diagrammed as follows:

FIGURE 5

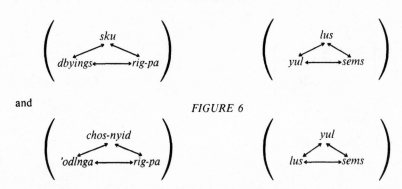

and

FIGURE 6

Although both figures 5 and 6 refer to transformations occurring within Being-*qua*-Existenz as it tends toward ontic levels of existence, they yet indicate a difference of emphasis. Figure 5 emphasizes the noetic pole of Being-*qua*-Existenz as the prethematically given presence of Experience-as-such, whereas Figure 6 emphasizes the noematic pole of Being-*qua*-Existenz (that which is as yet prethematically experienced)—both ending up in ontic objectification.

46.   Since the time of Einstein we know that what is called "matter" is a form of energy, and just as there are different aspects of energy, there are also different degrees of matter. The elemental forces *('byung-ba),* out of which the material world (including our physical body) is constituted, operate in a twofold manner. On the one hand, light values or frequencies *(dvangs-ma)* propagate radiant energy, while, on the other hand, this energy is transformed into various densities *(snyigs-ma).* In this process of radiation becoming matter, the physical-material world (and our own physical-material body) is formed. However, since radiation is not without excitatory intelligence, within this radiation transformation process the high energy phenomenon of excitatory intelligence *(rig-pa)* is transmuted into the low energy phenomenon of a mind *(sems).* Thus, a single process appears to operate with respect to both a body and a mind. *mKha'-yang* III, p. 188 states:

> ...the quincunx of light values or frequencies turns into domains (of interest) and the physical body (in interaction with these domains). Resonating concern (which operates by the energy of) excitatory intelligence goes astray into (a system of bifurcating) concepts. When this network of concepts has been fitted into the sheath of the body, body and mind are established as a duality, and this (body-mind complex) moves through the six kinds of living beings in the three world spheres.

47.   This "treasure" in it is said neither to increase nor decrease. See *mKha'-yang* III, p. 188; *Theg-mchog* I, p. 641.
48.   *Mahāyānottaratantraśāstra* I, pp. 112-113.
49.   The *rgyas-pa,* p. 280, explicitly states:

> If this mystery is revealed
> To (the followers of the) Hīnayāna or those who hold perverted
>   views
> They will, not understanding the real meaning of mystery,
> Take their daily behavior as
> The ultimately valid norm
> And pervert the very meaning of mystery.
> Since a person who does not understand it will go to hell,
> It has to be concealed from him.

According to a modern commentary on the *gSang-snying*, the *Zab-don lde'u-mig*, written by 'Gyur-med phan-bde 'od-zer in 1924, p. 99, it is the literalist from whom this mystery has to be kept away. He is unfit for it, as is a dirty vessel for "lion's milk" (a high-quality substance).

50. On the terms "act phase" and "object phase" see above note 3.

51. *gSang-snying*, fol. 5a. The sense of wonder has a double significance. On the one hand, it is an expression expressed; on the other hand, this expression serves as a means to recapture the sense of wonder, to raise the mind from its drabness to the level of pristine cognitiveness. All commentaries on the *gSang-snying*, regardless of which tradition, are unanimous on this point. In his *gNas-lugs*, p. 18, Klong-chen rab-'byams-pa uses the same five facets of wonder to indicate the undivided intensity *(phyal-ba)* of life's energy as man's existential value *(don-gyi snying-po)*:

> This then is life's energy whose undivided intensity can be
>   asserted:
> External things present the reach and range of that which is open
>   and has never come into existence (as some thing);
> Since (this reach and range itself) has no locus, and neither comes
>   nor goes, it is beyond predication.
> The images (expressive of it) have no bounds, retaining their free-
>   dom in their (ceaseless) rising;
> They are like the tracks of a bird in the sky, unnoticeable.

The auto-commentary, p. 122, states:

> From the perspective of excitatory intelligence, all the things (claimed to be) external objects have an open texture, like a reflection which, without existing as some thing, yet is a lucent coming-into-presence; and all the images (claimed to be) internal (features of psychic life), although coming-into-presence vibratingly, disappear by themselves without being objectively noticeable, like the tracks of a bird soaring in the sky. Since perceptions occur ceaselessly in (and on) the ground of excitatory intelligence, which is not the coming-into-existence (of some thing) because it is not found eanywhere (as any thing), Being's coming-into-presence has been dissociated from the perspective of representational thought.

52. These two aspects are termed *ji-lta-ba mkhyen-pa'i ye-shes* and *ji-snyed-pa mkhyen-pa'i ye-shes*. See *Theg-mchog* II, p. 19; *mKha'-yang* II, pp. 79f.;

Tshig-don, pp. 477f. In *Tshig-don,* p. 142 and *Theg-mchog* I, p. 645, these two operations are identified with the four lamps. See above note 11.

53.   *gSang-snying,* fol. 6a. The translation is based on Klong-chen rab-'byams-pa's commentary on this text, the *Klong-'grel,* p. 107.

54.   *gSang-snying,* fol. 6a; *Klong-'grel,* p. 108.

55.   *bde-(bar) gshegs-(pa'i) snying-po.* The connotation of this term as rendered above, is central to the existential (ontological) as contrasted with the epistemological (ontic) approach. On this difference see the reference in Chapter I, note 9. As Rong-zom-pa Chos-kyi bzang-po points out in his *Rong-'grel,* fol. 63b, in the common *(thun-mong)* presentation of Buddhist thought this term implies:

> Sentient beings carry within them an incorruptible seed acting as the cause for (momentum in reaching a state characterized as) limpid clearness and consummate perspicacity *(byang-chub).* In the profound *(zab-mo)* presentation, Experience-as-such *(sems-kyi rang-bzhin-nyid)* is this limpid clearness and consummate perspicacity, and hence the energy *(snying-po)* suffusing it.

It is important to note that when emphasis is on Experience-as-such, the indigenous Tibetan texts, mostly of the old tradition *(rnying-ma),* clearly distinguish between *sems-nyid* (Experience-as-such) and *sems* "mind" as a feedback mechanism for representational thought processes. For the old tradition *sems-nyid* (or as in the above quotation *sems-kyi rang-bzhin-nyid*) is synonymous with *ye-shes* and *rig-pa.* See for instance *Tshig-don,* pp. 116f.; *mKha'-yang* II, pp. 197f., 233; *Zab-yang* II, pp. 119f.; *Bla-yang* I, pp. 442f.; *Theg-mchog* I, p. 625 *et passim.* For a detailed discussion of the term *bde-gshegs snying-po* see *Theg-mchog* I, pp. 641ff.; *Tshig-don,* p. 122; *Yid-bzhin,* pp. 804ff., *Grub-mtha',* pp. 369f.; *dGongs-zang,* vol. 2, p. 384; vol. 4, p. 241. In *mKha'-yang* II, p. 197 the energy *(snying-po)* suffusing the whole process is equated with pristine cognitiveness *(ye-shes).*

56.   *gSang-snying,* fol. 6a.

57.   *gSang-snying,* fol. 6a.

CHAPTER III

1.   *Theg-mchog* I, p. 177.

2.   The *gSang-snying,* fol. 4b, qualifies the term *yid* (subjective mind) by *rdo-rje* (a symbol for indestructibility), and thereby indicates an ontological (in contradistinction to ontic) interpretation. "Indestructible subjectivity" is quite different from the metaphysical (ontic) subject of idealist philosophies. See also note 8.

3.   *Yid-bzhin,* pp. 70f. of the "root" text and pp. 793ff. in the commentary. For a discussion of the terms thematic and nonthematic see Calvin O. Schrag, *Experience and Being,* pp. 45ff.

4.   Klong-chen rab-'byams-pa points out in his auto-commentary to this text, pp. 794f., that "here" indicates the Vajrayāna. This aspect of Buddhism is also called "climax" *('bras-bu)* because as a spiritual pursuit it moves toward higher regimes ("climax"), but these higher regimes initiate, as it were, their

pursuit. Life is here seen as a self-regulatory, "self-explicating" system. This is technically termed "making the goal the path." See for instance *Grub-mtha'*, p. 273 and *Klong-'grel*, pp. 479f.

5. This image is meant to evoke the presential mode *(gnas-lugs)* of Being. In his *Bla-yang* I, p. 294, Klong-chen rab-'byams-pa speaks of this mode in the following images:

> This universal ground as the beginning (which is no beginning in the ordinary sense)
> Is the triad of facticity, actuality, and resonating concern.
> Since it never ceases in its being open, lucent, and the reason and ground for whatever may arise,
> Like the sky, the sun and moon, and a mirror,
> It has been there atemporally as an ultimate spontaneous presence.

The Tibetan language has a number of terms for the auto-initiatory dynamics of Being. The term *gdod-ma,* rendered in the above passage as "beginning (which is no beginning in the ordinary sense)" seems to imply a quasitemporal beginning, while the term *ye-nas,* rendered as "atemporally," has no such temporal or quasi-temporal connotation because what it refers to is there "before" the notion of time emerges. Another term, sometimes used with reference to a so-called "beginning" is *thog-ma,* which according to *Bi-ma* I, p. 76, is synonymous with *ye-nas.* The semantic boundaries of these terms, however, are somewhat fluid; they are more evocative than denotative.

6. *stong-pa.* Experientially this term refers to a "feeling" of openness, while analytically it may be understood as what in mathematics is termed an "empty set."

7. See Chapter I note 55.

8. *tshogs-brgyad.* They are the operations to which we give the generic term "consciousness." There are five perceptive functions coordinated with five sensory capacities and their domains. These five functions, however, are not adequate to account for the full range of consciousness. Long before Kant, the Indian tradition knew that no amount of abstraction from sensory data can yield the notion of, say, an elephant; such a notion is brought to the sensory data. This, the sixth function, or formative operation is termed *yid-kyi rnam-par shes-pa* (in Sanskrit *manovijñāna*). See also note 2 above on the term *yid* (which is often used as a shorthand term for the longer *yid-kyi rnam-par shes-pa*). Another, (seventh) operation concerns the fact that all perceptions are related to a center which, like the perceptions themselves, is an event and not an abiding entity. This central event is affectively toned and accounts for the fact that all perceptions are constituted against a background "mood" which then sustains them and gives them the specific ego-centeredness of consciousness. This operation is termed *nyon-yid* (in Sanskrit *kliṣṭamanas*) or *nyon-mongs-pa'i yid-kyi rnam-par shes-pa* (in Sanskrit *kliṣṭamanovijñāna*). The eighth operation is what may be called the genotype of conscious life *kun-gzhi'i rnam-par shes-pa* (in Sanskrit *ālaya-vijñāna*), constituting the "inherited program of instructions" *bag-chags,* (in Sanskrit *vāsanā),* which control the development of an individual.

9. The triple structure refers to virtual processes which assume a gestalt character:

a meaning-saturated gestalt *(chos-sku)*, which expresses the meaningfulness of Being and through which this meaningfulness is expressed; a scenario gestalt *(longs-sku)*, which is experienced as communication not in the sense of a transfer of bits of information to some other system, but as a kind of reorientation within a field of interactive processes; and a display gestalt *(sprul-sku)*, which is experienced as those cultural ideas and values which an individual aspires to realize in his life.

10. *snying-po'i khams.* The reasons for rendering this difficult term in this manner may be appreciated by a consideration of the highly complex understanding attached to the term *snying-po* in rDzogs-chen treatises. Here, the term *snying-po,* in its technical usage, seems to come closest to the modern quantum mechanical notion of energy. Klong-chen rab-'byams-pa says in his *Chos-dbyings,* fol. 159a:

> Energy *(snying-po)* has three states: (1) a naked energy *(rjen-pa'i snying-po)* that is atemporally free *(ye-grol)*—an open dimension *(stong-pa);* (2) a naked energy that is intrinsically free *(rang-grol)*—a lucent (radiating) dimension *(gsal-ba);* and (3) a naked energy that is abidingly free *(gnas-grol)*—a ceaseless process *('gag-med).*

Furthermore, the *Rang-shar,* p. 433, declares this energy to be specifically associated with excitatory intelligence *(rig-pa)* that operates on each of the three energy states of Being *(gzhi)*:

> Openness is the energy of pristine cognitiveness *(ye-shes snying-po)* as facticity, *ngo-bo;* lucency is the energy of light *('od-kyi snying-po)* as the field, *dbyings;* and self-existence as that which is beyond efforts, *rtsol-ba-las 'das-pa,* is the energy of excitatory intelligence *(rig-pa'i snying-po).*

Bearing in mind the operational equivalents of what has been termed "the ceaseless (ongoing) process" *('gag-med)* in the first quotation and "self-originated" *(rang-byung)* in the second quotation, we may now proceed to a schematic formalization of the above in terms of quantum mechanical theory. We use the model of the Schrödinger equation.

$$H\Psi = E\Psi$$

where H is the Hamiltonian operator, E is the eigenvalue, and Ψ is the eigenstate. In the context of the rDzogs-chen understanding, here discussed, Ψ is the wave function that contains all the information about the dynamic properties of that "system" termed Being (reality-as-such, *gzhi*). The energy values E of the system *(snying-po)* are the eigenvalues of the Hamiltonian operator termed "excitatory intelligence" *(rig-pa).*

In tabular form, one can indicate the three eigenstates of the wave functions termed Being Ψ *(gzhi)* and their corresponding eigenvalues E *(snying-po)* of the Hamiltonian as follows:

FIGURE 7

Eigenstates of functions $gzhi$ for system termed Being	Corresponding eigenvalues $E_{snying-po}$ of the Hamiltonian for the system
$gzhi_1$ = $ye\text{-}grol \longleftrightarrow stong\text{-}pa$	$E_{snying-po_1}$ = $ye\text{-}shes\ snying\text{-}po$
$gzhi_2$ = $rang\text{-}grol \longleftrightarrow gsal\text{-}ba$	$E_{snying-po_2}$ = $'od\text{-}kyi\ snying\text{-}po$
$gzhi_3$ = $gnas\text{-}grol \longleftrightarrow 'gag\text{-}med$	$E_{snying-po_3}$ = $rig\text{-}pa'i\ snying\text{-}po$

Here the sign " $\longleftrightarrow$ " signifies functional equivalence.

A cautionary note, however, seems to be in order, for, to regard these eigenvalues as easily and exactly determinable or, with respect to the Dzogs-chen understanding being discussed here, as state-specific experiences that are precisely measurable:

....Hamiltonians are very complicated, and their eigenvalue cannot be found exactly: the three major approximation techniques are pertur-bation theory, variation theory, and self-consistent field techniques.

(P.W. Atkins, *Quanta*, p. 89)

The only experiential "hints" regarding the "calculation" of these eigen-values are given in the quoted passage as glosses. Here, Ψ_{gzhi_1} is glossed by facticity *(ngo-bo)*, Ψ_{gzhi_2} glossed by field *(dbyings)* and Ψ_{gzhi_3} by beyond effort *(rtsol-ba-las 'das-pa)*. We leave it to the doggedly reductionist "behavioral" scientists to fabricate experimental approximation methods for more precise specifications of what these three glosses name.

Several important points should be brought out here regarding the signifi-cant implications of the Hamiltonian operation termed "excitatory intelli-gence" *(rig-pa)*. First, lest there be any doubt that this Hamiltonian operator here termed *rig-pa* "operates" over the *entire* range of the wave function Ψ_{gzhi}, one should note that this operator is also repeatedly characterized as "all-encompassing" *(kun-khyab)*. See for instance *Bi-ma* III, p. 4; *Theg-mchog* I, p. 175; and *Tshig-don*, p. 28.

Second, there is an intimate relationship between excitatory intelligence *(rig-pa)* and the naked *(rjen-pa)* dynamics *(lhun-grub)* of Being-*qua*-Existenz, about which Klong-chen rab-'byams-pa in his *Chos-dbyings*, fol. 158a has this to say:

The one and only place toward which excitatory intelligence tends, and where it will be settled in itself with no division occurring within it, is the naked initial purity *(ka-dag rjen-pa)* (of Being). The energy of its spontaneous presence *(lhun-grub)* (Existenz), is twofold: while its facticity remains the initial purity, its actuality is its very spon-taneity. Hence it is beyond (such predications as) eternalistic (eternalism *a parte ante*) and nihilistic (eternalism *a parte post*).

The third point regarding this Hamiltonian operator can be brought out by bearing in mind that the Hamiltonian is the operator for the total energy of the system and consists of a sum of terms corresponding to different contributions to the total energy. We may write this as

$$H = T + V$$

where H is the total Hamiltonian, T is the potential energy, and V is the kinetic energy of the system. This potential in the sense of intrinsic energy T is termed *khams bde-bar gshegs-pa'i snying-po*. It aptly describes the potential *(khams)* inhering "within" the very dynamics of the "system" termed a human being, as the energy *(snying-po)* which tends toward *(gshegs-pa'i)* optimization *(bde-bar)*. The so-called kinetic ("optimized") energy V, in this context, represents the totality of the various "optimized optimizers" *([bde-bar ~ de-bzhin] gshegs-pa)*, each with "their" vectorial specification *(rigs)*. Therefore, in "calculating" the total Hamiltonian, that is the totality of excitatory intelligence operating on the whole system (Being), one must include both the potential and kinetic energies.

This rather lengthy analysis of a single technical term *(rig-pa)* and its multilevel ramifications gives but a brief intimation of how the problem of mind's place in the universe has been probed by the rDzogs-chen thinkers.

11. This idea that all dichotomies are suspended is clearly stated in *Seng-ge rtsal-rdzogs*, pp. 286ff.

12. In his *mKa'-snying* I,p. 346, Klong-chen rab-'byams-pa indicates this individisibility *(dbyer-med)* as follows:

> Facticity is the indivisibility of a coming-into-presence and openness *(snang-stong)*; actuality is the indivisibility of lucency and openness *(gsal-stong)*; and resonating concern is the indivisibility of excitatory intelligence and openness *(rig-stong)*. Or, facticity is the indivisibility of excitatory intelligence and of openness; actuality is the indivisibility of a coming-into-presence and of openness; and resonating concern is the indivisibility of lucency and of openness.

13. *mKha'-yang* I, p. 462. *ka-dag* and *lhun-grub* are terms indicating the paradox of their being, so to say, "nothing" which yet turns out to be a "presence" not *of* something, but simply a sheer presencing. The fact that this paradox has both a field and pristine cognitive character, neither being separable, has been detailed by Klong-chen rab-'byams-pa in his "smaller" commentary on the *gSang-snying*, the *Yid-kyi mun-sel*, fols. 57a f. See also *mKha'-yang* II, p. 125; *Zab-yang* I, pp. 268, 279ff., 289; *Theg-mchog* I, pp. 380 ff.

14. *snang-srid*. Although all the standard Tibetan-English dictionaries give as the meaning "the visible, external world," the texts of the rNying-ma-pa tradition take this term as referring to both the external world *and* the interpretative perception of it. *Chos-dbyings*, fol. 150b, clearly states that this compound term *snang-srid* refers to both the world *(snod)* and the beings therein *(bcud)* in the sense that,

> *snod* (the container) is a coming-into-presence as the reflex of the five elemental forces, and *bcud* (the essence within the container) is the interpretive experiences constituting a mood spectrum ranging from happiness to misery, derived from actions and affective forces.

The *sNang-srid kha-sbyor*, p. 3, clearly states:

> *snang-ba* refers to the external object *(phyi'i yul)*,
>
> *srid-pa* refers to the internal mind *(nang-gi sems)*,
>
> *kha-sbyor* is their nonduality *(gnyis-su med-pa)*.
>
> *snang-ba* is the object selected by the five senses *(sgo-lnga'i rtog-yul)*,
>
> *srid-pa* is the five sensory perceptions *(rnam-shes rnam lnga)*,
>
> *kha-sbyor* is their invariance and unpremeditatedness *(mi-'gyur rtsis gdab med)*.
>
> *snang-ba* is the externalized biotic forces *(phyi'i dkar dmar yul)*,
>
> *srid-pa* is their inspection and cognition by the mind *(sems-kyi dran-rig)*,
>
> *kha-sbyor* is their indivisibility and (mutual) nonexclusion *(dbye-bsal med-pa)*.
>
> *snang-ba* is the world as container *(snod-kyi 'jig-rten)*,
>
> *srid-pa* is the sentient beings *(sems-can)* therein,
>
> *kha-sbyor* is the fact that (all this) has nothing to do with good or bad, affirmation or negation *(bzang-ngan dgag-sgrub med)*.

Rendering *sems-can* in the above quotation by "sentient being" is a concession to the traditional way in which Indo-Tibetan terms were translated. "Sentient being," with its emphasis on some being, is correct for the Sanskrit term *sattva*, but its Tibetan rendering emphasizes the character of representational thinking *(sems)* so that *sems-can* is someone who thinks thematically or has a mind (opinion). See also Chapter V, note 38.

15. This is the interpretation which Klong-chen rab-'byams-pa gives of the *yang-dag kun-rdzob* in *Yid-kyi mun-sel*, fol. 59a.

16. *gSang-snying*, fol. 18b.

17. That this distinction is one of direct action, implying a movement and a way, is most clearly stated in the *Rin-po-che 'phags-lam bkod-pa'i rgyud* (in *rNying-rgyud*, vol. 4, pp. 152-174), p. 162:

> In the ground (Being) that is atemporally pure,
>
> The two states of being a Buddha and being a sentient being
>
> Do not exist in such a duality.
>
> The ground itself (Being) is the state of being a Buddha, which is the understanding of (Being), and
>
> It is there as a formal gestalt and (its experience in) pristine cognitiveness.
>
> The ground itself (Being) is the state of being a sentient being which is the nonunderstanding of (Being);
>
> It is there as a body with its sedimented drives and tendencies.
>
> Therefore, where there is the understanding of the ground (Being)
>
> There is no differentiation between the state of being a Buddha and the state of being a sentient being.
>
> It is (only) when one embarks on a spiritual pursuit (path) that they

come-into-presence as different.

Here these states of being a Buddha or of being a sentient being can be understood in terms of what David Bohm has called holomovement. See Chapter II note 26.

18. *gSang-snying,* fol. 7b, as interpreted by Klong-chen rab-'byams-pa (*Klong-'grel,* pp. 155ff.) who sees the evolution of Saṃsāra as a kind of externalization or "misplaced concreteness"—to use Whitehead's diction—of the internal logic of Being. Quite a different analysis, apparently involving a rearrangement of the verse lines in the *gSang-snying* and taking five lines, instead of four, to form a conceptual unit, is offered by g.Yung-ston rdo-rje dpal bzang-po, *gSal-byed me-long,* fols. 62a ff.:

> On account of the subject (the grasping) and object (the graspable) dichotomy, which (represents the) bifurcating (power of) that stepped-down intelligence [which by virtue of not recognizing itself for what it is provides the momentum in the process, and by virtue of its divisive power ushers in the notion that individuals and objects have an ontic status]
> All [sentient beings residing in] this world constitute what is meant by mistakenness, [for Saṃsāra just is mistakenness].
> [Caught within both] an external and internal nexus
> Each and every one, [in constituting] a different [genus], experiences happiness and frustration;
> Yet this [whole] state of affairs has not slipped from Experience-as-such [which is a configuration of formal gestalt and pristine cognitiveness].

> Given the differentiation into the authentic [ultimate reality] and magic-like [conventionally accepted reality] modes,
> A self [as the eightfold cognitive ensemble] and a self's [possession as the psychophysical ensemble] and [all that is] other [than these, that is, the elemental forces] are not found [as something existent in the ultimate reality mode...The two reality modes, accessible as four identities, are in being]
> Diaphanously pure [not different with respect to] that continuum [which is identical with itself, and hence they constitute] a single mode.

> A self [as the eightfold cognitive ensemble operating as stepped-down intelligence] and a self's [possession as the fivefold psychophysical ensemble] and [all that is] other [than these, that is, the elemental forces manifesting as objects] are but absurd constructs and
> There is nothing subtle [such as an atomic particle as claimed by the Śrāvakas] or profound [such as a momentary cognitive entity as claimed by the Pratyekabuddhas] in them.
> There is but one absurd construction engaging with another absurd construction [forming a series],

But no moving into [or even becoming] something else.

g. Yung-ston rdo-rje dpal bzang-po understands the first verse as indicating the unitary character of Reality; the second verse as stating the logical reasons for such a unitary conception; and the third verse as highlighting the fallacies of reductionist philosophies.

19. *gSang-snying,* fol. 21a.

20. This rendering is the traditional one based on what the standard dictionaries indicate about the Sanskrit word *bhagavan.* Yet like most lexical transfers from Sanskrit, it fails to convey the rich semantic range of this term as hermeneutically interpreted by the Tibetans as *bcom-ldan-'das.* Though many interpretations are to be found in the indigenous Tibetan texts, that of Klong-chen rab-'byams-pa in *Klong-'grel,* pp. 29f. is exemplary:

> This is His nature: the four deadening powers have been in a state of having been atemporally vanquished *(bcom)* and so (He) possesses *(ldan)* the six qualitites of greatness, (meaning) that (He) is in a state of nonlocalizable Nirvāṇa *('das).* The manner in which the four deadening powers are in a state of having been vanquished is as follows: since the five affective forces are (actually) the five pristine cognitions, which have been atemporally operative, there exists nothing that can be accepted or rejected (regarding this fact). This is the (meaning of) vanquishing the deadening power of affective forces. Since there are no affective forces (as such), one cannot be born in Saṃsāra through their agency, and since there is no death for anyone who has not been born, there is no death (as such). This is the (meaning of) vanquishing the deadening power of death. If there is no death, the complex of the psychophysical constituents (constituting an individual) cannot reorganize itself (into a new complex). This is the (meaning of) vanquishing the deadening power of the psychophysical constituents. Since no forces that might upset such a complex can enter (a nonexistent complex), this is the (meaning of) vanquishing the deadening power of divine agencies.
>
> Nonlocalizable means the dignity of Kun-tu bzang-po through which the value and purpose of living beings is guaranteed, while (this dignity) itself is self-existent precisely because it does not reside either in interpretive schemata *(srid)* or in quietistic oblivion *(zhi).* Some claim that the word *'das* was added by the Tibetan (translators) and there is nothing corresponding to this in the Sanskrit term, but this is unjustified. The word *bhaga* applies to both Saṃsāra and Nirvāṇa. The point, however, is that (He) does not reside in either extreme.

Another interpretation is given by Klong-chen rab-'byams-pa on pp. 11f. of the same work:

> To have vanquished *(bcom)* the four deadening powers and the two obscurations together with their latent tendencies is (termed) the excellence of riddance. The four deadening powers are: the deadening power of the Lord of Death who impedes life; the deadening power of divine agencies who impede the in-depth appraisal (of Being); the deadening power of the psychophysical constituents that impede (the understanding of that sphere) where thematic formulations no more

obtain; and the deadening power of affective processes which impede freedom. Since these (four) have held no sway (over Him) since an atemporal beginning, the term *bcom* is used. The two obscurations are those presented by affective forces and those objectifiable features selected by representational thinking. These (obscurations) are the intellect obsessed with its notion that the five poisons (the affective processes) are distinct entities with distinct qualities, and (obsessed) with the countering notion that they have to be sublimated. As is stated in *Madhyāntavibhāga* [actually *Mahāyānottaratantraśāstra* V 14]:

> Notions like jealousy and so on
> (Constitute) what is said to be the obscuration due to affective processes.
> The notion of there being three (separable) facets of acting *('khor gsum)*
> (Constitutes) what is said to be the obscuration due to thematic formulations.

To possess *(ldan)* what is meant by the indivisibility of formal gestalt and pristine cognitiveness, is (termed) the excellence of understanding. As is stated in *Sampuṭi:*

> Lordliness and beauty,
> Splendor, fame, pristine cognitions and
> Effort (all are) excellences;
> These six features are what is meant by *ldan.*

Here "lordliness" is the meaning-saturated gestalt, the diaphanous purity *(dag-pa)* (of Being's) facticity (experienced in a pristine cognitiveness), which is the source of all meanings. "Beauty" is the scenario gestalt (experienced in) a pristine cognitiveness which is mirror-like. "Splendor" is a gestalt in which limpid clearness and consummate perspicacity come to-the-fore, (experienced in a pristine cognitiveness) that (preserves) its self-same identity. "Fame and pristine cognitions" are the cultural norms display gestalt, (experienced as a pristine cognitiveness) which—by being sensitively responsive to both what exists as such, and to the interconnectedness of what so exists—brings out the value of what is, and hence is individually selective. "Effort" is the invariant, indestructible gestalt *(rdo-rje'i sku)* (experienced in a pristine cognitiveness), which accomplishes tasks by auto-presencing—without ever moving from its source—in and through the activity of (the four) immeasurable catalysts (of kindness, compassion, joy, and equanimity). "Excellence" is added to this set of five qualities, such as lordliness, in order to point out that these are far superior, even to the pristine cognitions of noble aspirants.

Some people understand *bcom-ldan* in the sense of possessing that very value of having vanquished *(bcom-pa'i don nyid-ldan).*

To be beyond *('das)* means to have passed beyond all such qualifications processed through the mental-verbal field referred to as: Saṃsāra and Nirvāṇa, acceptance and rejection, existence and nonexistence. As is stated in the *Avataṃsaka:*

> Free from Saṃsāra and Nirvāṇa,
> An ocean of qualities, nondual,
> Far beyond the realm of mental-verbal proliferations—
> The *bcom-ldan-'das* is utterly serene (like) the cloudless sky.

In this lengthy passage Klong-chen rab-'byams-pa re-arranges the usual ordering of the six qualities of greatness so as to bring out their existential import.

One can note here the fact that what is termed a formal gestalt together with its experience in pristine cognitiveness is an indivisibly dynamic manifold. This is the import of the characterization that "a gestalt and pristine cognitiveness can neither be joined nor separated from one another" *(sku dang ye-shes 'du-'bral med-pa).* Yet one may, from an experiential and phenomenological perspective, speak of these interconnected modes separately, as the founding stratum *(sku)* and the founded cognitive operation *(ye-shes).* See my *Kindly Bent,* vol. 1, pp. 110-112.

There are, of course, many other indigenous interpretations of the term *bcom-ldan-'das,* but it would be outside the scope of this note to further elaborate. The interested reader, however, may consult one of the earliest hermeneutical interpretations of this term as found in the ninth century text *sGra-sbyor,* which laid down the translation principles on which the famous *Mahāvyutpatti* was compiled. See *Tibetan Tripiṭaka* (Peking edition), vol. 144, pp. 73-5-4f.

21. This work is in *rNying-rgyud,* vol. 5, pp. 525-601. The passage quoted is on p. 555.

22. The text uses the term *sems,* but from the context it is clear that *byang-chub-kyi sems* (which is synonymous with *sems-nyid, rig-pa,* and *rang-byung-gi ye-shes)* must be understood. In his *gNas-lugs,* p. 51, Klong-chen rab-'byams-pa complains that his contemporaries fail to see the difference between what these two terms connote:

> *sems* is the eight (functional groupings) together with the mental events relating to them, all of which are an adventitious contamination ranging over the triple world (of desire, aesthetic forms, and formlessness); *byang-chub-kyi sems* is excitatory intelligence, a self-existent pristine cognitiveness, and having no (predications such as) substance and attribute (which are constructs of representational thought [*sems*]), it is the source of all that is subsumed under Saṃsāra and Nirvāṇa.

Commenting on passages from the *Kun-byed rgyal-po,* in his *Chos-dbyings,* fol. 25b, he says that it is for metrical reasons that the term *sems* has been used instead of *sems-nyid,* and that the latter is synonymous with *byang-chub-kyi sems.* In brief, then, *sems* is a term for a feedback mechanism of thematic, representational thinking, whereas *sems-nyid* indicates Experience-as-such. On this crucial distinction see also Chapter II, note 55.

23. *rNying-rgyud,* vol. 4, p. 167.

24. *Theg-mchog* I, p. 281. Klong-chen rab-'byams-pa's choice of this definition seems to have been dictated by his esteem for the hermeneutical investigations by such famous rNying-ma-pa figures as Śrīsiṃha and Vimalamitra. Klong-chen rab-'byams-pa's definition of *dkyil-'khor* was apparently based

on a passage I have been able to locate in the *Rin-po-che 'phags-lam bkod-pa'i rgyud*, p. 167, a text said to have been translated by Śrīsiṃha and Vairocana. In this text one also finds the key terms *med-pa, lhun-grub, phyal-ba, gcig-pu.* These terms are taken as the basis around which Klong-chen rab-'byams-pa structures his *gNas-lugs rin-po-che'i mdzod.* It is on p. 41 of this work that he quotes the *Rin-chen spungs-pa yon-tan chen-po ston-pa rgyud-kyi rgyal-po* in support of his presentation. This text, available in *Ati,* vol. 3, pp. 73-114, and in *rNying-rgyud,* vol. 9, pp. 436-466, is said to have been translated by Vimalamitra and sKa-ba dpal-rtsegs. The quotation given by Klong-chen rab-'byams-pa in his *gNas-lugs,* p. 41, inaccurately reflects the corresponding passage of the two versions we have at our disposal. (See *Ati,* vol. 3, p. 107 and *rNying-rgyud,* vol. 9, p. 461.) The frequent discrepancies between Klong-chen rab-'byams-pa's quotations and the corresponding passages in the *rNying-rgyud* as well as in other quoted texts would seem to be due to his habit, not uncommon in the Tibetan tradition, to quote from memory without recourse to printed texts.

One should note, however, that the *rNying-rgyud,* both in the edition prepared under the auspices of Dingo Khyentse Rinpoche *and* the version preserved in the India Office Library, abounds in misspellings and omissions.

25. *Theg-mchog* I, p. 282.
26. Each of the three configurations corresponds respectively to the starting-point (as the ground in its double sense of basis and reason for), the path, and the goal. In particular, the path configuration has to do with ritual in the sense developed by J.Z. Young, *Programs of the Brain,* pp. 256f.:

> Humans probably need some formal rites both for individual develop-ment and to call attention to their responsibilities in society. Religious experience and moral conscience take many forms and are undoubt-edly engendered or helped in many people by rites, whether in commu-nal gatherings and worship or individual meditation.

These words quite admirably match what indigenous Tibetan texts indicate about the path as man's individual growth proceeding holistically in configu-ration images.

27. Alexander Gosztonyi, *Grundlagen der Erkenntnis,* pp. 68ff., distinguishes two characteristics of how the senses operate. He calls them *Realitätswert* (reality value) and *Evidenzwert* (evidence value). The latter is divided into a *formaler Evidenzwert* (formal evidence value) and an *existentieller Evidenz-wert* (existential evidence value). For a short summary of the significance of these values see Erich Jantsch, *Design for Evolution,* p. 134.
28. *Thig-le kun-gsal,* p. 230.
29. *mKha'-snying* I, p. 34, states:

> Self-existent means that something neither originates nor is dicovera-ble as a new thing; it is termed pristine cognitiveness because one understands the reality (of Being) that abides before there ever occurred a split into Saṃsāra and Nirvāṇa.

The term "self-existent" is later explained in the same text, p. 54:

> Since this pristine cognitiveness (which stems from) excitatory intelli-gence does not depend on causes and conditions but is self-existent, it

is termed self-existent.

30. *Theg-mchog* I, p. 394; see also p. 175.
31. *Chos-dbyings,* fol. 51a.
32. *mKha'-snying* I, p. 52.
33. *mKha'-snying* I, p. 18.
34. *mKha'-snying* I, p. 55.
35. *mKha'-snying* I, pp. 34f.
36. The texts use the term *thig-le* interchangeably with *ti-la*. This latter term seems to be an abbreviation of the Sanskrit work *tilaka*.
37. *mKha'-snying* I, p. 35.
38. In his *Zab-yang* II, p. 159, Klong-chen rab-'byams-pa discusses the difference between *mdangs* and *gdangs*. He says:

> Most people do not distinguish between *mdangs* and *gdangs* and let every *gdangs* get lost in *mdangs*. The fact is that *mdangs* in itself seems to have within its lucency a (single, uniform) light value and its color is bluish; on the other hand, *gdangs* is that aspect which radiates outward and has five light values of which one is whitish in color. The continuum (Being) is, in its internal lucency, termed *mdangs* and in its outward radiation it is termed *gdangs*. That which is indivisible from the facticity (of Being) is termed *mdangs,* that which arises (comes into the fore) from it is termed *gdangs*. Thus there is a difference.

Rendered in modern terminology this means that the "isotropic radiation" of the openness of Being *(mdangs)* sets up or comes in "radiation fields" *(gdangs)* each having its specific light frequency.

39. The character of an "envelope" is indicated by the term *sbubs*, which is sometimes used for *sku* (formal gestalt) and *lus* (the body-as-lived). See Chapter II, notes 39, 40, and 41. According to *Thig-le kun-gsal,* p. 246:

> The defining characteristic of *sbubs* is that it has become the site where (the energy of Being-*qua*-Existenz) has entered. This *sbubs* is a cover term (for specific forms of such an envelope).

Klong-chen rab-'byams-pa quotes this passage in his *Zab-yang* II, p. 445, but instead of *bzhugs-pa'i rten-du gyur-pa* he reads *bzhugs-pa'i klong-na brtan gyur-pa'o* "has become solidified in the area where it has entered."

40. See above note 38.
41. A favorite simile is the crystal. See, for instance, *Bla-yang* II, pp. 24ff.; *Theg-mchog* II, p. 325; *mKha'-yang* I, pp. 465, 467; III, pp. 171f., 186; *Zab-yang* I, p. 125; II, p. 210; *gNas-lugs,* pp. 128, 142, 152, 168; *Chos-dbyings,* fols. 33b, 41b, 51a, 125a.
42. *mKha'-snying* I, p. 18.
43. *mKha'-snying* I, p. 35. The hermeneutical explication of the term "pristine cognitiveness" *(ye-shes)* has already been discussed (in Chapter II, pp. 24ff. and notes). A good summary account has also been given by Klong-chen rab-'byams-pa in his *Theg-mchog* II, pp. 44f., and a more detailed one in his *Tshig-don,* pp. 470ff. This account is based on both *Thal-'gyur* and *Rang-shar*. This highly complex term can only be properly understood by carefully attending to the context of its occurrence. See *Klong-'grel,* pp. 452f. For previous discussions of this key term in rNying-ma texts, see the entries *s.v.*

ye-shes in the Index to my *Kindly Bent*, vol. 3.

44. The semantic resonances of the term *mnyam-nyid* are highly complex, embracing simultaneously the notions of reflexivity and identity. This has been discussed at length in *Chos-dbyings*, fol. 147b.

45. *mKha'-snying* I, p. 18.

46. *mKha'-snying* I, pp. 35ff.

47. *gSang-snying*, fol. 18b uses *ye-shes* and *thig-le* in a seemingly appositional manner in two consecutive lines:

> ye-shes thig-le de nyid-la
> ye-shes thig-le nyid snang-ba

The first occurrence of *ye-shes thig-le* is interpreted by Klong-chen rab-'byams-pa, *Klong-'grel*, p. 363, such that it presents a unitary notion: *ye-shes* is that pristine cognitiveness that as Experience-as-such *(sems-nyid)*, a diaphanous and pure continuum *(dbyings)*, has atemporally been in a state that is such that whatever has been of an obscuring and darkening nature has dissipated, and the inherent luminous potential has expanded far and wide *(sangs-rgyas-pa)*. Furthermore, *thig-le* is this very pristine cognitiveness, dissociated from the limits set by mental and linguistic horizons, as a virtual singularity *(nyag-gcig)* with respect to which neither affirmation nor negation have any meaning whatsoever.

The second occurrence is interpreted as meaning that *ye-shes* is the experiencer's awareness of that fact that, since the accidental (thematic) obscurations have dissipated, the momentum that has sustained them has run its course, and that no new momentum in this obscuring direction can ever again be generated. This awareness is both a "tuning in" and a state of "being tuned in" to the dynamics of Being-*qua*-Existenz—"like water poured into water"—and it is this very dynamic state, termed *thig-le,* that auto-presences in formal gestalt patterns in which the experience of our own existence in its multifaceted ramifications is included.

48. *Bla-yang* II, p. 5, speaks of Experience-as-such *(sems-nyid)* as a continuum of sheer lucency *('od-gsal-ba'i dbyings)*. It is likened to the bright sky in daytime in which all the stars are present though not visible. This indicates that Experience-as-such is, quantitatively speaking, a system containing all available information and can therefore be said to be constant. (In the universe as known to us the quantity of the information is about 10^{43} bits.) Qualitatively conceived, Experience-as-such ("the bright sky") becomes structured in formal patterns and configurations ("the stars and their constellations") whose operation is a revaluation of the available information. Such a conception of evolutions is offered by Rupert Riedl, *Die Strategie der Genesis*. Furthermore, *Chos-dbyings,* fol. 61b, likens Experience-as-such to the sky and describes its facticity as being a continuum, a point-instant virtual singularity *(dbyings thig-le nyag-gcig)*, in which all and everything is already embedded.

49. "Becoming enlightened" is a rendering of the verb *sangs-rgya-ba* (not listed in the standard dictionaries), which attempts to capture the sense of the term. The Tibetan term indicates the experiential event that the historical Buddha Śākyamuni described as "darkness has gone, light has arisen" *(tamo vigato āloko uppanno)*. See *Aṅguttaranikāya* I, p. 164. Thus, "becoming enlightened," rather than implying the intellectualistic connotation of the English term "enlightenment," describes what is an opening up to a wider perspective

and is a "more excited" state of excitatory intelligence—we light up with pleasure, we shine with joy, and we even brighten our environment. The term *sangs-rgyas*, the past tense of the verb *sangs-rgya-ba* used as a noun, denotes the resultant of this process of lightening up. This noun must be distinguished from the verbal-adjectival form *sangs-rgyas-pa* which we have seen to be descriptive of a dissipative structure. See Chapter II, note 19. On the hermeneutical interpretation of *sangs-rgyas* see below note 60.

50. The above condensed presentation of this complex phenomenon is based on *Theg-mchog* II, pp. 361ff.

51. *Rin-po-che spyi-gnad skyon-sel thig-le kun-gsal-gyi rgyud* (in *rNying-rgyud*, vol. 6, pp. 230-238), p. 233. The text then goes on to say that *thig* indicates that Being has nothing to do with origination and *le* indicates that Being has nothing to do with cessation.

52. *sGron-ma 'bar-ba*, p. 301.

53. *Mu-tig phreng-ba*, pp. 497f.

54. *Theg-mchog* II, p. 365.

55. This and the following account is based on *rDzogs-pa chen-po lta-ba yang-snying sangs-rgyas thams-cad-kyi dgongs-pa nam-mkha' klong-yangs-kyi rgyud* (in *rNying rgyud*, vol. 7, pp. 121-201), pp.176ff.; *Vairocana rgyud-'bum*, vol. 8 (pp. 1-85), pp. 59ff.; and *rDzogs-pa chen-po nges-don thams-cad 'dus-pa ye-shes nam-mkha' mnyam-pa'i rgyud* (in *rNying-rgyud*, vol. 8, pp. 124-478), pp. 362ff.

56. See note 8 above.

57. The world of desires *('dod-khams)*, comprising six possible life forms; the world of aesthetic forms *(gzugs-kyi khams)*, in the process of becoming ever more thematic; and the world of formlessness *(gzugs-med-kyi khams)* an as yet prethematic movement of radiant energy *('od-gsal snying-po)*. See *Yid-bzhin*, pp. 92ff.

58. More specifically this is a borderline state in which thematization has been suspended. Thematization may reassert itself at any time. It successively passes through four "prethematic" phases (which impose limitations on the free energy flow), then through four aesthetically experienceable phases, and finally becomes entangled in the concrete life-worlds. See also note 57 above.

59. The "state of having passed beyond" is Nirvāṇa and the "state of not having passed beyond (as yet)" is Saṃsāra.

60. This rendering of *Kun-bzang sangs-rgyas-nyid* by "the whole itself" is, of course, inadequate. There is simply no term in our language to convey the richness of meaning conveyed by the Tibetan phrase.

    Kun-bzang, which is the short form for *Kun-tu bzang-po*, has been interpreted in *Kun-tu bzang-po thugs-kyi me-long-gyi rgyud* (in *Ati*, vol. 1 pp. 233-280), pp. 243f. as follows:

> *kun* [all] because, in the dynamic reach and range of the understanding of the internal logic of Being, excitatory intelligence, having nothing to do with a coming-into-presence, comes about;
>
> —because, in the dynamic reach and range of (this) excitatory intelligence, not being amenable to fabrication, the meaning-saturated gestalt, having nothing to do with cessation, comes about;

—because, in the dynamic reach and range of pristine cognitiveness, which has nothing to do with any essent *qua* substance and
attribute, excitatory intelligence, having nothing to do with a
coming-into-existence, comes about;
  —because, in excitatory intelligence which is limpid clearness and
consummate perspicacity, all that comes-into-presence and is inter-
pretatively assessed, comes about.
tu [in/into] because, in the dynamic reach and range of excitatory
intelligence, which is spontaneously there, the goal, which is not
amenable to fabrication, lies coiled up;
  —because, out of the dynamic reach and range of excitatory intelligence which is open-dimensional, pristine cognitiveness emerges
embellished by lucency;
  —because, in the dynamic reach and range of lucency, which has
nothing to do with subjectivity, excitatory intelligence, which has
nothing to do with conceptualization, is settled;
  —because, in the dynamic reach and range of the indivisibility of
that which comes-into-presence and of that which is open, excitatory intelligence dissociated from all (thematic limitations) is
settled.
  Just as when a man arrives at the island of pure gold,
  All that which ordinarily appears as dirt and stones, turns into gold,
  So also when the meaning and value of Kun-tu bzang-po is understood, representational thought turns into pristine cognitions.
bzang [good/positive] because there is no moving from the dynamic
reach and range that is positive thoughout;
  —because in the dynamic reach and range of self-sameness neither
good nor bad exists;
  —because in the dynamic reach and range of indivisibility there is
unity;
  —because abiding in a nondual mode.

While this text does not give an interpretation of *po* (in *kun-tu bzang-po),* the
rDzogs-pa chen-po nges-don thams-cad 'dus-pa ye-shes nam-mkha' rgyud
(in *rNying-rgyud,* vol. 8), p. 333 explicates *po* in connection with the term
kun-bzang thig-le:

  kun is the whole of Saṃsāra and Nirvāṇa;
  bzang is pristine cognitiveness rising as meaning-saturated gestalt;
  po is playfulness coming in manifold guises;
  thig is the source for all and everything, self-existent;
  le is the source for the state of being a sentient being and the state of
    being a Buddha.

The same work explicates the term *sangs-rgyas,* usually rendered as "Buddha" or "Buddhahood," but actually a descriptive term for that experience in
which everything limiting and obscuring has dissipated *(sangs)* and everything positive expanded *(rgyas).* It says on pp. 412f.:

> *sangs* dissipated: the clinging to (and the belief in) mistaken iden-
> tities has dissipated;
>
> *rgyas* expanded: the meaning-saturated gestalt, unwavering, has
> expanded.
>
> *sangs*: the clinging to (and the belief in) thematizing mentation
> has dissipated;
>
> *rgyas*: the self-existent pristine cognitiveness has expanded.
>
> *sangs*: the mental operations that involve pitfalls and obscura-
> tions have dissipated;
>
> *rgyas*: pristine cognitiveness in which no conceptualization
> enters, has expanded.
>
> *sangs*: buoyancy and despondency have dissipated;
>
> *rgyas*: bliss and lucency have expanded.
>
> Therefore pristine cognitiveness, which does not derive from them-
> atizing mentation,
>
> Is (a process in which there is) dissipation by itself and expansion by
> itself.
>
> And, furthermore,
>
> *sangs*: languidness and inattentiveness have dissipated;
>
> *rgyas*: pristine cognitiveness deriving from excitatory intelli-
> gence has expanded.
>
> *sangs*: the clinging to Saṃsāra and Nirvāṇa has dissipated;
>
> *rgyas*: the meaning-saturated gestalt, flawless, has expanded.
>
> *sangs*: the sedimentations of (personal, ego-related) experience
> and the affective processes have dissipated;
>
> *rgyas*: excitatory intelligence in itself, the facticity (of Being-*qua*-
> Existenz), has expanded.
>
> *sangs*: the trickeries of *bdud* (Māra, the force that brings about
> spiritual death) have dissipated;
>
> *rgyas*: a vision that overcomes everything has expanded.
>
> Therefore this self-existent excitatory intelligence
>
> Has not come from thematizing mentation, but is (a process in
> which there is) dissipation and expansion.

The *Thig-le kun-gsal*, p. 177, declares *sangs-rgyas* to be "flawless pristine cognitiveness" and gives as its definition:

> The stains engendered by affective processes have been removed and a
> pristine cognitiveness that is sensitive (to everything) has expanded.

The text goes on to say that *sangs-rgyas* is twofold:

> As ground *(gzhi)* it is just there, and (as) understanding *(rtogs)* it is a
> coming-to-the-fore.

Finally, *Chos-dbyings*, fol. 129a, may be quoted:

When excitatory intelligence *(rig-pa)* has become dissociated from thematizing mentation *(sems)* then, because it has also become automatically dissociated from the presencing of mistaken identities that pertain to thematizing mentation, it has no other target *('gro-sa)* than this singularity (termed) *sangs-rgyas,* because (now) the facticity of Being, which is *sangs-rgyas,* has come to-the-fore due to the fact that it has become dissociated from that which had obscured it.

61. *Rang-shar,* p. 554. Also quoted with variant readings in *Theg-mchog* I, p. 282.

62. *tsitta* is also termed "a precious palace" *(gzhal-yas)* in *Thal-'gyur,* pp. 111, 126 and in *sGron-ma 'bar-ba,* p. 303; "a configuration" *(dkyil-'khor)* in *Rang-shar,* pp. 531, 533, 548, 558; "a center" *(dkyil)* in *Rang-shar,* pp. 460, 535. This term is an expression for an enclosing domain that "houses" a specific world experience.

63. *dung-khang.* This also is a term for an enclosing domain. On the relationship between *tsitta* and *dung-khang* see Chapter VII.

64. *lu-gu-rgyud.* A detailed explanation of this term is given in *Theg-mchog* II, pp. 164f. The expression "welling-up" renders the German *Zitterbewegung* (jitterbugging), a term used in quantum mechanics. See P.W. Atkins, *Quanta,* p. 190.

65. This term is discussed at length in *Theg-mchog* I, pp. 581ff., on the basis of the *sGron-ma 'bar-ba,* p. 307. See also *Seng-ge rtsal-rdzogs,* pp. 316f.

66. *Bi-ma* II, p. 38. This welling-up phenomenon is also intimately related to a formal gestalt pattern *(sku)* as indicated by the following passage in *mKha'-yang* II, p. 399:

Incandescence is envisaged as an indication of the presence of a field; the quantum of action as that of the operation of pristine cognitiveness; and the welling-up as that of a formal gestalt.

This passage is incorporated *verbatim* by Sangs-rgyas gling-pa (1340-1396) in his *Bla-dgongs,* vol. 9, p. 581.

67. *Theg-mchog* I, pp. 573ff.; *Tshig-don,* pp. 148ff.

68. For a nontechnical treatment of such virtual processes see B.K Ridley, *Time, Space and Things,* pp. 105ff. For a discussion of such virtual processes with regard to recursion see Douglas R. Hofstadter, *Gödel, Escher, Bach: An Eternal Golden Braid,* pp. 142ff.

69. *Rang-shar,* pp. 569ff.

70. *Rang-shar,* p. 536.

71. In this context we may mention an intriguing feature regarding both sound and color, pointed out by J.Z. Young, *Programs of the Brain,* p. 182:

The vowel sounds are thus the result of the balance of higher and lower frequency components *irrespective* of pitch-shifts.... [and] colors are reported as the psychophysiological products of contrasts of higher and lower wavelengths *irrespective* of their position in the frequency spectrum. (emphasis added)

72. *Thig-le kun-gsal,* p. 231, also associates "light" with formal gestalt and

"rays" with authentic utterance.

73. The term "spirituality" is at best evocative. On the inadequacy of the term "spirit" (of which spirituality is a derivative) and "consciousness" in a philosophical discourse see Calvin O. Schrag, *Experience and Being,* pp. 142ff.

74. *Seng-ge rtsal-rdzogs,* p. 267.

75. *Chos thams-cad rdzogs-pa chen-po byang-chub-kyi sems/kun-byed rgyal-po,* usually quoted in its abbreviated title *Kun-byed rgyal-po* (in *rNying-rgyud,*vol. 1, pp. 1-220), p. 197. Also quoted in *Klong-'grel,* pp. 225f. The alleged Sanskrit title of this work seems to have been a later fabrication, when it was compulsory to list the Sanskrit title of works translated into Tibetan as well. Of course, many "translations" were original Tibetan works.

Despite the anthropomorphic diction the text itself makes it quite clear that the "creator of universes" is *not* some form of super-person or God. This points to an important difference between Western and Eastern culture complexes. The Western cultural tradition, particularly the Judaeo-Christian version, is obsessed with the notion of a beginning in a historical sense, which reinforces the concomitant notion of a "who" as the author or manufacturer. The Eastern and particularly the Buddhist cultural tradition tends to understand the term "beginning" as merely a logical and heuristic term, for this tradition is primarily concerned with the existential question: "How has it happened that we as humans find ourselves in this or that context?"

76. Althought the text reads *rig-pa,* the context suggests *thugs.*

77. Authentic utterance *(gsung)* is always used in contrast with speech *(ngag)* in the sense of talk and chatter. This distinction is similar to the one made by existential thinkers who speak of authentic and inauthentic speech *(Sprache* and *Gerede).* Authentic utterance is communication, not so much in the sense of information transmitted from one entity to another, but rather in the self-referential context of Being-*qua*-Existenz informing itself of its state. Speech, on the other hand, is the "idle talk of chatter, gossip, and sterile repetition of cliches" (Calvin O. Schrag, *Experience and Being,* p. 183).

78. *Kun-byed rgyal-po,* p. 175. Also quoted in *Klong-'grel,* p. 226.

79. This idea has been taken up in one of the "songs" *(mgur)* by rGyal-ba Yang-dgon-pa rgyal-mtshan-dpal *alias* lHa-gdong-pa (1213-1258), a disciple of rGod-tshang-pa mgon-po rdo-rje (1185-1258). See *The Collected Works (gsuṅ-'bum) of Yaṅ-dgon-pa rgyal-mtshan dpal* (vol. 3, pp. 274f.) This song has been commented upon by 'Ba'-ra-ba rgyal-mtshan dpal-bzang (probably 1310-1391). See *A Tibetan Encyclopedia,* vol. 11, pp, 296ff. "Bliss supreme" *(bde-chen)* is a term for experience "before" it is converted into either Saṃsāra or Nirvāṇa and "after" it has been restored to itself by having become dissociated from this duality.

80. *Klong-'grel,* p. 409, where it is said to be a quotation from the *Kun-byed rgyal-po.*

81. On this notion and its application in various areas see Joe Rosen, *Symmetry Discovered,* pp.12ff.

82. The first course is indicated by the phrase *ye sangs-rgyas-la yang sangs-*

rgyas. See below Chapter VIII for a detailed explication. The second course is indicated by the statement in *Mu-tig phreng-ba,* p. 535:

> Although the reason (ground) for going astray has been explained in many ways,
> (It can be summed up as) spontaneous presence *(lhun-grub)* and resonating concern *(thugs-rje).*

Whatever constitutes our familiar world experience is thus the intersection of two movements: the possibility of an intersection (the spontaneous presence) and the response to this (open) possibility, the "concern" the experiencer has for the presence. On this idea of "intersection" in modern thinking see David Bohm, *Wholeness and the Implicate Order,* p. 153.

83. On this feature and the related problem of order through fluctuation see specifically Ilya Prigogine, *From Being to Becoming,* pp. 100f.

CHAPTER IV

1. This special sense of *yi-ge* is intimately connected with Experience-as-such *(sems-nyid)* (see note 7 below) and should not be confused with the understanding of the term *yi-ge* (Sanskrit *akṣara*) as discussed in the grammatical tradition of Tibet. The latter (more common) concept of *yi-ge* embodies both the notions of phoneme and grapheme—a fact that caused great problems for Tibetan grammarians. For a discussion of this and associated problems, see Roy Andrew Miller, *Studies in the Grammatical Tradition in Tibet* [Amsterdam Studies in the Theory and History of Linguistic Science, vol. 6], Amsterdam/John Benjamin B.V., 1976, pp. xiv, 41-42, 45, 53, 75, 121.

2. In this connection reference may be made to two passages in *What is Called Thinking?* by Martin Heidegger. On pp. 191f. he says:

> Language admits of two things: one, that it be reduced to a mere system of signs, uniformly available to everybody, and in this form be enforced as binding; and two, that language at one great moment says one unique thing, for one time only, which remains inexhaustible because it is always originary, and thus beyond the reach of any kind of leveling.

Again, on p. 128 he states:

> Thought and poesy never just use language to express themselves with its help; rather, thought and poesy are in themselves the originary, the essential, and therefore also the final speech that language speaks through the mouth of man.

The notion of a gnosemic language medium is based on the exhaustive treatment of *yi-ge* by Klong-chen rab-'byams-pa. He discusses this notion in a fourfold manner. First, there is the ontological dimension, Being's gnosemic level *(don-gyi yi-ge)*—the lucency of experience, a self-existent pristine cognitiveness. Secondly, there is the language of the system Being-*qua*-Existenz as constituted by our human body in its structural aspect defined by the conductors *(rtsa)* of Being's energy becoming embodied—the gnosemic level of the structuring process *(rtsa'i yi-ge)*. Thirdly, there is what is ordinarily termed language as articulated in common speech—the gnosemic level of phonemes *(sgra'i yi-ge)*. Fourthly, there is the melodious aspect of intentional speech—the gnosemic level of optimal performative utterance *('bras-bu'i yi-ge)*. See *Theg-mchog* I, pp. 198ff. In *Klong-'grel*, p. 172, he gives another fourfold division: that of (a) the structuring process *(rtsa'i yi-ge)*; (b) the iconic vision *(lha'i yi-ge)*; (c) the reassuring communication that we are part of a larger whole—the manifestly communicative gnosemic level *(sprul-pa'i yi-ge)*; and (d) phonemes *(sgra'i yi-ge)*.

'Gyur-med phan-bde 'od-zer, in his *Zab-don lde'u-mig*, pp. 245ff.,discusses the gnosemic language medium in terms of its ontological-existential *(don)*, its thematic-representational *(rtog-pa)*, and its symbolic, iconic vision *(lha)*, aspects.

3. *Klong-'grel*, p. 186. A detailed account of the sound-image correspondence is given by Nyi-ma'i seng-ge'i 'od in his *dPal gsang-ba snying-po'i rgya-cher 'grel-pa*, pp. 203 and 207f. The date of this work is unknown, yet it must be later than Lalitavajra's famous *Mahārājatantra-śrī-guhyagarbha-nāma-ṭīkā (gsang-'grel spar-khab)*, to which reference is made on p. 385.

4. See Hans-Georg Gadamer, *Wahrheit und Methode: Grundzüge einer philosophischen Hermeneutik*, pp. 443f., quoted in David E. Linge, transl. and ed., *Philosophical Hermeneutics*, p. xxxii.

5. Here, "Buddha" can be heard as that commanding silence, enigmatically termed the "lion's roar" *(seng-ge'i nga-ro)*, whereas "sentient being" is heard as existential stuttering in tones of logorrheic vapidity. Things unclearly and poorly said are unclearly and poorly thought. This observation has been discussed by Klong-chen rab-'byams-pa in *Theg-mchog* I, p. 200, and by Rong-zom-pa Chos-kyi bzang-po in *Rong-'grel*, fol. 80a.

6. *Klong-'grel*, p. 172.

7. *sems-nyid*. As previously noted (see Chapter II, note 26), within rDzogs-chen thought there is a clear distinction between *sems* and *sems-nyid*. The former term roughly corresponds to the notion of "mind" as a thematically-representational operation. The term *sems-nyid*, however, may be rendered as "experience as such" and corresponds to the phenomenological notion of "experience in its primitive presence." As Calvin O. Schrag, *Experience and Being*, pp. 3f., succinctly states:

> Experience has to do both with seeing into a situation and acting within it. It includes in its range perceptual acts and the anticipation of concepts. It involves both the knowledge and evaluation of objects, events, and situations. Thus experience in its primitive presence lies beyond any conflict between theory and practice, subject and object, intellect and will. It is with this notion of experience in its primitive presence that philosophical reflection begins, projecting as its peculiar task the penetration of experience with lucidity.

This "primitive presence" is indicated by the emphatic and reflexive particle *nyid*. It points to the very subject matter that is under consideration "as such," not yet filtered through mental constructs. For other references to the term *sems-nyid* as understood by rDzogs-chen thinkers, see *Kindly Bent*, vol. 3, Index *s.v.* See also Chapter III, note 22.

8. On the technical terms *rtsa, thig-le, 'khor-lo* see *Kindly Bent,* vol. 3, Index *s.v.*
9. *Theg-mchog* I, p. 198.
10. *gSang-snying,* fol. 10a. *Rong-'grel,* fol. 38b, explicates the "magic" of gnosemic language as follows:

> When the magic working of Buddhahood sets in, the movement into mistaking that which (actually) has no defining characteristics as having defining characteristics is (operationally linked to) gnosemic language. For example, when it begins to rain—jewels amongst gods and water amongst men—clouds appear in the clear sky due to the gusting of the wind. From these clouds, as has been previously mentioned (fol. 2b), various types of lightning, thunder, and rain come forth. Likewise, it is from out of the meaning-saturated gestalt, which has no defining characteristics, through the bestirring wind of ultimate resonating concern, that there arises the cloud of gnosemes as the first (moment of) magic. Just as a precious (rain) cloud serves as the basis for (providing for) all that is needed (for growth), so also this precious cloud of gnosemes establishes all that is needed for one's projects and spiritual realizations.

Furthermore, through an active contemplation *(sgom)* as a creative involvement with the gnosemic language medium, the practitioner relives, by bringing to life within himself, the magic working of Buddhahood. See *Rong-'grel,* fol. 79b.

11. *Theg-mchog* I, pp. 198f.; *mKha'-snying* II, p. 52. The conductors mentioned here have been discussed at length in *Theg-mchog* I, pp. 491ff.; and *Tshig-don,* pp. 130ff.
12. *Klong-'grel,* p. 173.
13. *Bla-yang* II, p. 246. The "affinities with Being" *(rigs)* may be understood as genotypes—programs of instructions that control the development and the life of an individual. In this passage, deity *(lha)* refers to an image in which the energy of mentation *(sems)* expresses itself. A deity is not to be construed as something outside or apart from the energy of such mentation. This point is clearly made in Dharmaśrī, *Coll. Works,* vol. 16, pp. 300, 340 and *Klong-'grel,* p. 436.
14. *Klong-'grel,* p. 192; *Rong-'grel,* fol. 73ab. The gnoseme *A* as a continuum that just is—having no temporal onset nor spatial dimension—may be likened to the vacuum field, and the gnoseme *KṢA,* with which the continuum resonates and which gives "shape" to the felt presence of the continuum, may be likened to the fluctuation of the vacuum field. The resonating inseparability of these primal gnosemic forces is iconically envisioned as a sensitive embrace, termed *yab-yum.* Masculinity *(yab)* and femininity *(yum)* are not formal abstractions. As the active shaping of felt presences they are lived patterns of world comprehension.
15. *gSang-snying,* fol. 8b; *Klong-'grel,* p. 183. The brackets here and in the following quotations indicate Klong-chen rab-'byams-pa's exegesis.
16. *Klong-'grel,* p. 183. For a detailed discussion of the technical term *chos-sku* and the related terms *longs-sku* and *sprul-sku* see Chapter VIII below.
17. *gSang-snying,* fol. 8b - 9a; *Klong-'grel,* p. 184.
18. *Klong-'grel,* p. 184.
19. *gSang-snying,* fol. 9a; *Klong-'grel,* pp. 184f.

20. The number forty-five results from adding the "initial ornamental stroke" *('go)*, the "dot" *(tsheg)* between syllables, and the "stop" *(shad)* to the forty-two grapho-phonemic elements. Here again one should note that the phonemic and graphemic aspects are fused. See note 1 above. For discussion of the number forty-five see also *Klong-'grel,* p. 186; *Zab-don lde'u-mig,* pp. 242ff.; *Coll. Works,* vol. 6, p. 119; *Rong-'grel,* fol. 70b.

21. *gSang-snying,* fol 9a; *Klong-'grel,* p. 185. *Rong-'grel,* fol. 71a, introduces a subtle distinction between gnosemic language as Experience-as-such, identical with "Buddhahood" *(sangs-rgyas-kyi rang-bzhin),* and gnosemic language as voiced, this voicing being identical with "Buddha-activity" *(sangs-rgyas-kyi mdzad-pa).* This distinction calls to mind Heidegger's assertion that the "essence of language" *(das Wesen der Sprache)* resides in "saying" *(Sagen).* In view of the nuances connected with the use of the term *sangs-rgyas,* the above distinction can, in the modern idiom of science, be rephrased as implying that if the universe (variously referred to as Being-*qua*-Existenz or Experience-as-such) is a dissipative structure (termed Buddhahood), then its evolution may be viewed as a giant fluctuation resulting in a new order, "Buddha-activity" being the specifics of this evolution.

22. Martin Heidegger, *On the Way to Language,* pp. 57-59.

23. *gSang-snying,* fol. 9a.

24. The number forty-five is derived from the following considerations. The "system" of an embodied individual is made up of a triadic ensemble of formal gestalt *(sku),* authentic utterance *(gsung),* and vibrant spirituality *(thugs),* each of which has five vectorial tendencies. Thus, the total number of vectorial tendencies for the whole system is fifteen. Furthermore, each of these fifteen vectorial tendencies also engenders a triadic ensemble, thus yielding a "grand canonical ensemble" of forty-five. See *Klong-'grel,* pp. 186f.

25. *ye-shes sems-dpa'.* Here, *ye,* in the term *ye-shes* (pristine cognitiveness) indicates the atemporally abiding, self-sufficient, nonderivative character of the universe as a whole. This conception is echoed by P.C.W. Davies in his *Space and Time in the Modern Universe* (p. 219), who quotes the German mathematician Hermann Weyl (1885-1955) to the effect that "the world doesn't happen, it simply is." Davies goes on to say:

> The world need not be started off, to run its carefully arranged course to some unknown destiny. Rather the world *is* space-time, matter and interactions, extending from past to future, from place to place, from event to event in a vast network of complexity and existence.

And, *sems-dpa'* indicates that experience *(sems)* is dominant *(dpa')* in that it is as yet unpolluted by dichotomic mentation. This is the interpretation of *ye-shes sems-dpa'* as given in *Bla-dgongs,* vol. 5, p. 59.

The term *sems-dpa'* is given a lengthy hermeneutical interpretation by Padmasambhava in *Kha-sbyor,* p. 27:

> *sems* is to think about the ultimately true value;
> *dpa'* is to courageously maintain the (this) value in which no duality obtains.
> *sems* is to think about that value which has no onset;
> *dpa'* is to courageously maintain that value which has no decay.
> *sems* is to think about that which is neither born nor dies;

dpa' is to courageously maintain that which has neither displacement nor transformation.

sems is to think about Saṃsāra and Nirvāṇa;

dpa' is to courageously maintain ultimate nonduality.

sems is to think about the dynamic reach and range which is
invariant:

dpa' is nonattachment as well as noninvolvement (in worldly
affairs).

sems is to think about that which has nothing to do with objects and
mentation;

dpa' is neither good nor bad, cannot be affirmed nor negated.

sems is to think about the internal logic of Being as mother;

dpa' is to courageously maintain the inseparability of mother and
child.

sems is to think about the invariant as a vortex;

dpa' is to courageously remain in the vortex of great bliss.

26. *gSang-snying*, fol. 9a. Compare this formulation with the remarks by Maurice Merleau-Ponty in his *Phenomenology of Perception* (p. 178): "Thus
speech, in the speaker, does not translate ready-made thought, but accomplishes it." He glosses this statement by saying:

> There is, of course, every reason to distinguish between an authentic
> speech, which formulates for the first time, and second-order expres-
> sion, speech about speech, which makes up the general run of empiri-
> cal language. Only the first is identical with thought.

In Buddhist texts, authentic (first) utterance is *A*. According to Klong-chen
rab-'byams-pa three phases are involved in the transformative process (see
notes 27 and 28 for the second and third phase respectively). The first phase,
indicated by the verse quoted, is that experience comes as spontaneous, first
utterance (primal gnoseme). *Klong-'grel*, p. 187, states:

> Experience-as-such, a sheer lucency, is gnosemic language as a spon-
> taneous presence. This primal gnoseme cannot be established as either
> a particular existent (substance) or a quality.

The *mTshan-brjod (Mañjuśrī-nāma-saṅgīti)* states:

> *A* is the most sublime of all gnosemes:
> It comes from deep within, having no onset.
> Of utmost significance it is the gnosemic language medium in an
> ultimate sense,
> The most sublime impulse for all speech;
> It makes all words (meaningfully) clear.

And in a Sūtra it is stated:

> Subhūti, gnosemic language is, in the ultimate sense, such that it
> has no onset. This is the facticity of *A*. Whatever is (the range of)
> *A*'s facticity, that is (the range of) experience's actuality. It is

completely beyond (the notions of) essent and nonessent.

27. *gSang-snying,* fol. 9a. This verse refers to the second phase in the transformative process in which the primal gnoseme *A* sets the tone for all existential features in the total phenomenon of experience. Thus *Klong-'grel,* p. 188, states:

> Experience-as-such is not objectifiable gnosemic language in the ultimate sense—it (presents), precisely because of its constitution by sheer lucency on various (levels), the glorious gyration of formal gestalt *(sku)* as the operational basis (for all activities); the glorious gyration of authentic utterance *(gsung),* which conveys (messages of existential significance); the glorious gyration of vibrant spirituality *(thugs)* as (sense-bestowing) intentionality; the glorious gyration of the culture-engendering creative potential *(yon-tan)* by virtue of the cognitive sensitivity to all and everthing; and the glorious gyration of (Buddha-hood) activity *(mdzad-pa)* because it cannot encounter any hindrances.
>
> Furthermore, this gyration, perpetually ornamented by formal gestalt, authentic utterance, and vibrant spirituality of all Buddhas, conjures up a superb miracle because of its spontaneous, atemporally abiding excellent qualities; it displays before itself its wondrousness—the marvel of (sense-bestowing) intentionality operating as gestalt and pristine cognitiveness which can neither be separated nor joined. The import (of this gyrating) is that by contemplating (reliving) this, the gestalt triad experientially comes to-the-fore by itself.

Here, the term gyration *('khor-lo)* refers to a whirling movement, which establishes a center and an environing. It may move in a direction that allows the gestalt triad *(sku gsum)* to be discerned either as an upward or downward spiralling. This movement, essentially a high-energy phenomenon, is, however, liable to gravitational collapse. Moreover such a collapsed state, a low-energy system operating as the ensemble of embodiment, speaking, mentation, always retains the statistical probability of being recharged to the high-energy state.

28. *gSang-snying,* fol. 9a. This verse refers to the third phase of the transformative process. *Klong-'grel,* pp. 188f. explicates this verse as follows:

> This very gnosemic language, which is thus coming into presence, is Experience-as-such, atemporally pure, a meaning-saturated continuum, a dynamically invariant reach and range. This is written (spelled out as such), atemporally, by the continuum which is pristine cognitiveness, spontaneously there and not being something that can be set up or tracked down. To this internal logic of Being, which never moves from itself nor changes into something other than itself, and which in itself is a sheer lucency, the designation gnosemic language is given. This does not mean that it is something newly fabricated or something newly arisen; rather, because it is nothing of this sort, gnosemic language—spontaneously like clouds swirling—is said to abide atemporally, in its own right, in the whole of Saṃsāra and Nirvāṇa.

29. *Rong-'grel,* fol. 24b. *Theg-mchog* I, p. 130, defines *sngags* as "protecting from affective forces and allowing for the speedy realization of limpid clearness and consummate perspicacity."
30. *Klong-'grel,* p. 194. *Rong-'grel,* fol. 73b f.

CHAPTER V

1. In-depth appraisal *(ting-nge-'dzin),* in the context of the existential approach to the problem of Being-*qua*-Existenz, is a tuning-in to special field effects within the cognitive-appreciative domain of an individual. These effects result from coordinating processes already operative in Being-*qua*-Existenz itself. It is these field effects which give one the impression of there being something happening. In figurative language, such field effects are termed gods *(lha). Rong-'grel,* fol. 27b, defines this "something" as:

   A gestalt with perceptible traits *(gzugs-kyi sku),* complete in its details, as it comes-into-presence out of the dynamic continuum *(dbyings)* in which all possible meanings *(chos)* abide, as yet utterly pure and diaphanous with respect to the noematic profiles *(rnam-pa)* these meanings may assume, operating coordinatively with pristine cogni-tiveness *(ye-shes),* which does not stray from the meaning-value *(don).*

   In-depth appraisal involves the experiential accessing and focusing on such a meaning-value. Its relationship to its objective reference is not appropriative, for it can, and does, move freely over both the nonthematic *(mtshan-ma med-pa)* and the thematic *(mtshan-ma dang bcas-pa).* As such, in-depth appraisal concerns itself with pure possibilities. On the notion of pure possibility see Edward S. Casey, *Imagining,* pp. 116ff.
2. *Klong-'grel,* pp. 202ff., explicating *gSang-snying,* fol. 10a.
3. *Rong-'grel,* fol. 74a f. and *Klong-'grel,* p. 202, both read *tshogs* instead of *sogs* as found in the printed version of *gSang-snying.* According to *Rong-'grel,* this ensemble is constituted by the various operations intending toward limpid clearness and consummate perspicacity, such as the united operation of openness and compassion, or the arousal of that awareness, which under-stands that the meaning-value of Being-*qua*-Existenz, in its infallibility, is the unity of the dynamic continuum and its pristine cognitiveness, or the opera-tion of mind as-is.
4. This is indicated in *Klong-'grel,* pp. 204 f. We are programmed this way because the gyrating display process discussed at length in the above quoted passage, takes place in our bodily existence *(lus-la gnas).* Feeling ourselves into this process is the unfoldment *(lam)* of our growth.
5. On the term autopoiesis see Chapter II, note 13.
6. The three kinds of in-depth appraisal are specific to the Mahāyoga. See *sNying-gi me-long* (in *Ati,* vol. 1, p. 328 and *rNying-rgyud,* vol. 10, p. 538). In both editions the passages explicating the second in-depth appraisal are textually corrupt. According to this work *(Ati,* vol. 1, p. 330), Mahāyoga is the foundation *(gzhi),* and is termed *bskyed-pa* (having raised [the mind] to a higher level, that is, having made the transition from mere ritualistic perfor-mance to an existential understanding). Anuyoga is the path *(lam)* as a holomovement and termed *rdzogs-pa* (complete). Atiyoga is the holistic

climax *('bras-bu)*, termed *rdzogs-pa chen-po (rdzogs-chen,* complete in an absolute sense). These three phases come as the climax of the ninefold division of the spiritual pursuit *(yāna)* as developed by rNying-ma thinkers. The traditional division into (1) Śrāvakayāna, (2) Pratyekabuddhayāna and (3) Bodhisattvayāna applies to persons of low intelligence; the *Dasein*-orientated aspects of (4) Kriyā, (5) Caryā, and (6) Yoga apply to persons of medium intellectual capacities; and the (7) Mahā (yoga), (8) Anu (yoga), and (9) Ati (yoga) are the domain for those of superior intelligence. For a discussion of these nine pursuits see *Theg-mchog* I, p. 106.

7. *Kun-byed rgyal-po,* p. 64.
8. *Kun-byed rgyal-po,* pp. 118f.
9. *gSang-snying,* fol. 5b. See also Chapter II, note 57.
10. *gSang-snying,* fol. 17b. *Klong-'grel,* pp. 304, 345 and *Rong-'grel,* fol. 79a.
11. *gSang-snying,* fol. 10a. *Klong-'grel,* p. 304, and *Rong-'grel,* fol. 79b.
12. *gSang-snying,* fol. 8b. *Klong-'grel,* pp. 177f., 305, and *Rong-'grel,* fols. 68b, 79b.
13. *Klong-'grel,* pp. 219f. There are four action patterns associated with such appropriate responsiveness. They are characterized as relieving, alleviating, and quieting *(zhi-ba)*; enhancing, increasing, and intensifying *(rgyas-pa)*; bringing under control, conquering, and subjugating *(dbang-du bya-ba)*; and rigorous, fierce, and forceful *(drag-po)*. These action patterns can be imaged in specific shapes and colors; they also present what may be called genotypic *(rigs)* and phenotypic *(las, phrin-las)* modes. See *Theg-mchog* II, pp. 48ff.
14. Experience-as-such *(sems-nyid)* is characterized (in *Chos-dbyings,* fol. 33b) as an open mode that accommodates and is endowed with all noematic profiles that may come-into-presence *(rnam-kun mchog-ldan-gyi stong-chen)*. This idea is also found in *Uttaratantra* I 92.
15. *gSang-snying,* fol. 11a and *Klong-'grel,* pp. 220f.
16. An excellent discussion of this important point has been given by Medard Boss, *Existential Foundations,* p. 120. Here he says:

> It is even possible that in death existence enters into something that is *prior* to all being; the dead may attain a relationship to Being-ness as such that is hidden from the living....It may be this possibility that enables certain rare human beings to accept death with a composed serenity, to experience it as the manifestation of an existential possibility encompassing and consummating all existence but based in a dimension not at man's disposal....

These statements bear a striking resemblance to the phases of death experience that the Tibetan tradition has exhaustively described under the technical rubrics of *'chi-kha'i bar-do* and *chos-nyid bar-do*. See, for instance, *Theg-mchog* II, pp. 402, 403; *Tshig-don,* pp. 379ff., and *dGongs-zang,* vol. 2, pp. 407, 414ff.

17. The term consciousness as used here, actually refers to an ensemble of perceptual operations involved. The inadequacy of the term consciousness has already been pointed out in Chapter II, note 64. On the problem of consciousness see also Medard Boss, *Existential Foundations,* pp. 132ff.; J.Z. Young, *Programs of the Brain,* pp. 38f.; and Ronald S. Valle and Mark King, *Existential-Phenomenological Alternatives for Psychology,* pp. 12ff. *et passim.*

18. For a discussion of space as a horizon-form see Calvin O. Schrag, *Experience and Being,* pp. 12, 49-56, *et passim.*

19. *gSang-snying,* fol. 11b and *Klong-'grel,* pp. 46f. *Rong-'grel,* fol. 80a indicates that this condensed passage is to be understood in the light of the longer description provided by *gSang-snying,* fol. 1b. *Rong-'grel,* fol. 42b lists a number of architectural terms connected with the gates of the palace: *sgo-legs* (door-wings), *sgo-khang* (porch), *sgo-khyud* (door superstructure?), *sgo-skyabs* (door support).

20. *gSang-snying,* fol. 1b and *Klong-'grel,* pp. 46f.

21. "The site of 'Og-min," according to *Rong-'grel,* fol. 42a, is not a place in the ordinary sense, it is a coming-into-presence of a specific richness operating through pristine cognitions that convey the meaningfulness of Being. The term *'og-min,* has been interpreted with respect to specific formal gestalt experiences in *Klong-'grel,* pp. 34ff. *Klong-'grel,* p. 42, quotes Buddhaguhya's *sPyan-'grel, (Vajrasattva-māyājāla-tantra śrī-guhyagarbha-nāma cakṣus-ṭīkā,* Peking edition, no. 4756), but the quoted passage bears virtually no resemblance to Buddhaguhya's discussion of *'og-min* as handed down in the Peking edition of this work. Nevertheless, Klong-chen rab-'byams-pa's words have been taken over, without stating the source, by Yon-tan rgya-mtsho in his *Yon-tan-mdzod-kyi 'grel-pa,* vol. 2, pp. 523f.

22. We have previously discussed (in Chapter II) the complex nature of pristine cognition *(ye-shes)* with respect to the omnidirectional, isotropic radiation oscillating outward from the point-instant virtual singularity *(thig-le nyag-gcig).* Here, too, in the context of that self-structuring process of transformation, which makes possible experiential imaging of this process as a palace, pristine cognitiveness is operative in all its modalities. We shall now provide another explication of pristine cognitiveness, based primarily on passages from the *Rang-shar,* the *Thal-'gyur,* and their elaboration in *Tshig-don.* The fact that the self-structuring process of transformation tends *toward* the formation of a center indicates that we here are dealing with a process which, although still virtual is yet beginning to establish differentiated orientational nuances (center, periphery, zenith, and nadir), which themselves may be experientially accessed (imaged).

The term *ye-shes* has been analyzed into the two components *ye* and *shes(-pa).* The former has been understood as a shortened form for *ye-nas* (indicating an atemporal primordiality) or of *ye-nas gnas-pa* (abiding in an atemporally primordial manner) or of *ye-nas gnas-pa'i don* (the meaning-value of Being-*qua*-Existenz as abiding in and with itself in an atemporally primordial manner). See *Tshig-don,* p. 122 and *dGongs-zang,* vol. 2, p. 515. The combination of *ye* and *shes(-pa)* indicates intentionality (Sinnsetzung) as it occurs on the level of Buddhahood *(sangs-rgyas),* where "Buddhahood" is to be understood in an ontological (not ontic) sense. Thus the *Rang-shar,* p. 736, declares:

> When atemporal primordiality *(ye)* and cognitiveness *(shes-pa)* are taken together (as a unit)
> This (indicates) true Buddhahood intentionality
> *[ye dang shes-pa gnyis 'dzom-na*
> *sangs-rgyas dgongs-pa dam-pa yin]*

For a hermeneutical interpretation of *sangs-rgyas* see Chapter II, note 52. The ontological character of *ye-shes* is clearly indicated in *Rang-shar*, p. 451:

> Such is the definition of *ye-shes*:
> Spontaneous operation—*ye*;
> Understanding having come to-the-fore—*shes*
> [*ye-nas rang-bzhin lhun-gyis grub*
> *shes-na(s) rtogs-pa mngon-du gyur*
> *ye-shes nges-tshig de-bzhin-no*]

The crucial distinction between the ontological character of *ye-shes* and the ontic character of *sems* is most clearly expressed in *Chos-dbyings*, fol. 48a.

23. As "object phase" *(yul)* it is clearly described in *dGongs-zang*, vol. 2, pp. 512f., 545f. See also *mKha'-yang*, vol. 2, p. 70.

24. This technical term is interpreted, in *Rang-shar*, p. 451, as comprising three inseparably fused aspects:

> The meaning-saturated field pristine cognition is such that
> It is/has as object (phase) an utter openness,
> It is radiant as the coming-into-presence of lucency,
> It is pristinely cognitive as the operational domain of excitatory
> intelligence;
> Since these three (aspects) operate together (as a unit) one speaks of
> field.

This interpretation is the basis for *Tshig-don*, p. 470. Here, lucency is explicated as the ground and reason for pristine cognitiveness shining in its own light. In very concise terms, *Chos-dbyings*, fol. 201a, defines this cognition: "an open, lucent, and excitatorily intelligent source" *(stong gsal rig-pa'i 'byung-gnas)*. The explication of the various pristine cognitions given in *Chos-dbyings* is strikingly similar to that given in *Tshig-don*. Klong-chen rab-'byams-pa seems to have written *Tshig-don* first, for in *Chos-dbyings*, fol. 48a, he refers to this work by its abbreviated title *'Od-gsal rin-po-che'i mdzod*.

25. Its essential nature *(ngo-bo)* in the sense of the German noun *Wesen*, is the openness of the meaning-saturated field cognitiveness; its functioning is its illumining character that allows things to appear as projections into an outside, like the phenomenon of mirror-images. See *Tshig-don*, pp. 471f., *dGongs-zang*, vol. 2, p. 515 and vol. 4, p. 104. A lucid analysis of the philosophical nuances embedded in the German word *Wesen* is given in Martin Heidegger, *The Question Concerning Technology* by the translator William Lovitt on p. 3, note 1.

26. For the notion of the thetic character of pure possibility see Edward S. Casey, *Imagining*, p. 111.

27. The interpretation of this pristine cognitiveness follows *Tshig-don*, p. 473, which itself is based on *Thal-'gyur*, p. 154 and *Rang-shar*, pp. 452f. A subtle distinction between identity and auto-reflexiveness (self-sameness) has been noted, but not further elaborated, by Martin Heidegger in his *Being and Time*, p. 150, note 2. The whole problem of identity and difference has been the subject of a separate study by Martin Heidegger, *Identity and Difference*.

28. *Tshig-don,* pp. 474f.
29. *Tshig-don,* pp. 475f.
30. *Klong-'grel,* pp. 229f. This is Klong-chen rab-'byams-pa's interpretation of *gSang-snying,* fol. 11a, which states:

> Pristine cognitiveness has been thematized into four directions with a center.
>
> The spontaneous presence of such a configuration surpassing the imagination
>
> Is the majestic wholeness (of Being-*qua*-Existenz). A yogi who understands (this)
>
> May well engage himself in the phenomenal world as (being) this grand configuration.
>
> *[ye-shes phyogs-bzhi dbus brtags te*
> *dkyil-'khor bsam-yas lhun-grub ni*
> *rdzogs-chen rtogs-pa'i rnal-'byor-pas*
> *kun-'byung dkyil-'khor chen-por spyod]*

In his commentary, Klong-chen rab-'byams-pa has substituted for the *kun-'byung* (the phenomenal world) of the verse text the term *rang-byung* (self-existent), and thereby interprets the passage as referring to what takes place on the nonthematic level. *Rong-'grel,* fol. 77a, takes *kun-'byung* as referring to the phenomenal world as it is organized with respect to the experiencing individual. It is interesting to note, however, that in another place Klong-chen rab-'byams-pa correctly quotes the verse text of the *gSang-snying* and says that this passage describes the spirituality configuration *(thugs-kyi dkyil-'khor),* which sees Saṃsāra in its primordial purity and transparency, a symbolic self-presentation of Being-*qua*-Existenz, rather than as something to be rejected. See *Klong-'grel,* p. 227.

31. In *Bla-yang* I, p. 423, Klong-chen rab-'byams-pa speaks of the "yogi who understands ultimate completeness" *(rdzogs-pa chen-po rtogs-pa'i rnal-'byor).* Although the same phrase occurs in an abbreviated form due to metrical exigency in *gSang-snying,* fol. 11a (see note 30 above), Tibetan commentators have split up the phrase into "majestic wholeness of Being-*qua*-Existenz" and "ultimate completeness" *(rdzogs-pa chen-po, rdzogs-chen)* as the predicate of the phrase *dkyil-'khor bsam-yas lhun-grub ni* (the spontaneous presence of such a configuration surpassing the imagination), and *rtogs-pa'i rnal-'byor-pa* (the yogi who understands this) as the subject of the phrase *kun-'byung dkyil-'khor chen-por spyod* (may well engage himself in the phenomenal world as being this grand configuration).

32. This surging occurs in a bimodal manner. In its open mode *(stong-pa),* it cannot be created nor destroyed and hence is symmetry-maintaining. In its coming-into-presence mode *(snang-ba),* it involves elemental forces, which themselves initiate discrete (symmetry-breaking) concretizations. See *Zab-yang* I, p. 282.

33. In the Tibetan term for palace *(gzhal-yas khang)* the bounded aspect is reflected by the term *khang* as "the site where all beings live," and the open aspect is reflected by the term *gzhal-yas,* which indicates that "representational thinking cannot fathom or measure it." See 'Ba-ra-ba, *A Tibetan*

Encyclopedia of Buddhism, vol. 7, p. 232. See also Khrag-thung Rol-pa'i rdo-rje, *Dag-snang,* p. 268. *Dag-snang,* p. 266, gives an interpretation of the important terms *zhing-khams*—the site on which the palace is situated and with which it is coextensive. Here, *zhing* (field) is so called because of its similarity with a vast expanse in which Saṃsāra and Nirvāṇa can spread and settle, and *khams* refers to the dynamics of the evolutionary process toward optimal operation *(bde-gshegs snying-po)* with which Saṃsāra and Nirvāṇa as its manifestations are identical. Furthermore, *Dag-snang,* p. 265, makes it quite clear that such terms as palace and field are to be understood as symbolic expressions.

34. *Chos-dbyings,* fols. 19a f. Only the verses have been rendered.
35. *skye-med (skye-ba med-pa).* This term is synonymous with *chos-kyi dbyings,* the meaning-saturated continuum. See *Klong-'grel,* pp. 104f.
36. *chos-kyi sku.* All and every experience has a formal gestalt character *(sku),* which cannot be reified. (See *Seng-nge rtsal-rdzogs,* p. 349). As such, experience is saturated with meaning *(chos).* The term *chos* (any particular kind of being) never loses its association with *chos-nyid* (the internal logic of Being). This understanding is also stated by Martin Heidegger, in his *On Time and Being,* p. 5, as: "Being, by which all beings as such are marked...." In *Dag-snang,* p. 254, *chos-nyid* is equated with *stong-pa-nyid,* indicating that the latter is not a barren emptiness, but rather something very active. Even more importantly, everything that can be thematized *(chos-can)* is continually interacting with everything else and is inseparable from the fluctuations of the "vacuum" *(stong-pa-nyid, chos-nyid).* The openness of Being *(stong-pa-nyid)* is also equated with the expansive space of the celestial horizon *(nam-mkha').* Thus, "space" is not to be seen as a passive container, but as an active structuring medium. As has been said by Peter S. Stevens in his *Patterns in Nature,* pp. 4ff.:

> For space itself has a structure that influences the shape of every existing thing... It turns out, however, that the backdrop, the all-pervading nothingness, is not so passive. The nothingness has an architecture that makes real demands on things. Every form, every pattern, every existing thing pays a price for its existence by conforming to the structural dictates of space.

37. *rin-chen.* Such preciousness is associated with the Wish-Fulfilling Gem. *Seng-nge rtsal-rdzogs,* pp. 218, 364, speaks of "the treasure of precious jewels that has come forth from the within without a within *(nang-med nang-nas nor-bu rin-chen mdzod phyung-ba).*" This preciousness is also associated with pristine cognitions, which are said to be precious jewels—"a palace ablaze in (the luster of) precious jewels (which are) pristine cognitions." See *gSang-snying,* fol. 1b. Inasmuch as *ye-shes* can be understood in a singular or plural sense, it is possible to render the passage as "a palace ablaze in the (luster of a) jewel (which is) pristine cognitiveness." The *lDe'u-mig,* p. 133, explicitly states that the precious jewel is the Wish-Fulfilling Gem. Furthermore, *Dag-snang,* pp. 308f., associates preciousness with the intending toward limpid clearness and consummate perspicacity *(byang-chub-kyi sems).* On this intending see Chapter III, note 22 and *Kindly Bent,* vol. 3, index, *s.v.*
38. *chos-nyid.* See also note 36 above. The internal logic of Being involves the

operation of excitatory intelligence, and where such intelligence is at work, whatever presents itself does so as a formal gestalt pattern *(sku)*. Because of its coextensiveness with Being, it has been equated with the expansiveness of the celestial horizon *(nam-mkha')*. Thus, the *Seng-nge rtsal-rdzogs*, p. 349, says:

> All this coming-into-presence of formal patterns *(sku)*
> Is not the coming-into-presence of (discrete) domains *(yul)*.
> Just as a young maiden
> Sees her face coming-into-presence
> In a bright mirror,
> So also in the internal logic of Being *(chos-nyid)*, (like) the sky in its expanse *(yul)*,
> The coming-into-presence of excitatory intelligence shines as a formal gestalt *(sku)*.
> This seeing of one's Existenz *(gnas-lugs)*
> Does not involve reification.
> It is an immediate lucency because of the transparency of the objective reference.
> Pristine cognitions, together with their centers and peripheries,
> In their true nature, do not reify,
> Yet it is when the state of a sentient being *(sems-can)* operates, that reifying occurs.

In this context one should perhaps say something about the danger of unthinkingly viewing Tibetan texts through Sanskrit semantic filters. The machine-like transfer procedure from Sanskrit to English is inadequate and often misleading with respect to the specific semantic nuances associated with "corresponding" Tibetan terms. Sanskrit *sattva* primarily denotes an "existent" and secondarily denotes a "living existent." The transfer from the Sanskrit *sattva* to the English "sentient being" fails to capture the specific semantic nuance associated with the Tibetan term *sems-can*. This term indicates the dominant activity of representational mentation and not merely the fact that we are dealing with an "existent" that happens to be sentient.

39. Klong-chen rab-'byams-pa indicates that the reference to height is merely a figure of speech. He implies that Experience-as-such moves along both horizontal and vertical axes. Thus the palace *(gzhal-yas khang)* or stronghold *(rdzong)* as which experience is imaged, is a vertical-horizontal axial complex.

40. *gSang-snying*, fol. 11b.

41. The following is based on the discussion in *Klong-'grel*, pp. 57f. See also *Rong-'grel*, fols. 43b f. *Klong-'grel*, p. 232, quotes a work with the title *'Od-rim* in which a peacock is mentioned instead of the mythical garuḍa bird. Both these animals are alike in that they are immune to and able to destroy poison. As previously noted, poison is a term for affective processes about which we, too, say that emotions "poison the atmosphere."

42. According to *Rong-'grel*, fol. 44b, the term jewel is used to indicate the preciousness of any and all thrones.

43. *gSang-snying*, fol. 1b. The four characterizations mentioned in this passage

have been given a fourfold hermeneutical interpretation with respect to the Pāramitā-Mahāyāna, the Yoga, the Mahāyoga, and the Atiyoga *(rdzogs-chen)* levels, respectively. See *rGya-cher 'grel-pa,* pp. 32-39.

44. The hermeneutical interpretation of *de-bzhin-nyid* has already been given above, pp. 77f. The *gSal-byed me-long,* fol. 17a, adds two further aspects to the as-is.

45. *Rong-'grel,* fol. 40a. The elative term *chen-po* ("great") in *longs-spyod chen-po* (thoroughly enjoying) conveys the meaning that there can be "nothing greater."

46. *Rong-'grel,* fol. 40a.

47. *Rong-'grel,* fol. 40b, mentions four kinds of sentients: those born from a womb, those hatched from an egg, those generated by heat and moisture, and those who appear spontaneously. He indicates that these symbolize imaginative processes.

48. *Rong-'grel,* fol. 40a. See also fol. 122a where the same analogy is used, and *rGya-chen* pp. 33f.

49. "Being wide awake" *(sangs-rgyas)* is also used with reference to a state in which two (seemingly) contrary notions are fused into a single dynamic whole. In this connection both *Klong-'grel,* p. 29 and *Rong-'grel,* fol. 40b, quote the following verse:

> The very state of nonoptimal *rig-pa*—radiant pristine cognitiveness;
> Affective processes and frustration—supreme limpid clearness and consummate perspicacity.

Nonoptimal *rig-pa (ma-rig-pa)* indicates a lowered state of excitation and hence lowered cognitive capacity. It does *not* involve a negation of cognitiveness. See Chapter II, note 9.

50. Dharmaśri, *Coll. Works,* vol. 6, p. 46, indicates that the *locus classicus* of this enumeration is the *Saṃpuṭika (alias Śrī-saṃpuṭikā Saṃpuṭodbhavakalparāja,* as yet unpublished). He relates these qualities to ways of being in the world *(sku)* and the corresponding ways of knowing *(ye-shes).* The following diagram results:

FIGURE 20

Qualities	Ways of being	Ways of knowing
lordliness *(dbang-phyug)*	*chos-sku*	*chos-dbyings*
beauty *(gzugs bzang-ba)*	*mngon-byang-gi sku*	*me-long lta-bu*
wealth and fame *(dpal dang grags-pa*	*longs-sku*	*mnyam-nyid*
knowledge *(ye-shes)*	*rdo-rje'i sku*	*so-sor rtog-pa*
diligence *(brtson-'grus)*	*sprul-sku*	*bya-ba grub-pa*

51.   *Rong-'grel*, fol. 41a.

52.   The esoteric approach *(gsang-sngags theg-pa*, Sanskrit *Guhyamantrayāna)*
      is the one that focuses on restoring Experience-as-such to the central position
      in man's life. In this approach it is the mystery *(gsang)* of Being that speaks
      (sngags). In rDzogs-chen teaching this approach is called *bka' rdzogs-pa
      chen-po* by Sangs-rgyas gling-pa (1340-1396). In his *Bla-dgongs*, vol. 10, pp.
      632ff. he says:

> That which has become the energizing quintessence of the esoteric
> approach is termed *bka' rdzogs-pa chen-po*. This epithet has been used
> because it refers to the authoritative pronouncement by the great
> teacher in his triadic gestalt personality. Does this mean that only this
> is authoritative and other pronouncements are not? (The answer is)
> that this is the ultimate completeness *(rdzogs-pa)*, the quintessential
> intentionality of all and every pronouncement. There can be no greater
> completeness than this totality, in which the essence of everything is
> contained, and therefore it is called great *(chen-po)* because it has
> become the greatness of the whole.

Sangs-rgyas gling-pa then characterizes the esoteric approach as follows:

> The *gsang-sngags*, in general, is like a milch cow; the *rdzogs-pa chen-
> po* is like the milk one gets from it, and the *yang-gsang snying-thig* is
> like the butter one gets from the milk.

The esoteric approach uses words drawn from life-experiences as the last
passage shows. Such words have, as do all words, general meanings—but, as
Louis Arnaud Reid, *Ways of Knowledge and Experience*, p. 49, has said,
these general meanings are:

> ...only a part of the references of the words, and may not be the most
> important part. The undefined fringes and overtones of meaning,
> ambiguous and ambivalent, are often more so.

The esoteric approach uses "embodying language" to express the existential
import of valuable experiences; it does not use "categorical language," which
in Reid's words (p. 115) is:

> the abstract discursive language of science and philosophy and to some
> extent of ordinary common sense. It is the language of propositions in
> which truths are affirmed or denied, hypotheses stated, deductions
> made, inferences examined and tested.

Unlike theory-bound ideologues, esoteric thinkers remain open to the
unbounded ground of their existence and, as true poets, they are creators of
worlds felt and known to be valuable.

53.   *rdo-rje btsun-mo'i bhaga*. The resolution of *rdo-rje btsun-mo* as a *tatpuruṣa*-
      compound rather than a *karmadhāraya* compound is based on the analysis
      given by Dwags-po Pan-chen bKra-shis rnam-rgyal (1512/13-1587) in his
      detailed commentary on the *Hevajra-tantra*, the *dPal Kye'i rdo-rje zhes
      bya-ba'i rgyud-kyi rgyal-po'i 'grel-pa legs-bshad nyi-ma'i 'od-zer*, p. 49:

> *rdo-rje* means energy; the indestructibility *(rdo-rje)* of this *rdo-rje* is
> the great rDo-rje-'chang (Vajradhara), (who), in this treatise, is the
> *bcom-ldan-'das* Kye'i rdo-rje (Hevajra). *bTsun-mo* means his
> consorts—sPyan-ma (Locanā) and the other (ladies-of-rank), or, as in

this treatise, (the ladies) Gaurī and the others.

54. Dwags-po Pan-chen's *Hevajra-tantra* commentary (p. 49) declares that the term *bhaga,* in conjunction with *btsun-mo,* carries sexual overtones so as to appeal to those who are under the sway of their passions. It should be born in mind, however, that this term must be understood in the context in which it is used. There certainly is a literal semantic core to the term *bhaga,* yet it has wider semantic resonances, which symbolize a wider appreciation of values. This wider connotation of the term is indicated by its synonymity with the term *chos-'byung* (origin of meanings) which Dwags-po Pan-chen (p. 50) explains as:

> It is the birth-place *('byung-gnas)* of all configurations together with their founding strata *(rten)* and their founded operations *(brten-pa).*

Dwags-po Pan-chen (p. 174), commenting on *Hevajra* (I v, 15), interprets the term *bhaga* in the attribute *bhagavan* to mean good fortune *(aṃśa)* and conquest. The semantic ambivalence of this term is again highlighted in his commentary on *Hevajra* I viii, 26 (pp. 267f.) where the difference between the imaged feeling of visualization *(bskyed-rim)* and that of felt imagery *(rdzogs-rim)* is brought out. An additional source demonstrating the semantic ambivalence of this term is the *gSang-sngags nang-gi lam-rim rgya-cher 'grel-pa Sangs-rgyas gnyis-pa'i dgongs-rgyan* by 'Gyur-med tshe-dbang mchog-grub (born 1764), pp. 212f.

55. *Klong-'grel,* p. 29. See previous discussion in Chapter III, note 20.

56. While the idea of four deadening powers (*bdud,* Sanskrit Māra) is a common one, Klong-chen rab-'byams-pa has clearly seen and stated their interrelationships. A short survey of these deadening powers, all of which are ultimately due to subject-object dichotomizing is given in his *Chos-dbyings,* fol. 170ab. This survey is based on *Rang-grol,* pp. 34-39, which he quotes. Dharmaśrī, *Coll. Works,* vol. 6, pp. 44f., gives a different relationship, which he derives from the expanded version of *gSang-snying,* the *rgyas-pa* (in *rNying-rgyud,* vol. 14, pp. 67-317), p. 261.

57. See Chapter III, note 60.

58. *Klong-'grel,* p. 30; *Rong-'grel,* fol. 41ab.

59. *gSang-snying,* fol. 1b and *Klong-'grel,* p. 30. Klong-chen rab-'byams-pa here indirectly criticizes Rong-zom-pa Chos-kyi bzang-po (see *Rong-'grel,* fol. 41b) for not noting that at this stage the prereflective nonthematic phase in experience is at work.

60. *Chos-dbyings,* fols. 4b-5a.

61. *gSang-snying,* fol. 2b.

62. A traditional account of these attributes and marks is given in *Abhisamayālankāra* VIII 13ff. A different interpretation is given in *Klong-'grel,* pp. 73f. and Dharmaśrī, *Coll. Works,* vol. 6, pp. 48f.

63. *Klong-'grel,* pp. 76f., explains these worlds, inconceivable in their qualities, as: the world that is the continuous field of Being in its dynamic polarity; the world that is the coming-into-presence as a virtual operation; and the world of various subworlds with their concrete life forms.

64. The six pristine cognitions are the five commonly known ones together with that pristine cognitiveness of which the meaning-saturated field pristine cognitiveness is, as it were, a first stirring.

The highly energetic information processing associated with the radial (omnidirectional) organization of the emerging structure termed the teacher requires a multilimbed apparatus for optimum utilization. In this connection reference may be made to a comment by the psychologist Joseph Royce, *Consciousness and the Cosmos* (in *Extra-terrestrial Intelligence: the First Encounter*, ed. by James L. Christian), pp. 188f:

> ... what might a manlike creature be like if he evolved in the context of radial rather than bilateral symmetry? It is conceivable that radial symmetry would have involved an even more efficient central nervous system than we have. For example, bilateral symmetry involves two interacting brains (the left and right hemispheres); a radially symmetric brain would be anatomically unitary and ideally suited for coordinating inputs from any direction. Since a radially organized man would not have a front or a back, he would be able to accommodate stimulus inputs from all directions. If such an organism were moving in all the possible directions of three-space, rather than in our typical two-space (i.e., the plane of the ground), a radial system of sensory intake would be necessary. Radial motor outputs (e.g., a multitude of limbs, perhaps roughly like legs with the prehensile characteristics of the hand) would also be required. Having such characteristics would probably constitute at least the beginnings of cognizing an *n*-space world.

65. Some of these emblems are discussed in *Rong-'grel*, fol. 46a and *Klong-'grel*, p. 79.

66. *Klong-'grel*, p. 80, indicates that the characterization of having three heads (or faces) applies to each of the rulers over the five affinities with Being *(rigs)* as genotypes of psychic life. These regents and affinities are discussed in Chapter VII, pp. 151f. *Rong-'grel*, fol. 46a, interprets this characterization as implying that it refers to the triad of formal gestalt, authentic utterance, and vibrant spirituality such that formal gestalt is the openness of Being *(stong-pa-nyid)*; authentic utterance is not thematically characterizable *(mtshan-ma med-pa)*; and spirituality has no thematically determinable intention. Since these three characteristics function as doors to Experience-as-such or Being and also serve as conduits for the emergence of Being's qualitites and capacities, they are imaged as the prominent and preeminent features of Being in the shape of heads or faces. Dharmaśrī, *Coll. Works*, vol. 6, p. 52, combines both of the above interpretations.

67. See *Abhidharmakośabhāṣya* ad III 85d. See also P.W. Atkins, *Quanta*, p. 276, Table 16.

68. William K. Hartman, *Astronomy: The Cosmic Journey*, p. 423.

69. See *Abhidharmakośabhāṣya* ad III 93d-94a.

70. *Zab-yang* I, p. 294. Similar accounts are given by Klong-chen rab-'byams-pa in *mKha'-yang* I, p. 18; II, pp. 35, 70; III, pp. 125f. *Theg-mchog* I, p. 387f. *Zab-yang* II, p. 102. *Bla-yang* II, p. 5.

70a. Paul Davies, *Other Worlds*, p. 133.

70b. Richard Schlegel, *Superposition and Interaction*, p. 183.

71. *Zab-yang* I, p. 294.

72. Klong-chen rab-'byams-pa has discussed in another work the emergence of the ground-totality *(gzhi-snang)* from the dynamics of the ground *(gzhi),* providing by the indeterminacy that marks the spontaneously present *(ma-nges-pa'i lhun-grub)* for the development of the pure possibility of exercising freedom and of the impure possibility of going astray. Thus he says in *Bla-yang* I, p. 295:

> Just as from a crystal rays of light burst forth,
> So also from the ground's dynamic reach and range the ground
>   itself comes-into-presence (as a whole)
> Further, the ground has three creative modes:
> The creative mode of its facticity is an opening up (so that)
> In its nonthematic sky-(like) vastness
> The creative mode of its actuality is (a set of) five colors
> Separating into their intrinsic outward-tending glowing of five
>   pristine cognitions.
> The creative mode of its resonating concern is a mere cognizing
> Which arises as the capacity to thematize.
> This is the ground for both exercising freedom and for going astray.
> It (is termed) indeterminate spontaneous presence.

He then addresses himself to the question of how the ground can serve as ground for two seemingly contrary developmental processes of "pure" and "impure." In *mKha'-yang* II, pp. 84f., he uses the phenomenon of mirroring to elucidate this question. Just as a mirror serves as the ground for mirroring quite different images such that they appear within a projective depth beyond the surface of the mirror, so also Being serves and acts as the ground for the projective emergence of the pure and impure. Here we must be careful to remember that these emergent processes termed pure and impure are but virtual projective tendencies borne by Being-*qua*-Existenz's indeterminate dynamics; they are not preestablished and invariantly fixed programs. To those persistent questioners who are perhaps unsatisfied by the mirror analogy and insist on again raising the problem of how a single ground can give rise to both Nirvāṇa (pure) and Saṃsāra (impure), Klong-chen rab-'byams-pa replies that one might as well ask how this single earth produces such a variety of fruit-trees *(mKha'-yang* II, p. 96).

73. *Zab-yang* I, p. 325. Another treatment of these three facets is given by Klong-chen rab-'byams-pa in his *gNas-lugs,* p. 52:

> Here, creativity *(rtsal)* is the power of intelligence (which initiates) the individual appearance of either Saṃsāra or Nirvāṇa, just as a single ray of the sun makes the lotus *(padma)* open its flower and the lily *(kumuda)* close its flower.
> Playfulness *(rol-pa)* is the playful frolicking of intelligence in its outward glowing, like the playful dance of a lamp's flame in its luster or that of the sun in its rays.
> Beauty *(rgyan)* is the ornate enrichment of the self-arisen intelligence when whatever auto-presences manifests itself as a display, just as the sky is adorned by a rainbow or by the sun, moon, and stars. So also it is stated in the *Thig-le kun-gsal* (p. 142):

The facticity of creativity is that it is ceaselessly active

and (p. 144):

Vigor which never ceases and has no duality is what I declare to be
the facticity of creativity

and (p. 144):

For this reason, to be beautiful is called adornment.

For further references to creativity and playfulness see *Chos-dbyings*, fols.
50b, 165b, 178ab.

74. *Thig-le kun-gsal*, p. 143. Also quoted in *Zab-yang* II, p. 228, which, on the
whole, appears to have the better reading.

75. This is the rendering of the text as it occurs in *Zab-yang* II, p. 228. The
rNying-rgyud version, vol. 5, pp. 143f., has *rang-sar dag-pas* instead of
don-la sbyor-bas, which in translation would be that the six kinds of sentients
are just "fine as they are." This would suggest that there is little need for
concern.

76. This is the rendering of the text as it occurs in *rNying-rgyud*, vol. 5, p. 144,
with the spelling *brgyan* corrected as *rgyan (de phyir mdzes-pas brgyan
zhes-bya'o)*. However, *Zab-yang* II, p. 228, where this passage is quoted, has
mdzes-pa'i rgyan, which misses the point that there is an ornamenting
process, not a statement about a "beautiful ornament." *gNas-lugs*, p. 52, has
mdzes-pa rgyan (beautiful—an ornament), which is a possible reading, but
does not conform to the syntax of the other lines in which *mdzes-pa* occurs.
This is only one example of the problems facing a translator in the absence of
any critical editions of Tibetan texts.

77. *Thig-le kun-gsal*, p. 146. A slightly different, though closely related, set of
comparisons regarding the three aspects of this transformation process is
given in *dGongs-zang*, vol. 2, pp. 517f. and vol. 4, pp. 105f. The former
passages state:

The meaning-saturated field *(chos-kyi dbyings)* and the formal gestalt
(expressing the) meaningfulness (of this field) *(chos-kyi sku)* and
pristine cognitiveness *(ye-shes)*—these three are present as an indivisible reality, even if each is spoken of separately. The analogy for the
meaning-saturated field and the formal gestalt (expressing the) meaningfulness (of this field), is the ocean and the (reflection of the) stars in
the ocean. The analogy for the indivisibility of formal gestalt and
pristine cognitiveness, is water and salt (dissolved in it). The indivisibility of (this total) reality is present such that one facet adorns the
other. In the *rDzogs-pa chen-po zang-thal-gyi rgyud* it is stated:

Since the pure meaning-saturated field is adorned by the formal
gestalt (expressing the) meaningfulness (of this field), it does not
become an empty vacuousness, but is made beautiful by a glowing
radiance. Since the pure gestalt (expressing the) meaningfulness (of
this field) is adorned by pristine cognition, it is made beautiful by

ceaselessly (operative) capabilities. Since these pure capabilities are
adorned by resonating concern, they are made beautiful by (attending to the needs of) the sentient beings ranging over six kinds (of
life-forms). It is because of "being made beautiful" that one speaks
of ornamentation *(rgyan)*. The triad of formal gestalts operates
such that each gestalt adorns the other in successive order. The
formal gestalt (expressing the) meaningfulness (of this field) rises as
the ornament of the meaning-saturated field-reality; the two distinctly shaped gestalts operate as the ornament of the gestalt
(expressing the) meaningfulness (of the field). The five light
(values), each retaining its specific characteristic, operate as the
ornament of the two distinctly structured gestalt patterns. The
analogy for the meaning-saturated field adorned by the gestalt
(expressing the) meaningfulness (of the field), is a turquoise set in
gold. The analogy for the gestalt (expressing the) meaningfulness
(of the field) adorned by pristine cognitiveness is a crystal with its
flashing in five-colored light rays. The analogy for pristine cognitiveness adorned by resonating concern is the warm and gentle rays
coming from the sun's energy and serving the needs of sentients. As
is said in the *gSang-ba spyi rgyud*:

> The beautiful ornaments on a Buddha's body.

78. *Theg-mchog* I, p. 429.
79. A hermeneutical interpretation of the term *phrin-las* is given in *Rang-shar*, p.
    652:

    > *phrin* is spoken of as Buddhahood as such;
    > *las* is to experience pristine cognitiveness;
    > *phrin-las* (therefore) is said to be Being-as-such.

80. Such unfoldment may be compared to the topological models developed by
    René Thom in his *Structural Instability and Morphogenesis*, especially the
    topological aspects of biological morphogenesis. See pp. 151f. and 294.
81. *Rong-'grel*, fol. 55a.
82. *gSang-snying*, fol. 3ab.
83. This threefold discussion in terms of value *(don)*, formulated energies *(lha)*,
    and specifically delimited operation and domains *(rtog-pa)*, is based on
    gSal-byed me-long, fols. 72b f. The hermeneutical interpretation of *lha* as
    "formulated energy" is based on *Rong-'grel*, fol. 9a. The traditional account
    of this fivefold grouping has been discussed in my *Philosophy and Psychol-
    ogy in the Abhidharma*, p. 54. A detailed discussion of the elemental forces
    ('byung-ba) is given in *Theg-mchog* II, pp. 4ff.
84. *Klong-'grel*, p. 86.
85. See also above note 44.
86. The term *snang-ba'i dbyings* is synonymous with *dbyings-kyi dbang-phyug-
    ma*.
87. There are fifteen subdivisions that make up the functional grouping termed
    the structuring and the structured *(gzugs)*, which constitute the relative

invariance of our world: four elemental field forces *('byung-ba)* out of which the physical world is built; five sensory domains *(yul)*; five controlling sensory operations *(dbang-po)*; and a character trait *(rnam-par rig-pa ma-yin-pa'i gzugs)*. These subdivisions have been discussed in my *Buddhist Philosophy in Theory and Practice*, p. 63. Only the character trait as the basic "in-built" invariance of a person's ethico-behavioral tendencies is imaged as Mi-bskyod-pa (Akṣobhya). The other fourteen subdivisions are associated with the field of the relatively invariant sensory operations, and hence are imaged as Sangs-rgyas spyan-ma (Buddhalocanā). See *Klong-'grel*, p. 84.

88. The interpretation given here follows the account given by Klong-chen rab-'byams-pa in his *Klong-'grel*, pp. 69f. He rejects the claim by others that Mi-bskyod-pa (Akṣobhya) should be understood as the operation of perception and hence centrally placed. The centrality of Mi-bskyod-pa was upheld by all Indian commentators, on the *gSang-snying* and by every Tibetan commentator, from the time of Rong-zom-pa Chos-kyi bzang-po to the present (see *Rong-'grel*, fol. 46b). Klong-chen rab-'byams-pa seems to be the only exception. He states that those who place Mi-bskyod-pa in the central position merely follow the common Tantra treatises, and that the superior understanding, which is in accord with the more advanced treatises, places rNam-par snang-mdzad (Vairocana) in the central position. He must be centrally placed, because as perception he belongs to that genotype affinity with Being which functions as the identity transformation of spirituality *(thugs-kyi thugs-kyi rigs)*, which is itself the auto-mirroring of that special resonating concern *(thugs-rje)* of the teacher Kun-tu bzang-po, through which he is linked to the universe.

The functionally grouped operation of perception *(rnam-shes)* is explicated by Klong-chen rab-'byams-pa as consisting of an eightfold cognitive ensemble *(tshogs-brgyad)*. See *Klong-'grel*, pp. 82f. and Chapter III, note 8.

89. The functionally grouped operation of feeling *(tshor-ba)*, more properly "judgments of feeling," comprises the three possibilities of being either pleasurable, unpleasurable, or neutral. See *Klong-'grel*, p. 83.

90. The functionally grouped operation of conceptualization *('du-shes)*, is said to be either wide, narrow, or medium. See *Klong-'grel*, p. 83. These subdivisions seem to refer to the scope and repertoire of one's concepts and categories, determining the "conceptual horizon" of one's world.

91. The functionally grouped operation of motivating *('du-byed)* consists of fifty-one mental events. Only forty-nine of these, however (excluding the functionally grouped operations of feeling and conceptualization) are the domain of Don-yod grub-pa (Amoghasiddhi). Also to his domain belong those factors which are collectively termed interpretative schemata. See my *Buddhist Philosophy*, p. 64, section d. See also *Klong-'grel*, pp. 83f.

92. Pioneering treatises on elemental imagining have been written by Gaston Bachelard. See, for instance, his *The Psychoanalysis of Fire*.

93. These three perspectives were first elaborated in *Uttaratantra* I, 47. They may be favorably compared to the three levels of inquiry developed by Erich Jantsch: the rational (the impure), the mythological (the pure), and the evolutionary (the utterly pure). See his *Design for Evolution*, pp. 84ff. *et passim*.

94. *Klong-'grel*, p. 81. *Rong-'grel*, fol. 48b.

95. This discussion of the three perspectives as phase-states is based on *Klong-'grel,* p. 65. See also his *Yid-kyi mun-sel,* fol. 60b. Given the current vogue for spiritual transformation of all varieties, it might be worth emphasizing how different an understanding is here involved. One is neither engaged—according to materialistic-reductionist interpretations of the alchemical enterprise—in changing the "base nature" of one's impure givenness into the "gold" of (hypothetical) spirituality; nor is one encouraged, as certain misguided "spiritually oriented" psychologists would advise, to realize one's "higher" nature (sublimate).

96. *Klong-'grel,* p. 81.

97. An important indication of such an awareness of the erotic structure of perception in Western thinking has been given by Maurice Merleau-Ponty. He says in his *Phenomenology of Perception,* p. 157:

> Erotic perception is not a *cogitatio* which aims at a *cogitatum....*

and

> There is an erotic "comprehension" not of the order of understanding, since understanding subsumes an experience, once perceived, under some idea...

See also figure 22 for the basic erotic structure of perception.

98. *Klong-'grel,* pp. 87f.

99. The term auto-presencing *(rang-snang)* is one of the key terms in rDzogs-chen thought. Specifically, it refers to the excitatory intelligence *(rig-pa)* setting up for its own cognition what may be said to be a virtual field. One aspect of this intelligence is resonating concern *(thugs-rje),* which has its own creative dynamics *(rtsal).* The creativity of concern expresses itself in the operation of pristine cognitions having as their domain the nonreductive meaningfulness of Being. See *Chos-dbyings,* fols. 54a and 117a.

100. There is a subtle pun in this quoted passage. The functionaries, making up the entourage of the central intelligence, are called *sems-dpa'* in this male aspect and *sems-ma* in their female aspect. Furthermore, they are qualified as *byang-chub,* which in rDzogs-chen thought has been understood as an integrative process involving refinement, clarification, hence limpid clearness *(byang)* and a falling into a pattern, consummateness, hence consummate perspicacity *(chub).* Since the functionaries are the integrative process *(byang-chub)* in their very nature, they are superior to "ordinary" spiritually advanced beings *(byang-chub sems-dpa';* Sanskrit *bodhisattva).* On *byang-chub* as an integrative process see, for example, *Chos-dbyings,* fol. 173a, and *bDe-ba chen-po byang-chub-kyi sems rmad-du byung-ba'i le'u* (in *rNying-rgyud,* vol. 2) pp. 63f., 66. This same understanding is also stated in *Rong-'grel,* fol. 56a.

101. A lengthy discussion of *rdo-rje* as a symbol for the indestructibility of the openness of Being is given in *Dag-snang,* p. 260.

102. *rNying-rgyud,* vol. 14, p. 302.

103. *Klong-'grel,* pp. 194, 289.

104. *Klong-'grel,* pp. 194, 289f. These female functionaries are also known as "goddesses (presenting the) object-phase" *(yul-gyi lha-mo).* The term *yul,* which usually refers to what is commonly called an object, is here used, however, in the sense of operational domain. See *Rong-'grel,* fol. 57a.

105. *Klong-'grel,* pp. 88f.
106. *Rong-'grel,* fol. 56b, emphasizes the desirability of these female functionaries as functional fulfillment. This functional fulfillment is imaged as four *sgeg-mo (lāsyā).* This technical term refers to the gentle and seductively alluring movement of dance, associated in the Indian tradition with the King of Dancers, Śiva Naṭarāja. See C. Sivaramamurti, *Naṭarāja in Art, Thought and Literature.* Although some have imaged these female functionaries distinctly as *sGeg-mo (lāsyā), Phreng-ma (mālā), Klu-dbyangs-ma (Gīti),* and *Gar-ma (nṛtyā),* there is no need to do so. They are but nuances of the gestalt patterns of a gentle dance. See *Klong-'grel,* p. 89 and *Rong-'grel,* fol. 56b.
107. *Klong-'grel,* p. 194. These female functionaries are also known as "goddesses (presenting) temporality" *(dus-kyi lha-mo).* See *Klong-'grel,* p. 291 and *Rong-'grel,* fol. 57a. On fol. 57b Rong-zom-pa Chos-kyi bzang-po relates these female functionaries to the four immeasurable catalysts of kindness, compassion, joy, and equanimity. On these catalysts see *Kindly Bent,* vol. I, pp. 106ff. The order in which Rong-zom-pa Chos-kyi bzang-po enumerates them differs from that given by Klong-chen rab-'byams-pa in *Klong-'grel,* p. 90.
108. *gSang-snying,* fol. 2b. Although this phrase is used in connection with the palace, *Klong-'grel,* p. 56, makes it quite clear that Experience-as-such is the referent, the palace being its symbol for it.
109. *Klong-'grel,* p. 91.
110. The Buddhist assessment of "body" is in striking agreement with the systematic phenomenology of the animate organism as developed by Gabriel Marcel and, above all, by Maurice Merleau-Ponty. See for a critical study of the body Richard M. Zaner, *The Problem of Embodiment* and Ronald S. Valle and Mark King, *Existential-Phenomenological Alternatives for Psychology,* pp. 242ff. Medard Boss introduces the term "bodyhood" whose dynamic quality he describes in his *Existential Foundations of Medicine and Psychology,* pp. 102f. as follows:

> Human bodyhood is *always* the bodying forth of the ways of being in which we are dwelling and which constitute our existence at any given moment. Thus, just as there can be no independently existing time, there can be no self-contained, fundamental, and final human bodyhood. And just as man's actual temporality emerges only in the particular modes of human existence, so his bodyhood occurs exclusively as the bodying forth of his existential dwelling amid the beings that address themselves at any given time to his perception and require of him an appropriate response. The borders of my bodyhood coincide with those of my openness to the world. They are in fact at any given time identical, though they are always changing with the fluid expansion and contraction of my relationship to the world.

111. This figure and its elucidation is based on *Klong-'grel,* pp. 91f. Rong-zom-pa Chos-kyi bzang-po also understands by body the ensemble of embodiment, speech, and mentation. In *Rong-'grel,* fol. 57b, he says:

> The scriptures repeatedly say:

> Undecaying, nonthematic cognizing,
> Nonverbalization, nonconceptualization—
> Bliss is realized when one knows (this to be)
> Buddhahood—limpid clearness and consummate perspicacity—
>   pristine cognitiveness.

Here, decay relates to embodiment, cognizing to mentation, and verbalization to speech. Together these features constitute the general nature of a living being. These features are given the symbol names of Death (*gshin-rje*, Sanskrit Yama), Appreciative Discrimination (*shes-rab*, Sanskrit Prajñā), Lotus Flower (*pad-ma*, Sanskrit Padma), and Obstacle (*'gegs*, Sanskrit Vighna). That pristine cognition which understands the nonentitative character of birth and death, is termed Yamāntaka; that pristine cognition which understands the nonentitative character of thematic cognition is termed Prajñāntaka; that pristine cognition which understands the nonentitative character of talk is termed Padmāntaka; and that pristine cognition which understands the nonentitative character of all the above mentioned features of a living being taken together, is termed Vighnāntaka.

112. This account is based on *rGya-cher 'grel-pa*, pp. 72ff.
113. This figure and the following elucidation is based on Klong-chen rab-'byams-pa's account in which he relates the appreciatively sensitive and felt quality of pristine cognitiveness in its outward-directed movement to the four catalysts and the four distinctive attractions as the manifest operation of this sensitivity. See *Klong-'grel*, pp. 92f. For a discussion of the catalysts see *Kindly Bent*, vol. 1, pp. 106ff., and for that of the distinctive attractions see *Mahāyānasūt-rālankāra* XVI 72-78. Although the Figure 24 and its elucidation follows the interpretation given by Klong-chen rab-'byams-pa, one must be careful not to regard these correspondences as rigidly fixed. Other commentators on the *gSang-snying* have given varying accounts. Thus, for example, Rong-zom-pa Chos-kyi bzang-po declares that both the appreciatively sensitive and felt quality of pristine cognitiveness and its manifest operation have a liberating effect and are emissaries *(pho-nya)* whose mission is to gladden and encourage those who occupy high positions in the hierarchy of Perception. However, he arranges the correspondences in the following manner: generosity is related to sympathetic compassion; the acting out of the intrinsic meaning and value of Being is related to loving kindness; the monitoring and selecting of that which is appropriate and effective with respect to the value of one's overall life plan is related to joyousness; and the beauty of diction and sound is related to equanimity (*Rong-'grel*, fol. 58a). g.Yung-ston rdo-rje dpal bzang-po in his *gSal-byed me-long* (fol. 29a) presents yet a different account in which he relates the appreciative sensitivity of cognitiveness to the traditional four axioms of transitoriness, frustration, the nonexistence of an ontic principle, and openness.
114. See his *Value Systems and Social Process*, as quoted in Erich Jantsch, *Design for Evolution*, p. 106.
115. *Chos-dbyings*, fol. 20ab.

CHAPTER VI

1. Thus *gSang-snying* (fol. 9a) says: "Being is written by Being." See also

Chapter IV, p. 72.

2. Posturing *(bzhugs-stangs)* is interpreted by Klong-chen rab-'byams-pa in his *Theg-mchog* II, p. 152, as follows:

> *bzhugs-pa* (to sit, to have sat down) is not to go beyond the in-depth appraisal that is just there, and *stangs* (stance, perspective) is to effect deliverance from Saṃsāra.

In his *mKha'-yang* III, p. 130, he discusses "in-depth appraisal" by stressing its existential character. This existential character is also emphasized in *Chos-dbyings*, fols. 107a, 112a ff.

3. *gSang-snying*, fol. 11b.

4. *Klong-'grel*, pp. 232f.

5. The verse text of *gSang-snying* (fol. 11b) only gives *rdzogs* and, accordingly, has been rendered as "in full (sovereignty)." Klong-chen rab-'byams-pa (*Klong-'grel*, p. 233) interprets this term as *rdzogs-pa'i sangs-rgyas*. He glosses this term (on p. 436) as "Experience-as-such in just abiding as it is, is complete Buddha(hood)." This "just abiding as it is" is associated with its in-depth appraisal, indicating that, insofar as man is by nature the openness of Buddhahood, its in-depth appraisal as an aesthetic perceptivity is the manner in which man is programmed to perceive fully. His endeavors are attuned to the implementation of this program as open-ended fulfillment. The number twelve is arrived at by counting the male-female aspects of Kun-tu bzang-po and his five vassals. It is important to bear in mind that the female aspects are of equal import in constituting what is a complete Buddha.

6. *Klong-'grel*, pp. 78f.

7. Figure 25 and its explication is based on Nam-mkha' rin-chen, *Yid-bzhin-gyi nor-bu*, p. 51. Nam-mkha' rin-chen's interpretation itself is based on the *Thugs-kyi thigs-pa'i man-ngag* (in *rNying-rgyud*, vol. 14, pp. 639-665), p. 647.

8. Calvin O. Schrag, *Experience and Being*, p. 144:

> Semantically, the terms "embodied spirit" and "incarnated consciousness" have a convertible form. One might, without loss of meaning, speak of "spiritual embodiment" or "conscious incarnateness."

9. For this reason, the mighty ones *(thub-pa)* are imaged without a female consort. While intentionality can be objectified into its two poles of masculinity and femininity as images of appropriate action and appreciative discrimination, respectively, the "I can" is not amenable to such objectification. This does not, however, mean that the interplay between appropriate action and appreciative discrimination is here lacking. Rather, the "I can" is fed by the unbroken and undivided whole, which cannot be turned into an object of representational thinking. Hence, the *gSang-snying*, fol. 16a, says:

> (Their) female consort *(yum)* is the meaning-saturated continuum which cannot be objectified.

See also *Klong-'grel*, pp. 286f., *Rong-'grel*, fol. 87b, *Yid-bzhin-gyi nor-bu*, pp. 344f.

10. This temporality as such is called the "fourth" kind of time *(dus bzhi-pa)*,

which is identical with the coming-into-presence of Being as Being-*qua*-Existenz *(gzhi-snang)*. This coming-into-presence may be interpreted as the emergence of Saṃsāra or Nirvāṇa, and in this interpretation temporality as such becomes amenable to the temporal structuring of past, present, and future. The idea of a "fourth" kind of time is only found in the rNying-ma tradition.

11. *Klong-'grel*, p. 230. Klong-chen rab-'byams-pa here interprets the four spokes as four pristine cognitions,which cut through impediments that are responsible for the stepped-down version of excitatory intelligence, and the rim of the wheel as signifying that pristine cognitiveness defies any reduction to propositions about it.

Nam-mkha' rin-chen interprets the term "a four-spoked wheel" as including the hub, and thus signifying five pristine cognitions; and he interprets the rim of the wheel as signifying the internal logic of being (*Yid-bzhin-gyi nor-bu*, p. 276).

12. This rendering follows *Klong-'grel*, pp. 233f.

13. *rtsibs-mtshan.*

14. Klong-chen rab-'byams-pa interprets the studs as the four immeasureably great catalysts (*Klong-'grel*, p. 233); Nam-mkha' rin-chen interprets them as the four truths (*Yid-bzhin-gyi nor-bu*, p. 276).

15. Klong-chen rab-'byams-pa interprets the corridor which is circumambulatory, as symbolizing the omnidirectionality of pristine cognitiveness (*Klong-'grel*, p. 231); Nam-mkha' rin-chen interprets the corridor as symbolizing the unity of ultimate and relative realities (*Yid-bzhin-gyi nor-bu*, p. 276).

16. The *rasa* theory of Indian aesthetics was first expounded in terms of eight sentiments in the *Bhāratīya-nāṭyaśāstra*, an encyclopedic work attributed to Muni Bharata. The *Viṣṇudharmottara* adds a ninth sentiment—silence or calmness or peacefulness *(śānti)*—which, from the third to fourth centuries onward, was considered to be the supreme sentiment. The *Samaraṅgana-sūtradhara* of Bhojarāja (ca. 11th century) lists eleven sentiments.

The most exhaustive treatment of sentiments *(nyams)* in Tibetan literature is found in Khams-sprul IV bsTan-'dzin chos-kyi nyi-ma's monumental commentary on Daṇḍin's *Kāvyādarśa*, the *rGyan-gyi bstan-bcos me-long pan-chen bla-ma'i gsung-bzhin bkral-ba dbyangs-can ngag-gi rol-mtsho legs-bshad nor-bu'i 'byung-khungs*, pp. 422ff.

17. This distribution of the nine sentiments is found in Yon-tan rgya-mtsho's *Yon-tan mdzod-'grel*, vol. 2, p. 187. Here, he substitutes *gshe-ba* (reviling) for the traditional *'jigs-su rung-ba* (frightening shrieks).

18. *gSang-snying*, fol. 11b.

19. These five "qualitites" are representative of the creative, beauty-engendering capacities of Being's facticity *(ngo-bo)*. The term "facticity" does not refer to a static essence—in rDzogs-chen thought it is synonymous with the dynamic open dimension of Being. The German *Wesen* perhaps captures the active sense of this term. See also Chapter V, note 25.

In marked contrast to Klong-chen rab-'byams-pa's exegesis, which understands these qualities in their existential dimensions as being unaffected by the vicissitudes of finite existence (birth and so on), Nam-mkha' rin-chen, *Yid-bzhin-gyi nor-bu*, pp. 284f., basing himself on g.Yung-ston rdo-rje dpal bzang-po, *gSal-byed me-long*, fols. 88a f., interprets these qualities as follows:

mnyen: the limbs pliable like molten gold—arrogance transmuted;
lcug(s): fingers tapering like a snake's tail—aversion transmuted;
'khyil: appropriate action and appreciative discrimination interconnected like a turquoise and its mounting—desire transmuted;
ldem: the waist straight like a pine tree—envy transmuted;
gzhon-tshul-can: like an eight-year-old child—bewilderment (mental darkness) transmuted.

20. *gSang-snying,* fol. 11b. According to *Klong-'grel,* p. 241, these radiant
qualities are representative of the creative, beauty-engendering capacities of
Being's multifacetedness *(rnam-pa'i yon-tan).* While Klong-chen rab-
'byams-pa understands these qualitites in their existential dimension, Nam-
mkha' rin'chen (*Yid-bzhin-gyi nor-bu,* pp. 284f.) associates them with the
affective processes.

21. A long hermeneutical interpretation of the term *phyag-rgya* has been given
by Rong-zom-pa Chos-kyi bzang-po in *Rong-'grel,* fols. 25b ff. and in his
rGyud spyi'i dngos-po, pp. 518ff. Both texts are very similar in diction and
interpretation. The basic idea is that *phyag-rgya* is a patterned energy pointing beyond itself to something unpatterned and only becomes accessible to
interpretation through its patterning. In that it is both a marking and a
being-marked by Being it allows for thematic differentiations. The dynamics
of marking is seen as fourfold:

phya-rgya chen-po
dam-tshig-gi phyag-rgya
chos-kyi phyag-rgya
las-kyi phyag-rgya.

The resultant of the marking, the being-marked, is seen as threefold:

rang-bzhin-gyis grub-pa'i phyag-rgya
ye-shes-kyi phyag-rgya
phyag-rgya chen-po.

Furthermore, the dynamics of marking and being-marked exhibits a circu-
larity that may be diagrammed as follows:

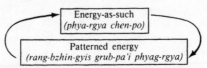

This is to say, energy-as-such *(phyag-rgya chen-po)* is a process of self-
patterning into patterned energy *(rang-bzhin-gyis grub-pa'i phyag-rgya)*
such that the energy (which is the universe in its totality) is split into two
interrelated modes; one presents the act phase, imaged as male, the other
presents the object phase, imaged as female. This marking-and-being-
marked, understood (because existentially felt), as a unitary process, is
termed a spontaneously present patterning-patterned energy *(lhun-gyis
grub-pa'i phyag-rgya).*

In his *Rong-'grel,* fols. 26b f., Rong-zom-pa Chos-kyi bzang-po equates *rang-bzhin-gyis grub-pa'i phyag-rgya* with *las-kyi phyag-rgya.* He says that this latter term indicates a woman's physical presence in contradistinction to the term *ye-shes-kyi phyag-rgya*, which indicates a dynamic qualitative pattern imaged in a female form, known as a mentally created goddess. He goes on to say that the term *phyag-rgya chen-po* indicates the meaning-saturated continuum as yet undisturbed by any perturbation through which it may become perceptible. He further indicates that the Tibetan term *phyag-rgya* was understood as encompassing three semantic modulations of the Sanskrit term *mudrā—mudrana* (sealing), *modana* (delighting), and *mudara.* This latter term (a Prākṛt form of Sanskrit *mudrā*) gave rise to a further interpretation which carries a dynamic connotation: *mu* indicates freedom and *dara* bondage; thus the term was understood to indicate either the operation of fettering and freeing oneself and others or the operation of removing each fetter individually.

22. *gSang-snying*, fol. 14b. The last line of this verse contains a reference to the full title of the *gSang-snying-gSang-ba'i snying-po de-kho-na-nyid nges-pa.* See *Klong-'grel*, p. 277.

23. This interpretation is based on Rong-zom-pa Chos-kyi bzang-po's statements in his *rGyud spyi'i dngos-po* (p. 518):

    (an individual) does not go beyond the realization of the needed aim which is his own

    and (p. 519):

    royalty, the indication of supreme patterned energy, means that it is not found in someone else (but in oneself), and this is what is meant by specific to the individual.

24. See his *Farbenlehre* § 175 and his letter of 3 March 1827 to Chr. D. v. Buttel. Cited in Hohannes Hoffmeister, *Wörterbuch der philosophischen Begriffe*, p. 636.

25. This renders the term Post-hoc-Zielgerichtetheit, coined by Rupert Riedel, *Die Strategie der Genesis.* Quoted in Erich Jantsch, *Erkenntnistheoretische Aspekte der Selbstorganization natürlicher Systeme*, p. 125, and Erich Jantsch, *The Self-organizing Universe*, p. 8.

26. *Rong-'grel*, fol. 26a. This verse is also quoted in *rGyud spyi'i dngos-po*, p. 521, where *rang-rig rgyas* is given as *rang-gi rgyas* which seems to be the better reading. But this version then concludes with the line which Rong-zom-pa Chos-kyi bzang-po says (*Rong-'grel*, fol. 26a) expresses the position of the ultimate Yoga approach.

27. See Rong-zom-pa Chos-kyi bzang-po's commentary on Padmasambhava's *Man-ngag lta-ba'i phreng-ba* in *Selected Writings*, p.76.

28. The distinction between an external Yoga approach and an ultimate Yoga approach is of utmost importance in connection with the idea of *mudrā* in the sense of delighting *(modana).* See above note 21. As Rong-zom-pa Chos-kyi bzang-po (in his *Rong-'grel*, fols. 26a f.) points out:

    According to both the ritually oriented *(bya-ba)* and the external Yoga approaches, the term *phyag-rgya* in the feminine gender refers to a gestalt in which goddesses have hidden. When this special feature is

pointed out to anyone, it is said to initiate delight (in this person) by
virtue of the fact that this is the way spirituality *(dam-tshig)* operates.
According to the ultimate Yoga approach an actual woman *(bud-med
nyid)* is spoken of as *phyag-rgya.* In this respect there is in both
approaches, whether one speaks of *phyag-rgya* as a woman or, as is the
case here of a woman as *phyag-rgya,* actually no difference in the fact
that delight is initiated. However, there is a difference with respect to
the levels of perceptivity on which a person in this world lives—he may
engage in the subtle and translucent or in the coarse and turbid.

The last sentence in this statement is of particular importance. Each participant in the drama we call life, is relatively situated within a meaning horizon
against which his life is acted out. Whatever the level of perceptivity and
perspective, the participant will see the world only within the parameters set
by this level which, however, he takes to be the whole of reality itself. Thus,
for example, since the universe in its polarity dynamics is imaged as exhibiting a "sexual" character, with respect to the phenomenon woman, according
to the level of perceptivity, one person will experience life only in terms of
genitalia, while another will be aware of the fact that there is more to it.

The term *dam-tshig* in the above quotation is short for *dam-tshig-gi
phyag-rgya.* It has been explained in *Rong-'grel,* fol. 27a, as follows:

Dam-tshig indicates the spirituality of True Individuality (in each and
every experiencer), which is pristine cognitiveness as the mystery (of
Being); *phyag-rgya* indicates that which (as mystery) has become
perceptible. In this respect *dam-tshig-gi phyag-rgya* is said to involve
the mutual differentiation (between the mystery as such and its
presence).

29. *Rong-'grel,* fol. 26a.
30. This interpretation of special *phyag-rgya*-s *(lhag-pa 'i phyag-rgya)* is based on
     gSal-byed me-long, fol. 103a.
31. *gSang-snying,* fol. 16a, illustrates this many-versions idea by the simile of a
     dancer who at any given moment is an ensemble of movements:

Like a dancer who
Performs many (movements)—not being restricted to any single
    movement of his body.
In brief, all these patterned energies
Cannot be said to be "this one" or to be "one only"
(For) there is a profusion of two and three and (more movements):
Movement (of the body as outer form) and delighting (in its inner
    spiritual and emotional content) are precisely this continuing
    (unity).
In brief, all movements and stirrings
Take place within the reach and range of Mahāmudrā *(phyag-rgya
    chen-po),*
But this "taking place" is neither an abiding nor a nonabiding.

The notion of the dancer as the ensemble of his movements is strikingly
similar to the modern notions of the "kinesphere," the "dynamosphere," and

the "choreutic shapes" as developed by Rudolf Laban. See his *The Language of Movement.*

32. *gSang-snying,* fol. 2b. The description is used with reference to the formal gestalt *(sku)* in which the central symbol is imaginally experienced. As Klong-chen rab-'byams-pa states *(Klong-'grel,* pp. 72f.), there is nothing solid or tangible about it; as pure spirituality it is omnipresent so that it is impossible to say that it has front or back.

33. *gSang-snying,* fol. 3a.

34. *gSang-snying,* fol. 11b.

35. *Klong-'grel,* pp. 237f. See also Figure 21.

36. Klong-chen rab-'byams-pa repeatedly states that rNam-par snang-mdzad (Vairocana) presents vibrant spirituality *(thugs),* central to the nature and development of man, and rooted in and operating from Buddhahood. See *Klong-'grel,* pp. 61 and 66. As previously indicated (see p. 107) Klong-chen rab-'byams-pa assigns the central position to rNam-par snang-mdzad (Vairocana), while all other commentators on the *gSang-snying* posit Mi-bskyod-pa (Akṣobhya) as the central figure. Their assignment of the respective emblems is, therefore, at variance with that of Klong-chen rab-'byams-pa. While Vairocana is taken as the symbol of spirituality *(thugs),* Akṣobhya is that of a formal gestalt *(sku),* Ratnasambhava that of creative potential *(yon-tan),* Amitābha that of authentic utterance *(gsung),* and Amoghasiddhi that of optimally executed activities *(phrin-las).* These activities are of four kinds, which reflect the different needs of those who have to be trained: calm and quietening *(zhi-ba),* expansive and bountiful *(rgyas-pa),* majestic and powerful *(dbang-po),* and stern and fierce *(drag-po).*

37. Sanskrit *dharmacakra.* This term is specifically used here as a symbol for the whole of the Buddhist transmission in all its nuances. The term *chos* (Sanskrit *dharma*) symbolizes the meaningfulness and valuableness of Being, and *'khor-lo* (Sanskrit *cakra*) symbolizes this meaningfulness spreading throughout. See *Klong-'grel,* p. 21; *Rong-'grel,* fols. 8b ff.

38. *Klong-'grel,* pp. 238f. See also Figure 22.

38a. Kun-tu bzang-po (Samantabhadra) as a functionary in the royal household, must be distinguished from Kun-tu bzang-po (Samantabhadra) as the supreme authority who is mankind's teacher, an image of the evolutionary principle.

39. *Klong-'grel,* p. 239. Although they are here given different names and iconographic attributes for purposes of visualization, as has been indicated before, they are all modulations of *sgeg-mo.* See Figure 22 and note 106 in Chapter V.

39a. On the distinction between reality value, formal evidence value, and existential evidence value see the detailed discussion by Alexander Gosztonyi in his *Grundlagen der Erkenntnis.*

40. *Klong-'grel,* pp. 240, 286. See also Figure 23.

41. *Klong-'grel,* pp. 240, 286. They are said to carry their respective emblems in their left hands, while embracing their consorts with their right hands formed as fists. See *Klong-'grel,* p. 286.

42. This idea of responsibility is expressed in the notion of karma. Literally this term means action. It has been traditionally linked up with the idea that no man can escape the consequences of his actions and that therefore also no

man can be held responsible for something he has not done. Therefore one has to act in a responsible manner, which is another way of saying that man is duty-bound to act in such a manner. The fact that the Sanskrit words *karma* (action) and *karuṇā* (compassion) are derived from the same root *kṛ* (to act) gives added significance to this central conception of Buddhism—to act compassionately.

43. *Klong-'grel*, pp. 239f.
44. *Klong-'grel*, p. 234. On p. 240, Klong-chen rab-'byams'pa remarks that there have been those who claim that Kun-tu bzang-po holds a diamond scepter and Kun-tu bzang-mo holds a lotus, which would thus transform them into something thematic. He goes on to say that such persons have failed to understand the thematic implication of *lha'i dag-pa*—*lha* is a specific formulation of psychic energy (see *Rong-'grel*, fol. 9a; *Klong-'grel*, p. 436) and *dag-pa* indicates the qualitative and imaginal character of the formulation. Kun-tu bzang-po and Kun-tu bzang-mo, however, are as yet unformulated energies. Klong-chen rab-'byams-pa's interpretation clearly indicates the aniconic character of Buddhist symbols. This has recently also been recognized in the excellent account given by Dietrich Seckel in his *Jenseits des Bildes. Anikonische Symbolik in der buddhistischen Kunst.*
45. *Klong-'grel*, p. 240.
46. *Klong-'grel*, p. 287.
47. *Yid-bzhin-gyi nor-bu*, p. 345.
48. The concise words of the *gSang-snying*, fol. 16a:

> Kun-bzang (in a state of) composure lets pristine cognitions burst forth;
> (What has) become (His) consort—alike (and) complete—(with) lotus gesture

has been elucidated by Rong-zom-pa Chos-kyi bzang-po in his *Rong-'grel*, fol. 87b, as follows:

> The patterned energy of Kun-tu bzang-po is a state of composure *(mnyam-par bzhag-pa)*, and from it light rays of pristine cognitions burst forth. The patterned energy of Kun-tu bzang-mo is identity-*cum*-completeness *(mnyam-rdzogs)* because She is spontaneously present in this state of composure. Her patterned energy is like that of Her consort. There is only a slight difference in posture. She sits in lotus posture.

Both Rong-zom-pa Chos-kyi bzang-po and Klong-chen rab-'byams-pa seem to have understood the term *padmo'i dkyil* as given in the verse of *gSang-snying*, as meaning *padmo'i skyil-mo-khrung* (lotus posture). Nam-mkha' rin-chen (see *Yid-bzin-gyi nor-bu*, p. 345), however, has interpreted the term *padmo'i dkyil* as indicating a position of the fingers. The positioning of the fingers plays an important role in Buddhist ritual, which is essentially a reenacting and reliving of processes that have engendered these outward (gestural) manifestations. Thus, far from having to do with magic, ritual is properly understood as a form of showing respect.

49. *gSang-snying*, fol. 3a. Color combinations are indirectly indicated on fol. 11b.
50. This has been stated poetically by Johann Wolfgang von Goethe:

> Wär' nicht das Auge sonnenhaft,
> Die Sonne könnt' es nicht erkennen
> [If the eye were not of the nature of the sun,
> It would not be able to perceive the sun].

51. The term formant is explicated by J.Z. Young, *Programs of the Brain*, p. 182, as follows:

> These damped resonances of the [supralaryngeal] tract are known as the formant frequencies of speech. The lowest peak frequency is known as the first formant, the next peak as the second formant and so on. The vowel sounds are usually recognizable by identifying the relative positions of the first two formants...Some consonants also have formant frequencies....

52. These five constitute genotypal encodement patterns on which see Chapter VIII. They may be envisaged as forming a configuration of horizontal connectiveness, yet also exhibiting a verticality indicative of a hierarchical order. This latter aspect has been detailed in *Thal-'gyur*, pp. 197ff.

53. *Klong-'grel*, pp. 240f. Klong-chen rab-'byams-pa seems to have been the only person who was aware of the subtle distinction between the inner and outer functionaries in the royal household and has arranged the color scheme accordingly.

54. The six greatnesses are given in *Klong-'grel*, p. 12. See also Chapter IV, note 4. The *dGongs-'dus* (in *rNying-rgyud*, vol. 11, pp.1-537), pp. 106f., gives a list of ten greatnesses.

55. *Klong-'grel*, p. 241. Mañjuśrī and Mañjughoṣa are interchangeable names.

56. *Klong-'grel*, p. 241. Paramāśva and Hayagrīva are interchangeable names.

57. Man is a spiritually concentrated *(bcud)* nexus of ongoing embodiment processes that creatively actualize in the concrete situations of everyday encounters, the preprograms of Existenz *(rgyud)*. This is but one of the interpretations of Existenz. See *Theg-mchog* I, p. 176 and Chapter II, pp. 17f.

58. *gSang-snying*, fol. 11b.

59. *gSang-snying*, fol. 11b.

60. *gSang-snying*, fol. 12a.

CHAPTER VII

1. *Klong-'grel*, p. 170.

2. *Rang-shar*, p. 400.

3. The terms *phrin-las* and *mdzad-pa* are closely related. Both refer to "activity" on the virtual level, which is indicated by the use of the term "formal gestalt" *(sku)* as the inseparable object phase of the act phase "pristine cognition" *(ye-shes)*. According to Klong-chen rab-'byams-pa's interpretation (in *Theg-mchog* I, p. 17), *mdzad-pa* is not a doing something, but Being's capabilities and creativity which, though still on this virtual level, tends to assume the modalities of task execution in being the energy in pristine cognitions.

The term *phrin-las* is explicated in detail (in *Theg-mchog* II, pp. 47ff.) on the basis of *Rang-shar*, p. 652, as follows:

> *phrin* is so termed with respect to Buddhahood;
> *las* is experiencing of and by pristine cognitions;
> *phrin-las* is said to be (Being) itself.

Insofar as *phrin-las* relates to Being in its totality, it is present in this its totality in and as each living being enacting, as it were, Being's program through an enchanting gracefulness (compare Greek *charis*) expressing the underlying wholeness. Such graceful activity, rooted in and borne by the whole, is, indeed, "charismatic" in the best sense of the word.

In *Klong-'grel,* p. 488, *mdzad-pa/phrin-las* is said to be the formal gestalt through which cultural features become intelligible *(sprul-pa'i sku).*

4. *Klong-'grel,* p. 488.
5. *Klong-'grel,* p. 488.
6. We have seen above, p. 84, that 'Og-min is the site upon which the palace of Kun-tu bzang-po is situated. In this context, 'Og-min is the site of the palace of the quincunx of Herukas. The various Herukas, specifically Che-mchog Heruka (the center of the quincunx), are but Kun-tu bzang-po in his fierceness. On the hermeneutical interpretation of the term Heruka see below, p. 280 n.24.
7. *Klong-'grel,* p. 488.
8. As to the character of the four modalities there is general agreement between Klong-chen rab-'byams-pa and Rong-zom-pa Chos-kyi bzang-po. The latter, however, lists resonating concern *(thugs-rje)* instead of *mdzad-pa*— actually the "quality" of the "activity"—and uses *mdzad-pa* instead of *phrin-las.* See *Rong-'grel,* fol. 115a. On the distinction between *mdzad-pa* and *phrin-las* see above note 3.

    g.Yung-ston rdo-rje dpal bzang-po (in *gSal-byed me-long,* fols. 163a f.) lists only three modalities: (1) the fierceness of appreciative discrimination *(shes-rab)* by which the belief in defining characteristics set up by thematizing thought as having an existence of their own is overcome; (2) the fierceness of pristine cognitiveness *(ye-shes)* which, in its sovereignty over what is held to be a duality, eradicates the germination into such a duality judged as Saṃsāra and Nirvāṇa; and (3) the fierceness of Mahāmudrā *(phyag-rgya chen-po)* through which the dynamics of Being-*qua*-Existenz expresses itself in the colors and emblems of the formal gestalts as they make themselves felt in experience in order to discipline recalcitrant beings. As previously noted (see Chapter V, note 113 and Chapter VI, note 19), g.Yung-ston rdo-rje dpal bzang-po's exegesis is minimally hermeneutic. By contrast that of Klong-chen rab-'byams-pa is profoundly hermeneutic. That this is so may be gleaned from a careful comparison of the exegesis by g.Yung-ston rdo-rje dpal bzang-po's given in this note with that of Klong-chen rab-'byams-pa as given in what now follows in the body of the text. Perhaps, it was precisely because of the more "profound" and hence more difficult hermeneutical endeavor of Klong-chen rab-'byams-pa that the presentation by g.Yung-ston rdo-rje dpal bzang-po was widely accepted. This acceptance can be demonstrated by the fact that his words have been taken over *verbatim* by Nam-mkha' rin-chen, *Yid bzhin-gyi mun-sel,* pp. 563f., and by Lo-chen Dharmaśrī, *Coll. Works,* vol. 6, p. 288. 'Gyur-med phan-bde 'od-zer, *lDe'u-mig,* p. 587, seems to attempt to combine the presentations of g.Yung-ston rdo-rje dpal bzang-po and Klong-chen rab-'byams-pa, his listing being:

shes-rab, ye-shes, thugs-rje, and *phrin-las.*

9. *Klong-'grel,* p. 489.
10. *Klong-'grel,* p. 489.
11. *Klong-'grel,* p. 489.
12. *Klong-'grel,* p. 489.
13. *dGongs-'dus,* p. 160; also quoted in *Klong-'grel,* p. 489.
14. Stepped-down excitation *(ma-rig-pa)* is itself the affective momentum that "engenders" and fuels the variety of affective processes that afflict man by enslaving him to the repetition of self-inflicted mistakes *(ma-rig bdag-tu 'dzin),* collectively termed Saṃsāra. It is in the wake of this affective momentum that affective processes, which vary in strength, have to be met by rectifying measures which are themselves of equal, if not superior, strength. Thus, the most strongly ("fiercely") agitating affective process, irritation-annoyance *(zhe-sdang)* easily developing into implacable hatred and spilling over into arrogance-egomania and envy, must be met by the strongest ("fiercest") rectifying measure *(khro-bo'i gdangs);* the calmer (less agitating) affective process of passion-addiction *('dod-chags)* can be rectified by milder measures *(zhi-ba'i mdangs);* the background affective process of dullness-infatuation *(gti-mug)* can be rectified by measures that are gentle or fierce *(zhi-khro)* in accord with the relative strength of the "background" affect. See *Klong-'grel,* p. 490.
15. See below note 23.
16. The close connection between open spaces and feelings of harmony and ease and closed-up spaces and feelings of disharmony and distress (dis-ease) is already embedded in the Sanskrit terms *sukha* (pleasure, happiness) and *duḥkha* (frustration, suffering). The word *sukha* is formed from the particle *su* (good, Greek *eu-*) and the noun *kha* (sky, open space); and the word *duḥkha* is formed from the particle *duḥ* (bad, Greek *dys-*) and the noun *kha.*
17. *gSang-snying,* fol. 24b; *Klong-'grel,* pp. 504f.; *rGya-cher,* pp. 375f.
18. The distinction and interrelation between the intrinsically mysterious mystery of Being *(gab-pa'i gsang-ba)* and the mystery of Being's concealment *(sbas-pa'i gsang-ba)* is quite subtle. It would seem that something akin to this subtlety has been glimpsed by Martin Heidegger in his discussion of the Greek word *aletheia* ("truth") as unconcealment. See, for instance, *An Introduction to Metaphysics,* p. 159.
19. For a critique of the classical psychoanalytical understanding of sadomasochism see Medard Boss, *Meaning and Context of Sexual Perversions.*
20. This story is told at length in *dGongs-'dus,* pp. 130ff. and summarized in *Klong-'grel,* pp. 496, 505. According to *rGya-cher,* p.377, Rudra (Rutra) is the son of Śiva and Umādevī.
21. The six realms and their associated affective processes are listed in Figure 24. Even the so-called "higher" realms of meditative states, which are imaged as being presided over by various gods, may cause harmful disruptions in those individuals who hypostatize these meditative experiences as being intrinsically important. See *Klong-grel,* pp. 495f.
22. On the term "chreod" see Conrad H. Waddington, *The Evolution of an Evolutionist,* p. 221. See also Erich Jantsch, *The Self-Organizing Universe,* p. 57.
23. C.H. Waddington, *The Evolution of an Evolutionist,* p. 223. Erich Jantsch,

The Self-Organizing Universe, p. 273.

24. *Rong-'grel,* fol. 117b. A different hermeneutical interpretation is given in *dPal Heruka'i thugs-kyi rgyud gal-po* (in *rNying-rgyud,* vol. 25, pp. 376-395), p. 377:

> *Śrī* indicates nonduality;
> *He* is laughter in delight;
> *Ru* is love supreme; and
> *Ka* is pristine cognitiveness as four (charismatic) activities.

25. *sgyu-'phrul dra-ba.* This term is also a name for a set of Mahāyoga Tantras amongst which the *gSang-snying* figures prominently.
26. *Klong-'grel,* p. 513.
27. *Klong-'grel,* pp. 513f.
28. *Klong-'grel,* pp. 516f.
29. *bcom-ldan-'das.* For the hermeneutical interpretation of this term see Chapter V, pp. 95f.
30. This feature refers to formal gestalt *(sku).*
31. This feature refers to authentic utterance *(gsung).*
32. The three releasements as gateways to Being are: (1) the openness of Being-*qua*-Existenz itself as a dynamic opening up *(stong-pa-nyid);* (2) the fact that such openness has no defining characteristics *(mtshan-ma med-pa)* which, traditionally subsumed under the categories of substance and quality, would limit openness; and (3) the fact that such openness cannot be biased *(smon-pa med-pa)* in favor of either of the two deviant trends of Saṃsāra and Nirvāṇa.

     The six transcending functions are the commonly listed ones of (1) liberal generosity (specifically in the sense of sharing), (2) self-discipline (as expressing itself in ethics and manners), (3) patient acceptance, (4) strenuous and vigorous striving, (5) meditative concentration (leading to the in-depth appraisal of one's being), and (6) appreciative discrimination (as both a climax of one's development and a sustaining power giving meaning and direction to the exercise of the preceding five functions).

     The four bases for success are: (1) taking a serious interest in what one is doing (and not acting in a routine fashion), (2) persevering in one's undertaking, (3) remaining motivated, and (4) critically assessing the context of one's engagement. See *Klong-'grel,* pp. 52, 57ff. For the complexity of these four bases see also *Kindly Bent to Ease Us,* vol. 1, pp. 242f.

33. In g.Yung-ston rdo-rje dpal bzang-po's account (in *gSal-byed me-long,* fols. 167a f.) the position of the legs is reversed. Those who accept this account, in which the left leg is drawn in and the right leg stretched out, are criticized by Klong-chen rab-'byams pa, without elaboration, as not correctly understanding the underlying imagery of appropriate action *(thabs)* and appreciative discrimination *(shes-rab).*
34. *Zab-yang* II, p. 71.
35. This figure is based on *Klong-'grel,* p. 517.
36. *Klong-'grel,* pp. 518, 548.
37. *gSang-snying,* fol. 27a.
38. *Klong-'grel,* p. 520.
39. See *Rong-'grel,* fol. 99a. The complementarity of *sgrol* and *sbyor* is discussed at length, though in concise terms in the *rDo-rje gsang-ba'i snying-po rtsa-*

ba'i rgyud de-kho-na-nyid nges-pa (in *rNying-rgyud,* vol. 16, pp. 1-138), p. 82. See also *rGya-cher,* pp. 314f.

40. This term is used synonymously with Kun-tu bzang-po in male-female complementarity. See *Klong-'grel,* p. 452. According to Rong-zom-pa Chos-kyi bzang-po, *Collection of Writings,* p. 253, this term is one in a set of three: *ngang, rang-bzhin,* and *bdag-nyid chen-po.* Here, *ngang* (the reach and range of Being) is synonymous with *ma-byas-pa* (uncreated); *rang-bzhin* (actuality) is synonymous with *ma-bcos-pa* (uncontrived); and *bdag-nyid chen-po* (True Individuality) is synonymous with *lhun-gyis grub-pa* (spontaneously present). Furthermore, "uncreated" means that, however much (Being) may be falsified by the mistaken notions of sentient beings about it, its actuality as mind cannot be turned into something other (than Being's pervasive intelligence). "Uncontrived" means that whatever means as appropriate action are deployed by the Victorious Ones (the Buddhas), Being's potential, which is the intent on limpid clearness and consummate perspicacity, cannot be used for ulterior purposes. "Spontaneously present" means that in view of this fact Being is beyond the notion of being a place where one may go or the notion of being something that has to be refined.

41. *gSang-snying,* fol. 27b.

42. *gSang-snying,* fol. 27b.

43. *Klong-'grel,* p. 527.

44. Here, the term "social" is not to be construed as a classificatory concept. It is used rather in the sense that the experiencer is always installed in a world and interacts with others. See also Calvin O. Schrag, *Experience and Being,* pp. 182ff.

45. This chart is based on Ngag-dbang bstan-'dzin rdo-rje's *rGyud-don snang-ba,* p. 74. However, it must not be assumed that this correlation between affective processes and inhabitants in their environments is of a rigidly fixed nature, and that there is a clear demarcation between these processes and their correlates. The affective processes are multifrequency pulsations within the system Being-*qua*-Existenz, each surging in a wave-like manner. To use the analogy of quantum mechanics, within an individual any such affective process may be understood as an operator having an eigenvalue corresponding to the observation of the state in a given eigenstate. For example, if we take irritation-aversion *(zhe-sdang)*—itself a summary term for every possible variation ranging from slight irritation to implacable hatred—as an operator for the determinable under consideration (in this context designated as hell), then the value for the state in which the system finds itself as either hot or cold, is the eigenvalue of the operator. Hot anger or cold rage aptly describe such a state in experiential terms. The expectation value of the operator irritation-aversion would be the result of experimenting with irritation-aversion, which would then be observed as the value of the state of the system determined and labeled hell. The same holds good for the other affective processes.

46. See *Klong-'grel,* p. 535 and *Rong-'grel,* fol. 116b. Both passages are almost identical in diction.

47. *gSang-snying,* fol. 31a.

48. While the *gSang-snying* text uses the term *dkyil-'khor* "configuration," Klong-chen rab-'byams-pa *(Klong-'grel,* p. 540) specifically emphasizes the

idea of a center *(dkyil)* and its periphery *('khor)*, for in this context it is the center or zero point that is of primary importance. The image itself is indicative of the reticular pattern of the five involvement domains *(rigs)*.

49.   They serve as symbols for the catalysts of kindness, compassion, joy, and equanimity. For a discussion of their operation see *Kindly Bent*, vol. 1, pp. 106ff. The wheel studs may also serve as symbols for the four axioms of transitoriness, frustration, the invalidity of the assumption of an ontic principle (ego/Self), and the fact that ecstatic bliss, which is felt when whatever has been restrictive and debilitating has faded away, is not a mere judgment of feeling. See *Klong-'grel*, p. 544; *Yid-bzhin-gyi nor-bu*, p. 602.

50.   They serve as symbols for the releasements *(thar-pa)* and the access to them. The releasements are both processes and states of being. See *Klong-'grel*, pp. 52f. and *Rong-'grel*, fol. 42b.

51.   They symbolize the conventionally accepted reality and the ultimately valid reality modes. See *Klong-'grel*, p. 544.

52.   *gSang-snying*, fol. 31a. Klong-chen rab-'byams-pa *(Klong-'grel*, p. 545) amends the text by reading *zung* (couple) instead of *bzung* (clutching). As he points out, the evil forces imaged anthropomorphically are trampled upon by the Herukas, they are not grasped by the claws of talons of the wild animals. The translation follows Klong-chen rab-'byams-pa's interpretation.

53.   *Klong-'grel*, p. 544.

54.   *Rong-'grel*, fol. 120a.

55.   *Yid-bzhin nor-bu*, p. 603. It seems, however, that Nam-mkha' rin-chen does not clearly distinguish between the Herukas and their relationships to the involvement domains.

56.   *gSang-snying*, fol. 31a.

57.   In connection with the "colors" mentioned, reference may be made to Johann Wolfgang von Goethe's *Farbenlehre* (theory of colors), which is based on man's interaction with reality as an integral physical-psychic process, both aspects shaping each other. See also Johannes Itten, *The Elements of Color*.

58.   *gSang-snying*, fol. 31a. The inversion of the lines of the original text is made by Klong-chen rab-'byams-pa *(Klong-'grel*, pp. 545f.) so as to provide logical coherence. For the symbolism involved see also *gSal-byed me-long*, fol. 179a.

59.   On the terms act phase and object phase see Edward S. Casey, *Imagining*, pp. 38ff.

60.   *tshogs*. Rong-zom-pa Chos-kyi bzang-po *(Rong-'grel*, fol. 118b) discusses the use of this term. He mentions other commentators, though not by name, who in accord with a grammatical convention consider *tshogs* as an honorific. He himself explains his preference for *tshogs* being a plural marker. In this specific context, *tshogs* as a plural marker indicates that for every single "generic" endorsement carrier there are actually a plurality of specific endorsement carriers corresponding to the plurality of specific individuals in whom they operate. Klong-chen rab-'byams-pa *(Klong-'grel*, p. 527) agrees.

61.   The hermeneutical explication of the term *phyag-rgya* follows *Rong-'grel*, fols. 25b ff., 85b f., and 119a.

    The term *ma-mo* which is used interchangeably with *phyag-rgya* (see also note 65 below), is explicated by Ngag-dbang bstan-'dzin rdo-rje *(rGyud-don snang-ba*, p. 15) as follows:

ma means (Being's) energy, the thrust toward limpid clearness and consummate perspicacity; *mo* means self-existent pristine cognitiveness.

62. *Klong-'grel,* pp. 527, 539, 547.
63. There is here a remarkable similarity between the Buddhist conception of the "body" as an ongoing process of embodiment and modern phenomenological studies. Calvin O. Schrag, *Experience and Being,* p. 132, calls the body an "incarnated project"; M. Merleau-Ponty, *Phenomenology of Perception,* p. 144, declares that "the body is our anchorage in a world," and pp. 249f.: "What counts for the orientation of the spectacle is not my body as it in fact is, as a thing in objective space, but as a system of possible actions, a virtual body with its phenomenal 'place' defined by its task and situation." Richard M. Zaner has made a book-length study entitled *The Problem of Embodiment.*
64. The ordering of these endorsement carriers follows *Klong-'grel,* p. 539. The same ordering is found in *gSal-byed me-long,* fol. 175b. The correlation with affective tone is based on *Rong-'grel,* fol. 119a.
65. *gSang-snying,* fol. 31b. The commentaries use the term *phra-men* for *yul-gyi phyag-rgya* ("object phase" endorsement carriers) and *ma-mo* for *gnas-kyi phyag-rgya* ("act phase" endorsement carriers). This difference in diction reflects their distinguishing between pure functionality and formulated energy *(lha).*
66. The names given here are those in *gSang-snying,* fol. 28b. In the same work, fol. 30b, however, vulture-faced one is given instead of goose-faced one, and crow-faced one instead of egret-faced one. This reflects the fact that there is no mechanical rigidity in symbol-formation. Whichever symbolic form the intrapsychic process will assume depends very much on the disposition of the individual. This is clearly stated in *Klong-'grel,* p. 550 and *Yid-bzhin-gyi nor-bu,* p. 609.
67. *Rong-'grel,* fol. 119a states:

   The four (female figures) having the faces of fierce carnivorous animals are said to be the endorsement carriers who overcome the four deadening powers (by virtue of) the charismatic activities pertaining to the four involvement domains. The four (female figures) having the faces of wild birds are said to be the endorsement carriers who act for the sake of sentient beings (so as to bring out their intrinsic value) by means of four pristine cognitions.

68. *gSang-snying,* fol. 29b f.
69. *gSang-snying,* fol. 31b.
70. *slas.* The commentaries explain this term by *chung-ma,* which usually means "wife." However, the central Heruka has his *btsun-mo,* "female consort" who is superior in rank and inseparable from him.
71. This number refers to the individual consorts of the defeated powers who, when what held them trapped was broken up, rushed to the quincunx of Herukas. Out of these twenty-eight, twenty were constituted into: eight *ma-mo,* eight *phra-men,* and four *sgo-ma,* thereby indicating that at least a portion of their energy was recycled. This partial recycling may be understood as indicating that the emergence of a new regime occurs through the utilization of what may be seen as the gene pool of available information.

CHAPTER VIII

1. *gSang-snying,* fol. 12b.
2. *Chos-dbyings,* fol. 30a. In the same work, on fol. 66a, Klong-chen rab-'byams-pa states that "Experience-as-such *(sems-nyid)* in just being experience *(ji-bzhin-pa),* is the facticity of the meaning-saturated gestalt." See also *gNas-lugs,* pp. 127f.
3. *gSang-snying,* fol. 12b.
4. *gSang-snying,* fol. 12b.
5. This idea of "one flavor," which is elaborated in *Zab-yang* I, pp. 213, 225, highlights the experiential character of Being's dynamics, preserving its unique identity in all its ramifications. The unified coherence of three seemingly separable entities (which may be designated by *a, b,* and *c)* may be likened to the mathematical concept of an abstract group *G* such that the operation "*" assigns to any element *a* and *b* of *G* an element *a*b* which also belongs to *G.* This operation must satisfy the following three conditions:

    (1) It is associative; that is, for any *a, b, c* E *G* we have
    $$a*(b*a) = (a*b)*c.$$

    (2) *There is an identity element I* E *G such that I*a = a = a*I for any a* E *G.* This identity is unique, which means that there is only one such element.

    (3) There are inverses; that is, for any *a* E *G* there exists a^{-1} E *G* such that $a*a^{-1} = I = a^{-1}*a.$

6. *Chos-dbyings,* fol. 195a.
7. See also *Chos-dbyings,* fol. 194a, where Klong-chen rab-'byams-pa refers to the *gSang-snying,* which uses the term four(fold) time *(dus bzhi).* In his *Klong-'grel,* p. 33, he explicates this term as meaning "indeterminate as to any of the three (distinct) aspects of (ordinary) time" and as being the very process of Being-*qua*-Existenz. See also Chapter VI, note 10.
8. *Rang-shar,* p. 443. See also *Tshig-don,* p. 448 and *Chos-dbyings,* fol. 122b.
9. *Yi-ge med-pa,* p. 273, explicitly states:

    > The meaning-saturated gestalt does not exist in and as a domain of manifest presencing

    and it continues:

    > The scenario gestalt does not exist as an objectifiable domain having specific characteristics (such as substance and quality);
    > The display gestalt does not exist as an ego or self.

10. This idea is also found in *Chos-dbyings,* fol. 33b; *gNas-lugs,* pp. 127f.; and *Bla-yang* II, p. 24.
11. *Klong-drug-pa,* pp. 183f. The printed version of this text and the quotation by Klong-chen rab-'byams-pa differ in a few minor variant readings. The overall intent of the passage is not affected.
12. See also *Chos-dbyings,* fols. 65b f. and *Seng-ge rtsal-rdzogs,* p. 293.
13. The term *dag-pa* is used with reference to both the diaphanous, aesthetically

moving and qualitative character of what is experienced, and the individual who is capable of such an experience by virtue of having refined sensibilities. By contrast, the term *ma-dag-pa* refers to the opaque, coarse, and quantitative to which experience is reduced by whomsoever lacks in refined sensibilities.

14. *gNas-lugs*, p. 52. See also *Zab-yang* II, pp. 221ff., where each of these three terms is explicated with reference to the *Thig-le kun-gsal*, pp. 140f. The very diction of the *Zab-yang* makes it abundantly clear that despite the concrete associations these terms elicit in us, they refer to virtual processes.

15. *Chos-dbyings*, fol. 12a.

16. See for instance *Chos-dbyings*, fols. 4a; 22a f.

17. *Thig-le kun-gsal*, p. 143; also quoted in *Zab-yang* II, p. 228. In this connection reference may be made to the following passage in *dGongs-zang*, vol. 2, pp. 517f.:

> Although one may speak of the triad of meaning-saturated field, meaning-saturated gestalt, and pristine cognitiveness, one at a time, (the triad) abides indivisibly. An analogy for the indivisibility of meaning-saturated field and meaning-saturated gestalt is the ocean and (the reflection of) the stars in it; an analogy for the indivisibility of (meaning-saturated) gestalt and pristine cognitiveness is water and salt (dissolved in it). Each enhances the other in beauty and all abide indivisible. The *rDzogs-pa chen-po zang-thal-gyi rgyud* states:
>
> > Since the diaphanous meaning-saturated field is splendorously adorned by the meaning-saturated gestalt
> > Its openness does not turn into an utter nothingness but (abides) beautifully enhanced through lucency.
> > Since the diaphanous meaning-saturated gestalt is splendorously adorned by pristine cognitiveness
> > It (abides) beautifully enhanced by ceaselessly vibrant qualitites.
> > Since the diaphanous qualities are splendorously adorned by resonating concern
> > (They display their) beauty to the sentient beings in the six life-worlds.
> > Because of this beauty one speaks of splendorous adornment and
> > An enhancement in beauty through a gradation (in the) triad of gestalts.
>
> Thus the meaning-saturated gestalt serves as a splendorous adornment for the meaning-saturated field; the two formative gestalts serve as a splendorous adornment for the meaning-saturated gestalt. Although the light values (pertaining to the five pristine cognitions constituting the cognitive-spiritual character of the scenario gestalt) each retain their specific hue, they emergently presence as the splendorous adornment of the two formative gestalts. An analogy for the meaning-saturated field splendorously adorned by the meaning-saturated gestalt is a turquoise with gold mountings; an analogy for the meaning-saturated gestalt splendorously adorned by pristine cognitions is a

crystal with its five (prismatic) colors of light; an analogy for pristine cognitiveness splendorously adorned by resonating concern is the sun rays which by their warmth and gentleness fulfill the need of sentient beings.

18. *Chos-dbyings*, fol. 196a.
19. Strictly speaking, "Being's primordial expanse" *(gdod-ma'i dbyings)* synonymous with meaning-saturated field *(chos-[kyi] dbyings)*, is the point-instant (singularity). See *Rong-'grel*, fol. 109b. In his *Collection of Writings*, pp. 217ff., Rong-zom-pa Chos-kyi bzang-po distinguishes between *chos-nyid-kyi thig-le*, the singularity that is the internal logic of Being, and *dbyings-kyi thig-le*, the singularity that is the meaning-saturated field. The former is a constant in the manner of a quantum of action, (as previously discussed in Chapter II), while the latter is this quantum of action, as it stretches out to encompass all that which virtually already is and thus collectively makes up Being.
20. On this idea and term see also above, p. 179.
21. See *Chos-dbyings*, fol. 196a. The same ideas are expressed in *dGongs-zang*, vol. 4, p. 226, which are supported by quotations from *Thal-'gyur*, (pp. 127f.), *Rang-shar*, (pp. 529f.) and *Klong-drug-pa*, (pp. 178f.).

In his *Bla-yang* I, pp. 295f., Klong-chen rab-'byams-pa says that in this process of Beings's auto-presencing *(gzhi-snang)* each of its three facets, facticity, actuality, and resonating concern, has its own creative dynamics:

> The creative dynamics of (Being's) facticity is an opening up—
> In its reach and range, (spacious as) the sky, without dichotomization,
> The creative dynamics of actuality is (a set of) five colors
> Emerging as the (prismatic) diffraction of the outward-directed glow (of this actuality in and as) pristine cognitions.
> The creative dynamics of resonating concern is a mere excited cognitiveness
> Emerging in the manner of being capable of differentiating between objective data.
> This (whole movement) is the ground and reason for (man's moving into the direction of) either freedom or straying (into the confines of bondage).
> This is (Being's) indeterminate spontaneity.

22. *Chos-dbyings*, fol. 196b.
23. In purely mathematical terms "the primordial Lord Kun-tu bzang-po" can be said to present an abstract group consisiting only of the identity element *I*. One possible realization of this group is the number 1 and ordinary multiplication as the composition. However, there is another realization, which is the number 0 and ordinary addition as the composition. This is indicated by the statement that "the facticity of this uniquely singular meaning-saturated gestalt cannot be established anywhere as something; it is the arrival at that level where everything and anything has ceased (to be something)" *(Chos-dbyings*, fol. 196b). In supporting this statement references are made to *Thal-'gyur* (p. 37), and *Klong-drug-pa* (p. 198).

One further important point may be brought out by reference to mathematics. It follows from the definition of an abstract group as a set of elements that it may have one other element *a* which must be its own inverse. The realization of such a group is the set of numbers 1, -1 under multiplication. Here the number 1 serves as the identity, while -1 is its own inverse, that is

$$(-1) \times (-1) = 1$$

In metaphoric language, Kun-tu bzang-po is the identity transformation *a* and rDo-rje 'dzin-pa, as the reflection transformation (of Kun-tu bzang-po), is his inverse a^{-1}, such that

$$a*a^{-1} = a^{-1}*a = I$$

where * denotes the operator and *I* is the identity element.

24. *Rang-shar* p. 431.
25. *Chos-dbyings*, fol. 197a.
26. *Rang-shar*, p. 431. The rendering reflects Klong-chen rab-'byams-pa's quotation which, however, is incomplete. The printed text of the *Rang-shar* inserts a line to the effect that the meaning-saturated gestalt is "complete as to all operations." This full passage is quoted by Klong-chen rab-'byams-pa in his *Tshig-don*, pp. 455f. and *Theg-mchog* II, p. 25.
27. *Chos-dbyings*, fol. 197a.
28. *Chos-dbyings*, fol. 197b.
29. It must be borne in mind that this is only a functional analysis and as such is not meant to be considered as attempting to establish entities within these complex processes. That this is so is amply borne out by those passages that explicate the reflexivity transformations. See, for instance, *Chos-dbyings*, fol. 197b; *Tshig-don*, p. 461; *Rang-shar*, pp. 763f. How these reflexivity transformations have been imaged, has been detailed in my *Tibetan Buddhism in Western Perspective*, p. 223.
30. *Chos-dbyings*, fol. 197b; *Theg-mchog* II, p. 572. It is significant that in this fivefold structuring the center which, as previously noted (see above, p. 111), is occupied by the teacher, is designated here as being an in-depth appraisal *(ting-nge-'dzin)*. This reflects the profound insight that here on the level of the virtual, we deal with deep-structures that precede, as it were, actual formulations that are imaged in anthropomorphic shapes.
31. *Chos-dbyings*, fol. 198b. See also *Tshig-don*, pp. 467f.
32. *Chos-dbyings*, fol. 199b.
33. See, for instance, *Chos-dbyings*, fol. 196b.; *Bla-yang* II, p. 236; *Thal-'gyur*, p. 127.
34. The explication here follows *Chos-dbyings*, fol. 200a, which summarizes the lengthy hermeneutical interpretation of this gestalt in *Rang-shar*, pp. 435f. See also *Theg-mchog* II, p. 29; *Tshig-don*, p. 456, where gestalt is concisely defined, on the basis of *Seng-nge rtsal-rdzogs*, p. 396, as "having radiance and brilliance."
35. Compare with the idea of subsystem, system, and super-system, suggested by D.J. Bohm and B.J. Hiley, "On the Intuitive Understanding of Nonlocality as Implied by Quantum Theory" (in *Foundations of Physics*, Vol. 5 No.1, 1975, pp. 93-109), p. 102.
36. *Chos-dbyings*, fol. 202b.
37. *Chos-dbyings*, fol. 202b.
38. *Rang-shar*, p. 438.

39. Analytically speaking, the former aspect is known as *ji-lta-ba mkhyen-pa'i ye-shes*, the latter as *ji-snyed-pa mkhyen-pa'i ye-shes*. Their specific operations are detailed in *Thal-'gyur*, p. 126; *Klong-drug-pa*, p. 182; *Theg-mchog* I, p. 645; *Tshig-don*, pp. 477f. Since these two pristine cognitions are the operation of resonating concern, their operation may be conceived of as a kind of intersection of two orders, as suggested for perception by David Bohm, *Wholeness and the Implicate Order*, p. 153.

40. This is implied by the term *grol-sa* which, literally rendered "freedom level," points to the dynamics of Being. See *Theg-mchog* I, p. 606; II, pp. 427, 543; *Tshig-don*, p. 454. *Mu-tig phreng-ba*, p. 536, explicitly states that *grol-sa* means an atemporal beginning *(thog-ma)*. On *thog-ma* as an atemporal beginning see *Bi-ma*, vol. 2, p. 76.

41. *Tshig-don*, p. 28.

42. See *Chos-dbyings*, fols. 185b f.; *Bla-yang* I, p. 296; *Zab-yang* I, 297; *Tshig-don*, p. 35.

43. *mKha'-yang* II, p. 224. See also *Bla-yang* II, p. 235.

44. *Thal-'gyur*, p. 84.

45. *Theg-mchog* I, p. 391.

46. *Thal-'gyur*, p. 127. See also *Theg-mchog* I, p. 605; II, p. 19; *Bi-ma*, vol. 3, pp. 4f.; *Tshig-don*, p. 102.

47. *Chos-dbyings*, fol. 196a f.

48. *Thal-'gyur*, p. 128.

49. In the highly technical language of rDzogs-chen thought this is expressed as follows: Being's auto-presencing as Being-*qua*-Existenz constitutes an instability phase such that the process as a whole in its self-reflexivity, which may become expressed in function and structure, either becomes self-cognition and self-discovery as freedom *(grol-lugs)* or self-oblivion ("mistaken about itself," *'khrul-lugs*) by becoming ever more engrossed in an identifying itself with its constructs. See, for instance, *Tshig-don*, pp. 18, 272f.; *Theg-mchog* II, pp.263ff.; *Chos-dbyings*, fols. 101a,177a; *Bla-yang* II, pp. 6ff.; *mKha'-yang* II, p. 142.

50. *Zab-yang* II, p. 102; *dGongs-zang*, vol. 4, p. 206. Other passages such as *mKha'-yang* II, p. 68; III, p. 74; *Bla-yang* II, p. 3, have "before there was Saṃsāra as a downward movement and Nirvāṇa as an upward movement."

51. *Chos-dbyings*, fol. 187a.

52. *Chos-dbyings*, fol. 187b. Klong-chen rab-'byams-pa is quite emphatic in stating that any "doing" merely holds the "practicing" person within the already existing confines and prevents his self-transcendence. See *Theg-mchog* I, p. 626.

53. *Chos-dbyings*, fol. 188a.

54. *Chos-dbyings*, fol. 188b.

55. *Chos-dbyings*, fol. 189b.

56. *bag-chags sbubs*. See *Seng-ge rtsal rdzogs*, p. 283, quoted in *Chos-dbyings*, fol. 190a; *Thig-le kun-gsal*, pp. 268, 275. See also above Chapter Two, p. 25.

57. *rnam-rtog*. See *Seng-ge rtsal-rdzogs*, p. 283, quoted in *Chos-dbyings*, fol. 190, and also above Chapter Two, p. 25.

58. *Chos-dbyings*, fol. 190a.

59. This term has been used in order to emphasize the process setting up experiential horizon-forms within an indeterminate horizon encompassing

other possible horizons of "world"-engagement.

60. This is summed up in the terse statement concerning man's straying into the various niches or regions of his enworldedness, in *Mu-tig phreng-ba*, p. 535. See above Chapter Two, note 3. The verse is quoted in *mKha'-snying* I, pp. 349, 488; II, p. 38; *mKha'-yang* II, p. 142.

61. *Chos-dbyings*, fol. 190b.

62. *gSang-snying*, fol. 12b. See also *Klong-'grel*, p. 253.

63. *gSang-snying*, fol. 12b.

64. These endeavors and the existential awareness occur in what Calvin O. Schrag, *Experience and Being*, p. 186, has so aptly termed "sociality of situation." It is "my situation as lived through with the other. It is the situation of awareness and action in which meanings contributed by the other both limit and enrich my own existence as a project of meaning."

65. *Thal-'gyur*, p. 153. Also quoted in *Chos-dbyings*, fol. 192a. A similar idea is found in *Klong-drug-pa*, pp. 181f.

66. See, for instance, *Tshig-don*, pp. 458, 465.

67. See, for instance, *Tshig-don*, p. 457.

68. *Rang-shar*, p. 443. The passage is incomplete in the otherwise excellent *rNying ma'i rgyud bcu bdun* edition (New Delhi 1977). The complete passage is found in *Chos-dbyings*, fol. 195a and *Tshig-don*, p. 455.

69. *Thal-'gyur*, p. 202.

70. *Phenomenology of Perception*, p. 250.

71. The primacy of the mind understood as a feedback mechanism facilitating the observable activities of bodily and vocal engagements was long ago recognized in the famous opening stanza of the *Dhammapada*.

72. The term "prior" is not to be understood temporally prior to the overt activities. There is an interplay between all activities, and attention can be directed toward any one activity which, in this attending, constitutes a temporalization.

CHAPTER IX

1. The decisive passage is *gSang-snying*, fol. 23a:

> *dkyil-'khor ldan-pa'i dkyil-'khor-gyis*
> *dkyil-'khor-la ni dkyil-'khor bsgom*
> *dkyil-'khor dkyil-'khor-las byung-ba*
> *thugs-kyi dkyil-'khor dkyil-'khor mchog*
> *gsang-ba'i thig-le dkyil-'khor dbyings*

This passage has been interpreted in different ways. Klong'chen rab-'byams-pa's interpretation (*Klong-'grel*, pp. 448f.) is holistic-experiential. He associates the first two lines with *thabs*, which in this context he understands as the internal dynamics of Being; the second two lines with *shes-rab*, as the deeply felt appreciation of the process; and the last line with *'od-gsal*, the sheer lucency of Being-*qua*-Existenz. According to his interpretation the above passage is to be understood as follows:

[The underlying order constituting man's being is Being-*qua* -Existenz's*] configurational character, (which) through a configuration [constituting a deeply probing in-depth appraisal]
Is to be cultivated (illumined as) a configuration [which knows the ground] to be a configuration.

The configuration [which is bliss, lucency, and nondichotomy] emerges from a configuration [which has taken a firm hold on what presences as dichotomic mentation and affective processes].
[Since this presencing is the pure actuality of the ground, it is termed] vibrant spirituality's configuration—the most sublime (among all) configurations.

[The atemporal presence of the ground in and as the indivisibility of formal gestalt and pristine cognitiveness is the very mystery of Being], the mysterious [and ultimate] point-instant binding energy, the continual source of the configurations [of formal gestalt, authentic utterance, and vibrant spirituality in ceaseless ornamental gyration].

Although in many respects similar, the interpretation by g.Yung-ston rdo-rje dpal bzang-po (*gSal-byed me-long,* fols. 152b f.) and those who follow his tradition, is analytic-classificatory.

2.   The fierce nature, as will be shown later on, is introduced by the equally melodious *HŪM. Rong-'grel,* fol. 121a, discusses this difference of intoning the eulogies.
3.   *Rong-'grel,* fol. 113b, explicitly states that each facet comprises all other facets.
4.   *gSang-snying,* fol. 24a. *Rong-'grel,* fols. 113b f. associates the formal gestalt encodement program with the three formal gestalts of meaning-saturated gestalt *(chos-sku),* scenario gestalt *(longs-sku),* and cultural norms display gestalt *(sprul-sku).* This interpretation is continued by g.Yung-ston rdo-rje dpal bzang-po and those who follow him.
5.   *Rong-'grel,* fol. 114a, states that in this specific context this term also has the meaning of unoriginatedness.
6.   *gSang-snying,* fols. 24a f. *Rong-'grel* fol. 114a, states that the term king is a metaphor for True Individuality *(bdag-nyid).*
7.   *gSang-snying,* fol. 24b.
8.   *gSang-snying,* fol. 24b. *Rong-'grel,* fols. 114a f., sees in the phantasmic play the unity of *thabs* and *shes-rab.*
9.   *gSang-snying,* fol. 24b.
10.   *gSang-snying,* fol. 24b. *Klong-'grel,* p. 487.
11.   *gSang-snying,* fol. 35b.
12.   *gSang-snying,* fol. 35b.
13.   *gSang-snying,* fol. 35b.
14.   *gSang-snying,* fol. 35b.
15.   *gSang-snying,* fol. 35b.
16.   *gSang-snying,* fol. 35b.

Bibliography

A. BOOKS AND ARTICLES IN WESTERN LANGUAGES

Atkins, P.W. (1974). *Quanta. A Handbook of Concepts.* Clarendon Press, Oxford.
Bachelard, Gaston (1964). *The Psychoanalysis of Fire.* Translated by Alan C.M. Ross. Beacon Press, Boston.
Bohm, David (1980). *Wholeness and the Implicate Order.* Routledge & Kegan Paul, London.
——— and Hiley, B.J. (1975). "On the Intuitive Understanding of Nonlocality as Implied by Quantum Theory" (in *Foundations of Physics,* Vol. 5, No. 1).
Boss, Medard (1979). *Existential Foundations of Medicine and Psychology.* Translated by Stephen Conway and Anne Cleaves. Jason Aronson, New York.
——— (1949). *Meaning and Context of Sexual Perversions.* Grune and Stratton, New York.
Casey, Edward J. (1976). *Imagining. A Phenomenological Study.* Indiana University Press, Bloomington.
Davies, Paul (1980). *Other Worlds. A Portrait of Nature in Rebellion. Space, Superspace and the Quantum Universe.* Simon and Schuster, New York.
Davies, P.C.W. (1977). *Space and Time in the Modern Universe.* Cambridge University Press, Cambridge.
Gadamer, Hans-Georg (1976). *Philosophical Hermeneutics.* Translated and edited by David E. Linge. University of California Press, Berkeley.
——— (1960). *Wahrheit und Methode: Grundzüge einer philosophischen Hermeneutik.* C. Mohr, Tübingen.
Gosztonyi, Alexander (1972). *Grundlagen der Erkenntnis.* C.M. Beck, München.
Guenther, Herbert V. (1971). *Buddhist Philosophy in Theory and Practice.* Penguin Books, Baltimore; Shambhala Publications, Boulder.
——— (1976). *Philosophy and Psychology in the Abhidharma.* Shambhala Publications, Boulder.
——— (1972). *The Tantric View of Life.* Shambhala Publications, Boulder.
——— (1975-76). *Kindly Bent to Ease Us.* 3 vols. Dharma Publishing, Emeryville, CA.
Hartmann, William K. (1978). *Astronomy: The Cosmic Journey.* Wadsworth

Publishing Company, Belmont, CA.

Heidegger, Martin (1961). *An Introduction to Metaphysics.* Translated by Ralph Manheim. Anchor Books, Doubleday & Company, Garden City, New York.

———(1962). *Being and Time.* Translated by John Macquarrie and Edward Robinson. Harper & Row, New York.

———(1968, 1972). *What is Called Thinking.* Translated by Glenn Gray. Harper & Row, New York.

———(1971). *On the Way to Language.* Translated by Peter D. Hertz. Harper & Row, New York.

———(1972). *On Time and Being.* Translated by Joan Stambaugh. Harper & Row, New York.

Hoffmeister, Johannes (1955). *Wörterbuch der philosophischen Begriffe.* Felix Meiner, Hamburg.

Itten, Johannes (1970). *The Elements of Color.* Translated by Ernst Van Hagen. Van Nostrand Reinhold Company, New York.

Jantsch, Erich (1975). *Design for Evolution. Self-organization and Planning in the Life of Human Systems.* George Braziller, New York.

———(1978). "Erkenntnistheoretische Aspekte der Selbstorganisation natürlicher Systeme" (in *Wahrnehmung und Kommunikation,* edited by Peter M. Hejl, Wolfram K. Köck und Gerhard Roth). Peter Lang, Frankfurt am Main.

———(1980). *The Self-Organizing Universe. Scientific and Human Implications of the Emerging Paradigm of Evolution.* Pergamon Press, Oxford.

Laban, Rudolf (1976). *The Language of Movement. A Guidebook to Choreutics.* Plays, Inc. Boston.

Merleau-Ponty, M. (1962). *Phenomenology of Perception.* Translated by Colin Smith. Routledge & Kegan Paul, London.

Prigogine, Ilya (1980). *From Being to Becoming. Time and Complexity in the Physical Sciences.* W.H. Freeman and Company, San Francisco.

Reid, Louis Arnaud (1961). *Ways of Knowledge and Experience.* George Allen & Unwin, London.

Rosen, Joe (1975). *Symmetry Discovered. Concepts and Applications in Nature and Science.* Cambridge University Press, Cambridge.

Royce, Joseph (1976). "Consciousness and the Cosmos" (in *Extra-Terrestrial Intelligence: The First Encounter,* edited by James L. Christian). Prometheus Books, Buffalo, NY.

Schlegel, Richard (1980). *Superposition and Interaction. Coherence in Physics.* The University of Chicago Press, Chicago.

Schrag, Calvin O. (1969). *Experience and Being. Prolegomena to a Future Ontology.* Northwestern University Press, Evanston.

Seckel, Dietrich (1976). *Jenseits des Bildes. Anikonische Symbolik in der buddhistischen Kunst.* Carl Winter, Heidelberg.

Sivaramamurti, C. (1974). *Nataraja in Art, Thought and Literature.* National Museum, New Delhi.

Stevens, Peter S. (1974). *Patterns in Nature.* Little, Brown and Company, Boston.

Thom, René (1975). *Structural Stability and Morphogenesis.* W. A. Benjamin, Reading, Mass.

Vail, L.M. (1972). *Heidegger and Ontological Difference.* Pennsylvania State

University Press, University Park.

Valle, Ronald S. and King, Mark (1978). *Existential-Phenomenological Alternatives for Psychology.* Oxford University Press, New York.

Waddington, Conrad H. (1975). *The Evolution of an Evolutionist.* Edinburgh University Press, Edinburgh.

Young, J.Z. (1978). *Programs of the Brain.* Oxford University Press, Oxford.

Zaner, Richard M. (1964). *The Problem of Embodiment. Some Contributions to a Phenomenology of the Body.* Martinus Nijhoff, The Hague.

B. WORKS IN TIBETAN

Collections

Ati
 = rNying-ma'i rgyud bcu-bdun
 New Delhi, 1973-77

Collected Writings
 = An Encyclopaedia of Tibetan Buddhism: Collected Writings of 'Ba-ra-ba
 Dehradun, 1970

Collection of Writings
 = Gsung-'bum of Rong-zom-pa chos-kyi bzang-po
 n.p., n.d.

Dharmashri Coll. Works
 = Collected Works of Lo-chen Dharmashri
 Dehradun, 1976

rNying-rgyud
 = rNying-ma'i rgyud-'bum
 Thimbu, 1973

sNying-thig ya-bzhi
 Klong-chen rab-'byams-pa
 New Delhi, 1970

Selected Writings
 = gSung-thor-bu of Rong-zom-pa chos-kyi bzang-po
 Leh, 1974

Vairocana rgyud-'bum
 Leh, 1974

Works by Known Authors

Klong-chen rab-'byams-pa
 Klong-'grel
 = phyogs-bcu'i mun-pa thams-cad rnam-par sel-ba
 Paro, 1975

mKha-snying
= mKha'-'gro snying-tig
IN: sNing-thig ya-bzhi, vol. 2-3

mKha-yang
= mKha-'gro yang-tig
IN: sNying-thig ya-bzhi, vol. 4-6

Grub-mtha'
= Theg-pa mtha'-dag-gi don gsal-bar byed-pa grub-pa'i mtha rin-po-che'i mdzod
Gangtok, n.d.

sGron-ma snang-byed
= Dung-yig-can rgyud-kyi dhras-don bsdus-pa sgron-ma snang-byed
IN: sNying-thig ya-bzhi, vol. 8, pp. 1-159

Chos-dbyings
= Chos-dbyings rin-po-che'i mdzod
Gangtok, n.d., rDo-grub chen

Theg-mchog
= Theg-pa'i mchog rin-po-che'i mdzod
Gangtok, n.d.

Nam-mkha' klong-yangs
IN: sNying-thig ya-bzhi, vol. 1. (= Bla-ma yang-tig, part 1, pp. 279-294)

gNas-lugs
= gNas-lugs rin-po-che'i mdzod
Gangtok, n.d.

Bi-ma
= Bi-ma snying-thig
IN: sNying-thig ya-bzhi, vol. 7-9

Bla-yang
= Bla-ma yang-tig
IN: sNying-thig ya-bzhi, vol. 1.

Man-ngag mdzod
= Man-ngag rin-po-che'i mdzod
Gangtok, n.d.

Tshig-don
= gSang-ba bla-na-med-pa'i 'od-gsal rdo-rje snying-po'i gnas-gsum gsal-bar byed-pa'i tshig-don rin-po-che'i mdzod
Gangtok, n.d.

Zab-yang
= Zab-mo yang-tig
IN: sNying-thig ya-bzhi, vol. 10-11

Yid-kyi mun-sel
= dPal sGang-ba snying-po'i spyi-don legs-par bshad-pa'i snang-bas yid-kyi mun-pa thams-cas sel-ba
n.p., n.d.

Khrag-thung rol-pa'i rdo-rje
Dag-snang ye-shes dra-ba-las gnas-lugs rang-byung-gi rgyud rdo-rje
snying-po
Dehradun, 1970

mKhan-po nus-ldan
mKhas-'jug-pa'i tshul-la 'jug-pa'i sgo'i mchan-'grel legs-bshad snang-ba'i
'od-zer
Delhi, 1974

'Gyur-med phan-bde 'od-zer
Zab-don sgo-brgya 'byed-pa'i lde'u mig
Delhi, 1974

'Gyur-med tshe-dbang mchog-grub
dGongs-rgyan
= gSang-sngags nang-gi lam-rim rgya-cher 'grel-pa sangs-rgyas gnyis-pa'i
dgongs rgyan
Leh, 1972, Smanrtsis Shesrig Spendzod, vol. 25

'Jam-mgon 'Ju Mi-pham rgya mtsho
mKhas-'jug
= mKhas-pa'i tshul-la 'jug-pa'i sgo
Kalimpong, n.d., Dingo Mkhyen-brtse

Nyi-ma'i seng-ge'i 'od
dPal gsang-ba snying-po'i rgya-cher 'grel-pa
Gangtok, 1976

Bstan-'dzin chos-kyi nyi-ma, IV Khams-sprul
rGyan-byi bstan-bcos me-long pan-chen bla-ma'i gsung-bzhin bkral-ba
dbyangs-can ngag-gi rol-mtsho legs-bshad nor-bu'i 'byung-khungs
Thimphu, 1976, Kunsang Topgay

Dwags-po Pan-chen bKra-shis rnam-rgyal
Legs-bshad nyi-ma'i 'od-zer
n.p., n.d.

Nam-mkha' rin-chen
gSang-ba'i sning-po de-kho-na nyid nges-pa'i rgyud-kyi 'grel-bshad rgyud-
don gsal-bar byed-pa'i sgron-ma yid-bzhin-gyi nor-bu
IN: Commentaries on the Guhyagarbha Tantra and Other Rare Nying-
mapa Texts, vol. 2, pp. 1-709
New Delhi, 1978

Padmasambhava
Kha-sbyor
= sNang-srid kha-sbyor bdud-rtsi bcud-thigs 'khor-ba thog-mtha' gcod-
pa'i rgyud phyi-ma
IN: rNying-rgyud, vol. 6, pp. 1-52

lTa phreng
= Man-ngag lta-ba'i phreng-ba
IN: Selected Writings (gSung thor-bu) of Rong-zom-pa chos-kyi bzang-
po, pp. 1-18

Brag-phug dge-bshes dGe-'dun rin-chen
Kyai rdor rgyud-kyi tshig-don rnam-par bshad-pa man-ngag-gi mdzod
= Tshig-don rnam-bshad
Thimphu, 1978

Yon-tan rgya-mtsho
Yon-tan mdzod 'grel
= Yon-tan rin-po-che'i mdzod-kyi 'grel-pa nyi-zla'i sgron-me
Gangtok, 1969-71, Sonam T. Kazi

g.Yung-ston rdo-rje dpal bzang-po
gSal-byed me-long
= dPal gsang-ba snying-po'i rgyud-don gsal-byed me-long
n.p., n.d.

Rong-zom-pa chos-kyi bzang-po
rGyud spyi'i dngos-po
IN: Collection of Writings

Rong-'grel
= rGyud-rgyal gsang-ba snying-po'i 'grel-pa dkon-cos 'grel
n.p., n.d.

Sangs-rgyas gling-pa
Bla-ma dgongs-'dus
Gangtok, 1972, Sonam T. Kazi

Works by Unknown Authors

Kun-tu bzang-po thugs-kyi me-long-gyi rgyud
IN: Ati, vol. 1, pp. 233-280

Kun-byed rgyal-po
= Chos-thams-cad rdzogs-pa chen-po byang-chub-kyi sems kun-byed
rgyal-po
IN: rNying-rgyud, vol. 1, pp. 1-220

Klong-drug-pa
= kun-tu bzang-po klong-drug-pa'i rgyud
IN: Ati, vol. 2, pp. 111-214

bKra-shis mdzes-ldan chen-po'i rgyud
IN: Ati, vol. 1, pp. 207-232

dGongs-'dus
= sPyi-mdo dgongs-pa 'dus-pa
IN: rNying-rgyud, vol. 11, pp. 1-537

dGongs-zang
= rDzogs-pa chen-po dgongs-pa zang-thal
Leh, 1973, Smanrtsis Shesrig Spendzod, vols. 60-64

sGron-ma 'bar-ba
= Gser-gyi me-tog mdzes rin-po-che'i sgron-ma 'bar-ba'i rgyud
IN: Ati, vol 1, pp. 281-313

sNying-gi me-long
= rDo-rje sems-dpa' snying-gi me-long-gi rgyud
IN: Ati, vol. 1, pp. 365-388

Thal-'gyur
= Rin-po-che 'byung-bar byed-pa sgra-thal-'gyur chen-po'i rgyud
IN: Ati, vol. 1, pp. 1-205.

Thig-le kun-gsal
= Thig-le kun'gsal chen-po'i rgyud
IN: rNying-rgyud, vol. 5, pp. 124-289

dDe-Ba chen-po byang-chub-kyi sems rmad-du byung-ba'i le'u
IN: rNying-rgyud, vol. 2, pp.1-68

Nor-bu phra-bkod
= Nor-bu phra-bkod rang-gi don thams-cad gsal-bar byed-pa'i rgyud
IN: Ati, vol. 2, pp. 1-75

sNang-srid
= sNang-srid kha-sbyor bdud-rtsi bcud-thigs thob-mtha' gcod-pa'i rgyud
IN: rNying-rgyud, vol. 5. pp. 526-601

dPal Heruka'i thugs-kyi rgyud gyal-po
IN: rNying-rgyud, vol. 25, pp. 376-395

sPungs-pa yon-tan
= Rin-chen spungs-pa yon-tan chen-po ston-pa rgyud-kyi rgyud-po
IN: Ati, vol. 3, pp. 73-114 and also rNying-rgyud, vol. 9, pp. 436-466

sPyi-gnad skyon-sel
= Rin-po-che spyi-gnad skyon-sel thig-le kun-gsal gyi rgyud
IN: rNing-rgyud, vol. 6, pp. 230-238

sPyi-phud
= Theg-pa kun-gyi spyi-phud klong-chen rab-'byams-kyi rgyud
IN: rNying-rgyud, vol. 4, pp. 174-416

'Phags-lam bkod-pa
= Rin-po-che 'phags-lam bkod-pa
IN: rNying rgyud, vol. 4, pp. 152-174

Mu-tig phreng-ba
= Mu-tig phreng-ba zhes-bya-ba'i rgyud
IN: Ati, vol. 2, pp. 417-537

rDzogs-pa chen-po nges-don thams-cad 'dus-pa ye-shes nam-mkha' mnyam-pa'i rgyud
IN: rNying-rgyud, vol. 8, pp. 124-478

rDzogs-pa chen-po lta-ba yang-snying sangs-rgyas thams-cad-kyi dgongs-pa nam-mkha' klong-yangs-kyi rgyud
IN: rNying-rgyud, vol. 7, pp. 121-201 and also Vairocana rgyud-'bum, vol. 8, pp. 1-85

Yi-ge med-pa
= Yi-ge med-pa'i rgyud chen-po

IN: Ati, vol. 2, pp. 215-244

Ye-shes nam-mkha'
= rDzogs-pa chen-po nges-don thams-cad 'dus-pa ye-shes nam-mkha'
mnyam-pa'i rgyud
IN: rNying-rgyud, vol. 8, pp. 124-478

Rang-grol
= Rig-pa rang-grol chen-po thams-cad grob-ba'i rgyud
IN: Ati, vol. 3, pp. 1-72

Rang-shar
= Rig-pa rang-shar chen-po'i rgyud
IN: Ati, vol. 1, pp. 389-855

Seng-ge rtsal-rdzogs
= Seng-ge rtsal-rdzogs chen-po'i rgyud
IN: Ati, vol. 2, pp. 245-415

gSang-snying
= rDo-rje gsang-ba'i snying-po rtsa-ba'i rgyud de-kho-na-nyid nges-pa
IN: rNying-rgyud, vol. 16, pp. 1-137

gSang-snying rgyas-pa
= gSang-ba'i snying-po de-kho-na-nyid nges-pa
IN: rNying-rgyud, vol. 14, pp. 67-317

Indexes

A. Tibetan Technical Terms
(In Tibetan alphabetical order)

phyal-ba, 227 n.51
phyi'i dkar dmar yul, 233 n.14
phyi'i yul, 233 n.14
phra-men, 283 n.65, 71
phrag-dog, 88f., 152, 160
phrin-las, 3, 104, 136, 140, 142,
  151f., 181, 199f., 204, 253 n.13,
  265 n.79, 275 n.36, 277 n.3,
  278 n.8
phrin-las drag-po, 149

bag-chags, 229 n.8
bem-stong, 223 n.37
bya-ba, 273 n.28
bya-ba grub-pa'i ye-shes, 52, 86,
  88f., 152, 259 n.50
by-ba nan-tan-gyi ye-shes, 52
bya-ba byed-pa'i sprul-sku, 184
bya-ba rdzogs-pa'i sprul-sku, 184
byang-chub, 3, 111, 228 n.55,
  267 n.100
byang-chub-kyi sems, 237 n.22,
  257 n.37
byang-chub chen-po, 111
byang-chub sems-dpa', 267 n.100
byams-pa, 118
byin-gyis brlabs, 14
byol-song, 160
dbang, 167
dbang-du bya-ba, 253 n.13
dbang-po, 266 n.87, 275 n.36
dbang-phyug, 259 n.50
dbyings, 18, 48, 53, 105, 174, 180f.,
  224 n.45, 230 n.10, 240 n.47,
  252 n.1
dbyings-kyi sgron-ma, 58
dbyings-kyi thig-le, 286 n.19
dbyings thig-le nyag-gcig, 240 n.48
dbyings-rig, 18
dbye-bsal med-pa, 233 n.14
dbyer-med, 7, 38, 186, 216 n.30,
  220 n.26, 232 n.12
'byung-gnas, 261 n.54
'byung-ba, 11, 105, 226 n.46,
  266 n.87
'bras-bu, 8, 184, 198, 215 n.20,
  228 n.4, 253 n.6
'bras-bu'i yi-ge, 247 n.2

sbas-pa'i gsang-ba, 279 n.18
sbubs, 223 n.38, 239 n.39
sbyin-pa, 118
sbyor, 156, 280 n.39

ma-skyes-pa, 13
ma-nges-pa'i lhun-grub, 263 n.72
ma-bcos-pa, 281 n.40
ma-dag-pa, 109, 284 n.13
ma-byas-pa, 281 n.40
ma-mo, 282 n.61, 283 n.71
ma-rig bdag-tu 'dzin, 279 n.14
ma-rig-pa, 17, 22, 26, 214 n.11,
  219 n.9, 259 n.49, 279 n.14
mi,160
mi-'gyur, 53, 151
mi-'gyur rtsis gdab med, 233 n.14
mi-sdug-pa, 126
ming, 64
me, 88f., 108
me-long lta-bu'i ye-shes, 51, 85,
  88f., 107, 152, 259 n.50
med-par skur-ba gdab, 129
mo-rgyud, 156
dmyal-ba, 160
smon-pa med-pa, 280 n.32

tsitta, 57, 59, 68, 139, 244 n.63
btsun-mo, 283 n.70
rtsa, 65, 67, 69, 247 n.2
rtsa-ba, 53
rtsa'i yi-ge, 247 n.2
rtsal, 51, 54, 101, 177f., 185,
  218 n.5, 224 n.45, 263 n.73,
  267 n.99
rtsibs-mthan, 271 n.13
rtsol-ba-las 'das-pa, 230 n.10
brtson-'grus, 259 n.50

tshig, 64
tsheg, 249 n.20
tshogs, 8, 214 n.16, 282 n.60
tshogs-brgyad, 229 n.8, 266 n.88
tshor-(ba), 88f., 105, 108, 152,
  266 n.89
mtshan-nyid, 216 n.32
mtshan-ma, 117
mtshan-ma dang bcas-pa, 252 n.1

B. Subject Index

(Entries followed by a Tibetan term indicate rDzogs-chen key notions and/or ideas hermeneutically developed by rDzogs-chen thinkers. See also *A. Tibetan Technical Terms*.)

Act phase, 28, 113, 167, 176, 217 n.3

action, 148, 198; appropriate, 75, 93, 97, 103, 114, 122f., 165, 280 n.33

activity, 142, 277 n.3; creative, 184; karmic, 143; modes of, 3; optimally executed, 104, 131, 136, 140, 152, 180, 199, 204, 207; psychic, 167

actuality (*rang-bzhin*), 17, 20f., 99, 175f., 179, 185f., 218 n.5, 232 n.12

addiction, 88, 91

adornment (*rgyan*), 177f.

affinity with Being (*rigs*), 106f., 136, 149, 175, 183, 248 n.13, 262 n.66

all-encompassing (*kun-khyab*), 53

anger, 142f.

animal, 124, 134, 137, 160, 163

Anuyoga, 252 n.6

apparition, 12f.

appreciation, 119, 156, 198

appreciative discrimination (*shes-rab*), 75, 93, 97, 103, 114, 122f., 165, 213 n.11, 214 n.12, 269 n.111, 278 n.8, 280 n.33

Apsaras, 152f.

arrogance, 88; -egomania, 152, 160

as-is (*de-bzhin*), 76f., 94, 104, 107, 146, 215 n.26

atemporal (*ye, ye-nas*), 185, 214 n.17, 218 n.5, 229 n.5

Atiyoga, 209 n.1, 252 n.6

atom, 98

atomic distance, 98

audience, 20, 183,

auto-presencing (*rang-snang*), 3, 18, 100, 202, 267 n.99, 286 n.21

auto-reflexive, 86

avarice, 160

awareness, 187, 193; optimal, 22; stepped-down, 22

Beauty, 43, 101f., 127, 130, 132, 263 n.73

Being (*gzhi*), 5f., 12, 16, 22, 28, 32, 35, 37f., 40, 44f., 62, 71f.,103, 148, 183, 189, 192, 222 n.37, 257 n.36; as presence, 33f.; atemporal spontaneity, 75; auto-elucidation, 10; autopoietic structuring, 200f.; dynamics, 129; engagement, 96; facticity, 47, 75f.; internal logic, 42, 48, 57, 91f., 102f., 141, 178, 185, 219 n.12, 257 n.38; intrinsic intelligence, 9, 12; mystery, 7f., 12f., 75, 198, 201, 208; projectivity, 90; resources, 7f.; totality, 194

Being-*qua*-Existenz (*rgyud*), 22, 33, 45f., 48, 53, 56, 58, 61, 63, 66, 72f., 76, 93, 121, 129, 141, 156,

C. Names

I. Sanskrit (in English alphabetical order)

Akṣobhya, 106f., 131, 136, 164,
266 n.87, 88, 275 n.36
Amitābha, 106, 108, 131, 137,
275 n.36
Amoghasiddhi, 106, 108, 131, 137,
266 n.91, 275 n.36
Amṛtakuṇḍalin, 106, 133, 137
Aṅkuśā, 118
Avalokiteśvara, 112, 132, 137

Buddhalocanā, 106, 108

Caṇḍālī, 168
Caurī, 167

Dhātvīśvarī, 106f.
Dhūpā, 112, 132
Dīpā, 112, 132

Gaganagarbha, 112, 132, 137
Gandhā, 112, 132
Gaurī, 167
Ghaṇṭā, 118
Ghasmarī, 168
Gīti, 132, 268 n.106

Hayagrīva, 133, 137, 277 n.56
Heruka, 141, 147f., 152f., 155f.,
161, 164f., 206, 278 n.6, 280 n.24,
283 n.70,71. See also Śri Heruka;
Buddha-, 151f., 162, 164; Karma-,
152f.; Padma-, 152f.; Ratna-,

152f.; Vajra-, 153, 162, 164, 166f.

Indra, 134. See also Śatakratu

Jvālamukhadeva, 134

Krodheśvarī, 152f.; Buddha-, 152f.;
Karma-, 152f.; Padma-, 152f.;
Ratna-, 152f.; Vajra-,152f.
Kṣitigarbha, 112, 131, 136

Lāsyā, 112, 268 n.106

Mahābala, 116, 133, 137
Mahādeva, 150, 153
Maitreya, 112, 131, 137
Mālā, 132, 268 n.106
Māmakī, 106, 108
Mañjughoṣa, 137
Mañjuśrī, 112, 131, 277 n.55

Nivaraṇaviṣkambhin, 112, 132
Nṛtyā, 132

Pāṇḍaravāsinī, 106, 108
Paramāśva, 116, 133, 137, 277 n.56
Pāśā, 118
Pramohā, 168
Pukkasī, 168
Puṣpā, 112, 132

Ratnasambhava, 106, 108, 131, 137,

II. Tibetan (in Tibetan alphabetical order)

sNang-gsal-ma. *See* Dīpā

sPyan-ras gzigs dbang-phyug. *See*
Avalokiteśvara

Phyag-na rdo-rje. *See* Vajrapāṇi
'Phreng-ba-ma. *See* Mālā

Byams-pa. *See* Maitreya
dByings-kyi dbang-phyug-ma. *See*
Dhātvīśvarī

Mar-me-ma. *See* Dīpā
Mi-bskyod-pa. *See* Akṣobhya
Me-tog-ma, *See* Puṣpā

Wa-gdong-ma, 169

Zhags-pa-ma. *See* Pāśā

bZhad-dgong-ma, 170

'Ug-gdong-ma, 170
'Od-dpag-med. *See* Amitābha

Rin-chen 'byung-ldan. *See*
Ratnasambhava

Śākya thub-pa. *See* Śākyamuni
gShin-rje-gshed. *See* Yamāntaka

Sa'i snying-po. *See* Kṣitigarbha
Sangs-rgyas spyan-ma. *See*
Buddhalocanā
Seng-ge rab-brtan, 234
Seng-gdong-ma, 169

A-wa glang-mgo, 134